D0336193

THE CHALLENGE OF PROMOTING HEALTH:
EXPLORATION AND ACTION

Biomedical Library
Queen's University Belfast
Tel: 028 9097 2710
E-mail: BiomedicalLibrary@qub.ac.uk

For due dates and renewals:

QUB borrowers see 'MY ACCOUNT' at
http://library.qub.ac.uk/qcat
or go to the Library Home Page

HSC borrowers see 'MY ACCOUNT' at
www.honni.qub.ac.uk/qcat

This book must be returned not later
than its due date but may be recalled
earlier if in demand

Fines are imposed on overdue books

This book forms part of the core text for the Open University course *Promoting Health: Skills, Perspectives and Practice* (K301) and a new qualification, The Certificate in Health Promotion. It has been produced with support from the Health Education Authority and Health Promotion Wales, although the content of the course is the sole responsibility of The Open University.

If you are interested in studying the course and gaining the new Certificate please write to the Information Officer, School of Health and Social Welfare, Walton Hall, Milton Keynes MK7 6AA, UK.

Other texts required for the course and also published by Macmillan in association with The Open University are:

- the first core text, *Promoting Health: Knowledge and Practice,* edited by Jeanne Katz and Alyson Peberdy

- the course reader, *Debates and Dilemmas in Promoting Health*, edited by Moyra Sidell, Linda Jones, Jeanne Katz and Alyson Peberdy

- the set book, *Health Promotion: Professional Perspectives,* edited by Angela Scriven and Judy Orme.

The Challenge of Promoting Health

Exploration and Action

Edited by

Linda Jones and Moyra Sidell
The Open University

MACMILLAN

in association with

The Open
University

Cover photo: Tony Stone Images (Jeremy Walker)

Copyright © The Open University, 1997

All rights reserved. No reproduction, copy or transmission of this publication may be made without written permission.

No paragraph of this publication may be reproduced, copied or transmitted save with written permission or in accordance with the provisions of the Copyright, Designs and Patents Act 1988, or under the terms of any licence permitting limited copying issued by the Copyright Licensing Agency, 90 Tottenham Court Road, London W1P 9HE.

Any person who does any unauthorised act in relation to this publication may be liable to criminal prosecution and civil claims for damages.

The authors have asserted their rights to be identified as the authors of this work in accordance with the Copyright, Designs and Patents Act 1988.

First published 1997 by
MACMILLAN PRESS LTD
Houndmills, Basingstoke, Hampshire RG21 6XS and London
Companies and representatives throughout the world

ISBN 0–333–68173–8 hardcover
ISBN 0–333–68174–6 paperback

A catalogue record for the book is available from the British Library.

This book is printed on paper suitable for recycling and made from fully managed and sustained forest sources.

10   9   8   7   6   5   4   3   2   1
06 05 04 03 02 01 00 99 98 97

Printed in the United Kingdom by J.W. Arrowsmith, Bristol

15165B/k301b2p1i1.1

Contents

Preface

The Open University Team have perceived precisely one of the major challenges facing health care today. They have approached the challenge with insight and inspiration. The increasing importance of health promotion means that promoting health has become the business of all those engaged in health and social care. This book will be invaluable for a wide range of practitioners, policy makers, academics and other lay and professional people interested in enhancing the nation's health. The text will prove to be particularly timely for large numbers of nurses in roles which actively embrace preventive care and the promotion of health.

This practice-led book illuminates the complexity of health promotion as a concept and focuses appropriately on key approaches to working in this area. Issues associated with ways of working and building collaborative relationships and alliances are carefully addressed. Readers are eased into examining the paradox between empowerment and the traditional medical model and lifestyle approach.

The principles of analysis and critique pervade the text and encourage innovation and progressive practice. Some deeply held assumptions about definitions of ownership and control in health are challenged.

Emancipation and partnership are presented as key determinants of effectiveness and the need to rigorously evaluate health promotion activity is emphasised.

This book is itself a testimony to the value of collaboration and open-mindedness. Its content has been debated and vetted by a range of individuals and organisations. The Open University course, Promoting Health: Skills, Perspectives and Practice, of which this book and its sister publication *Promoting Health: Knowledge and Practice* form core texts, has evolved in partnership with potential consumers, HEA and Health Promotion Wales.

The Challenge of Promoting Health: Exploration and Action truly breaks new ground. It provides the building blocks for progressive health promotion through skilfully helping readers to apply theory to practice. It offers exactly what is needed by all those charged with a responsibility to enhance health. It stimulates provocation and challenge to turn thinking into action.

Professor Jill Macleod Clark
The Nightingale Institute
King's College London

Acknowledgements

Grateful acknowledgement is made to Liverpool City Council for their help, co-operation and input to Chapters 3 and 4. Also to the Greater London Association of Community Health Councils for the use of their material from *A review of health promotion in primary care: from the GP health promotion contract to promoting health with local communities* for Chapter 1. Also to the Health Education Authority for numerous case studies.

Grateful acknowledgement is made to the following sources for permission to reproduce material in this book:

Text

Bedford, B. (1996) Letter to *Health Services Journal*, 25 April 1996; Smithies, J. (1995) *Moving On – A Report of the National Community Health Conference*, Labyrinth Training and Consultancy; *The SCCD Charter – A Working Statement on Community Development* (1992), reproduced by courtesy of the Standing Conference for Community Development, 356 Glossop Road, Sheffield, S10 2HW; Labonte, R. (1993) 'Community development and partnerships', *Canadian Journal of Public Health*, **84** (4); Department of Health (1993) *Working Together for Better Health*, © Crown Copyright is reproduced with the permission of the Controller of Her Majesty's Stationery Office; *Boxes 5.3, 5.4:* Beattie, A. (1991) 'Knowledge and control in health promotion: a test case for social policy and social theory', in Gabe, J., Calnan, M. and Bury, M. (eds) *The Sociology of the Health Service*, Routledge; *Box 6.1:* Riley, J.C. (1987) *The Eighteenth Century Campaign to Avoid Disease*, Routledge; *Box 8.1:* Department of Health (1992) *The Health of the Nation – A Strategy for Health in England*, © Crown Copyright is reproduced with the permission of the Controller of Her Majesty's Stationery Office.

Figures

Figure 2.1: adapted from Blennerhasset, S., Farrant, W. and Jones, J. (1989) 'Support for community health projects in the UK', *Health Promotion*, **4** (3), Oxford University Press. By permission of Oxford University Press; *Figure 3.1:* Reproduced with the kind permission of Pavilion Publishing (Brighton) Ltd., from 'Managing user involvement' in *Roots and Branches – Papers from the OU/HEA*; *Figure 4.1:* Draper, R. (1992) *Reflections on Progress – Health for All 2000*, World Health Organisation; *Figure 5.2:* Beattie, A. (1991) 'Knowledge and control in health promotion: a test case for social policy and social theory', in Gabe, J., Calnan, M. and Bury, M. (eds) *The Sociology of the Health Service*, Routledge; *Figure 5.3:* Bracht, N. and Tsouros, A. (1990) 'Principles and strategies of effective community participation', *Health Promotion International*, **5** (3), Oxford University Press. Reprinted by permission of Oxford University Press; *Figure 5.4:* Smithies, J. and Adams, L. (1993) 'Walking the tightrope: issues in evaluation and community participation for Health for All', in Davies, J.K. and Kelly, M.P. (eds) *Healthy*

Cities: Research and Practice, Routledge; *Figure 6.1:* WHO (1986) *Ottawa Charter for Health Promotion*, World Health Organisation; *Figure 6.2:* Tones. B.K. (1990) *The Power to Choose: Health Education and the New Public Health*, Health Education Unit, Leeds Metropolitan University; *Figure 6.3:* Milio, N. (1987) *Promoting Health Through Public Policy*, Canadian Public Health Association, Ottawa, Canada; *Figure 6.4:* Macdonald, G. and Bunton, R. (1993) *Health Promotion: Disciplines and Diversity*, Routledge; *Figure 7.1:* adapted from Easton, D. (1965) *A Systems Analysis of Political Life*, John Wiley and Sons Ltd. Reprinted by permission of John Wiley and Sons Ltd; *Figure 9.1:* adapted from Beattie, A. (1991) 'Knowledge and control in health promotion: A test case for social policy and social theory', in Gabe, J., Calnan, M. and Bury, M. (eds) *The Sociology of the Health Service*, Routledge; *Figure 9.2:* Wilkinson, R.G. (1994) *Unfair Shares*, Barnardos; *Figures 9.3 and 9.4:* Jones, L.J. (1994) *The Social Context of Health and Health Work*, Macmillan Press Ltd, © Linda J. Jones 1994; *Figure 10.1:* Maglund, B. et al. (1991) *"We Can Do It" Sundsvall Handbook from 3rd International Conference on Health promotion, Sundsvall, Sweden, 9-15 June 1991*, Stockholm, Karolinska Institute/WHO; *Figures 12.1 and 12.2:* Leathard, A. (1994) *Going Inter-Professional: Working Together for Health and Welfare*, Routledge; *Figure 12.3:* Audit Commission (1993) *Their Health Your Business: The New Role of the District Health Authority*, © Crown Copyright. Reproduced with the permission of the Controller of Her Majesty's Stationery Office; *Figure 12.4:* Audit Commission (1994) *Finding a Place: A Review of Mental Health Services for Adults*, © Crown Copyright. Reproduced with the permission of the Controller of Her Majesty's Stationery Office.

Tables

Table 3.2: Eardley, A., Elkind, A., Hobbs, P. and McGuinness, H. (1989) 'Encouraging participation in breast-screening', *Health Education Journal*, **48**, (4), Health Education Authority; *Table 7.1:* White, M. (1996) 'Who's who in public health?', *Healthlines*, May 1996, Health Education Authority; *Table 8.1:* National Audit Office analysis reproduced in *Health of the Nation, Progress Report*, (1996), © Crown Copyright. Reproduced with the permission of the Controller of Her Majesty's Stationery Office; *Table 8.3:* SHEPS (1994) *Roles for Health Promotion Specialists in Purchasing and Providing in the NHS Definition of Specialist Health Promoters' Roles*, Society of Health Education and Promotion Specialists; *Table 9.2:* Central Statistical Office (1994) *Social Trends*, © Crown Copyright is reproduced with the permission of the Controller of Her Majesty's Stationery Office and the Office for National Statistics; *Table 10.1:* Munn, R.E. (1992) 'Towards sustainable development', *Atmospheric Environment*, **26a** (15), Elsevier Science Publishing Company Inc; *Table 10.2:* Brown, V., Ritchie, J. and Rotem, A. (1992) 'Health promotion and environmental management: a partnership for the future', *Health Promotion International*, **7** (3), Health Education Authority.

General Introduction

This book explores ways in which health promotion may be 'mainstreamed' within services, localities, organisations and policy-making processes. It investigates the experience of working for health at different levels and encourages would-be health promoters to review their own practice and consider how far it is possible to work in new ways and forge new health alliances. It is a partner volume to *Promoting Health: Knowledge and Practice*, which investigates the range of knowledge, skills and understanding which would be useful to those involved in promoting health. These include an understanding of key health promotion debates and models, assessing, planning and evaluating health promotion actions, interpreting health statistics, communicating with people, counselling skills and developing a systematic understanding of the nature and determinants of health.

In *The Challenge of Promoting Health: Exploration and Action* we examine debates and dilemmas as they arise in a range of practice contexts and approaches. These include debates about the reorientation of primary health care, the role of community development, the potential of health alliances and the scope for influencing public policy. We look also at some key dilemmas in practice: for example, the inherent difficulties of building empowerment and participation, the problems in reconciling an individual and a collective focus and the essentially contested nature of 'healthy public policy' work. In doing so we highlight three fundamental challenges facing health promotion as it enters the twenty-first century. The first of these is to persuade the public that health promotion is relevant to their everyday lives; the second challenge is to persuade professionals, in and outside the health sector, that health promotion should be an essential element of their everyday work. There is also a third challenge, perhaps the most difficult of all, which lies in breaking down the barriers between 'professional' and 'lay' work so that the insights and strengths of each may be harnessed in the struggle for better health.

Three challenges for health promoters

Public perceptions of health promotion are still confused and contradictory. On the one hand, findings from researchers such as Davison, Frankel and Davey-Smith (1992) indicate a deep scepticism towards health promotion and suggest that a complex lay logic of 'luck' and 'fate' may be a more potent influence on people's thinking. On the other hand, for many people health promotion means targeting behaviour. People in the street who are asked about health promotion often reply with conventional comments about changing behaviour and mention one of the 'big' four – smoking, drinking, diet or exercise (BBC, July, 1996). This does not mean that they will make a change; indeed, people may then go on to explain why change is difficult or impossible for them.

Such evidence presents a challenge to would-be health promoters which is not initially or even primarily about changing public attitudes but about changing their own thinking and practice. It is not surprising that the public perceive health promotion as attempted behaviour modification, if we reflect on the narrow emphasis there has been within most professional groups on 'lifestyles' and on offering heavy-handed health advice to individuals. If the relevance of health promotion to people's everyday lives is to be recognised health promoters need to challenge the 'lifestyles' orthodoxy and its marginalisation of socio-economic and environmental influences on health.

Would-be health promoters also need to think about process change rather than just product change. A survey of 'best practice' in the Health of the Nation areas reported that 'initiatives for new services accounted for by far the greatest number of examples. In these cases a need was identified and a service planned and delivered by nurses, midwives and health visitors, or at least with major input from them' (DoH, 1993: 13). New services may, of course, be important but this notion of health promotion as 'add on' services, with needs assessed and met largely by professionals, has served to perpetuate a view of health promotion as another health product. Opening another clinic or organising another advice session may be important, but it may also distract attention from the more basic objective of re-orientating statutory and voluntary services. Extensions of services are often much easier to achieve than a reorientation of current practice, which may be difficult and threatening.

The chapters that follow demonstrate how a broader approach to health promotion may be developed and examine the potential for health promoters to use this to review and reorientate their practice. They explore some key building blocks in improving health: health advocacy, community action, healthier public policies and supportive environments. In doing so they respond to the third challenge we noted above, which is to break down the barriers between 'lay' and 'professional' work for health.

Health promotion, it has been claimed, is 'everybody's business' (DHSS, 1976) and voluntary and community groups have been in the forefront of innovative work for health in recent years. Some have built strong alliances with professionals but others have been greeted with suspicion. The preference of professional groups, on the whole, has been for docile 'patients' and 'clients' rather than active partners. Self-help has been characterised in individual terms much more than in terms of active groups or communities. Yet a fundamental objective in health promotion is to achieve change within the wider society so that health has a higher priority and is better protected. This cannot be achieved without the commitment and participation of lay people in the process of challenge and change. This book, therefore, is also about ways of working in partnership with people in a range of agencies and localities, in order to make health promotion more sensitive to people's needs and more effective in bringing about change.

Action at the local level

Part 1 focuses on the interface between health and welfare professionals and local communities. It investigates how far the model of primary health care based health promotion, endorsed by the WHO as appropriate for developing countries, can be translated into the general practitioner services which form the basis of primary health care in the UK. The model of community-oriented primary health care advocated by the King's Fund (Gillam, 1994) represents a shift from attending to the patient who walks through the surgery door to adopting a whole practice view. This takes the local community's health as its brief and involves reaching out into the community to discover the community's health needs and priorities. Mainstreaming health promotion within primary health care and taking a community-oriented approach requires new ways of working for the primary health care team. The community is not a passive entity waiting to be acted upon. Avoiding 'cultural invasion' and achieving 'cultural synthesis' is as much a challenge for health promotion into the twenty-first century as it was at the time Paulo Freire (1972) was writing about the role of education in deprived communities in the 1960s and 70s.

Community development for health has a well established tradition within health promotion of supporting and enabling local communities to work together to improve their collective health and well-being. Community health development workers have attempted to avoid an emphasis on the individual lifestyle change approach to health promotion and instead have focused on the conditions of people's lives, trying to find ways through collective action that they might change their local health environment.

Recent government strategy, encouraging user involvement, consultation and participation in health and health care has put community development health workers under the spotlight and changed their role in many ways. Community development workers now have to represent the statutory agencies to the local community and the local community to the statutory agencies. They truly have a foot in both camps enabling statutory agencies and local communities to work together to promote health. Building health alliances which achieve a balance between a top-down and a bottom-up approach is a challenge with which many are now grappling.

Many would see the mainstreaming of community development work as a contradiction in terms. However, if community development is to be more than an exercise in Do-It-Yourself health, then it must bring about real participation by communities in decisions made at all levels which affect their health and well-being. The third challenge to health promotion identified earlier, of breaking down the barriers between lay people and professionals, requires health professionals at all levels to work in new ways and ways which many may find threatening to professional autonomy.

Promoting health through public policy

Part 2 explores the potential for improving health through the use of public policy. Traditionally, health and welfare work has been focused on individuals, with the assumption that it takes place within a given policy framework. Health promotion questions this view by focusing on groups and populations, and by seeking to transform policies so that health can be protected and enhanced. This suggests a role for would-be health promoters in challenging and modifying unhealthy policies and working to change them.

One response to such a demand might be to argue that building 'healthy public policy' is rather too ambitious a task for the average health promoter, who may associate policy making with managers, politicians and civil servants rather than 'grass roots' workers. A key message of Part 2 is that everyone is potentially a policy maker. Policy decisions are made and executed at many levels and a sound understanding of the policy process can enable health promoters to become more skilled in seizing opportunities to influence policy change. We look at the political bargaining around health, both through a case study of smoking policy and by exploring debates about national health strategies and welfare restructuring.

How has 'health promotion' been conceptualised and realised in public policy? This Part investigates its origins and growth and the contribution of public health, social policy and the environmental movement to its realisation. In particular, we explore the emergence of 'healthy public policy' and 'supportive environments' as key ideas in contemporary health promotion and discuss how far health promoters can build these ideas into their everyday work. There is a systematic analysis of the relationship between social welfare and health, which highlights how accounts and models of health promotion have drawn on welfare typologies and examines the shifting debates about welfare entitlement through a case study of poverty.

Finally, the incorporation of a 'green' dimension into health promotion is analysed and evaluated. How high a priority should health promoters attach to environmental interventions and what can be achieved at local level? Some of the attempts to integrate environmentalism into health, such as the 'Greening the NHS' initiative, are assessed. Struggles over health promotion territory, we suggest, are still continuing and health promoters need to decide where they stand in contemporary debates about the 'new public health' and the 'healthy public policy'.

Debates and dilemmas in promoting health

The discussion in Parts 1 and 2 of the practical and policy implications of new ways of working to promote health, enabling people to participate in the decisions which affect their health and mainstreaming health promotion, highlights many contradictions. The final Part of this book picks up and dissects some of the debates and dilemmas facing health promotion as it moves into the twenty-first century. The ethical assumptions which underlie alternative ways of working are explored. A searching sociological analysis based on the surveillance and modernisation critiques asks difficult questions about the relationship between health promotion and wider social and political forces. Gender issues are brought into perspective by the recent emphasis on privileging men's health. The need for inter-professional collaboration which must underpin attempts at inter-sectoral and inter-agency working is subjected to scrutiny. The implications of a shift to user involvement with its emphasis on lay perspectives is critically analysed, asking how far it is possible to install a new lay epidemiology in health promotion.

The final chapter explores possible futures for health promotion. A range of people working in the field at national and international level put forward their own predictions and speculations about health promotion as it moves into the twenty-first century. Their different priorities and visions suggest that health promotion will continue to be an essentially contested territory.

Linda Jones and Moyra Sidell
1st November 1996

Part 1
Promoting health at the local level

Introduction

The collective approach to promoting health aims to involve people not only in their own health and well-being but in acting together upon their physical, social, political and economic environment for the sake of health. It attempts to avoid the pitfalls of both 'victim blaming' and the paternalism and top down approach of much health service provision. Community participation has always been a central tenet of WHO strategy. The Alma Ata declaration from the International Conference on Primary Health Care explicitly stated that:

> ...people have a right and a duty to participate individually and collectively in the planning and implementation of their health care.
> (WHO, 1978)

And the Ottawa Charter further developed these principles:

> Health promotion works through effective community action in setting priorities, making decisions, planning strategies and implementing them to achieve better health. At the heart of this process is the empowerment of communities, and the ownership and control of their own endeavours and destiny .
> (WHO, 1986)

In the UK we tend to equate primary health care with General Medical Practice but in its widest sense the primary health sector encompasses community health practitioners, community and self-help groups and local government as well as general medical practitioners. The primary health sector therefore is fertile ground for collective action for health.

This Part begins by looking at the potential for health promotion within the professional setting of General Practice and explores ways of involving and reaching out into the wider community. Chapter 2 moves further into the territory of community action for health to examine other types of groups who are working for health at the local level. Chapter 3 then looks at the possibilities for meeting in the middle, exploring partnerships and collaborations which build health alliances to promote health through community participation. This is not a simple matter and the second part of Chapter 3 analyses the issues involved and goes on to

ask how far community participation can achieve the goal of empowerment. Chapter 4 explores the role and skills of community workers who
aim to improve the health of communities through participation and
Chapter 5 examines issues of how we can evaluate community initiatives.

Chapter 1
The potential for promoting health with local communities: general practice and the primary health care team

1.1 Introduction

When the words 'health' and 'local' are considered together, many people think of their GP or the primary health care team (PHCT) at their local health centre. And so it is assumed that, at a local level, general practice is a natural and particularly suitable setting for promoting health. This has certainly been the UK government's thinking in recent years – *Health of the Nation, A Strategy for Health in England*, prioritises the role of the PHCT in promoting better health and preventing sickness (DoH, 1992), and the renegotiation of the GP contract in 1990 made health promotion a formal and distinct part of a doctor's duties (DoH, 1990). Furthermore, as part of the UK government's policy of promoting a primary-care-led NHS, GPs have been given a central role in needs assessment and commissioning for the health of local populations. But, what is health promotion within a general practice context?

> Think back to the consultations you have had with health professionals at your local surgery. Which components would you identify as health promotion?

There exist a multitude of activities that could be placed under the banner of health promotion – a GP advising a patient to give up smoking, a health visitor facilitating a reminiscence group for elderly people linked to the practice, a practice nurse collecting routine data on patients' housing conditions, a public health nurse conducting a local needs assessment through community development, a group of GP fund holders offering complementary therapy clinics, and so on.

This chapter explores the current and potential role of GPs and the core PHCT in promoting health, and discusses the advantages and drawbacks of general practice as a setting for health promotion. It draws upon a range of theories and models of health promotion to contrast the mainstream, conventional approach to health promotion in general practice (risk factor screening of individuals and lifestyle advice), with examples of health promotion practice by PHCTs that move beyond an essentially medical model of health, emphasise the significance of subjective knowledge about health and risk, and see health promotion as having a key role to play in addressing inequalities in health.

1.2 The organisational framework for health promotion in general practice

During the 1990s the government developed an explicit policy on health promotion in general practice. Of course, many activities in general practice which might be defined as health promotion had gone on before this time, and health promotion in general practice continues to be much more than that framed by official policy. Nevertheless, the organisational arrangements have been highly significant in defining the approach to health promotion in general practice and, some would argue, in preventing other approaches from flourishing (GLACHC, 1995).

In 1990, for the first time, health promotion became part of the GP's terms of service. The new GP contract defined the basic role of health promotion within the relationship between the patient and the GP (DoH, 1990). However, attempts to formalise health promotion in general practice through the vehicle of the GP contract have not had an easy passage – by 1996 the contract had been reformed twice in its short history. In part this reflects the widespread lack of agreement on what constitutes appropriate and effective health promotion within general practice. It also reflects the way in which health promotion policy in general practice became the battleground for tensions between government and doctors over the control of general practice. Taylor and Bloor (1994) suggest that many doctors believed that the main purpose of the 1990 contract was ultimately to weaken the authority of the profession, and that health promotion policy in general practice has 'come to symbolise the entire issue of professional judgement and commitment versus government/management "interference".'

The 1990 contract included an obligation for doctors to invite patients aged 16–74 not seen in the previous three years to attend for a health check. A fee was offered for each newly registered patient given a health check, and GPs were also obliged to write to patients aged 75 and over, offering health checks at yearly intervals. Most significantly, financial incentives were offered for GPs to hold health promotion clinics and to employ a wider range of ancillary staff than hitherto to carry out health promotion. The clinic system was not cash-limited and allowed GPs to earn considerable amounts of money from health promotion. There was widespread reporting of 'abuse' of the clinic system of payments. Abuse was defined in terms of GPs setting up clinics in order to make money rather than necessarily to meet a defined need. Griffiths (1990) has argued that the old system provided 'incentives to maximise the number of health promotion clinics regardless of their appropriateness or effectiveness'. There were some interesting examples of GPs using clinic money to fund innovative health promotion clinics based on needs identified by users (such as complementary therapies, counselling and self-help groups for victims of domestic violence). Yen (1995), however, argues that, in the main, the guiding interest in what to obtain health promotion monies for was not patients' needs but the self-interest of GPs in extending the capacity of primary care services in order to increase their visibility as a provider within the emerging primary care market of the 1990s.

There were other problems with the first attempt to introduce health promotion into general practice. GPs in well-off, middle-class areas found it fairly easy to establish and attract patients to clinics and did so in abundance, whilst those in deprived inner-cities found it far more difficult and inappropriate to run clinics (Gillam, 1992). A system of funding had therefore been established that shifted resources away from inner-city practices where need is greatest to middle-class areas with less need. Finally, the scientific validity of the 1990 arrangements for health promotion was seriously questioned by many in the medical profession, particularly the requirement to provide health checks for patients (Fowler and Mant, 1990; Noakes, 1993).

In 1993 the GP contract was revised. The new arrangements placed a moratorium on health promotion clinics and abolished the obligations to provide health checks in the structured way laid down in the 1990 contract. The focus shifted to opportunistic screening of individual patients for coronary heart disease (CHD) and stroke risk factors. The term 'opportunistic' meant that health promotion took place within, or as part of everyday consultations rather than within separately organised clinic sessions. A 'banding' system was introduced for activity and payment which allowed practices to opt into one of three bands (National Heart Forum, 1995). The scope of health promotion activities within each band was defined by government policy.

Many commentators were highly critical of this second attempt to formalise health promotion within general practice. The type of health promotion fostered by the new system was seen as based within a traditional, and some would say out-of-date paradigm of health promotion, whereby knowledge about health and risk is seen as lying within the expert disciplines of epidemiology and clinical medicine, and the role of the health promoter is to give information to bring about behavioural change in relation to established risk factors. The banding arrangements were described by Cowley (1995), using a phrase from Andrew Tannahill, as 'state of the ark practice, not state of the art'.

This approach can be contrasted with that fostered by the WHO Health For All movement and by current thinking on good practice within the disciplines of health promotion and primary care. Here, emphasis is placed on the role of empowerment and social change in promoting health, with professionals working as enablers alongside local communities to articulate lay definitions of health need. Health is seen as much more than an absence of risk factors, and health promotion is perceived as having a key role to play in addressing inequalities between social groups.

Other commentators, however, argue that it is artificial and unhelpful to polarise approaches to health promotion into conventional behavioural and medical approaches versus empowerment and social change approaches. They argue that in health promotion, the various layers of activity can reinforce and complement each other. But commentators such as the Greater London Association of Community Health Councils (GLACHC, 1995) have argued that different approaches may actually be antithetical to each other. For example, an approach that sees expert knowledge about health as belonging to the professional, will be unable to recognise lay knowledge as another legitimate form of expert knowledge (Williams and Popay, 1996). Furthermore, in a world of finite resources, a focus on certain approaches inevitably means that resources are not directed at other approaches.

Some doctors were highly critical of the banding system, arguing that it encouraged little more than ritualistic data collection (Stott, 1994). Others were more optimistic. Daykin *et al.*, (1995) point out that the banding system was not as restrictive as critics suggested and in fact offered scope for innovation and good practice. They summarise the positive features of the banding system identified by their research: 'useful and appropriate guidelines and protocols, the development of a practice information base to support planned health promotion activities, opportunities for in-creased income, better teamwork and increased external liaison'. However, whilst in theory the health promotion contract stated that all activities should encourage 'working with other individuals and agencies', there was little evidence to suggest that this was happening in practice. The picture often found was that, faced with competing demands and pressures, GPs were doing the minimum necessary to obtain their health promotion payments.

Box 1.1

Some GPs in Hackney provided an illustration of how the banding system could be used flexibly by health workers committed to highlighting the role of socio-economic factors in patient health and moving beyond a medical model of health promotion. Aware of the housing problems of many of their patients and the time they spend as doctors on housing-related health problems or on writing letters to the local housing department, they decided to take the opportunity offered by the data collection requirements of the banding arrangements to collect additional data on patients' housing status. The aim is eventually to use this data in conjunction with other local statutory bodies and community groups and in this way become involved in campaigning for improved housing conditions in the area.

The GP health promotion contract has also been widely criticised for the way it has influenced the division of labour between doctors and nurses in general practice. The contract remunerates doctors for health promotion, even though in most practices the tasks of health promotion are delegated to practice nurses (the number of practice nurses has expanded by over 50 per cent since the introduction of the GP contract in 1990). However, the prescriptive nature of the banding arrangements, and the power relations within general practice, have meant that nurses have had limited independence to develop their own ideas and approaches.

A further issue is whether practice nurses, most of whom come from a clinical rather than a community background, are the most appropriate nursing group to be undertaking health promotion. A study by the Social Policy Research Unit at the University of York showed that only 3 per cent of practice nurses were health visitors (Atkin *et al.*, 1993). Another study has shown the lack of knowledge of practice nurses in the area of health promotion and their wish to receive more training (Cowley, 1995). Health visitors, on the other hand, have specific training in health promotion and see it as integral to their role, yet the GP health promotion contract failed to acknowledge this potential resource in primary care. This does not mean that health visitors are not active in health promotion. Examples later in this chapter illustrate ways in which health visitors have often been at the vanguard of working with local communities to promote health in primary care. However, as one GP notes, the GP contract has had a perverse effect on working relationships in general practice:

> The 1990 contract restructured the way GPs were paid, ... incentive payments [were introduced] for health promotion, immunisation, cytology, new patient checks and child surveillance. Many health visitors found their change of role to 'GP income generators' difficult to handle, and saw no benefit for themselves in helping GPs 'to earn more' as some saw it. We [doctors] found it difficult to convince health visitors that, as self-employed small businesses, we were simply trying to claim our legitimate but reconstructed earnings... Practice nurses became our preferred business allies, a sad reflection on beneficial and effective relationships.
>
> (Bedford, 1996)

At the time of writing this chapter, the government has just announced yet another reform of the arrangements for health promotion within general practice, with the *British Medical Journal* reporting that the health secretary was 'persuaded by the profession's argument that the banding system hindered good practice' (*BMJ*, 1996). In October 1996 the tightly defined banding system was replaced by a system which allows individual general practices to define their own health promotion activities. Under the new arrangements, practices submit a description of their proposed activities for approval by a local health promotion committee. Initial reactions indicate that GPs see this reform of health promotion arrangements in general practice as a victory in their negotiations with government for the control of health promotion activities. To what extent GPs will continue to practise mainly a conventional type of health promotion, and whether the new arrangements will foster initiatives that move beyond a medical model and allow other health professionals and patients more say in health promotion activities is unclear.

1.3 Debates about conventional health promotion activity in general practice

Beyond the specific issues of the organisational arrangements for health promotion, some health professionals and commentators express fundamental concerns about the conventional approach to health promotion in general practice, particularly when health promotion is considered within the wider context of the competing demands on primary care.

First, there is concern over the scientific basis for health promotion in general practice and whether or not there is sufficient evidence of benefit to justify the expenditure of resources. Williams and Calnan (1994), reporting on a survey of GPs, concluded:

> ...knowledge within this area is characterised by a high degree of uncertainty... doctors may become subject to criticisms by patients who become more aware of the uncertainties which characterise medical knowledge. Hence, doctors may become increasingly reluctant to become involved in health promotion due to the considerable uncertainties and the threat to professional status which this entails.

In an attempt to reduce levels of uncertainty, with the introduction of the banding system, the Department of Health (1993) sent an extensive and impressive review of evidence in favour of risk factor intervention, entitled *Better Living, Better Life*, to every general practice in the country. More recently, general practice has had access to the findings of two large-scale studies – the OXCHECK Study (1995) and the Family Heart Study (1994) – both set up to determine the effectiveness of nurse-conducted health checks, screening and lifestyle counselling in general practice, in changing CHD risk factors. The consensus opinion, prepared by the National Heart Forum (1995), is one of cautious optimism. Both studies showed a small but worthwhile benefit, with the interventions leading to declines in cholesterol and blood pressure levels among men and women, but not in smoking rates. To achieve these modest results, the interventions were far more resource intensive than anything currently found in general practice.

At the same time, there has been a great deal of media and professional debate about the studies, with a wide range of interpretations of the findings. On the whole, those who believe that conventional interventions in general practice are of benefit have interpreted the findings as indicating such programmes should continue. Those who are sceptical about particular approaches to screening and risk factor modification have interpreted the findings as indicating failure of that particular approach. Those who are against health promotion *per se* have interpreted the findings as proving that health promotion does not work. The various reactions illustrate well how scientific results can be used to draw very different conclusions. Michael Marmot (1986) suggests that 'when facts collide with theories, scientists are far more likely to discard or explain away the facts than the theory'.

Secondly, there is the problem that 'opportunistic health promotion' can have two distinct meanings, with very different implications (Huntington and Killoran, 1991). On the one hand, every consultation or contact with a patient can be seen as an opportunity to collect risk factor data or discuss health promotion, even if unrelated to the original reason for consultation. Some general practice practitioners feel uncomfortable with this interpretation of the term 'opportunistic', and see health promotion in this context as negative and intrusive on the practitioner-patient relationship and thus inappropriate. Unfortunately, the banding system, by setting population coverage targets, tended to encourage this approach. Research conducted by Stott and Pill (1990) found that patients only wanted preventive advice from their GPs *when it was relevant to the presenting problem*, and furthermore that they were keen to assert their right to accept or reject the advice given. This is the second, more appropriate meaning of the term 'opportunistic'. Indeed, Stott (1994) goes further to suggest that truly opportunistic health promotion is part and parcel of good everyday clinical practice in general practice, and it is inappropriate for government policy to define it as a bolted-on extra.

Stott and Pill's findings lead us to a third point. Some are concerned that conventional health promotion can be a moral intrusion on people's lives. In its tendency to see 'healthy' behaviour as synonymous with rational behaviour and health as a metaphor for self-control (Kickbush, 1984), conventional health promotion implies a moral judgement on a person's 'choice' of behaviour and their rationality. Kelly and Charlton (1992) ask whether people have a right not to experience such interference in their lives.

What might be an unfortunate consequence of this perceived interference?

Opportunistic health promotion within a consultation may put people off going to the doctor for fear of being lectured or confronted with their obesity, smoking or drinking habits, etc. Furthermore, could screening for risk factors sometimes do more harm than good by raising public anxiety levels for relatively little health gain?

Finally, there is the concern that an overemphasis on health promotion in general practice could be at the expense of attention to what is commonly perceived to be the mainstay of general practice – treating and supporting people in ill-health. Opportunistic health promotion within a consultation could be seen as taking away from the much needed and already very small amount of time that GPs have with their patients to discuss the presenting problem. Findings from a national survey of GPs (General Services Medical Committee, 1992) indicate that GPs feel overburdened by the additional roles and responsibilities being placed at their door at present. Within such a context, many feel that health promotion cannot be afforded a priority. Doctors such as Julian Tudor Hart (1993) argue that the priority for promoting better health has to be ensuring that 'the basics' of general practice are adequately resourced. In a similar vein, Taylor and Bloor (1994) caution that the current focus and interest in health gain in primary care policy must not result in investment in prevention being seen as an alternative to, as distinct from an addition to, investment in other health care activity.

1.4 Broader approaches to health promotion in general practice: some innovative case-studies of PHCTs working with local communities to promote health

We now describe some innovative initiatives where GPs and PHCTs, along with health authorities, health promotion units and community health initiatives have found ways of working that represent a very different kind of health promotion to mainstream practice. These initiatives tend to acknowledge the role of socio-economic factors in health and to see professional power and control over knowledge and resources as issues to be challenged. A central component of their activity is usually self or community empowerment, and this often involves validating and supporting community health initiatives.

Community health projects linked with general practice

The Wells Park Health Project in Sydenham, South London is an example of a community health project linked to general practice which has developed organisational structures and ways of working that enable a community development approach to health to be integrated with the day-to-day activities of the surgery with which it shares premises. The project was founded in 1984 with the aim of promoting health and empowering people to take more control over their lives.

A Wells Park community worker describes the thinking behind the project:

> Often people visit the doctor because it's the only place they know to find help. This is often inappropriate when their problems, while affecting their health, are non-medical ones, and GPs do not have the time or information to help. The project provides services which GPs and other practice staff are unable to provide, like extensive information, counselling and group support – and these are essential components of PHC services. Our role is to empower patients by providing as much

knowledge as possible to deal with what is wrong, to make informed
choices, and to feel happy about the decision they've made.

(Gosling, 1992)

The project employs community health workers to undertake and develop
a wide range of activities: facilitating self-help groups; weekly drop-in
sessions for general advice, assistance with form-filling, and counselling; a
health information library for use by local residents, patients and health
professionals; a summer play scheme; and a free acupuncture and
osteopathy service. One major strand of work is that of lay needs
assessment: uncovering the health issues that matter to local people from
their point of view and feeding the results into the commissioning
process.

The project has formal and informal links with the general practice but
is independent of it. It is run by a management committee of local
residents and interested primary health care staff, including staff from the
general practice. The project is represented at practice meetings. In
addition there is informal communication between the project and
practice staff. Financial support has come from a variety of statutory and
charitable trust sources. Some staff costs have been reclaimed under the
arrangements for GP reimbursement for ancillary workers. Prior to 1993
some of the group activities were funded as health promotion clinics
under the old arrangements of the GP contract. The FHSA provided
additional funding to Wells Park for the employment of project workers to
assess the needs of the Vietnamese and African Caribbean communities.

A GP at Wells Park reflects on the fact that 'one of the recurring
surprises of working with a health project is the solutions provided by its
different perspective':

For example, our practice area is very hilly and our response to the
bronchitic and angina-ridden patients was to increase their medication.
The project's response was to negotiate with the local council to provide
a bus route through the estate to Sainsburys!

(Fisher, 1994)

Welfare rights advice projects

As it is increasingly recognised that poverty is a major determinant of
health in a community, so welfare rights casework for patients, and
associated advocacy and training, is becoming a growing area of activity
within primary care and many GPs now perceive it as a legitimate activity
for general practice (Paris and Player, 1993). The impetus for the work has
often come from outside general practice (from Citizen Advice Bureaux,
local 'Health for All' initiatives etc.) where anti-poverty strategies are still
much higher on the agenda than in general practice. Those involved with
anti-poverty work have argued that general practice is a particularly

suitable setting for welfare rights advice because it is seen as non-stigmatising and because of the high proportion of the population who visit their GP. GPs' willingness to be involved in these initiatives indicates their explicit recognition of the links between poverty and health. GPs are reporting high numbers of their patients living in poverty whose health is clearly affected by lack of money, and are frequently finding that these patients, especially those who are chronically sick, are not receiving benefits to which they are entitled (*Independent*, 1994).

The Southwark Benefits Advice Service is one example of a welfare rights initiative in general practice. This service is run by the local authority, and funded by the local health authority. The aim is to remove some of the pressures on GPs and other primary care staff by offering patients a comprehensive benefit take-up service within GP practices. The Benefits Advice Service provides weekly 'clinics' in surgeries by specialist welfare rights advisers giving welfare benefits advice to patients by appointment, and offers home visits for patients unable to attend surgery. It also provides follow-up casework and representation at tribunals as necessary, and training and consultancy on welfare rights issues to PHC staff (Southwark Council, 1995).

Between April 1994 and May 1995 the Benefits Advice Service was able to generate a total of £123,715 extra benefit income for the 327 patients who consulted it. A similar health and benefits project which operated in Islington for six months in 1993 calculated a projected average weekly gain for each of the 157 people advised of £39.59, or £2,058 a year (Griffiths, 1993).

Box 1.2: An individual case-study from the Southwark Benefits Advice Service

Mr Andrews is a pensioner who was diagnosed as having terminal cancer. His wife visited the Southwark Benefits Advice Service to find out if they could claim any benefits to ease the financial pressures caused by Mr Andrews's illness. When the adviser checked his benefits, she found that Mr Andrews should have been receiving the higher rate of Disability Living Allowance but was only being paid the lower rate. The Benefits Advice Service arranged a review of the original decision by claiming under special rules for people with terminal illness. The review was successful and resulted in Mr and Mrs Andrews receiving an extra £45.70 a week and a backdated lump sum of £500. Mr Andrews had believed that the Disability Living Allowance he was receiving disqualified him from claiming Housing or Council Tax Benefit. In fact, he could have been claiming these benefits for some years so the Benefits Advice Service have applied for a backdated payment. Claims are backdated only up to 52 weeks, regardless of the length of time the claimant should have been getting benefits. Even so, this will result in another lump sum of £650.

Other welfare rights initiatives in general practice are choosing to place computer hardware and software in general practice settings for joint use by health professionals and patients, rather than employ specialist advisers. A computer allows for privacy but it also requires computer literacy. This way, therefore, would need back-up support and advice for welfare rights experts as and when necessary.

Occupational health advice in general practice

The concept of providing occupational health advice within a general practice setting has been pioneered by four occupational health projects in the UK, based in Liverpool, Sheffield, Bradford and Camden. Their origins relate to campaigning by trade unions active in the occupational health field, and to the broader context of community development work initiated by the WHO-inspired Healthy Cities programme. The projects provide another useful illustration of the way in which health promotion in general practice can, in a very practical sense, start from an understanding of, and intervene to tackle, social causes of ill-health.

The Camden Occupational Health Project (COHP) aims to raise awareness in general practice of occupational health issues by providing support to patients and by supporting practice staff who deal with health and safety problems experienced by patients. It is funded by the local health authority.

The core of COHP work is interviewing patients in GP surgeries. The objective is to raise patient awareness about occupational health and safety and to give patients concrete practical help. Through interviews (which may be project-initiated by invitations or initiated by GP referral or self-referral) a full occupational history is taken which is later summarised on a record card for inclusion in the patient's medical records. Where hazards or problems are identified during the interview the Occupational Health Adviser gives detailed advice on what can be done in the workplace to prevent the problem. Further information is sent if needed and occasionally the project intercedes on a person's behalf by contacting an enforcement agency or writing to an employer (COHP, 1993).

A growing area of the project's work is the provision of training initiatives for GPs and practice nurses to increase their knowledge and awareness of how work may be affecting the health of their patients. The project has worked with practice nurses to include occupational health issues on the new patient registration forms, and to assist them in assessing whether patients would need to be referred to the project or should be provided with information leaflets.

An unresolved issue for COHP, highlighted by a recent evaluation (Shipley, 1993), is whether it can be most effective by encouraging a change in professional behaviour by giving GPs and practice nurses the knowledge, confidence and skills to incorporate more appropriate preventive occupational health work into their consultations, or whether this work is best carried out by specialist occupational health project staff, working within, and collaborating with, general practice.

Public health nursing in general practice

> In essence, public health is a collective view of the health needs and health care of a population rather than an emphasis on an individual perspective... Health analysis is the first stage of taking public health perspectives forward into nursing practice... Another essential feature of public health action relates to community action or development.
>
> (Royal College of Nursing, 1994)

> Public health can be seen as an approach to tackling health and social problems with a clear political dimension. It is a philosophy of care and a strategy for action ... We need to find ways of responding directly to the structural factors which affect our clients' health, exploring approaches which allow us to address the root causes of ill health. In short, we need a public health approach.
>
> (Savigar and Buxton, 1993)

There are those within community nursing, particularly health visiting, who see the increasing focus on purchasing for primary care and GP fund holding, together with the attention given to health promotion by the Health of the Nation policy, as an exciting opportunity to develop a 'public health nursing' role as an integral part of general practice (as well as in other settings). The SNMAC (Standing Nurse Midwife Administrative Committee) emphasised the need for nurses and midwives as well as health visitors to adopt a public health approach 'to achieve commonly shared goals for improving the health and wellbeing of people' (DoH 1995: 31). GP fund holders are now in a position to purchase community nursing services and could therefore purchase nursing services to include a public health function. It offers an interesting alternative model to that of practice nurses where the focus of their role is on more conventional screening programmes.

What do you think might be the strengths and weaknesses of the view of public health nursing given in the quotations above?

One case study of this approach which indicates some of the possible strengths and limitations is provided by the Public Health Nurse Project initiated by a general practice in Castlefields, Runcorn. The project began in 1990, funded for two years by Mersey Regional Health Authority. During the course of the project, the practice became a fund-holding practice.

The post of public health nurse was seen as a way of stimulating the PHCT to utilise community development and community advocacy ways of working to research, identify and address the health needs of the local practice population. The job involved:

- establishing a database by compiling, analysing and interpreting information gathered to produce a health profile
- being a community development facilitator
- having an educative role for both the community and the PHCT
- being a community research person for primary care
- auditing the public health perspective of primary care.

The thinking behind the project was that the public health nurse should not be seen as an additional PHC worker, but rather as a new approach to health visiting:

> Many would in fact argue that this was the health visitor's original role, long lost in the mists of NHS reorganisation. We felt that... the public health nurse role could emancipate health visiting from the rather narrow approach to primary care which currently confines the work of many health visitors.
>
> (Colin-Thomé, 1993)

However, when the pilot project finished, the health visitors attached to the practice, already overburdened, felt unable to take on the additional public health role and incorporate it into their everyday work. A decision was therefore taken by the project to employ a nurse practitioner, whose role is to: be available to patients as an alternative to consulting GPs, be a health promotion co-ordinator, and undertake the community development work of the public health nurse.

The practice feels that, in this particular case, the role of public health nurse has been subsumed by the whole of the PHCT, rather than it becoming a separate, distinct entity. In larger practices, a separate role of public health nurse may be more applicable and more viable.

1.5 Moving a broader view of health promotion from the margins to the mainstream: obstacles and opportunities

In this final section we explore how feasible and appropriate it would be for the broader health promotion initiatives described here to be more widely adopted within general practice.

First, it is worth looking at the findings of a survey of innovative general practices undertaken by Hilary Neve, a GP in Plymouth (Neve, 1996). Most of the GPs she interviewed felt that their work was more satisfying as a result of closer links with the community. With the information they gained about local health resources beyond general practice they felt empowered in their role as doctors:

> Most doctors recognise that many patients' problems are rooted in poverty, loneliness and poor housing; but they often find it easier to treat the symptoms than to delve into problems for which they have no solution. Once they can suggest a welfare rights worker, a reminiscence group or housing action association they are often more prepared to address these issues... Several doctors [said] they now prescribe fewer drugs: they might suggest a relaxation class instead of benzodizepines, a support group instead of a course of antidepressants and osteopathy or yoga rather than painkillers. Many also spoke of the benefits of having closer links with other agencies – they no longer saw themselves as responsible for all patients' problems but recognised that these were shared problems which needed shared solutions.
>
> (Neve, 1996)

Perhaps the most obvious obstacle to working in this way is lack of time. General practice staff involved in initiatives working with local communities stress the amount of time and commitment involved. It is understandable, given the pressures on general practice, that staff feel they do not even have the time to undertake the conventional health promotion indicated by the banding arrangements, let alone get involved with local community groups and setting up welfare rights projects.

But more fundamentally, broader health promotion initiatives involve a basic paradigm shift for general practice and its staff. They involve a belief that health promotion, and PHCTs, should find ways of focusing on the socio-economic factors which influence people's basic foundations for achieving better health. They require recognition that interest in and validation of people's experience and views can be health enhancing in their own right, and ultimately require an act of faith that trusts people to say what they want and need for their health. Broader approaches also involve adopting an evaluative framework that enables benefit to be assessed in terms of what 'ordinary' people define as important for their health rather than what professionals think is important for people's health.

What effects do you think this paradigm shift would have on the traditional doctor/ patient relationship?

These broader approaches to health promotion require a reconceptualisation of the traditional relationship between professionals and patients in general practice. Concepts of empowerment and participation and validation of lay knowledge do not sit comfortably with the way in which the majority of professionals perceive and conduct their role as 'experts' in general practice interactions. Hilary Neve reports that 'some GPs find even the idea of a suggestion box in the waiting room quite threatening. GPs' training teaches them to "know the answers". It does not equip them to learn from the community and actively seek out their views.'

It is argued that another obstacle to the more widespread adoption of broad health promotion initiatives in general practice is the present-day gap between the rhetoric of 'team working' within the PHCT and the reality:

> In many practices the term 'team' is at best a euphemism for a situation in which individuals and professional groups are in reality working in isolation, with occasional encounters or communications between each other, but no real collaboration or integration of effort.
>
> (Taylor and Bloor, 1994)

Health promotion has in fact acted as an important catalyst for change in the development of PHCTs. The Health Education Authority's PHCT workshop programme, established in 1987 as a tool for encouraging general practice to reflect upon and enhance their health promotion and disease prevention activities, primarily focuses on team development and group management skills in general practice (HEA, 1993a).

The following two quotes, from mainstream commentators on general practice and prevention, suggest that such a paradigm shift may be increasingly considered appropriate for general practice:

> Because [PHCTs] are in a position to know more than most about the specific health problems of their local community, they have an important role to play as advocates, ensuring that health becomes an important part of the local and national political agenda. In order to achieve this aim, GPs and other members of the PHCT will need to develop strong links with their local community. They could assist local community groups to define their health needs and to press for change...'
>
> (Coulter, 1993)

> The challenge is for PHC providers to look beyond the confines of the one-to-one consultation or even of family care, and to accept that their role is to work with others to enable the community as a whole to increase its control over the determinants of health.
>
> (Anderson, 1993)

The publication by the Royal College of General Practitioners of an occasional paper on community participation in primary care (Heritage, 1994), describing several of the case-studies of innovative practice identified in this chapter, can be seen as another sign of more awareness within the profession of broader approaches to health promotion, and adds a legitimacy to these broader ways of working.

Backett *et al.* (1994) suggest that the paradigm shift required by general practice for a different approach to health promotion may not be so great, since they believe that GPs are in an ideal position to mesh individual health concerns with a wider, community-oriented view of health. They describe how PHCTs are constantly reminded in their everyday work of the interconnections between the individual and the social:

> Because GPs and their teams are community-based and see members of local populations as individuals, they are in an excellent position to develop an understanding of the environmental, social and personal factors influencing their patients' thoughts about the maintenance of good health and the avoidance of illness. This essentially local knowledge is sometimes at odds with the current goals of health promotion, which tend to underplay environmental and collective issues and to focus more on personal health-related behaviours in the overall context of centrally devised national targets. This approach to health promotion may be in danger of failing to utilise the particular strengths and advantages of the general practice setting. These are that the primary care team has the ability to build up an essentially holistic understanding of both the health of individual patients and the health profile of their community.
>
> (Backett *et al.*, 1994)

Others argue that effective community-oriented initiatives for health gain in general practice require that it be reorganised on a locality rather than a practice population basis. Practice premises and catchment areas have grown up in a haphazard fashion over the years, so that identification with a defined community and collaboration with other services which are organised on a locality basis are difficult (Hughes and Gordon, 1992).

If general practice is to shift towards a more community-oriented approach to health promotion, it is necessary that improved links are made with local authorities and the wide range of organisations and groups that exist within the community. A common cry of professionals outside general practice and of community organisations is that the majority of GPs appear untouched by calls for intersectoral working, links with community groups and the development of healthy alliances. Ashton and Seymour (1988) comment:

> ...whereas some progressive practitioners are keen to develop participative styles and intersectoral working, most are still tightly locked into a medical model. ...When it comes to the kind of community-development linkage with primary health care which is to be found in non-industrial countries and which should be regarded as just as important in, for example, inner-city areas of the UK, there is nothing to suggest that GPs regard this kind of work as having anything to do with them.

Finally, broad approaches to health promotion in general practice will need more resources than the short-term, piecemeal funding they receive at present, and a more supportive organisational structure than the banding system provided (National Heart Forum, 1995; GLACHC, 1995). Whether the new arrangements introduced in 1996 will facilitate PHCTs to work in innovative ways with local communities to promote health, rather than perpetuate a limited conventional health promotion practice remains to be seen.

1.6 Conclusion

This chapter has explored the range of roles for GPs and PHCTs in promoting health within a general practice setting. It began by documenting the influence of national policy on health promotion in general practice since 1990, and described how health promotion in general practice is dominated by risk factor screening and lifestyle advice for CHD and stroke prevention. The second part of the chapter described some initiatives where GPs and PHCTs have moved beyond a medical model of health promotion, and have worked with local communities to promote health in innovative ways. These initiatives, it is suggested, offer exciting models for PHCTs to exploit their unique position to mesh their knowledge of individual health concerns with a wider community-oriented view of health, and work in ways that make explicit the interconnections between the individual and the social in promoting health.

Chapter 2
Community action for health

2.1 Introduction

In the previous chapter the role of the primary health care team in promoting the health of their community was examined and some innovative strategies were suggested for PHCTs to be much more active in the community. In this chapter we explore how the *community* can act to promote its own health. Community action for health is based on the premise that health chances and health choices are shaped to a great extent by the social, political and economic conditions in which people live. The ability of individuals to control and shape these wider structures is limited. Community action involves individuals in collective activity to change the socio-economic environment and to redistribute power and resources in order to enhance the health chances of hitherto disadvantaged groups. It requires the participation of local people in working together to promote health: their own and that of others, and is based on the principles of collectivism rather than individualism. Within a collectivist ideology individuals combine and take responsiblility for each other's health and well-being. The individual is not submerged or lost in the collective but is located within it rather than existing in isolation and competition with others (Collins, 1997). A more individualistic approach lays responsibility firmly on individuals. They, therefore, may need to compete with others to improve their own health and well-being.

There are many ways that people work collectively for health. The umbrella term 'community action' begs the question what constitutes community? The term is used in so many contexts that we need to think a little about the various meanings associated with it. The term community implies a common bond. It may be based on geography or locality. But there are other characteristics which might create common bonds such as identity or sharing a common problem or interest.

2.2 The meaning of community

What does community mean to you and what communities do you consider you belong to?

You could have identified a number of communities to which you belong. Maybe you identified the area where you live, but if so did you identify your road or street or was it your estate or neighbourhood in general? Perhaps it was a school catchment area or a political ward, a parish or village, a district or county, or a nation or even a group of nations. If you live in a large town or city you may not feel part of any geographical community, you may not even know your neighbours or want to know them. Perhaps you feel you belong more to another form of community based on age, gender, ethnicity or nationality. Or maybe you have more in common with other groups of people based on a common interest. A love of music or drama may have motivated you to join a drama or operatic or orchestral group. Religion or politics may bind you to a group of like-minded people. It could be that your workplace feels like your community. Or you may feel you belong to a group of people on the basis of a shared problem.

Of course none of these are mutually exclusive and your communities will probably intersect. If you belong to a particular ethnic community this may or may not coincide with a particular locality. If you belong to a religious group again this may also provide a geographical community based on the church, temple, mosque or synagogue. Gender or sexuality may coincide with a political grouping such as a women's group, gay rights movement or political party.

Community tends to have quite a positive image. It evokes a sense of closeness and warmth – 'the face-to-face close comfort of regular personal contact with valued others' (Heginbotham, 1986: 10). But Heginbotham goes on to describe a less attractive side to community which can be both punitive and coercive. Community norms or the values of a small clique can be imposed on others who perhaps do not share or welcome them. We may be part of a community which is in conflict and which is experienced as alienating rather than binding, maybe even suffocating. Neighbourliness can sometimes feel like an invasion of privacy. Close-knit communities can serve to make us feel valued or excluded and communities can be at war on the basis of some other grouping which may follow class, ethnic or religious affiliation.

Community action for health operates within a diverse range of communities and because they are not always harmonious, part of community action for health may well involve attempts to reconcile various conflicts. The relationship of health to these various notions of community may be strong or extremely weak, even non-existent. On the other hand health is often a motivating force for bringing people together. Alan Beattie describes community action for health in the following way:

> A group or groups of like-minded people, who recognize themselves as having common experiences in health matters, come together to discuss and review their concerns, to take stock of their situations, to identify mutual problems and to share in the process of clarifying options, working out appropriate joint action and setting about the process of trying to change their circumstances.
>
> (1991: 176)

Have you been involved in or do you know of any community action for health? Was this based on a locality or some other grouping?

Perhaps you have been involved in a women's health group which campaigned for a Well Woman Clinic. Maybe you have been active in campaigning for traffic calming measures to be put in your road. Perhaps you are caring for an older relative and you belong to a carers' group which is working to get better day-care facilities. On the other hand you may be a health professional working on a particular housing estate to improve the living conditions.

Community action for health can involve both lay and professional people. Before we address the issue of who participates and how, we will try to draw together the various strands of what has been identified as a community health movement.

2.3 A community health movement

Alison Watt and Sue Rodmell (1988) reviewed a range of community health initiatives and identified over 10,000 which might be said to come under the umbrella of a community health movement. They identified three distinct strands:

- self-help groups, e.g. bereavement support groups
- community health groups, e.g. campaigners against environmental pollution
- community development health projects, e.g. neighbourhood projects with a paid community health worker.

Jane Jones (1991) has suggested a way to understand these different strands. That is to see each as part of a larger grouping but having a distinct health component. She has also widened the net to include social movements such as the women's movement and black and minority ethnic action groups and also health professionals working in more radical ways. Figure 2.1 conceptualises the way in which the health components constitute a community health movement.

The one feature they all share is, as Watt and Rodmell point out, *an understanding of, and commitment to, the process and value of collectivity* (1988: 360). This collective action aims to achieve greater equality and social justice and to break down the unequal power relationships which exist between health professionals and the 'lay' public. As such it is a particular form of collectivity: not that of troops dragooned into battle but based on the full participation in the decision-making process of those concerned. It is characterised by a bottom-up rather than a top-down approach to bringing about change.

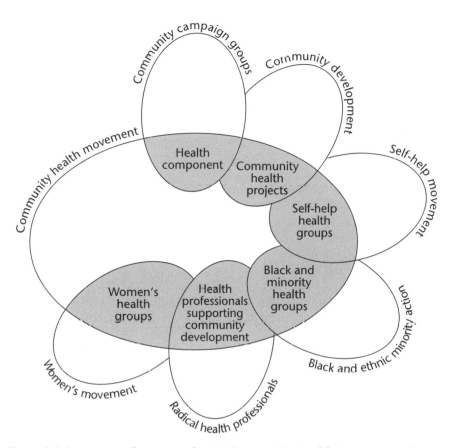

Figure 2.1 **Some contributors to the UK Community Health Movement** (Jones, 1991, adapted from Blennerhassett, *et al.*, 1989)

We will examine each of the groups identified in the diagram in more detail to explore their characteristics.

Community campaign groups with a health component

These groups come together to campaign on a specific issue in their locality which may not be primarily about health. It may, however, have a health component within it even though the main motivation was not health. It may be an environmental issue such as pollution from a local factory which has wider implications, health being one of them. It may be a pensioners' group concerned about the transport needs of older people; or a parent's action group campaigning for a safe play area for their children.

Think of any such campaigns in your locality and try to identify the health component.

Residents of housing estates sometimes get together to campaign for better facilities or to improve existing facilities such as lifts in blocks of flats. Malfunctioning lifts can render older people or parents with young children homebound and have a direct effect on their health and well-being. People who live near airports are constantly vigilant of any increase in flights, especially at night, and will organise a petition or lobby the local authority or their MP to fight any increase. Noise pollution can have a very negative effect on health, especially if sleep is disturbed.

Community campaigns can be reactive or proactive but they tend to come together for a particular purpose and do not necessarily form long-term groupings, although some do form lasting links and campaign over many years. Undoubtedly such campaigns are prime examples of collective action but the acronym NIMBY (Not In My Backyard) could well be applied to many campaigns, especially those which campaign against the siting of an undesirable object. If the fact that this object may be placed in another less articulate or active territory is of no concern, then in ideological terms they are exhibiting many of the features of individualism. If on the other hand, a chain of community protest is set up such as with the anti-road protesters then the ideals of collectivism are being met. Similar contradictions can be located within self-help groups.

Self-help groups

Self-help groups are many and varied. They mainly revolve around a specific problem or condition and are based on the premise of 'being in the same boat' and 'knowing what it's like'. A shared understanding of the situation is founded on the basis of common experience. The Society of Compassionate Friends is a national self-help agency for those who have suffered the loss of a child. Bereaved parents offer support and help to other bereaved parents. Other counsellors or professionals are thought not to be able to understand what it feels like to lose a child if they have not had that personal experience. Similarly members of Alcoholics Anonymous find mutual trust because they have all 'been there'. Mutual aid, therefore, is provided on the basis of common experience. The benefits are reciprocal, helping yourself while helping others. This acknowledges that giving and receiving support is equally beneficial. Where the problem or condition carries an element of stigma the self-help group serves to reinforce self-concepts of normality and validates feelings and attitudes.

As well as the supportive functions of sharing, self-help groups aim to promote the health of participants through increasing understanding and knowledge of the particular problem or condition. Through their collective will-power they may also engage in some form of action towards shared goals. The campaign for greater access for disabled people has achieved some degree of success in getting ramps and lifts installed in buildings. This campaign not only aims to get something practical done but also to expose the disabling nature of modern society and de-stigmatise disability.

Most self-help groups are thoroughly participatory in that they are usually set up and organised by the members themselves. They are therefore genuine, grass roots organisations. But Gareth Williams (1989) has questioned the degree to which they are collectivist in the ideological sense. He claims that most self-help groups are 'janus headed' in that they straddle both the individualist and collectivist ideologies and that an 'uneasy compromise exists between different impulses ... self-care or social support, counselling or activism, personal change or political change (p. 154) .

In similar vein, Watt and Rodmell suggest that self-help groups are usually well regarded by the medical profession in that they provide services which the medical profession has no vested interest in providing. It is only when self-help groups make demands on professional services that they are perceived as challenging. Self help has generally been better at providing help than pressurising the statutory services.

The women's health movement

The women's health movement emerged from the women's liberation movement of the 1970s. By giving women access to information about their own bodies it aimed to enable them to take greater control over decisions about their health and well-being. It also played a part in demanding services such as well women clinics where a woman could be attended to by a woman doctor. More importantly it has taken seriously the health concerns of women in ways which women found acceptable.

Three major strands can be identified in the women's health move-ment. One is the acquisition of knowledge and power over decisions about women's own health discussed in Katz and Peberdy (1997), Chapter 10. The second is the reproductive rights campaign which is concerned with giving women real choices in relation to their own fertility. Gains were made in the provision of free contraception and the availability of abortion on the NHS. The third is the provision of well women clinics which have become an integral part of much community action for health.

Well women clinics

By the 1980s three types of well women clinics had emerged from the women's health movement:

1   **The medical model clinic**. This was largely a screening clinic based on a preventive model of health. Typically it would offer a medical check consisting of a full medical history, urine test, test for anaemia, blood

pressure check, heart soundings, chest and abdomen check, weight, breast examination and a cervical smear test. This service was provided usually by an all female professional staff by the NHS. Treatment was not available at the clinic so the woman had to be referred to her GP if treatment was recommended. This gave rise to a good deal of difficulty in relation to the confidentiality of these clinics. The clinics were seen as threatening to local GPs. In response they set up their own screening clinics so that most GPs nowadays have regular well women clinics.

2   **The holistic model clinic**. This was the preferred option of the activists in the women's health movement. A great deal of campaigning went on to persuade health authorities to provide this model of clinic. They were organised and monitored by the women's health group who usually provided volunteers for each clinic session. The users saw a nurse and a female doctor but the volunteers filled in a questionnaire and did a preliminary interview before the women saw the professionals. This questionnaire was designed to elicit the women's own health agenda to make the process as participatory as possible. A full physical examination was available but in practice doctors found themselves dealing with a great deal of social and emotional stress, with each appointment taking about an hour. Debriefing sessions were held with volunteers and professional staff after each session and an evaluation questionnaire was given to each woman as she left the clinic. This type of clinic was a real attempt to break down the power relationship between doctors and lay public and doctors found themselves working in very different ways. In this way it was a more radical option than the third one.

3   **The self-help model clinic**. This type of clinic was organised and run by the activists without funding from the health service and without professional input. It provided the opportunity for women to talk over their health problems but did not provide any medical examination or advice. Sometimes these clinics offered pregnancy testing but the emphasis was on sharing health education and knowledge so that women would be in a better position to make their own health choices. These clinics were often the catalyst for the formation of discussion groups on women's health matters.

The early 1980s were a time of maximum activity in the founding of well women clinics. By 1987 a survey carried out by the Labour Party women's organisation found that 381 clinics were in existence which had some funding by the health authorities. Of these, 76 per cent resembled the medical model and only 23 per cent the holistic model. (Self-help clinics were not accessible to the survey.) Much of the provision was being taken over by GPs who, as discussed in the previous chapter, were also encouraged by financial incentives to carry out their own cervical screening. The holistic model was beginning to be squeezed out by the late 1980s and the tantalising vision of a more radical partnership between women and their doctors began to fade.

The Women's Health Movement was criticised for expressing the needs of mainly white and many would argue white middle-class women and black women felt that it had little relevance for them. The black and minority ethnic movement for health developed separately and focused on the experience of black men and women (Douglas, 1996).

Black and minority ethnic health action

A major threat to the health and well-being of people from black and minority ethnic groups is racism and racial discrimination. Health is inextricably bound up with issues such as employment, poverty, welfare rights, immigration legislation and racial harassment. So health is a part of all community action to combat racial disadvantage and discrimination. As Douglas says:

> A meaningful exploration of the experiences of black and minority ethnic communities in Britain in relationship to health or many other issues must incorporate the relationship of black and minority ethnic communities to the social organisation of British society. Within British society racism and racial discrimination are central features in the lives and experiences of black and minority ethnic communities. A black minority culture is often compared to white majority culture in a detrimental way such that beliefs and values of minority cultures are undervalued.
>
> (Douglas, 1991: 21)

Much of the impetus for black and minority ethnic health action arose out of the institutional racism experienced by both service users and workers within the NHS. It was claimed that this institutional racism adversely affected the health and well-being of black and minority ethnic people. The response to this can be traced in two forms of action; the campaign for racist awareness education within the health sector and in single issue campaigns organised around a specific condition such as sickle cell anaemia or diabetes.

Training in health and race was set up to enable NHS workers more effectively to recognise and meet the needs of black and minority ethnic communities (Douglas, 1991). The strategy adopted was to develop racism awareness and anti-racist training programmes. As Douglas points out, this 'represented a shift from "cultural awareness" training and the position of viewing minority ethnic cultures as being problematic' (p. 23). Although there is now a growing literature on the health of black and minority ethnic communities much of this falls within a biomedical model of health and focuses on particular diseases which affect those communities (Smaje, 1995). Douglas (1996) claims that the health inequalities which undoubtedly exist between the white and the black and minority ethnic communities are much more to do with racially disadvantaged economic and social conditions.

The health agenda coming from black communities has tended to focus on conditions such as sickle cell anaemia and thalassaemia, particularly in terms of the lack of appropriate service provision which is linked to racial discrimination. But the wider association between poverty, racism and ill health has received rather less attention. Drawing on research into the health and social needs of black and minority ethnic communities in Smethwick, Birmingham, Douglas (1996) argues that health promotion workers need to address both the broad and narrower health agendas. She believes that focusing on the lack of provision for specific conditions such as sickle cell anaemia builds up community support and trust which can be harnessed to tackle the wider issues such as poor housing and racial discrimination.

Radical health professionals

All the groups discussed so far are grass roots organisations with a bottom-up structure. How can health professionals fit into that kind of structure?

Health visitors work *in* the community but the extent to which they work *for* the community is debatable. Yvonne Dalziel (1994), a health visitor who has tried to incorporate a community development approach in her work, poses three fundamental questions for radical health visitors to ask themselves:

1 In what ways can I help the community respond to difficulties so that they become collectivised rather than individualised?
2 How can I use individual knowledge and experience and help it to be shared with others in a way that leaves families and their community more empowered?
3 As a health visitor, how can I tap into the everyday support and learning that occurs naturally as part of human contact?

How do you think Dalziel's focus differs from the traditional health visitor role?

Dalziel compares this approach with the traditional health visitor role in child health clinics, which she claims is that of expert in child development and parenting. The parent is largely passive in the face of this 'overwhelming power of knowledge' (1994: 355). Dalziel believes that the best way to shift this balance of power is to use and value the expertise and knowledge of parents. She proposes to get parents to take responsibility for assessing their own child's development and to share their experiences with other parents. The health visitor's role is to facilitate this sharing of knowledge and to support it.

Other health professionals such as occupational therapists who have traditionally worked with individuals, are taking on more community-focused health promoting roles. The Canadian Association of Occupational Therapists states that:

The integration of individuals with families, families with communities and communities with the larger social context, is a fundamental component of occupational therapy, client services and research .

(CAOT, 1996)

2.4 Community development health projects

Community health projects emerged in the late 1970s. They have their roots in the Community Development Projects which were set up in 1969 by the government as 'a neighbourhood-based experiment aimed at finding new ways of meeting the needs of people living in areas of high social deprivation' (quoted in Jones, 1991: 32). Jan Smithies (1995), at a recent conference of community development workers held in Bradford, charted the history of Community Development for Health.

1970s and 80s:
- Local projects emerging out of women's and Black movements.

1981:
- Development of London Community Health Resource (LCHR) (funded by King's Fund/Greater London Council)

1982:
- National Council for Voluntary Organisations (NCVO) Inner Cities Unit publish *Community Based Health Initiatives*

1983:
- Community Health Initiatives Resource Unit (CHIRU) established at NCVO (funded by DoH)

1986:
- CHIRU and LCHR merge to form National Community Health Resource (NCHR)
- First national Community Development and Health (CDH) Conference, Bradford

1987/88:
- NCHR established and set up:
  - Women's Health Network
  - Black Health Forum
  - CDH Training Project and Regional Training Groups
- Second national conference (Salford)

1988:
- Health Education Authority (HEA) sets up Professional and Community Development (PGG) Division – £250K budget for CD, including some funding for NCHR

1988/89:
- PCD Division attempts to establish a national (England) CDH Strategy

1989:
- Third national conference (Newcastle)

1990:
- *Roots and Branches* Winter School, Open University (funded by HEA)
- HEA drops CDH as specific budget and post

1991/92:
- *Community Development and Health – Reclaiming the National Agenda –* National Seminar (Sheffield)
- NCHR loses HEA funding

1992/93:
- Community Health UK (CHUK) established out of NCHR. CHUK loses DoH funding

1994:
- N. Ireland establishes Community Health Network
- Scotland establishes Community post at the Health Education Board for Scotland (HEBS)
- Health Promotion Wales establishes 'Communities for Better Health' Network

1995:
Some current opportunities for CDH work
- Health for All/Healthy Cities
- Community Care/Advocacy
- Standing Conference for Community Development
- *Local Voices* – an important aspect of purchasing agenda
- 'Locality planning' taken on by many Health Commissions
- Local Authority Community Forums
- Agenda 21 focuses on community involvement in developing sustainable environments
- Childrens Act emphasises childrens' rights and involvement
- HIV/AIDS work
- etc.

The first community development health projects were mostly funded by inner city partnership money, the Urban Aid programme or by charitable trusts (Jones, 1991). More recently Healthy City and Health for All initiatives have led to the development of more projects. Projects are now likely to be funded by mainstream NHS budgets or linked directly to primary care centres or health promotion units. The focus on a needs-led service and the commitment to listen to local voices has put community work more centre stage. Community development workers who once saw themselves on the other side of the battle lines attacking statutory provision or state bureaucracy now find themselves on the pay role acting as go-between. Is this a welcome development? Does it represent a new awareness on the part of the statutory services? The late Wendy Farrant was sceptical about the new rhetoric of user participation and community involvement, She wrote:

> The belated interest of the NHS in community development needs to be seen in relation to the crisis in the welfare state, and broader debates around such issues as community care, volunteerism, decentralisation and consumerism.
>
> (Farrant, 1994: 14)

She goes on to argue that this new interest is largely concerned with consumerist notions of community participation which she believes 'undermines the fundamental principles of community development' (1994: 17)

Community development embraces a set of principles which are embodied in the Charter of the Standing Conference for Community Development (SCCD). These are set out in Box 2.1.

What do you think are the essential themes emerging from the charter in Box 2.1?

Participation and involvement are recurrent themes. The charter stresses the collective and active involvement of people in issues which affect their lives.

It is concerned with issues of powerlessness and disadvantage and it is no accident that community development projects were not set up in affluent residential areas. The process is concerned with 'the empowering and enabling of those who are traditionally deprived of power and control over their common affairs'.

Translated into health the aims of the community health projects were to set up a process whereby the community defines its own health needs, works out how those needs can best be met and collectively decides on a course of action to achieve the desired outcomes.

Lee Adams has distinguished the main features of a community development approach to health. These are:

(a) A whole person, holistic approach is emphasised in contrast to depersonalised topics, diseases or parts of the body.

(b) It is something done with people, not to them, the members of the group or community are involved at all stages.

Box 2.1: A working statement on community development

This is adopted as a move towards our understanding of Community Development.

Community Development is crucially concerned with the issues of powerlessness and disadvantage: as such it should involve all members of society, and offers a practice that is part of a process of social change.

Community Development is about the active involvement of people in the issues which affect their lives. It is a process based on the sharing of power, skills, knowledge, and experience.

Community Development takes place both in neighbourhoods and within communities of interest, as people identify what is relevant to them.

The Community Development process is collective, but the experience of the process enhances the integrity, skills, knowledge and experience, as well as the equality of power, for each individual who is involved.

Community Development seeks to enable individuals and communities to grow and change according to their own needs and priorities, and at their own pace, provided this does not oppress other groups and communities, or damage the environment.

Where Community Development takes place, there are certain principles central to it. The first priority of the Community Development process is the empowering and enabling of those who are traditionally deprived of power and control over their common affairs. It claims as importantly the ability of people to act together to influence the social, economic, political and environmental issues which affect them. Community Development aims to encourage sharing, and to create structures which give genuine participation and involvement.

Community Development is about developing the power, skills, knowledge and experience of people as individuals and in groups, thus enabling them to undertake initiatives of their own to combat social, economic, political and environmental problems, and enabling them to fully participate in a truly democratic process.

Community Development must take a lead in confronting the attitudes of individuals and the practices of institutions and society as a whole which discriminate unfairly against black people, women, people with disabilities and different abilities, religious groups, elderly people, lesbians and gay men, and other groups who are disadvantaged by society. It also must take a lead in countering the destruction of the natural environment on which we all depend. Community Development is well placed to involve people equally on these issues which affect all of us.

Community Development should seek to develop structures which enable the active involvement of people from disadvantaged groups, and in particular people from ethnic minorities and black groups.

(SCCD, 1992)

(c) The public are encouraged to identify their own needs rather than receiving a professionally prescribed list of priorities. Problems are seen to be interrelated not compartmentalised into 'health', 'housing', 'education' etc.

(d) The outcomes of such approaches are to a certain extent unpredictable and this has important implications for evaluation.

(e) Lay understanding is emphasised in contrast to professional mystification.

(f) More stress is placed on issues common to many members of a community rather than concentrating upon individuals and their problems in isolation.

(g) It seeks to achieve greater participation by communities in their own health and health care delivery.

(Adams, quoted in Cox and Findlay, 1990: 6)

A community development approach takes time, perhaps two or three years, to build up trust, involvement and understanding of local issues and concerns. Some projects start by setting up in a local community centre or shopping precinct. Or the community development worker may visit local groups, knock on doors, or frequent play areas or launderettes. Undertaking a community profile or needs assessment by involving local people and groups in the process is becoming increasingly popular. This then becomes not only an information-gathering exercise but allows people to learn new skills as well as share experiences. The project worker may become involved in setting up mutual support groups and action groups. They may wish to influence statutory service provision, or they may become involved in setting up their own initiatives (such as food co-operatives) or they may campaign around a particular issue (such as improving the safety of children on their own estate).

Those who work within CDH projects are very positive and sometimes evangelical about their work but they are not without their critics. Alan Beattie, who is mainly very positive about the contribution of CDH projects, nevertheless points out some areas of criticism. CDH is, as he says, 'sometimes unforgivably naive in its claim to be able to transform the lives and social prospects of deprived groups' (1991: 178). Beattie also points out that there is 'the persistent doubt whether local action can ever achieve more than marginal and token victories in the face of the larger social inequalities and social injustices which, of course, reflect policies at national level' (1991: 178).

Proponents of CDH would counter that, although they recognise the need to change policy at national and international level, their endeavours are focused on helping deprived and oppressed groups to 'find a voice' (Rosenthal, 1983). The following 'pyramid diagram' shows a six category classification of CDH activity shown as a continuum with an increasing degree of community influence and control, from the community being provided for, consulted or co-opted at the bottom of

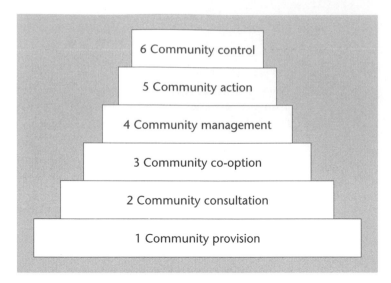

Figure 2.2 (Baites, 1991)

the pyramid to devolvement of management with the community taking action and having control at the top of the pyramid.

A community group's 'purpose' might not be primarily to redress social inequalities. It may be to provide a community centre where local people can meet and organise local activities. There are many small steps on the road to achieving the CDH workers' aim to empower communities to take control over their own affairs. Although an ultimate aim would be to promote equity, they would identify many other categories of activity which achieve a health gain. The issues of empowerment and achieving equity are developed in the next chapter.

It is the role of the health promotion community development worker which is particularly ambiguous. If paid by the state they are therefore accountable to it. Yet the worker is nevertheless expected to provide a service to the local community and motivate that community to work collectively for change. There is thus a possible contradiction that in trying to give a voice to the underprivileged that voice may well challenge and be in conflict with the state and the bureaucracies through which it works thus being inclined to 'bite the hand that feeds them' (Loney, 1983).

CDH project worker's loyalties are usually firmly located in their community and they see themselves as having a pivotal role in supporting the community and facilitating group action as well as securing resources and access to policy makers. Thus the role ambiguity can be construed as positive as well as negative.

The following account from a community development worker illustrates some of the dilemmas of the role.

Box 2.2: A vision of health promotion

So, here I am then, a community health worker on the Bournville Estate, Weston-super-Mare, with a remit to reduce the factors which contribute to morbidity from heart disease over a three year period. I'm interested in heart disease, but my problem is that no one here gives a toss about it. They're much more interested in other factors in their lives: about how to make ends meet from day to day, how you pay the bills, how they buy food in the afternoon. They don't think about tea-time three weeks in advance, and go down to the local supermarket and fill up the hatch-back with healthy foods. They think about tea-time at half past three, send little Willie over to the chip shop and buy the food then, depending on what's in their purse.

No one here's interested in heart disease. It's my remit to make them interested – how do I go about that? Do I become the lifestyle thought police, following people round the supermarkets, following them home, seeing what they're eating, seeing if they're taking enough exercise, seeing what they're smoking? Is that the way?

No. We looked at a completely different approach here. We've not looked at those lifestyle factors at all initially. We've said a healthy community is a community where people feel they're a part of it, they've some control over their daily lives, they feel empowered to make some decisions which affect them.

Traditional health promotion approaches have tended to blame the victim for the diseases they're suffering from. If you're a smoker or drinker, you don't eat the right diet, you're overweight, don't take enough exercise – it's your fault, you've done these things, you contributed to your own ill-health.

What we tried to do on the Bournville is get away from that image of health promotion and instead promote a positive image of people in a community organising for themselves. We feel if they do that, this will be a much more positive approach to improving their health than blaming them for aspects of their lifestyle.

(Bruce *et al.*, 1995: xix)

What similarities do you see between this community health worker's approach and the community-oriented approach to PHC discussed in Chapter 1?

The acknowledgement of the importance of paying attention to local people's own perspectives on their health and to understand the impact of the conditions of their lives on their health is essential to community development and to communitiy-oriented approaches in general practice.

Community development goes a step further in actively trying to organise communities to take action on their own behalf.

2.5 Conclusion

Community action for health takes many forms. Some action is based on conflict, battling against state bureaucracies for better services or changes in policy. Other forms are more consensual, working together to improve conditions. Collective action is the unifying factor based on the premise that the whole is more than the sum of the parts and that powerless individuals can have more influence if they work together. Community development is a way of working which aims to encourage communities to identify their concerns and to find ways of working collectively. Chapter 4 takes a more detailed look at how community development workers go about this task but, before that, the next chapter focuses on how communities can form partnerships and collaborations to achieve their goals by forming health alliances.

Chapter 3
Partnerships and collaborations: the promise of participation

3.1 Introduction

The last chapter focused on groups of people working at the local level to define and promote their collective concerns in relation to health. Enabling and encouraging people to participate in that process is a key aim. If community groups operate in isolation they will not make an impact on the organisations and agencies which affect their health and well-being. Indeed many of the criticisms and potential handicaps of the community action approach are that it marginalises the community and does not challenge or influence wider stakeholders and policy makers. Chapter 1 on the other hand explored the potential within general practices for a community-oriented approach which would explore the health needs and encourage the involvement of local communities in their services. How providers of services and local communities can 'meet in the middle' to define their needs and plan and provide services is the subject of this chapter.

3.2 Health alliances

Building health alliances has become a favourite theme within health promotion. The term 'healthy alliances' was coined following the advent of the government's Health of the Nation strategy. A health alliance has been described as a process which involves networking, co-operation, collaboration and integration (Powell, 1993). Lee Adams, Director of Health Promotion, Sheffield Health Authority, defines the term:

A 'healthy alliance' is a partnership of organisations and/or individuals to enable people to increase control over and to improve their health and well-being

- emotionally
- physically
- mentally
- socially/environmentally.

A partnership for health gain that goes beyond health care and attempts collectively to change social and environmental circumstances which affect health.

(Adams, quoted in Powell, 1993)

The wider policy implications of health alliances and the issues of intersectoral and interagency working are the subject of Part 2, Chapter 8. Here we are concerned with the alliances, partnerships and collaborations that are available to groups at the local level.

Implicit in the notion of partnerships and collaborations is that the partners and collaborators are fully participant. This process of participation is not the same as the process of consultation where a government agency, local authority or planning group consult with members of the community on an issue which is on their agenda. There is an important distinction to be made between the terms 'participation' and 'consultation'. The fundamental characteristics are:

Consultation	Participation
1 information gathered from citizens	1 shared decision making
2 dialogue controlled by government or agency	2 negotiated relationships
3 on-going dialogue	3 no on-going dialogue
4 problem/issue/plan name given	4 open problem/issue/plan naming
5 no agreement on power sharing	5 resources for less powerful groups to aid their participation.
	(adapted from Labonté, 1993)

Forming partnerships and collaborations and building health alliances is a two-way process. Both a push and pull aspect are possible. The push effect is prominent when the impetus for the partnership or collaboration comes from a community group that wants to widen its sphere of influence, mobilise resources or gather support from other groups. The pull effect is apparent when groups in the community are consulted or invited to participate in activities which affect their community or to make the delivery of services more accountable to local needs. Although in practice the distinction is rarely clear cut, the push effect of a community seeking a partnership is a 'bottom-up' alliance, the pull effect of inviting in the community represents a more 'top-down' alliance.

3.3 'Bottom-up' alliances

Community groups might find it useful to develop a partnership with local authorities, the education sector, other voluntary groups, the NHS, including health professionals and GPs, business and employees, trade unions or the media.

To a great extent the reasons for the alliance will determine which groups are involved and who initiates the partnership.

Self-help groups may want to provide a telephone help line to others who share their concerns. They may therefore approach the local authority for a grant or for the use of premises from which to operate. A campaign group for a safe children's play area may elicit the help of the local newspaper to gain support for their scheme. Activists in the women's health movement who campaigned to set up well woman clinics which provided professional as well as voluntary help had to engage with the local health authority. It was important to form a partnership in which the health authority provided premises and professional help for the clinic but which still allowed the women's group to run the clinic.

Black and minority ethnic community groups may work with local schools to promote racial awareness or with the family doctor service to improve the accessibility of the service for their community.

The DoH manual *Working for Better Health* (1993) notes the following possible benefits to forming partnerships:

- mobilising resources
- generating networks
- exchanging information
- breaking down barriers
- broadening responsibility for health.

Three community development projects from Liverpool are good examples of 'bottom-up' alliances.

As you read through the three case studies think how far they achieved the benefits suggested in the DoH manual.

The Ellergreen Centre

Ellergreen is a community centre in one of the largest satellite housing estates in Liverpool with a population of over 21,000. The estate covers approximately one square mile with very low car ownership. It has no clubs or traditional pubs so there is no place where community activities could take place. The estate is economically and socially deprived with high unemployment rates. Various self-help groups tried to offer mutual help but had no base from which to operate. Two local groups, PADA (Parents Against Drug Abuse) and a women's health group, were so frustrated with having no base that when a local school was re-located they took over part of the empty building. Supported by Liverpool Healthy Cities neighbourhood health team, they formed an alliance with other agencies such as the police, churches and local councillors and set up the Norris Green Community Health Forum. The resulting community working group negotiated with the local education authority which owned the empty school and were given permission to stay. The Health Forum then took up residence in the school, organising slimming groups, bereavement support groups, healthy budget cookery courses, dance and exercise classes. The City Council had hoped to sell the site and so this action had financial implications for the Council.

Although gaining access to the building was a great step forward for the community group the actual building was far from satisfactory and it has been a struggle to maintain morale with inadequate heating and sometimes no water or electricity. The building has been frequently vandalised and many windows are broken or boarded up. However, over a period of five years, the Norris Green Health Forum and the City Council have worked together with other local groups and the Health Authority and developed plans for a complete refurbishment of the site. The plans are very ambitious and include a medical centre from which local GPs will operate, a swimming pool and leisure facility, integrated childcare facilities, a managed workspace and training facility and a community café. The Health Alliance between the local people of the Norris Green Health Forum, the City Council and the Health Authority has put together funding bids to various English and European funds.

Supported Independent Living Project Housing (SILPH)

In late 1990 a small group of parents who had sons and daughters with a learning disability living at home approached the Croxteth Health Action Project (CHAP). They were concerned about what would happen to their sons and daughters when they were unable to care for them. With Lorraine Rowlands, a neighbourhood development worker from CHAP they devised a questionnaire which was sent to all local carers to find out what their concerns were, and from that they carried out a series of focus group discussions with other carers. The main need which emerged was for some local accommodation for adults with learning disabilities which also provided support. They approached social services, the housing department, the police, local clergy, the health authority, local community representatives and tenant organisations. From this they formed a multi-disciplinary management advisory board.

The group worked closely with the social services and housing departments from Liverpool City Council. Social Services made a commitment to provide the care costs which would pay for the support to enable tenants to live in their own homes. The housing department's role was to identify and secure appropriate accommodation within the local community that had the potential to be refurbished to meet the needs of the tenants and to identify and secure the funding to carry out the refurbishment. Throughout the process the views and needs of the parents and their children were paramount. Five years later and after many disappointments and false starts accommodation was found and refurbished and the tenants moved in. Five people with learning disabilities now have their own front door key and are living independently, with some support, in their own homes.

The Asian Women's Swimming Project

The Asian Health Forum in Liverpool had identified a worrying degree of isolation and depression amongst Asian women in the area. Joanne McKain, a neighbourhood development health worker, became involved in helping to find ways of alleviating some of this isolation and depression. She worked with Sanjeeda Nabi, an Asian woman worker with the Health Forum who could speak many of the community languages. After discussions with some of the local Asian women who expressed a desire to take part in leisure activities, they decided to approach a local sports centre manager about the possibility of the Asian women attending the centre for swimming lessons. They explained the cultural and religious needs of the women. For instance they would need total privacy, the windows to be blacked out and the sessions to be staffed only by women. The centre manager was co-operative and even managed to get funding from local sports development funds to subsidise the pool for one session a week and to provide an instructor. Although the funding was for one month, an alliance had been formed between local Asian women, the sports centre and the sports development fund.

The scheme proved to be popular. In fact it was almost too popular as 30 women turned up on the first day and many brought their children. This tested the goodwill of the centre manager and Joanne had to work hard to defuse his anxieties. They re-arranged the timings of the sessions to late on sunday afternoon so as not to conflict with other pool activities and managed to accommodate the children. At the end of the trial period the sports development fund agreed to pay for another three month's of sessions and about 20 women and 20 children attended regularly throughout the summer. Joanne was able to delegate responsibility for the sessions to some of the participants. The women became interested in other sports activities and Joanne moved onto trying to open up other sports facilities to increase the choices available to the women.

In terms of the benefits achieved they were all able to mobilise resources and support from departments within Liverpool City Council, e.g. SILPH from housing and social services. They both generated networks between the local community groups and the statutory bodies involved. This allowed for an exchange of information which broadened the base of information and increased the range of skills, ideas and approaches. In so doing they were also broadening the boundaries of responsibility for health and through co-operation achieved common goals. Resources were mobilised for the Asian women from the sports development fund and so again this was broadening responsibilities for health. Through exchanging information about the cultural needs of the Asian women they were also breaking down barriers by opening up a range of facilities hitherto unused by the community of Asian women.

All three managed to keep going, sometimes against considerable odds. But alliances are not easy to sustain. They sometimes collapse after a few meetings, are mere 'talking shops', fail to make decisions, become inward looking and exclusive, have vague or unrealistic goals or are insensitive to different points of view.

Draw on your own experience of working with others to assess the difficulties you think alliances might face.

The parties involved may not have the same outlook or share the same goals. There may be an imbalance in what each party is putting into the alliance and what each is getting out of it. They may lack an understanding of their different organisational structures. In order to succeed, the core group must have a shared vision, a common agenda, agreed priorities, openness about self-interests, mutual respect, trust, the ability to learn from others, and cultural sensitivity.

A great deal depends on achieving consensus. Although PADA and the women's health group at Ellergreen initially took direct action by taking over the building, they were always willing to leave peacefully when the Council decided they needed the building. By negotiating with the Council they gained legitimate access to the building and entered a partnership to provide better community facilities for their area. However it could be argued that the Council might not have been able to sell the site and would have had a derelict building to manage. It therefore may have suited the Council to hand over the building. Had the Council been unwilling to negotiate, the squatters' decision to act peacefully would have lost them their centre.

Road campaigners tend to take a more conflictual approach, occupying houses and treetops along the route of a proposed road building scheme. They often have to be forcibly removed, thus risking arrest by their protest. Invariably they *are* removed *and* the roads are built. But they would argue that their impact is much wider than one particular road building scheme and that they have influenced general road building policy with a number of projects being cut. Some would argue that the government might be glad of the opportunity to cut down on public spending and so are using the protesters as an excuse.

Community groups who build health alliances are working within a consensus model of action and claim that this is the way forward to improve the circumstances of disadvantaged groups. Others would claim that this type of action is essentially reformist and never actually challenges the existing power structures. Local people are being helped in a compensatory way rather than fundamentally changing their situation (Tomlinson, 1996). On the other hand there is a growing climate within the health sector of responsiveness to local and community participation. The document *Local Voices* published by the NHS management executive in 1992 urged health authorities to involve local people in decision making.

Setting up an alliance

Working Together for Better Health (DoH, 1993c) provides some useful guidelines for setting up and maintaining an alliance.

Box 3.1: How to get started

The following steps provide a framework for setting up a successful alliance:

- identify where your own organisation wants to improve health and achieve this through joint working
- contact existing alliances in the area to avoid duplicating effort, aims or purpose
- identify and choose potential partners
- set an agenda
- agree common aims and goals between partners, and ensure your partners are committed to those aims and goals
- communicate between and within partner organisations, especially regarding the five Health of the Nation key areas (coronary heart disease, cancers, mental illness, accidents, and HIV/AIDS and sexual health)
- clarify who will take the lead on specific pieces of work and ensuring that agreed work is done
- identify and agree tightly defined tasks for each partner
- agree a procedure for monitoring the effectiveness of the alliances by deciding what work is to be done, what 'milestone' achievements should be reached by when, how quickly the results should be achieved, and what the final results of the joint working should be
- agree between partners how to measure success
- train and educate alliance partners where necessary
- identify and commit resources
- ensure that partner organisations are accountable to those people and groups targeted for health promotion, and that the decision-making process is open.

Box 3.2: How to keep an alliance going

- communicate effectively between the partners about progress and problems

- meet regularly to review progress, letting partners express concerns and make new proposals; regularly compare the intended 'milestone' achievements with the actual achievements

- ensure that partners remain accountable, and that those who stand to benefit from the healthy alliance are able to make comments and suggestions

- review progress by each partner on their particular tasks

- make sure that training and education of partners, their employees and volunteers is continuing, and is available for those who get involved after the healthy alliance is established

- find a means by which differences of opinion can be raised easily and without conflict, and encourage partners to be committed to resolving those differences

- nominate a co-ordinator to make sure all the above are carried out.

Do alliances which are initiated by policy makers and providers of services have a different motivation from the more 'bottom-up' initiatives? The new needs-led, user-responsive NHS is aiming to be sensitive to 'consumer' interests. The next section looks at what can be achieved by this 'top-down' approach.

3.4 'Top-down' approaches

In an attempt to break down barriers which might exist between providers and recipients of services the rhetoric of building health alliances is frequently called upon. This is often motivated by a genuine desire to involve recipients of services in determining what should go into that service. A process of consultation is set up to elicit the views of the community at the planning stage in the hope that those views will be reflected in the eventual outcome. One of the main difficulties faced by those who would consult with communities is first to gain access to the community and secondly to define who is knowledgeable about that community. Rapid appraisal methods are frequently used where key informants in the community are interviewed using qualitative interview techniques to try to build up a number of perspectives which are representative of the community. Key informants are defined as:

1 people who work within a community and have a professional understanding of issues, and often interpret communities from their particular disciplinary vantage point: for example, school teachers, police, health visitors, and so on

2 people who are recognized community leaders and seen to represent (a section of) the community: for example, councillors, church leaders, chairs of self-help groups

3 people who are important within informal networks and often play a central role in local communications: for example, a corner-shop owner, bookie, lollipop person.

(Ong and Humphris, 1994: 66)

What do you think are the main problems associated with these types of consultations?

The common practice of identifying key community activists may focus on people with their own strong agendas which may or may not reflect the agendas of the local population. A local needs assessment survey carried out in Kirkstall, Leeds, found that lay and professional groups held different views about the value of different aspects of health and differed on their assessment of the underlying influences on health. The community representatives also held different views to 'ordinary people' on what were the health needs of the community (Percy-Smith and Sanderson, 1992)

Holroyd (1991) reported on another attempt at collaboration which aimed to improve the mental health services in Salford and make them more sensitive to user's needs. A senior health promotion officer for mental health, was appointed by the regional health authority. Part of his remit was to consult with users of the service to influence future planning. On the positive side Holroyd notes that 'the person whose need is being met will gain in stature and self-esteem if he is at the same time able to meet a need. Therefore the person who is being helped is "dignified" when it is observable that he, too, is helping'. But Holroyd also sounds a few warning notes, asking how representative are the actual people who get involved in the planning. He estimates that out of a patch with a population of 25,000 there will typically only be about 25 people involved or just 0.1 per cent of the population. Another key issue which Holroyd identifies is whether the service has the resources and the will to respond. Without the ability to respond, consultation and collaboration represent mere tokenism and reinforce the power imbalance between provider and user of the service. Holroyd suggests that the flow diagram overleaf may be helpful in establishing effective consultation.

Coke, reflecting on the experiences of black women, is quite sceptical about the consultative and collaborative processes initiated by local and health authorities. She writes as a community health worker in the London Borough of Lambeth and feels that many such consultations left

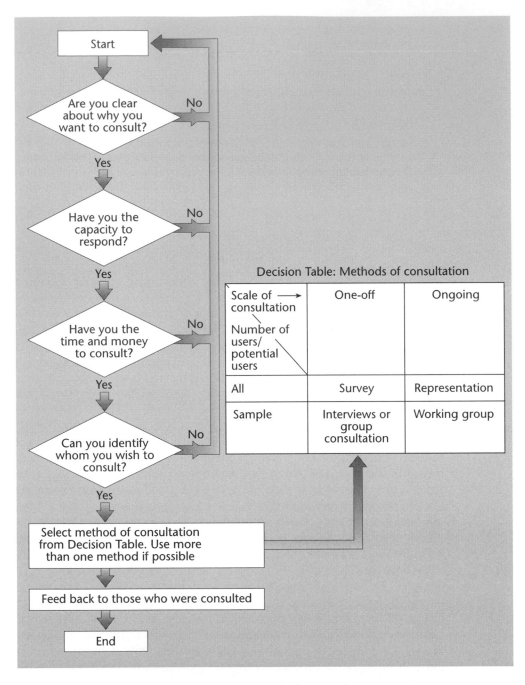

Involving groups of users can be a time-consuming and expensive exercise. Getting it right is important. Users will feel that their views are *genuinely* being listened to and staff will feel the confidence to repeat the exercise.

Figure 3.1 **Managing user involvement** (Holroyd, 1991: 170)

people feeling more powerless, both as individuals and as communities. She cites the example of the local authority going into the community and telling people what it has decided to do rather than asking what the community would like it to do. As she says, 'This experience brought home for many people the reality that knowing what is about to happen is meaningless unless individuals and groups have the power to influence it'. (1991: 162). However she describes an equally disempowering situation when, after many years of consultation about the building of a new health centre, the views and wishes of the local women who had in good faith given time, energy and enthusiasm were not reflected in either its design or management structure. She concludes that:

> Until the health authority begins to change its ethos and see that the idea of building alliances is about a dialogue between two separate entities, with each group having something to offer in their own terms, then the experience of building alliances... will continue to be one of conflict and confrontation.
>
> (Coke, 1991: 165)

One of the basic criteria for evaluating health alliances identified by Funnell *et al.* (1995) was the degree to which it achieved the participation of local people. Much is made of the need to involve communities, but enabling the participation of local people is not an easy matter. We need to reflect on what is meant by the term and why it is so important.

3.5 The promise of participation

Participation is a necessary element in building health alliances and lies at the heart of the community health movement. As well as having the direct effect of enhancing health and well-being, claims are made about empowering communities and reducing inequalities in health.

What is participation?

Participation is yet another term which can have different meanings for different people in different circumstances. It is a term often used synonymously with involvement and it can apply to both individuals and collectives. Croft and Beresford (1992) maintain that enthusiasm for participation waxes and wanes and that the late 1980s saw a resurgence of interest in participation in relation to service provision in health and social care with a shift from provider-led services to user-centred provision, made possible by the increased involvement of users. They attribute this interest in user-involvement to a number of factors in the British post-war welfare state as follows:

- the rise of the political right and the election of Conservative governments from 1979, with their concern with the cost of public services, dislike of a 'nanny' welfare state which was perceived as creating and perpetuating dependency, their objections to government intervention and preference for a greater role for the private market.

- the struggle for equal opportunities highlighting the frequent failure of welfare services to ensure equal access, opportunities and appropriate provision for women, black people and members of other minority groups.

- progressive professionals and other service workers who wanted to work in different more egalitarian ways...

- the appearance of new kinds of support services... women's, black and gay organisations, for example, set up lesbian lines, rape crisis centres, women's and Black women's refuges, advocacy schemes and buddy schemes. These established different relationships between service users and providers, met needs that had previously been ignored and were often run in more collaborative ways

- the development by disabled people of a new politics of disability based on a critique of existing services, a redefinition of the problem and an attempt to create an alternative service structure controlled by disabled people.

(Croft and Beresford, 1992: 30–31)

Participation within the community health movement is concerned to bring about change in the conditions of mainly disadvantaged communities. By acting collectively, marginalised or disadvantaged groups can pool resources in order to influence the social context which may be damaging to their health and well-being. This might be achieved either by acting politically to bring about a change in policy or by taking direct action themselves to bring about the necessary change. For example, people on a local housing estate might campaign to persuade the local council to provide a safe play area for young children or alternatively they may construct one themselves.

The WHO sees community participation as an essential way of unlocking valuable knowledge:

> With recognition that there is a conventional wisdom in every community, and that people are able to think and act constructively in identifying and solving their own problems, the emphasis on health education is shifting from 'intervention' to 'community involvement'.
>
> (WHO, 1983)

There is certainly a great deal of rhetoric attached to the notion of community participation, but how far is it achieved and what are the dilemmas posed? At the beginning of this chapter you were briefly introduced to the difference between consultation and participation. Different degrees of participation are charted in Table 3.1.

Table 3.1 **Degree of participation, participant's action and illustrative modes for achievement**

Degree	Participant's action	Illustrative mode
Low	None	The community is told nothing.
	Receives information	The organisation makes a plan and announces it. The community is convened for informational purposes; compliance is expected.
	Is consulted	The organisation tries to promote a plan and seeks to develop the support which will facilitate acceptance or give sufficient sanction to the plan so that administrative compliance can be expected.
	Advises	The organisation presents a plan and invites questions. It is prepared to modify the plan only if absolutely necessary.
	Plans jointly	The organisation presents a tentative plan subject to change and invites recommendations from those affected. It expects to change the plan at least slightly and perhaps even more subsequently.
	Has delegated authority	The organisation identifies and presents a problem to the community; defines the limits and asks the community to make a series of decisions which can be embodied in a plan which it will accept.
High	Has control	The organisation asks the community to identify the problem and to make all of the key decisions regarding goals and means. It is willing to help the community at each step accomplish its own goals, even to the extent of administrative control of the programme.

(Adams, 1989: 180)

What do you think is the likely effect on professionals of a high degree of community participation?

Achieving a high degree of participation is very challenging and some-times threatening to professionals who may resist the implicit transference of knowledge and power. Adams (1989) counters that both professionals and communities bring their own knowledge and ability, and emphasises the need to value and share each other's knowledge.

Another dilemma raised earlier in relation to consultation is the question of who gets to participate. Communities do not necessarily speak with one voice. Some interest groups can be dominant and serve to exclude others. Traditionally the more well educated middle-class elements in the community have had their voices heard. If the rhetoric of participation is in place then the non-participation of certain groups gives fuel to the view that their difficulties are to do with their own inadequacies. Adams maintains that it is essential to discriminate positively to encourage those who are least likely to participate, such as the poor and disadvantaged groups in society. This might involve the allocation of resources such as baby sitting or creches, travelling expenses, training and administrative help.

A more sceptical view of the recent focus on participation and user involvement maintains that it can serve other functions, although not necessarily intentional (Croft and Beresford, 1992). The need to involve users can become a device for procrastination and delay. Co-opting people into participatory arrangements can serve to limit their activity and divert them from more radical action. Participation can be little more than a window-dressing activity which gives the impression of open and democratic decision making. The participation of minority groups can be mere tokenism which perpetuates the unrepresentativeness of the organisation. On the other hand there are several practical and philosophical reasons why it is important to try to increase people's involvement and participation apart from the expressed desire of people to be involved. It:

- makes for more efficient and cost-effective services
- ensures accountability
- reflects the democratic ethos of our society
- encourages people's independence and self-determination
- is consistent with people's human and civil rights.

(Croft and Beresford, 1992: 36)

At the heart of both the problems and the possibilities of participation lies the issue of power and control over the decision-making processes. Much of the rhetoric of community action is concerned with empowerment, particularly the community development model. Working with disadvantaged groups, problem solving, achieving participation and helping people gain control over their own health are all stated aims. What do we actually mean by empowerment and is it a realistic goal for community action?

3.6 Community empowerment

At a very basic level empowerment involves gaining power, either by being given it or by taking it. In order to understand empowerment we need to understand the nature of power. According to Lukes (1974: 34) there are three dimensions of power held by groups or individuals. One is the ability to 'modify the conduct of others', two 'to control the issues on the agenda' and three to 'prevent people from having grievances by shaping their perceptions in such a way that they accept the existing order of things'. Power in this account is about the domination of a person or group by another person or group against their will. Kenny distinguishes two types of power or control:

- Coercion: a dominant group maintains its power by forcing people to do things against their will.

- Consent: a dominant group maintains power by gaining the consent of subordinate groups. It can do this by distorting, concealing and deflecting a real understanding of power relations and the ways things work. Subordinate groups can unwittingly enter into an alliance with dominant groups, and this allows the maintenance of unequal relations of power. At other times subordinate groups are complicit in their own subordination because they believe that they are inferior or have no right to power and that this stage of affairs is natural, legitimate and inevitable.

(Kenny, 1994: 115)

Coercion is overt and explicit, whereas maintaining power by consent is a much more subtle exercising of power where people collude in their own subordination. Empowerment is said to work by raising awareness of the ways in which power is exerted.

Swift and Levin (1987) proposed a three stage model of empowerment. For people to become empowered they first need to recognise their powerlessness. They then need to feel strongly enough about their inequitous situation and seek interaction with others in the same position. Finally the group gains sufficient strength to take action aimed at changing the social conditions which have created their powerlessness.

One major problem with that three stage model seems to lie in how people who perceive themselves as powerless can feel motivated to make the leap into joining up with others if there are no structures in place for that to occur. Community development approaches aim to create the structures by which communities recognise their oppression and are motivated to act to change things.

It has been argued that there exists a 'fundamental paradox in the idea of people empowering others because the very institutional structure that puts one group in a position to empower also works to undermine the act of empowerment' (Gruber and Tricket, quoted in Rissel 1994: 40). Grace (1991) goes so far as to suggest that empowerment is the health establishment's response to demands made by communities to gain control over their own health, and that attempts to empower actually mask attempts by health professionals to maintain control. Community development distinguishes between 'power over' and 'power to', and aims to overcome the fundamental paradox of empowerment by introducing the notion of 'power with'. Community workers talk of 'meeting in the middle'.

Community development has been much influenced by the work of the Brazilian, Paulo Freire (1972). Although working within a different cultural environment, his thinking has been applied to all oppressed groups. Freire argued that human fulfilment can only be achieved when people are liberated from oppression. In order to be liberated they need to acquire a critical awareness of the world in which they live. This *conscientisation* is the process of change in consciousness where people gain the knowledge to make an accurate and realistic awareness of their place in the world in relation to others. From that position of awareness they are enabled to act to transform their world. For Freire this means not only having control over the decision-making processes that affect people but also having control over the problem posing. This involves ordinary people in identifying problems as they see them, not as those in positions of power see them.

The notion of having control over the problem posing is very much in tune with Foucault's analysis of the relationship between knowledge and power (1980). For Foucault it is not so much the acquisition of knowledge which bestows power but the designation of a body of knowledge or 'discourse' as the dominant discourse which then has the power to set the agenda. In relation to health, medical knowledge has become the most powerful. Lay knowledge about what constitutes health has been relegated to the realms of folk or 'old wives' tales. So knowledge about people's own bodies as well knowledge about the effects of their social and economic environment has until quite recently had little status and has not been listened to. The effect of this is to create an unequal power relationship between medical and lay personnel with medical personnel and institutions having control over both the problem posing and the problem solving. In order for people to participate in the decision-making processes that affect their health there has to be some shift in that unequal balance of power with power being shared. In order for the balance to be redressed and for people to be able to participate in the problem posing as well as the problem solving they have to feel confident about the status of their knowledge.

Much of community development work for health is about creating healthy and equitable power relations between community groups and institutions (Labonte, 1993). In order to participate, communities need access to the political structures, organisations and institutions which affect their lives. Community workers see their role as facilitating that access, and the creation of health alliances is part of the process. They act as go-betweens with other statutory and voluntary agents and the community. A major part of the role of the community health worker is to work in the community, mobilising and supporting local groups so that they are able to participate. Four essential elements in supporting communities have been identified:

- personal development: to increase people's expectations, assertiveness, self-confidence and self-esteem
- skill development: to build the skills they need to participate and to develop their own alternative approaches to involvement
- practical support: to be able to take part, including information, child care, transport, meeting places, advocacy etc.
- support for people to get together and work in groups: including administrative expenses, payment for workers, training and development costs.

(Croft and Beresford 1992: 39–40)

Enabling people to participate by raising their consciousness and confidence has been characterised as pychological empowerment (Rissel, 1994). Political and economic empowerment, on the other hand, is bound up with the unequal distribution of resources. It is here that community development approaches have been found most wanting. Modifying the structural conditions of disadvantaged communities and reallocating resources, it has been argued, is much more difficult to achieve at the local level. Curtice (1991) has questioned whether the social and economic correlates of poor health are susceptible to change through collective participation which operates mainly at the local level. Removing the health disadvantages of deprived communities requires attention to national issues such as taxation and welfare benefits. Although local authorities have the ability to provide decent housing and services or can make improvements in road safety or education, they are constrained by central government policy. Curtice maintains that:

Many community health workers have recognised that even within a locality the resources that they have available are insufficient to deal with many of the problems in the communities in which they are working. Similarly, it may be recognised that even if fully realized the potential of local community intitiatives alone to achieve many of the community health movement's objectives may be inadequate – and will certainly be so if the initiatives remain isolated beacons of what can be done.

(1991: 262)

Community participation alone will not tackle inequalities in health. The new public health movement calls for intersectoral action on all fronts. Action at the level of public policy is an essential part of the equation and these issues are fully developed in Part 2 of this Book.

3.7 Conclusions

Whilst not expecting too much of community participation the fostering of partnership ways of working can only be welcomed. It has been suggested that achieving a society that is at one with itself is only possible through community ownership, accountability and democracy (Beck, 1995). Whatever the motivation, participation through partnerships and collaborations is heralded as a new way of working for the health sector. It has long been on the agenda of health promotion and community health workers are finding themselves in a new situation where they are in a position to facilitate a dialogue between local people and the statutory agencies as well as voluntary agencies and business. This is not an easy role. They have to convince professionals who may feel very threatened as well as deal with communties who can feel very frustrated if their demands are not met – it can sometimes be very uncomfortable in the middle. The next chapter focuses on that role through the work of community workers whose projects, the Ellergreen Centre, Supported Independent Living Project Housing and the Asian Women's Swimming Project, you were introduced to earlier in this chapter.

Chapter 4
Working at the local level

We gratefully acknowledge Sharon Abdul and Lorraine Rowlands for their advice and support; and Lorraine Rowlands, Joanne McKain and Christine Gardner who contributed the case studies and to the discussions.

4.1 Introduction: setting the scene

Previous chapters have charted how over the last decade there has been an accelerating interest, particularly among health professionals, in how to enable and encourage people to participate in and take action to improve the health status of their community.

This interest in community participation and collective action and the growth of community health projects has embraced the notion of community development as an effective means of achieving this. Central to the principles and philosophy which underpin community development is the way in which inequalities in health are acknowledged and addressed through the empowerment of local communities, so that they can have more power and control over their everyday lives and the factors which influence these. It is a process of working which encompasses a number of stages which are progressed through, some of which may be step by step and others simultaneously. Although this chapter focuses on community development workers and draws on examples of community development work it is a process of working which can be applied to all people who work in the community. The skills explored here are relevant to a wide spectrum of health promoting work which would include social workers, health visitors, community nurses, occupational health workers, environmental health workers, occupational therapists and many others.

The following stages in the community development process have been identified by Healthy Sheffield 2000.

Box 4:1: Stages in the community development process

A community development approach incorporates certain identifiable stages which build upon and inform the overall community development process. Any community development initiative, whether at grass roots, city-wide or planning/policy development level, will need to work through this process, though some of the stages may occur simultaneously rather than step by step. This process is equally relevant to individual workers, community groups and other organisations.

It is critical at each of the stages identified below that work is developed in conjunction with people from the particular community which is its focus.

- Getting to know the community, its needs, concerns and priorities; by drawing up a community profile, talking to local people, both individually and in existing groups; talking to local workers, e.g. housing, youth and community workers, health visitors; looking at statistics, such as census data, Director of Public Health Reports, unemployment figures.

- Building up contacts, trust, and identifying formal and informal networks and structures within the community; clarifying role of workers with a community development brief.

- Working with people from the community to identify main concerns/ areas of common interest, recognising the possibility of conflicting interests and the need to make every effort to make contact with and involve the most groups.

- Identifying what needs to change, in negotiation with people from the community, and developing support for possible action.

- Clarifying opportunities for change and potential obstacles, and developing appropriate strategies.

- Taking action as agreed with the community.

- Evaluating the effectiveness of the action, e.g. what was achieved, who was involved, positive and negative outcomes, unexpected developments.

- Reflecting on the lessons learnt and reviewing aims and objectives.

- Planning new strategies for the future in the light of all the above.

(Healthy Sheffield 2000, 1993: 15)

Hand in hand with this process will be the expectation of organisational development and change. It is at this interface of community and organisational development and change that the dilemmas and contradictions begin to emerge. Central to this is the ownership and control of knowledge and information, the mechanisms for improving a community's health status, together with the prioritising of resources. The length of time it takes to achieve that change requires patience and commitment and can be a source of a great deal of frustration. For example, Ron Draper (Consultant to the WHO European Region), in his report *Reflections on Progress – Health For All 2000*, Copenhagen 1992, visualises the achievement of health gains as being a process of change which requires a ten year perspective (see Figure 4.1).

Liverpool has a long history of community activism and, latterly, community development aimed at addressing a range of health and

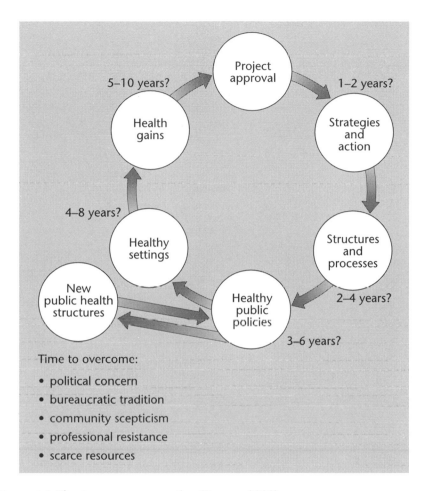

Figure 4.1 **The ten-year perspective** (Draper, 1992)

related issues. It has certainly gathered pace through the Healthy Cities Initiative and the partnership approach to identifying health needs and solutions to these, and more recently as a result of European-funded initiatives. Central to this wealth of activity and effective community action, whether that be in general or around health and quality of life, is a set of core skills and values which underpin this process. A route of community development work and some of the tasks and skills involved is summarised in Figure 4.2. The following sections will identify and define those core skills and illustrate them in practice through the voices of the neighbourhood development health workers employed by Liverpool City Council who were involved in the three case studies of community action in Liverpool introduced in the first half of the last chapter, Christine Gardner of the Ellergreen Centre, Lorraine Rowlands, of the Supported Independent Living Project Housing (SILPH) and Joanne McKain of the Asian Women's Swimming Project.

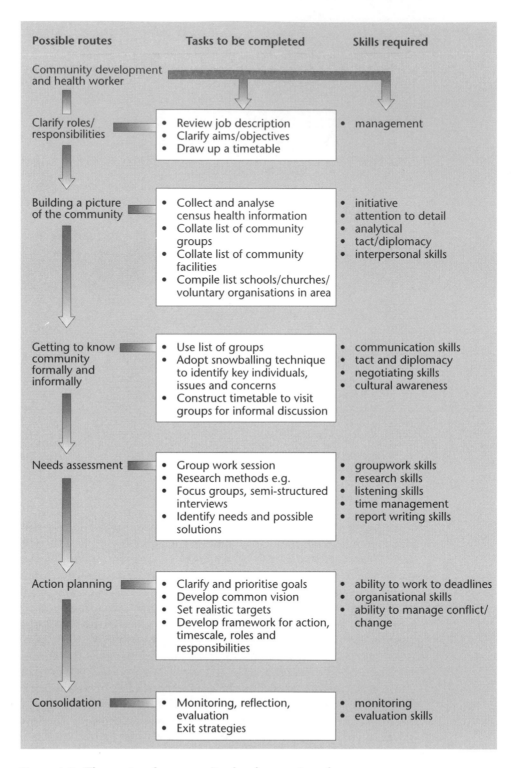

Possible routes	Tasks to be completed	Skills required
Community development and health worker		
Clarify roles/ responsibilities	• Review job description • Clarify aims/objectives • Draw up a timetable	• management
Building a picture of the community	• Collect and analyse census health information • Collate list of community groups • Collate list of community facilities • Compile list schools/churches/ voluntary organisations in area	• initiative • attention to detail • analytical • tact/diplomacy • interpersonal skills
Getting to know community formally and informally	• Use list of groups • Adopt snowballing technique to identify key individuals, issues and concerns • Construct timetable to visit groups for informal discussion	• communication skills • tact and diplomacy • negotiating skills • cultural awareness
Needs assessment	• Group work session • Research methods e.g. • Focus groups, semi-structured interviews • Identify needs and possible solutions	• groupwork skills • research skills • listening skills • time management • report writing skills
Action planning	• Clarify and prioritise goals • Develop common vision • Set realistic targets • Develop framework for action, timescale, roles and responsibilities	• ability to work to deadlines • organisational skills • ability to manage conflict/ change
Consolidation	• Monitoring, reflection, evaluation • Exit strategies	• monitoring • evaluation skills

Figure 4.2 **The route of community development work**

4.2 The role of the community worker

Community workers wear many hats. They are facilitators, enablers, researchers, mediators, fund-raisers and managers. In a typical week a community worker may:

- prepare a submission for funding an additional programme at the community centre
- talk to a group of residents about changes to social security legislation
- write a regular column for a local newspaper on coming events at the community centre
- respond to referrals for emergency accommodation in the locality
- advise on the establishment of a food co-operative, including legal, financial and municipal constraints and regulations
- address a local organisation of people from non-English-speaking backgrounds on equal opportunity issues in the local council
- attend a meeting of local housing workers
- take phone-calls from other agencies requesting up-to-date information on such matters as domestic violence, co-operatives, and action research.

(Kenny, 1994)

Which of the above list of activities are applicable to your own experience?

The work is very diverse and community workers need to be clear about their roles and responsibilities, lines of accountability, professional and managerial supervision, together with an awareness of their own strengths and limitations. Lorraine Rowlands of the SILPH project explained how:

> Throughout the phases of the project and the development of the management of the organisation the worker's title changed several times from Development Worker to Project Co-ordinator to Project Manager and now to Manager. This also shows the phases of development within the organisation and had implications on the worker's role and the ability and adaptability of the worker to be able to progress through the roles and meet changing needs and demands.

They also need to recognise and value the similarities and differences between unpaid and paid community workers, and those who work for voluntary/community organisations and statutory agencies, together with the differing strengths and constraints that these roles and functions bring. Similarly, it is important to be clear about the role of the community activist.

A community activist can be defined as:

- a volunteer/person who is actively engaged in community activities but without being paid for it.
- a person who gets involved in campaigns to influence policies/ services that affect them.

Whereas, a community worker can be defined as:

- a paid or unpaid worker who works as a partner with others in a co- operative venture. A community worker must be skilled in acting as an enabler, a facilitator, a catalyst for action, an energiser. S/he must be able to bring information, support and advice to people so that they make choices about what they want to do.

(quoted in Harris, 1994)

Community workers also need to know and understand who or what has identified or triggered the need to facilitate local action to promote health. This is particularly important if the trigger has been a statutory agency (who may also be their employer), as it could lead to the organisational objectives being incorporated into the community worker's role. Whilst local communities may acknowledge these as important they may prioritise their objectives differently. This could lead to initial dilemmas and conflict of interests for the community worker. A community worker needs to tread very warily until she or he has a thorough grasp of the issues, local politics and sensitivities of the local community.

4.3 Planning and negotiating entry into the community:

There are two main elements to this which could naturally run in parallel with each other:

- building an initial picture and profile of the community
- getting to know the community, both formally and informally.

Building an initial picture and profile of the community

The aim of the community worker is to develop a written snapshot of the community's natural and built environment together with the social, economic, political, cultural and religious structures of support within this. There are a number of sources both nationally, such as the census data which gives information on a regional basis, and more locally, such as the reports from the health authority and public health reports. The Community Health Council might be another source of information as well as the local authority. This information, coupled with a list of services and activities provided by statutory and non statutory agencies, voluntary organisations and community organisations/groups, is a tool which provides the worker with an initial insight and understanding of the community. However, it is only through understanding the community's perception of all this that the statistics and other such information can become a living reality.

> **Why do you think it is important for health promotion work to get the perspective of local people as well as the statistical information?**

From the discussion in Chapter 3 it was clear that if communities are to be enabled to participate in the decision-making processes and achieve partnership ways of working then health promoters have to work with the community and understand and value their needs and perspectives.

Getting to know the community, both formally and informally

This can take time and patience as well as a great deal of tact and diplomacy. The community worker needs to be aware of the cultural and political sensitivities of the area. Networking is a frequently heard term in community work. Basically it is about making contacts, building trust, developing alliances, tapping into local knowledge and listening and learning from as wide a range of people within the community as possible. The following ideas have been suggested for building good networks:

1 Walk, don't ride. Always try to walk from A to B, and ensure that you visit areas that are unfamiliar to you.
2 Never pass up the opportunity to make or renew a contact (unless you are fairly sure that to do so at that point will damage another area of work).
3 Learn how to listen and notice.
4 In order to get you must give. People are prepared to give best when it is clear that they will get something in return.

(Twelvetrees, 1982: 23–28)

Snowballing is a useful technique in building networks. Essentially, it is about using existing contacts to suggest others that might be contacted, who in turn are asked to suggest others. One of the drawbacks of this technique is that you could end up with only one real network based on the original person contacted. To avoid this it is best to set off more than one snowball. Community workers who are very unfamiliar with an area will need to immerse themselves in the community by frequenting local shopping centres, sitting in cafés or pubs and generally talking informally to as many people as possible.

Making both formal and informal contacts will allow the community worker the opportunity to talk, and more importantly to listen, to people who live and work in the community about what they think constitutes a 'healthy' person and community; what the particular health needs of their area are; whether they think that these are being met and, if not, what they think might be the solution to these; and whether they might want to get involved with future developments. In order to do this, the community worker can use a range of methods, such as one-to-one discussion, questionnaires, workshops, focus groups and public meetings. S/he must be able to talk to a range of people in different situations and from a variety of backgrounds and s/he will need good written, verbal and non-verbal communication skills.

The community workers from SILPH and the Ellergreen Centre told how they discovered the needs of their particular communities.

> The first task for the worker was to research into the concerns/needs of local carers of adult sons/daughters who have a learning disability. This was done by first constructing a questionnaire with the ultimate aim of finding out what the main concerns for these parents/carers were, their long-term plans if any for their sons/daughters and what they saw as a need for themselves...

> From the results of the questionnaire those people who responded and expressed the same need for local long-term accommodation with support were contacted and ask to attend a small group meeting where future discussion took place.
>
> (Lorraine Rowlands)

> Facilitated by the team, community representatives met to prioritise their needs in relation to the overall environmental problems within the area at that time. The meetings took place on a weekly basis and, although formal in the sense that agenda, minutes, relevant accompanying paper work would always be available, an informal atmosphere encouraged representatives, particularly women, to assess, evaluate, and basically take stock of what resources were already 'out there'.
>
> (Christine Gardner)

The process of networking and building up community contacts can also raise a number of issues including the dilemma of representation and who can be said to represent the community's views and interests. As discussed in the previous chapter at a practical level 'community leaders or representatives' will be able to give a particular perspective or overall view, but it may not be representative of the totality of the community. The skill of the community worker is to recognise and understand this and to seek as many views as is practically possible. They also need to be aware of the community's existing organisational structures; and to clarify what local residents see as the boundary to their community, which may be different to the geographical one based on the electoral ward.

Although this initial phase can be seen as laying the building blocks for effective community action, these may already be in place because of the community's past and present history of taking collective action. It is important to work within existing organisational structures if these are in place.

Other issues that may emerge are those related to what can be achieved and how this is to be done, particularly if the proposed local action is an 'intervention' based on a time limited project. Local residents and/or community groups may have low expectations as to what may be achieved, particularly if they have had little or no resources in the past or, in their view, statutory agencies have 'failed to deliver'. Lorraine Rowlands told how the parents/carers from SILPH had poor experiences in the past in their dealings with the social services department.

> They claimed that for years they had received inadequate support from the department and had been accused by many people of being over-protective. This they resented and from this first meeting it could be seen that it would be a long slow process establishing trust, and forming a partnership as the basis to work from.
>
> (Lorraine Rowlands)

Christine Gardner also noted how the residents of the estate had found it hard to make any impression on the local council in the past.

> It was understandable why some people sometimes expressed concern and were apathetic towards the local authority and statutory bodies. The problems they faced on a day-to-day basis failed to have the same impact on politicians and press as those experienced by the old inner city areas. Yet poor housing, poverty and high unemployment were common to both.
>
> (Christine Gardner)

At the other end of the scale what do you think might be some of the pitfalls of having high expectations?

'Unrealistic' expectations of what is achievable can eventually lead to demoralisation when time-scales and outcomes do not match those expectations. However low expectations are a more common problem. For various reasons (such as lack of confidence, the inaccessibility of an organisation, or institutionalised racism) local people may feel unable to raise the issues that they feel strongly about with the appropriate agency. This may particularly be so if the need being identified challenges either the way in which that need is already being met by the agency or indeed is not seen as a priority. Joanne McKain who organised the swimming sessions for Asian women makes this point in relation to racism:

> Racism, particularly that of institutional racism... often results in a lack of cultural awareness among service providers and/or a lack of commitment to equal opportunities. As a result, the services provided

are neither sensitive nor appropriate, and can lead to members of the black and racial minority groups experiencing barriers in accessing services.

(Joanne McKain)

In such situations the community worker would need to act as a conduit or communication channel to enable those voices to be heard and the issues put on the relevant 'agenda'. They would also need to work with local people to develop their skills and confidence. This process of empowerment is crucial if local people are to be able to determine how they want to take action to get their needs met. The worker's role would be to enable them to develop appropriate ways of taking action, such as campaigning and lobbying, or developing activities to suit their needs. Local people would start to take action to set the 'agenda' rather than having it set for them. Joanne McKain saw the provision of leisure facilities for Asian women as having such a longer-term aim:

> It was felt that if the women had more opportunities to meet outside the home, e.g. leisure facilities, social gatherings and day trips, this would begin to address the issue of isolation and depression. It was agreed that if these activities took place this would begin to improve the mental and physical health of the women. This would also provide an opportunity to hear and raise other health concerns with the women and begin to make recommendations for change within the statutory agencies, in particular Liverpool City Council and Liverpool Health Authorities.
>
> (Joanne McKain)

The role of the community worker is to build on initial research and contact with people living and working in the community, so that the needs identified can be expanded upon and solutions developed. The worker's overall role would be to support and facilitate that process, particularly in terms of existing organisational structures and the creation of new ones.

4.4 Action planning: bringing people together

The community worker has a developmental role in the process of bringing together a group of people who share a common need/interest to explore how they could take action to address their needs. Task groups or sub-groups can be set up to work on particular issues. Within this structure, focus groups could be organised to enable more in-depth research of the needs and solutions identified. Either or both of these groups could, through the composition of their membership, provide the foundations for developing a partnership between the local residents, the statutory, non-statutory, voluntary and community organisations. Christine Gardner describes how the Ellergreen group took shape:

> Volunteers formed a Community Working Group which included representatives from local churches, police, local housing office, and community groups. ... By 1992 the groups, under the banner of the local health forum took responsibility for the day-to-day running of the sixth form block. An inter-agency working party had also been set up which included senior officers from education, economic initiatives, legal services, community development and equality unit, the health sector, local ward councillors and community representatives. The primary role was to co-ordinate the contributions of both community groups and key statutory agencies in developing a multi-purpose centre.
>
> (Christine Gardner)

Lorraine Rowlands tells how the management group for SILPH was formed:

> The small group of seven carers decided that in order to progress any supported housing initiative they would need to bring on board people who could offer relevant expertise and advice. A Management Group was formed comprising parents/carers, local community representatives, local clergy, housing, social services, Merseyside police and Centec.
>
> (Lorraine Rowlands)

The setting up and development of a group, whether it be to deal with a single issue or a variety of issues, requires the community worker to have a range of skills to enable it both to develop, as a cohesive group with a shared vision and common identity, and to achieve its objectives. Community development workers often seem like the glue which keeps people working together. Good organisational skills and the ability to manage both people and budgets are important. Skills in fund-raising and marketing are also useful. Group members will bring different skills and experiences together with their different commitments outside the group process. This can raise a variety of issues in terms of ownership and control, the development of an equitable partnership and the commitment expected from the members. This will particularly be the case if it is an inter-agency group, as its members may have differing expectations, as well as competing needs, interests and priorities.

The group may have a natural life span with a beginning, middle and end. This might be because:

- it has a particular task to achieve
- it is part of a time-limited project for which the funding ceases
- there is no longer a perceived need for this particular type of group and something else might replace it.

Working together: prioritising needs, agreeing and progressing solutions

Once the community worker has brought the group together, their first task will be to define its purpose, clarify and prioritise its goals, set realistic targets for action, and agree the mechanisms for monitoring and reviewing the outcomes. In the light of this, they will also need to review the group's membership in terms of the skills mix and training needs, particularly if they see the group as working towards a long-term future. This stage will form the basis for developing a framework for action which will include a time-scale and timetable for meeting their agreed objectives, and a common agreement and shared understanding of the members' roles and responsibilities within this. It will also start the process for establishing effective team building and developing partnership ways of working, as well as providing opportunities for flagging up potential areas of conflict when particular dilemmas and contradictions may emerge for group members.

Central to this will be the issue of the group achieving its objectives whilst building and developing the organisational structure to enable this. A prime example would be the emphasis on delivering concrete measurable outcomes as a measure of achievement.

What other achievements do you think should be taken into account?

Whilst important, quantifiable measures of concrete outcomes do not acknowledge the importance of the building of organisational structures and the empowerment of individuals and communities which this entails. It can therefore be difficult to translate the rhetoric (about community development and community action) into the concrete reality of achieving action and change. The group's action plan should include the development of an organisational structure to meet its particular needs and what it sees as its terms of reference. This may be done informally, agreeing the processes of recruitment/membership, decision making, communication and accountability, or more formal arrangements may be made which, as a first step, include a written constitution with agreed policies and procedures. However, the group may also wish to seek limited company status and/or charitable status. Whilst this provides the group with a legal framework and also other opportunities for fund-raising and income generation, it also brings additional levels of responsibility and accountability. Lorraine Rowlands describes her experiences:

> In terms of working with the Management Group as the Development Worker the role was to set up the Management Group by bringing relevant people together, servicing the group, formalising the group by

drawing up a constitution and registering as a Charity with Limited Company status, drawing up the group's policies and procedures, ensuring that enthusiasm was maintained and all people contributed to the planning and running of the group – building partnerships, gaining trust, and supporting the group in periods of highs and lows.

(Lorraine Rowlands)

The process can be quite lengthy and time-consuming, demanding high levels of commitment, particularly if the group also needs to raise funds, in order to support its activities. Indeed, at this point, the original purpose of the group can become subsumed under these demands, and members may become disenchanted and disillusioned as they struggle with their other various competing commitments outside the group. The worker's skills in supporting these processes will be crucial, in terms of maintaining the impetus of the group and the commitment of its members. There is a need for perseverance, a good deal of realism and a sense of humour. The community worker will also need the ability to collect and provide information, give administrative and organisational support and enable the group to network and liaise with other organisations so that the relevant expertise, advice and support can be either be brought into or made available to the group. They may also need to resolve areas of conflict which may be internal or external to the group.

Conflict management

Any vibrant community organisation will experience conflict and so dealing with conflict is likely to be a daily activity for a community worker. Conflict can be a healthy feature of community action but it can also be disruptive and destructive.

Several steps to conflict management have been identified:

- Identify the protagonists and analyse the problem or issue.
- Get the protagonists to meet together.
- Negotiate the terms of that meeting.

(Kenny, 1994: 183)

Sometimes it is possible to address the underlying source of the conflict but it may not always be possible to resolve all conflict and it may be that it just has to be accepted. But it does need to be acknowledged and not denied. Christine Gardner and Lorraine Rowlands draw attention to this important aspect of their role.

The structure of the organisation needs to be given plenty of thought and should be flexible/adaptable enough to meet needs as the organisation moves through various phases/stages. There has been a need to look at conflict resolution as some members of the Management Group wear different hats being parents of tenants of the organisation and Officers of the Board. This can at times be confusing for any community worker and it is essential that the worker has a clear job description and lines of accountability. It is also essential that training is provided to a community organisation wishing to become a community business employing staff, and that clear roles and responsibilities of management group members are defined. Some members may find it difficult to operate within a given framework and may often digress. In many cases a conflict of interest/self-interest may occur and it is essential to mediate any conflict. Much of this is to do with power and control, and the worker must have a clear understanding of the workings of the group and the abilities/expertise/skills that each group member brings and ways in which those skills and talents can be harnessed and used constructively and not to the detriment of the organisation. It is also essential that, although sometimes difficult, the worker continues to identify new people who can sit on the management group, bringing new ideas and strengthening the organisation.

(Lorraine Rowlands)

Working alongside the groups, their personal development was beginning to emerge quite effectively. Conflict and criticism arose quite frequently and there had been a stage of ill feeling between sections of the community concerning the project.

This may have been due to differing views on how the project should be developed and whether representatives would be able to sustain what clearly could become a worthwhile ambitious scheme.

(Christine Gardner)

Managing conflict and the effective harnessing of the skills, talents and experiences within the group, together with the development and extension of these by training and/or additional members are crucial to building and maintaining the group's credibility and 'track record' of achievements. This process can also be facilitated by raising awareness and gaining and maintaining the active involvement and support of the community through effective campaigning and the use of the mass media, together with gaining and maintaining the support of decision-makers.

What do you think are the benefits of publicising a group's achievements?

Publicising the group's achievements is important both in terms of individual and group self-esteem and confidence, and also for the positive messages that this conveys to others about the value of community action and working together. It also enables the group to take stock regularly, reminds them of to whom they are accountable, and enables them to record their 'story' and celebrate. All too often, people living and working in the community are so busy 'taking action' that they do not have the time to write about their experiences. This record of the process and outcomes of community action is then lost, or perhaps written up by an outside professional. Whilst this is valuable, it is important that the group also have ownership and control, or at the very least, a common agreement about how this is produced and circulated. This process of active reflection can also provide the means of enabling the group to continue to evolve and develop in response to changing needs and priorities.

4.5 Consolidation and sustainability

The process of consolidation will be crucial to the long-term future of a group and the ways in which it can sustain and possibly continue to develop its services/activities. Joanne McKain talks about some of the difficulties she encountered in trying to sustain and develop her work with Asian women:

> I had to work through an Asian woman worker as she had personal contact with many of the women and could speak the different languages. This gave me access to the women. Generally this went well as we began to develop trust and were working towards the same goals. However there were difficulties. The Asian woman worker who worked part-time secured full-time employment, and so had other demands on her time. Not having direct access to the women or speaking the different languages often led to misunderstanding. The sessions were originally for women who did not speak a lot of English and who were generally isolated. However, very few women in this category attended; the majority were fluent in English. More work needs to be done to ensure that the target group is not missed, and does get access to the facilities provided. It is vital to get another woman who will work to ensure that this happens, and also to look at securing resources. Many of the women experienced racial name calling outside the sports centre, which we informed the centre manager about, and we are beginning to look at ways to address this issue.
>
> (Joanne McKain)

Any type of group whose objective is the provision of long-term services/ activities, whether or not they complement or fill a gap in existing provision, has to be extremely creative in terms of the sustainability of these. Funding is also always a problem. Joanne managed to get funding for one month, then three, but securing a longer-term commitment can be difficult. Despite commitments to partnership ways of working and the promotion of health through the empowerment of communities, it may be difficult for statutory agencies to put these into practice. The current economic climate, with its emphasis on the contract culture and income generation, can provide various opportunities, particularly in terms of job creation and the development of small businesses. However, it can raise dilemmas and contradictions for groups such as: the integration of the philosophy and values of the 'market-place' and its emphasis on competitiveness with those of community development; the increasing professionalisation of community action and volunteering; and the increasing responsibilities for management committees based on volunteers' commitment and goodwill. Lorraine Rowlands cautions against too ambitious a project:

> The worker must be able to recognise the potential within the organisation and, whilst the demand for services can be great, it is essential that for any organisation, the worker must advise and recommend to members of the group that any initiative should be small and of good quality, rather than to take on too much and provide lesser a quality of services.
>
> (Lorraine Rowlands)

The community worker's role will be to enable the group to draw on the relevant expertise, advice and support, so that they set manageable aims and objectives. In setting these positively and creatively, the group can adapt and survive in a way that meets their needs, particularly in terms of influencing future service provision.

Letting go and moving on

The various stages of initiating, developing, managing and consolidating the process and outcomes of community action requires the community worker to adopt a number of roles. These include acting as a catalyst, energiser, facilitator and manager and, as such, to have a range of skills and the flexibility which would enable them to move between these roles when the need arises. In order for community development and, by definition, community action to remain a dynamic process, the community worker and the group must be able to 'let go' and 'move on'. The community worker's role will have been evolving and changing in response to the various needs of the group and their consolidation of ownership and control; it may no longer be possible or practical for the community worker to continue his or her current role, as Christine Gardner noted:

> Their expectations of my role have also changed. For example, they no longer expect me to speak solely on their behalf, as they are quite capable of speaking on their own terms. They now have sufficient networking skills, but still require day-to-day community development to acquire the related skills to enable them to take forward the project to the next stage, and ultimately to its completion.
>
> (Christine Gardner)

In terms of time-limited projects exit strategies need to be devised to ensure either the group's survival, or that the activities and/or the ways of working are incorporated into the statutory agencies' objectives, and by definition their mainstream budgets. The community worker/s may effectively cease to be employed; or, in terms of those employed by statutory agencies, it may be agreed that the lessons learnt from that project will be disseminated further, through the creation of mainstream posts. Similarly, a group's organisational structure may have evolved, so that they are now functioning as an independent autonomous group which employs or is in the process of employing its own staff.

In any of these situations, the community worker may still continue to offer support and advice to the group, if this is appropriate. However, they must be clear about the changing nature of their role and make sure that boundaries and responsibilities are defined and recognised. This would be equally relevant whether or not the community worker had been employed to support the community action which resulted in the group's development and this was to continue; or they were an unpaid worker undertaking this role; or indeed they were subsequently employed by the group.

Similarly, a group's individual members must be able to 'let go' and 'move on', as their roles/functions may change as the group evolves and develops in response to changing demands (and also as new members are brought in) as Lorraine explains:

> Projects such as these do not develop in isolation, they have a history and background that may or may not influence their future development. Whilst it is important to acknowledge the roots of the project, in order for it to continue to evolve and remain responsive to the needs that it was set up to serve, there has to be an acceptance and a willingness to move on and change.
>
> (Lorraine Rowlands)

4.6 Conclusion

Community work is a dynamic process which can provide the framework and foundations for innovatory and creative approaches to health promotion. However, whilst community action can be a force to influence change and, as such, presents a challenge to professional autonomy, it may be extremely difficult for communities to achieve fundamental change. Therefore, in order to maximise this potential, it needs to be harnessed with partnership ways of working and organisational development. These processes are fundamental to achieving improvements in the community's health status.

Partnership ways of working are a challenge to all, community, lay and professional alike. Implicit in partnership ways of working is the notion of equity, which by definition implies that not only does each member have both rights and responsibilities but also their skills, knowledge and experience are acknowledged and valued equally. It requires the development of openness, trust and a willingness to take action and change existing ways of working. The commitment to and pursuit of a common vision maximises the resources available by effectively harnessing the skills and talents of those who live and work in the community. Evaluating these ways of working is very difficult and the final chapter in this Part looks at ways of attempting to do this.

Chapter 5
Evaluating community action

5.1 Introduction

This chapter discusses the main questions that need to be addressed when planning, carrying out or just using evaluations of the types of activity we have described as community action for health. Very often it is the people most directly involved in community action, rather than external 'experts', who initiate and conduct evaluations in this field, frequently with few resources and, perhaps, feeling insufficiently trained. When a sample of health education officers, for instance, were asked about their current work and training needs in community development initiatives, they identified 'methods of evaluation and monitoring' as among the top three areas of training need. (Adams *et al.*, 1989). This chapter aims to meet some of that need and begins by looking at the reasons for evaluation and the different forms evaluation may take.

5.2 Reasons for evaluating community action

Evaluation is fundamentally about judging the worth of an activity. What sort of reasons do people have for wanting to make this kind of judgement? To some extent the answer to this depends on who is calling for an evaluation and, in particular, on their relationship to the activity in question. Funders, managers, community workers, the community itself, and different sections within the community, may well each have different reasons flowing from different values, expectations, interests and experiences.

Evaluations required by funders are often concerned with issues of accountability. Funders usually want to know that their money has been used wisely and as expected, which means they need an evaluation which describes what happened (the process). They may also wish to know what the impact and outcomes were. Has the activity achieved what it set out to do? Does it represent value for money? Employers and managers of community development workers tend to want evaluations for very similar reasons. This may simply mean recording the use of money and time or it may mean providing a full account of the process.

For people directly engaged in community action for health the reasons for carrying out evaluation are many and varied. They range from a visionary desire to promote the underlying philosophy of community action activists and to 'validate community development work in the health field' (Cox and Findlay, 1990: 29) to more mundane attempts to learn from experience, improve practice, skills and understanding and inform decision making. All of these will almost always involve evaluation of process and sometimes also evaluation of impact and outcome. The difference and relationship between process and outcome evaluation is summarised below.

Box 5.1

Evaluation may:

1 Be concerned with **process** – recording and describing how the activity or project works, providing information that may improve what happens.

2 Identify impact and **outcomes**:

   (a) ask whether the activity or project achieved what it set out to do

   (b) identify additional or unintended consequences.

3 Consider cost and/or efficiency.

Members of the community meant to benefit from an activity are likely to be especially concerned with the extent and ways in which an activity actually involves and benefits them. One reason for evaluation may be to discover whether and how participation actually happens. As Baum notes, 'Some commentators have suggested that participation is often more spoken about than practised.' (1992: 11). How to go about answering this question is an issue we return to later in this chapter.

Amongst practitioners, planners and academics concerned about the development of health promotion practice and theory, a major long-term reason for encouraging thoughtful, critical evaluations is the building up of a collective body of experience which might help to answer key questions relating to community action for health (some of which have been mentioned in previous chapters). These include:

- Is community participation real or rhetorical?
- Can community action bring about any meaningful shift in power?
- Who initiates community action and community development projects? Are they essentially about social engineering in a more progressive garb?
- Is community development more about social amelioration than radical change?
- Is community action and community development more for the careers of health workers than for the community?

(Baum, 1992: 14)

The reasons for evaluation are clearly many and various. When planning an evaluation, or reading about evaluations that are complete, it is important to try to identify the underlying reasons and values which influence the questions that are asked.

5.3 Forms of evaluation

When and who?

Designing an evaluation involves making decisions about when evaluation will take place and who should carry it out. An evaluation that records and describes what happens (the process) would be well advised to start early and, if possible, be built in from the beginning. Of this kind of evaluation and in the context of community development projects, Somerville notes,

> ...on the whole project workers have to carry out evaluation themselves. It seems crucial therefore that evaluation complements ongoing project work, strengthens it and can be carried out as part of day-to-day community work activities using existing skills.
>
> (1984: 89)

Sometimes, however, evaluation takes place just towards the end of a project or entirely retrospectively. This may be because those involved have neither the time, skills nor interest in integrating evaluation with day-to-day activities. Or perhaps the questions being considered call for a more distant or external evaluation, or the evaluation is something of an afterthought.

Goal achievement or process description?

More deliberate decisions about the general design of an evaluation, such as whether the focus is on process or outcome and whether the methods are to be predominantly qualitative or quantitive, also have to be addressed. The figure below represents these options as a choice between two very different cultural systems.

People directly involved in the field of community action for health usually tend to favour qualitative approaches which emphasise and explore processes, shifts in power, fulfilment of human potential and so on; but the wider environment in which they operate increasingly emphasises value for money and requires evaluation to incorporate quantitive information and analysis relevant to this end.

The goal-oriented approach to health is one that has specific, clearly identified aims which can be measured in a numerical way, for example halving the number of smokers in a population or increasing by ten per cent the number of people cycling to work. Where the emphasis is mainly

Figure 5.1 **Goal achievement or process description?**   (adapted from Beattie, 1991: 230)

on achieving set goals, evaluation means discovering whether the goal has been met so little importance is attached to describing the process. In contrast, the process-oriented approach to health places a high value on aspects of health that are not easily measured numerically, such as the quality of relationships, or an increase in individual self-confidence or group solidarity. In this perspective, what people learn in the process of involvement in community action for health is regarded as at least as important as achieving a previously determined goal – so describing and understanding the process is the key feature of evaluation.

Different approaches to evaluation are not random but rooted in ideological predispositions. So, for instance, a health service manager whose working life revolves around the smooth running of a given system will tend to approach evaluation with a broadly centrist, bureaucratic mind-set, assuming, perhaps, that evaluation is necessarily about measuring the extent to which clearly defined goals have been met. In contrast, a community development worker will usually take a more radical or democratic view of what evaluation involves. Often the actual shape of an evaluation is the result of a compromise between community workers' perspectives and those of managers, funders and doctors, as Box 5.2 illustrates.

This evaluation was designed with goal-oriented presuppositions in mind because these were what counted to health service managers. But at the same time it was also possible to incorporate a qualitative, process-oriented approach.

Frames of reference

To tease out further the choices available in the evaluation of community action for health, Alan Beattie has proposed that in addition to the goal versus process contrast there is a further contrast depending on whether or not the evaluation includes consideration of relationships between the community and the wider context. If, for example, the evaluation focuses on what happens to the individuals involved in a project Beattie describes it as having internal terms of reference, but if it asks how these people are relating to wider power structures then it is operating with external terms of reference. By cross-tabulating these two main axes he arrives at a four-

---

Box 5.2: Evaluation of a health-oriented community development project in Bristol

Decisions about how best to evaluate a health-focused community development project on a council estate in Bristol were influenced by the knowledge that 'traditional professionals in control of resources' in the health service doubted that the employment of a community worker was a legitimate health service activity. How might an evaluation of the project change that view? It was thought that measurement of changes in health, perhaps in terms of infant mortality, birth weight or GP consultation rates would provide convincing evidence, but for different reasons each of these indicators could not be used. The number of expected infant deaths was too small to provide an indicator sensitive to health changes in the population, people moved in and out of the area too much for birth weight to provide a reliable measure and reduction in the use of GPs can indicate things other than improved health. It was recognised that many community workers believe it is inappropriate to evaluate community development projects using quantitive data and that qualitative recording of the processes involved and the progress made is a more appropriate approach. But it was also recognised that such an approach would not 'count' in the eyes of those holding the purse strings. A compromise was made. Those responsible for the evaluation write, 'In the end we opted for collecting descriptive data together with counting heads. We have found that this combination of qualitative and quantitative information, although it falls short of demonstrating a change in community health status, has gone some way to satisfying local managers that the project has been effective...'

(Stewart-Brown and Prothero, 1988: 157)

---

fold map of evaluation studies which identifies four ideologically-based evaluation models: economic, developmental, systems and cultural.

This map can be helpful in understanding some of the tensions and conflicts between different interest groups and also provides a way of designing evaluations that meet, to some extent at least, the expectations of several parties. In the Bristol evaluation with its combination of quantitive and qualitative design, there is evidence of all four models:

1 Case-studies describe the way in which access to a community flat, which provided a meeting place and health visitor support for parents with young children, enabled isolated young mothers to form friendships and grow in self-confidence (the developmental model).

2 Detailed records give the numbers of people who had contact with the project so, for example, it was possible to calculate that about two-thirds of under-fives used project facilities in some way (the systems model).

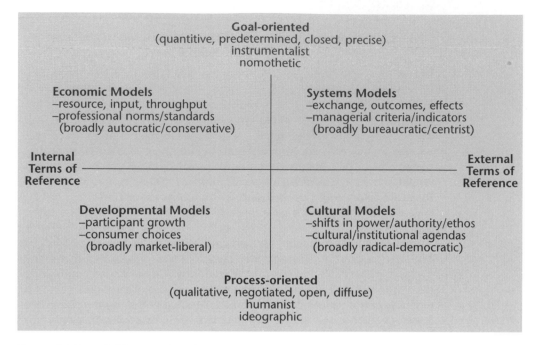

Figure 5.2 **Four-fold map of evaluation studies** (Beattie, 1991: 230)

3 Income and expenditure accounts for the project show that the health
   authority's contribution was more than doubled by successful applica-
   tions for funding from other sources (the economic model).

4 Project worker reports document the way in which some residents have
   taken over the management of parts of the project and have initiated
   new groups and activities (the cultural model).

Diversity

A detailed review of over 40 reports recording attempts to evaluate local
community development initiatives in health promotion paints an
equally diverse picture (Beattie, 1991). Whilst some were addressed to
other practitioners and/or local communities, others were directed
towards funders, managers, policy makers and more general audiences.
The tendency was very much towards qualitative design but within this
any of ten major styles of evaluation were employed and in a variety of
combinations.

> **Box 5.3: Styles of evaluation used in a sample of reports 1979–89**
>
> Historical – assembling a chronological narrative of the project.
>
> Participatory – giving priority to involvement of lay people in the process of evaluation.
>
> Negotiated – checking accounts with key informants.
>
> Objectives-based – systematic checking of progress in reaching aims and objectives.
>
> Goal free – focusing on process.
>
> Decision-led – a briefing for specific management decisions.
>
> Action research – external evaluator making a formative contribution to management of the project.
>
> Critical – professional judgement by one or more experts.
>
> Practitioner as evaluator.
>
> Independent external evaluator.
>
> (Beattie, 1991: 225–6)

Which parts of the four-fold map would each of these styles fit into?

Most are more process- than goal-oriented, with the objectives-based and decision-led approaches being the most obvious exceptions. Some are in practice compatible with any of the four models identified on the map.

5.4 Methods

When people involved in community action for health favour a process-oriented perspective but find themselves operating in predominantly goal-oriented contexts the most sensible approach to evaluation is likely to be pluralistic, combining different approaches and methods. Beattie recommends gathering a 'mixed bag' of information, both quantitative and qualitative, as things proceed, thus forming a resource or portfolio that can later be used in different ways for different audiences. This portfolio might include:

- basic work records: attendance, costs, diaries, logs, minutes, work-plans
- needs database: local health statistics, local community survey findings, interviews

- project file: time charts, job descriptions, agendas and minutes of meetings
- customer audits: summaries of feedback sessions, comments sheets, complaints, letters
- follow-up data: learning contracts, action plans, digests of follow-up surveys
- external monitoring: press cuttings, testimonials, conference presentations etc.

(adapted from Beattie 1991: 230–1)

At the same time there needs to be a word of caution. Too much attention to record-keeping can get in the way of the main activity. This certainly has been the experience of some people. In a report about a community development project in Cambridge, the two workers, Rosemary Cox and Gail Findlay, comment:

> In the early stages of this project, we attempted, almost literally, to make evaluation a continuous part of the dynamic process. For example, we kept comprehensive daily diaries of our work and also developed a 'contact sheet' which recorded the nature and origin of our daily contacts with individuals and groups in community and professional networks.
>
> It soon became clear that both the diary and the contact sheet were intrusive and unmanageable on a daily basis and therefore not feasible data collection instruments for evaluation over the whole period of the project. They were however... very useful, though time-limited, tools.

(1990: 30)

With the help of a consultative group a more manageable and varied evaluation strategy was arrived at. So, for instance, it was agreed that the diary would take six month snapshots to illustrate the nature of the work and the way it was changing over time. It was also decided to select particular themes and initiatives as a focus for the diary keeping.

Sometimes, it may be necessary to draw on particular areas of expertise from outside. In their evaluation of the Bristol project mentioned earlier, Stewart-Brown and Prothero noted that richer and more informative qualitative material would have been gathered had they sought advice and help in interviewing. They write:

> Collecting... comments and case-histories was, however, not easy and some of the users who appeared to make great use of the centre were unable to comment succinctly on why they found it helpful. In a future evaluation, we would consider recording interviews between users and a researcher skilled in such methods.

(1988: 161)

Given the diversity of evaluation styles and methods that may be relevant, is it possible to agree on some basic principles of good practice? Here is one attempt designed mainly for evaluation of community development approaches within the health service.

Box 5.4: Developing a code of practice for evaluation in community development for health

Any evaluation of a community development initiative:

1   should keep rich descriptive records

2   should ask a few powerful questions

3   should seek explanations and do essential detective work

4   must be valid/authentic/verifiable/checkable (or must make limitations explicit)

5   must be fair and impartial (and/or make the value position explicit)

6   must not damage/distort/interfere with the programme

7   must have clear rules of confidentiality or disclosure

8   must offer feedback to project workers/managers for decisions

9   must be firmly linked to problem-solving and remedial action

10 must be intelligible to external audiences.

(Beattie,1991: 232)

Do you think these guidelines are realistic and appropriate?

My own view is that whilst they provide ideals to strive towards there will be situations in which some of the guidelines are unrealistic. For instance, the notion that evaluation should not interfere with the programme or project being evaluated might well prove difficult or even impossible to sustain in many evaluations. Perhaps evaluation always influences those being evaluated? Proposing a less neutral and more committed model that extends community development practice and principles into evaluation, Smithies and Adams advocate what they describe as a radical rethink of evaluation and research.

> **Box 5.5: Principles for evaluation and research in health promotion**
>
> - It should engage with participation as a dynamic in the process of the research and the way communities and the researched receive the research outcomes.
>
> - Equal opportunities policies should be integrated into research methodologies.
>
> - Researchers and evaluators should work in partnership with their subjects creating new methodologies.
>
> - Researchers need to be accountable to their subjects.
>
> - The research process and intended outcomes should aim to contribute to reducing inequalities in health.
>
> (Smithies and Adams, 1993: 70)

5.5 Evaluation, empowerment and participation: issues and methods

Measuring empowerment

It has already been argued that empowerment is a slippery and contested concept, which makes the notion of *measuring* empowerment sound as though it is out of the question. But it is worth bearing in mind that in many evaluations the issue of what would count as success and which measures and indicators seem most appropriate is one that has to be teased out and argued about. Rarely is the answer obvious and straightforward. Indeed, when planning an evaluation, the very process of discussing aims and indicators can help clarify and improve aspects of the project and its operation. The exercise of inviting people involved in a project to be more precise about what they mean by a very broad aim or value-stance, such as empowerment, may well reveal conflicting views which need to be aired not only for evaluation to occur but also for the project to develop.

Here are some of the main questions that may need to be addressed:

What kind of power is at issue?

Will empowerment of this group involve others letting go of power?

What dimensions of empowerment is the action/intervention intended to affect?

- attitudes: self-esteem, self-confidence, perceptions of hopelessness or helplessness

- consciousness: awareness of disparities in power, awareness of larger context
- skills: gaining information, lobbying, influencing the media, organisational skills
- structural: resource redistribution, participation in decision making, changing structures.

Who is involved and/or affected?

(adapted from Hawe, 1994: 206)

This kind of discussion involves considering which dimensions are the major focus of concern and then what would count as evidence of movement in that direction. In addressing these questions it is likely that very different expectations will emerge but in identifying these differences and making deliberate choices between them it may become possible to clarify values, specify objectives and agree on indicators which can be used to 'measure' progress in relation to empowerment. In this way empowerment 'becomes less daunting, more "do-able" and potentially more evaluable' (Hawe,1994).

Participation

Community action and participation are closely linked. One important role for evaluation in the area of community action is the documentation of the processes and the extent to which they enable participation to occur. But first there has to be some clarity about what kind and nature of participation is intended and enacted. Bracht and Tsouros (1990) suggest there are five basic questions regarding participation:

- what is the meaning of participation?
- where and at what level does participation occur?
- who participates? for how long? who does not?
- why is participation important? benefits/obstacles?
- how is participation facilitated?

These questions can be used as a framework for a process evaluation of participation in community action for health. Figure 5.3 expands on the questions listed above and identifies the options and dimensions that might be considered within these questions.

The figure maps out the areas an evaluation might need to look at in order to document and analyse the kinds of participation that are taking place in order to compare these with the hopes and aims of the various parties concerned. But asking such questions does not, of itself, make an evaluation participatory in style and method as advocated by Smithies and Adams.

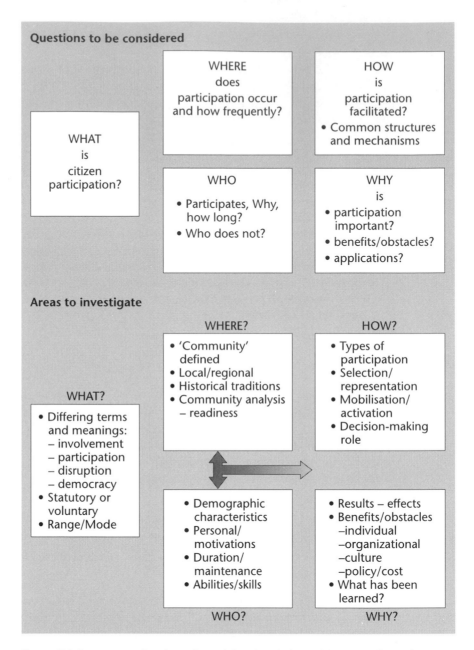

Figure 5.3 **Process evaluation of participation** (adapted from Bracht and Tsouros, 1990: 200)

Participatory evaluation

Because of the link between community action and participation, there is a special affinity between community action for health and participatory evaluation. In its most thorough form, participatory evaluation means that those who are meant to benefit from an action or project play the major part in planning and controlling the evaluation and make the crucial decisions about its focus, timing, purpose and so on. It may or may not involve external evaluators, depending on the decision of the community. An evaluation which is planned and controlled by funders, managers or project workers, but in which members of the community are asked their views, is probably best described as consultative rather than participatory.

Similarly it is important to distinguish between partnership and participation. Verhagen's definitions of different sorts of evaluation of community development projects may help here (Verhagen, 1989). In any project there are at least three parties: the members of the community, the staff or workers, and the funders. With evaluation which is concerned to foster partnership between the various parties there are four possibilities:

1 Self-evaluation, in which each party evaluates itself.

2 Joint-evaluation, where two or more parties jointly carry out an evaluation.

3 Mutual evaluation, where two or more parties evaluate each other's performance.

4 Participatory evaluation, in which those intended to benefit from the project have most say.

Whilst the first three options may foster partnership (a concept which presupposes a basic equality between the parties), it might well be argued that only the fourth is really concerned with empowerment and the redressing of a basic inequality between the various parties. But, at the same time, it is important to bear in mind that participatory evaluation is not simply distinguished by *who* conducts the evaluation but also by *how* the evaluation is conducted. So, for example, research and evaluation that seeks to enable participation by those with least power and influence has to give a great deal of consideration to questions of how best to communicate with people in terms and images with which they feel at home. An evaluation which managed to put childrens' views on the agenda illustrates this point well.

The evaluation involved finding out what a group of primary school children thought about their neighbourhood through group discussions, individual interviews with a play worker and written work, but was not proving very fruitful until an alternative method was chosen. Each child was given a disposable camera and invited to take photos of their favourite places, the places they steered clear of and the places that featured in the daily lives of members of their families. When the photographs were

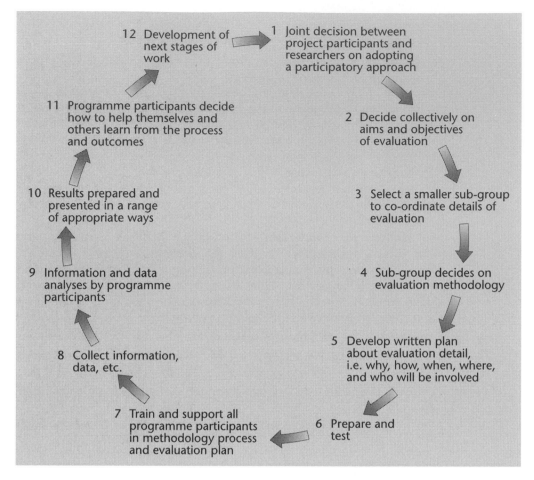

Figure 5.4 **The participatory approach to evaluation** (Feurstein, as adapted by Smithies and Adams, 1993: 63)

processed the children discussed the pictures and places saying what they thought of them. Their words and pictures were put together as an exhibition which was subsequently displayed at various centres in their community (Green, 1994).

The point is that participatory methods such as this are not simply more effective in identifying people's views, they also offer relatively powerless groups an opportunity to articulate and reflect on their experience in public contexts from which they are normally excluded and thus in some measure 'create the texts of practice' (Freire, 1972). Thus an evaluation that is neither designed nor executed by those meant to benefit from community action for health can, in the hands of evaluators committed to participatory methods, work towards active participation and even, perhaps, empowerment.

An evaluation that aims to be as participatory as possible will, however, take a participatory approach from the outset and continue this through all the key stages of planning, conducting and reporting. Figure 5.4 illustrates what this involves.

One illustration of an evaluation that aimed to follow this pattern is MESMAC (Men Who Have Sex With Men-Action in the Community), a three year project funded by the HEA. Gay men were involved in the planning, consultation, management and development of the project and the particular interests of different communities of gays were represented in all these stages. Positive targeting was employed to ensure involvement of under-represented groups such as black and ethnic minority men and disabled men. The design of the evaluation followed the principles of community development, incorporating the knowledge and insights of all project members and giving full feedback at all stages and levels of the project. Evaluators were primarily facilitators who employed skills of negotiation, communication and relationship building as well as research methodology (Smithies and Adams 1993: 68–69)

Look back at Figure 5.2 to identify the kinds of situations most likely to welcome a participatory approach to evaluation and those which would probably regard it as unscientific and cumbersome.

5.6 Conclusion

This chapter has teased out some of the main issues that need to be considered in evaluation of projects that pursue a community development approach to health. It has noted that there are likely to be very different perspectives on what counts as evaluation. Many of these differences are linked with different perspectives on the nature of health and what makes for good health and with different views about the nature of knowledge. The chapter has also looked at situations in which funders and development workers have found ways of combining their very different expectations. Nevertheless a fully participatory evaluation is by definition unable to make this kind of compromise and, perhaps for this very reason, is particularly likely to encounter funding difficulties.

Enabling the participation of local people in the decisions which affect their health and well-being must remain high on the health promotion agenda. This needs to be supported and complemented at the level of public policy. The public policy arena is the subject of the next Part.

Part 2
Promoting health through public policy

Introduction

This Part explores the prospects for creating health through public policy. It examines the promotion of 'healthy public policy' and 'supportive environments' as major objectives of international health promotion and considers the philosophical and practical dilemmas of putting in place strategies and programmes to meet these objectives. It connects to students' own experience of working within a policy framework and discusses how practitioners might seek to influence policy making for health.

Why study public policy? It could be argued that the main task for those wanting to promote health is to work with individuals and communities rather than spend time in analysing policy. The chapters that follow challenge this view by demonstrating that understanding policy making and change can form a vital part of effective health promotion practice. In health promotion, policy really matters. Decisions about welfare benefits, the availability of housing, the level of employment or access to appropriate health care have a vital influence on people's health and quality of life.

A policy analysis offers a new 'way of seeing' everyday work, highlighting why and how it is constructed. Understanding how policy is made will also help in planning how it might be influenced and changed. Policy decisions are made at many levels and, while it may seem extremely difficult to influence national or international policy making, health promoters can and do challenge and modify such policies at local level. Since this often involves alliances and collaboration with other agencies, knowledge of broader welfare frameworks can be important to success.

The five chapters in this Part explore the contribution made to promoting health within the public decision-making arena. The analysis focuses not only on international, national, regional and local government policies but on policy developed by major players in the health field, such as large corporations. Such organisations not only make policy decisions which impinge on health but influence public policy outcomes by creating frameworks within which politicians have to respond.

Chapter 6 discusses why and how healthy public policy has emerged as a central concern in health promotion and examines how public health, social policy and environmental politics have shaped contemporary views about what healthy public policy should be. Chapter 7 investigates the policy-making process and discusses its significance for health promotion practice. It suggests that much of what health workers accept as a taken-for-granted policy framework is the result of negotiation and can continually be challenged and modified. Chapter 8 explores the political bargaining that takes place around health through an exploration of the politics of health promotion in the UK, including national health strategies. Chapter 9 discusses the shifts in social welfare strategies in the UK, the withdrawal of the state from some areas of welfare provision and the rise of market principles. It considers the implications for health promotion of debates about the proper limits of welfare through a study of poverty. Finally, Chapter 10 considers the rise of 'green' politics and the linking of these to the health agenda through a 'global' and 'local' politics of health analysis. Throughout the chapters the opportunities for health and welfare workers to influence policy change through professional action, campaigning and strategic alliances are emphasised.

Chapter 6
Health promotion and public policy

6.1 Introduction

Promoting health through public policy is not a new concept. What is novel is the call to act 'in the name of health' rather than in the cause of industrial development, economic growth or national efficiency. There has been a long-standing acceptance in industrialised countries that the creation of some type of welfare infrastructure – health services, social support, education, income maintenance – is the price to be paid for a reasonably healthy, productive and amenable labour force. In early twentieth century Britain, for example, concern about the poor quality of British army recruits was a significant factor in persuading governments to introduce school meals and medical inspection (Hay, 1975).

In this view health policy can be seen in functional terms as enabling people to be productive workers and is underpinned by a concept of health as 'absence of disease'. In contrast to this, promoting health through public policy could result in prioritising health goals over other national goals: for example, unchecked economic growth which might be damaging to people's health. The call to create 'healthy public policy' and 'supportive environments' for health, therefore, is not value-free or consensual but essentially political and contestable. It is underpinned by a vision of health as positive and dynamic. This builds on the World Health Organisation definition of health as 'a positive concept emphasising social and personal resources as well as physical capabilities' and as related to 'the extent to which an individual or group is able, on the one hand, to realise aspirations and satisfy needs and on the other hand, to change or cope with the environment' (WHO, 1984).

This chapter examines the increasing interest in policy change as a means of promoting health, noting how the concept of healthy public policy has emerged and how it relates to a much longer public health and social welfare tradition. It looks at ideas for creating supportive environments for health through policy interventions at national and international levels. In all these areas debates have centred on how far legislation and regulation, as opposed to voluntary codes of practice, should be invoked to promote health and how far health needs should be paramount, as opposed to other priorities.

6.2 The public policy dimension in health promotion

Most models of health promotion have wider public policy intervention as an essential part of the framework. Policy interventions to promote health have been variously characterised as 'health protection and prevention', the 'politics of health' and 'social change' (Tannahill, 1990; French, 1990; Ewles and Simnett, 1995). These models mainly see action in terms of legislative and regulatory interventions designed to protect people's health and tend to be 'top-down' approaches.

Since the 1980s policy change has been growing in importance in World Health Organisation deliberations. The WHO Health For All targets for health in Europe (1985) set targets on 'lifestyles conducive to health' (targets 13–17) and on 'healthy environment' (targets 18–25) and in both categories regulatory measures were envisaged. Healthy environment, for example, called for target setting for health protection against environmental hazards, adequate monitoring mechanisms to control water, air and food quality, housing quality, workplace risks and waste disposal (WHO, 1985). Lifestyles targets focused mainly on health education for

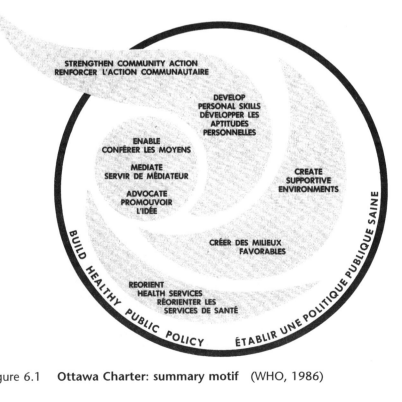

OTTAWA CHARTER FOR HEALTH PROMOTION
CHARTE D'OTTAWA POUR LA PROMOTION DE LA SANTÉ

Figure 6.1   **Ottawa Charter: summary motif**   (WHO, 1986)

behaviour change but they also included target 13, 'Healthy public policy', which was conceptualised in the following terms:

13 Healthy public policy

By 1990, national policies in all Member states should ensure that legislative, administrative and economic mechanisms provide broad intersectoral support and resources for the promotion of healthy lifestyles and ensure participation of the people at all levels of such policy making.

(WHO, 1985, European Region target)

The definition acknowledged not only that economic and social policies influenced lifestyle choices but that intersectoral policy change and public participation were needed to build healthy public policy. What it did not do was to link together environmental interventions and other policy actions as part of a wider public policy approach.

The linkage was made through the Ottawa and Adelaide conferences of the later 1980s, which played a key part in redefining and broadening the concept of healthy public policy. In the Ottawa Charter on Health Promotion healthy public policy became the driver of health promotion (Figure 6.1). This vital connection was made through the concept of participation and the role that individuals and communities would play in increasing control over the determinants of health and their own health (WHO, 1986). This reflected a growing attachment to community action and a belief that the political change required to make 'healthy choices easier choices' involved the mobilisation of public opinion at a whole range of levels, from global to local. Building healthier public policies, it was argued, required mediation and the development of co-operation between the various, often conflicting groups, sectors and agencies involved in creating conditions for improved health. Professionals might facilitate and support this process but individuals, communities and organisations became the central players. This generalised health promotion and healthy public policy building as 'everybody's business'.

The other significant policy shift was the linking together of healthy public policy and supportive environments. In 1990 it was claimed that 'the main aim of Healthy Public Policy was to create supportive environments which would make healthy choices possible or easier for the citizens and enable them to lead a healthy life' (WHO, 1990). The Sundsvall conference reinforced this message, responding to growing environmental concerns which were expressed during the late 1980s through a wave of national government and international reports. The conference declaration emphasised 'interdependence', 'the global perspective' and environmental protection as 'the challenge of our times' and emphasised the need for 'global accountability' to secure equity within societies and between the 'industrialised' and the 'developing' world (WHO, 1992). 'Think globally, act locally' gradually became incorporated into health promotion strategy (Rutten, 1995).

Once again an important feature was the identification of community empowerment, alliance building and mediating between conflicting interests as key 'health action strategies'. The Sundsvall declaration argued that reaching the goal of healthy public policy involved not just national and international action but community action for health. Strongly linked with this was the emergence of a more pluralist approach to policy making, in which the state became one of many players and agencies in the policy-making arena – giving rise to notions of 'healthy alliances' and 'intersectoral collaboration'. In some member states there was a growth of formal mechanisms to support health policy development, for example inter-departmental government committees. But, reflecting the fact that the state was becoming less central in the provision of health and social services, there was a concurrent emphasis on the role of private and voluntary agencies in providing for health.

The ideology of 'healthy public policy'

Exhortations to build 'healthy public policy' and 'supportive environments' are inevitably ideologically charged. We have already noted an emphasis not only on public participation as 'a good thing' but on community action and intersectoral alliances between private and voluntary sector agencies. In addition, it was seen as important for public policy to improve equity and accountability. The Adelaide Recommendations emphasised that 'an explicit concern for health and equity in all areas of policy and ... an accountability for health impact' were essential aspects of health promotion (WHO, 1988).

The problem for health promotion is that not all these ideas pull in the same direction. For example, communities may press for health policies that professionals consider 'unhealthy' and alliances between business organisations may result in decisions which downgrade health in favour of economic growth. Workplace health schemes run by employers, even NHS employers, have tended to focus on narrow lifestyle changes at work rather than on workplace health issues (Eakin, 1992). In addition there is a tendency to assume that governments are neutral players who, because they are 'ultimately accountable to their people' can be trusted to assess, monitor and inform the public about shortcomings in healthy public policy. A 1990 WHO briefing paper spelled this out:

> Public accountability for health is an essential nutrient for the growth of healthy public policy. Governments and all other controllers of resources are ultimately accountable to their people for the health consequences of their policies, or lack of policies. A commitment to Healthy Public Policy means that governments must measure and report the health impact of their policies in a language that all groups in society readily understand. Health information systems that support this process need to be developed at all levels. This would encourage informed decision-

making over the future allocation of resources for the implementation of Healthy Public Policy.

(WHO, 1990: 23)

In reality the politics of health policy making are not as straightforward as this and for any government health is going to be one of several political priorities. More fundamentally, however, what the ideology of healthy public policy demonstrates is that its intellectual roots lie in European and North American political traditions. It makes assumptions about the role of the state and the democratic process which would not be applicable in countries with different political priorities or one-party state traditions. It identifies a need to trade off economic growth against health goals which would be rejected by many developing countries for whom economic development seems an obvious route to northern hemisphere-style prosperity. To poor countries, creating healthier public policy and supportive environments may be a luxury compared with industrial growth, even if such growth brings about environmental degradation. Moreover, it may be northern multi-national enterprises who are instrumental in causing both the health hazards and new industrialisation prospects. Chemical, pharmaceutical and tobacco multi-nationals are all manufacturing intensively in Africa and South-East Asia, for example.

Health promoters themselves are not all agreed on the role of healthy public policy. There are differences of emphasis about where to make the major effort. Should the focus be on critical consciousness raising and empowerment in communities in the expectation that they will pressure for 'healthy' change? Should high risk strategies or whole population approaches take precedent? As one strategy is brought into focus there is a tendency for others to be marginalised, so there is no simple answer to these questions.

6.3 The anatomy of healthy public policy

How has 'healthy public policy' been defined and evaluated by health policy analysts? Some writers have emphasised the importance of multi-sectoral policies, whereas others have highlighted public participation or have viewed healthy public policy as any health-making policies (Pederson *et al.*, 1988). Dutch health researchers offer a definition which equates healthy public policy with health policy as 'a long-term, continuously used, standing decision by which more specific proposals aimed at, or related to [improving health] are judged for acceptability...' (De Leeuw and Polman, 1995) This is clearly a reflection of their concern that all policies for health should satisfy healthy public policy principles and it represents a normative goal rather than a detached definition.

There is also disagreement about the relationship between healthy public policy and other approaches, such as public health. Some writers have distinguished between 'public health policy' and 'healthy public policy', arguing that public health policy has historically focused on the maintenance of a health system mainly to care for ill people whereas healthy public policy is concerned to create a 'healthy society' (for example Hancock, 1982). This requires not only a much broader 'social' vision of health and an acknowledgement that it is influenced by social, economic and cultural forces, but also a readiness to intervene across the range of government sectors outside health and in the wider environment so that health is protected and promoted. This echoes the distinction made by the WHO between 'traditional public health policy [which] is mainly geared towards securing and improving medical care and prevention... uni-sectoral and short-term in nature' and healthy public policy which 'is basically multi-sectoral in nature, moving beyond health care with a long-term view to create a healthy society' (WHO, 1990).

Some would see healthy public policy as one aspect of a radical and 'new' public health approach (Ashton and Seymour, 1988; Public Health Alliance, 1994). The 'new' public health movement emerged in the UK in the 1980s, drawing inspiration from the traditions of nineteenth century public health and its concern to improve the physical environment of cities. The 1980s movement, however, had a broader and more radical agenda. The Public Health Alliance, formed in 1985, echoed the WHO's declaration (1977) that basic necessities such as security, equal opportunity and adequate food, homes, work and income were prerequisites for health. Their charter also called for environmental protection, adequate public services, a comprehensive health service and supportive social policies which help to sustain health.

The independent multidisciplinary committee which produced *The Nation's Health* set out a public health philosophy along broadly similar lines, recognising not only that basic necessities and services are necessary but that 'the promotion of public health will depend crucially on whether we can survive the worst consequences of the human propensity for disputation and contrive to live at peace' (Jacobson *et al.,* 1991: 3). The role for healthy public policies is seen as central in the new public health movement:

> Many contemporary health problems are... social rather than solely individual problems; underlying them are concrete issues of local and national public policy, and what are needed to address these problems are 'Healthy Public Policies' – policies in many fields which support the promotion of health. In the New Public Health the environment is social and psychological as well as physical.
>
> (Ashton and Seymour, 1993: 21)

In a parallel way, a distinction has been made between health promotion policy and healthy public policy. Health promotion policy is focused on 'specific health promotion programmes such as the development of no-smoking policies or healthy diet policies, or even the establishment of health promotion organisations or structures. Healthy public policy, by contrast, refers to multi-sectoral and collaborative processes involving the participation of all groups and populations affected' (Bunton, 1993: 131).

This is part of a wider claim made by Bunton that healthy public policy and indeed health promotion as a whole might be seen as part of social policy.

Health education and healthy public policy

Health education, it has been claimed, is an essential building block of healthy public policy (Tones and Tilford, 1994). Health education creates knowledge, critical consciousness and the pressure to change to healthier policies. In turn, this process creates the institutional frameworks and supportive environments within which people are enabled to change to healthier lifestyles and institutions can become more health supporting. In this view, health education, without an underlying commitment to creating healthier public policy, can come close to blaming the individual for illness when part (or all) of the explanation lies in the wider socio-economic environment. Public policy acts on the socio-economic and physical environment to create the conditions in which people can be more healthy and choose more healthy ways of life, but it is public pressure, networking, lobbying and so on – the products of raised consciousness and community action – that are seen as the essential building blocks to force the legislators and regulators to act (Figure 6.2).

The example of working at a local level to reduce child accidents highlights many of the key issues in Figure 6.2. It would include a health education dimension: for example, educating children about making safer choices when they cross roads and negotiate traffic. Another aspect of health education would be critical consciousness raising in the local area,

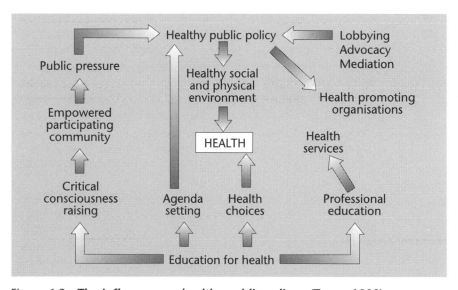

Figure 6.2 **The influences on healthy public policy** (Tones, 1990)

not only about accidents as a health issue but about the infrastructural changes that might be developed at a political level to reduce accidents. This could result in public pressure (by the 'empowered participating community') and active agenda setting for change. Another way of working for change could be evidence gathering, lobbying and mediation by professionals who worked on child safety issues. For example, there may be opportunities to write targets for change into health contracts. The outcome of the whole process, if successful, could be the introduction of healthier public policies, such as traffic calming or new speed restrictions by the local highway authority.

In the 'real world' of transport policy making such policies might be (and have been) resisted on the grounds that, while they might be safer for children, they would bring economic disbenefits by slowing up traffic and adding to congestion (Davis and Jones, 1996). So one important part of a health-promoting role might be to demonstrate why, in this case, health considerations should outweigh economic considerations.

Critically review Figure 6.2 in the light of your own experience of working for change on a particular health issue.

Smoking offers another example and here there is already a regulatory framework: for example, an age limit for tobacco sales, restrictions on advertising and a requirement to state the health effects of smoking on the packaging. But from a health promotion viewpoint there is still considerable room for regulatory initiatives. The health education emphasis has been on persuading individuals to quit, and on conscious- ness raising of the dangers of smoking through special projects, programmes and general awareness campaigns. These approaches appear to have been partly successful, although it is difficult to tell how far tax and regulatory measures have also played a part. Certainly, between 1972 and 1990 the percentage of male smokers fell from 52 to 31 per cent and female smokers from 41 to 29 per cent (*Social Trends*, 1994). However, a marked social class gradient in smoking-related deaths still exists (even if smoking incidence is taken into account) and rates of smoking among young people, especially young women, are now rising. Concern about the impact of smoking on cancers and circulatory diseases has led to the setting of targets for smoking reduction in all national health promotion strategies.

The call for a complete ban on advertising has been made by a range of health campaigning bodies such as Action on Smoking and Health (ASH), and has received support from smoking surveys. For example, 76 per cent of adults support a total ban on advertising and 70 per cent or more would support a ban on smoking in all public places, excluding workplaces, restaurants and pubs (HEA, 1995a). Despite campaigning initiatives and shifting public attitudes, however, the thrust of UK policy remains on self- regulation by the tobacco companies, and the consequence has been that advertising is still widespread, purchasing tobacco is easy even for under-age smokers (HEA, 1992) and prices are still (relatively) low. In other words, although health education has probably had a real effect in changing behaviour and raising public consciousness, and campaigning and lobbying is in place, these have not yet resulted in a change in legislation. This draws attention to other likely pressures on policy makers: from producers and retailers, European Union agricultural policies, economic pressures (for example, the government revenue acquired from tobacco sales) and ideological pressures towards 'free choice' rather than regulation.

The healthy public policy environment

Milio (1987) emphasised that healthy public policy must be 'ecological in perspective, multi-sectoral in scope and participatory in strategy'. In particular, for healthy public policy to be realised, it is argued that there is a central imperative for governments to evaluate all policies for their health impact (gain or loss) just as governments already review the financial implications of policies. In the UK, health impact appraisals and the recent development of a UK-wide environmental health action plan are beginning to enable such assessments to be made (see Chapter 10).

The objective is to steer through policies which offer maximum 'health gain' and this begins by recognising how people operate within a complex environment which is social, cultural and economic as well as physical. Within this 'ecological system' environmental and behavioural factors are constantly interacting at various levels. 'Implicating circumstances and activities', as Milio termed environmental influences, may be responded to by people in very different ways and may or may not be linked to health-damaging responses or lead to illness (see Figure 6.3). The need for policies which operate at different levels – global, regional national and local – is therefore seen as crucial.

Milio also drew attention to the extent to which 'typical personal behaviour among Americans, even as variations occur, is closely linked to a growth-oriented, industrial economy. It is a reflection at the personal level of directions taken on the national scale. The lavish use of energy for production brings more sedentary jobs and modes of transportation which reduce physical exercise and calorie expenditure'. She argued that competition and the pace of life 'makes for greater use of readily available "solutions" such as cigarettes, alcohol and tranquillisers' and that intense industrial production of these and other consumer products endangers workplace, food, air and water quality.

Researchers at the Unit for the Study of Health Policy at Guy's Hospital, London, in the 1970s and 1980s contested the claim that economic growth of itself would improve health, suggesting that 'we must develop economic policy, social policy and health policy in an integrated way rather than putting economic considerations first and thus creating health

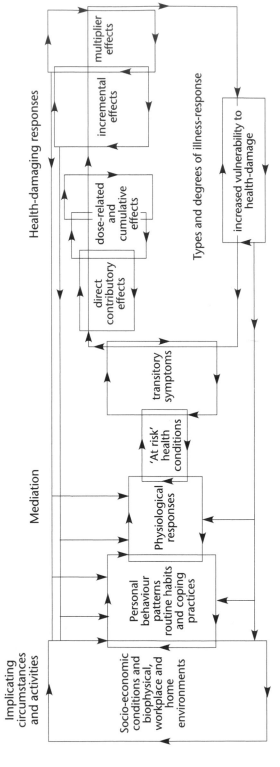

Figure 6.3 **The environment of healthy public policy** (Milio, 1987)

and social problems' (Popay *et al.*, 1993). For example, they argued that overreliance on capital intensive, high energy forms of agricultural production brought higher health risks through overuse of pesticides, growth hormones and intensive animal rearing, whereas a switch to national self-reliance and less industrialised production methods would improve consumer nutrition and cut pollution, resulting in decreased levels of diverticulitis and obesity.

From your reading so far, assess what you see as the most important elements of a 'healthy public policy' approach. One such list of ideas is set out below. Compare it with your own.

A healthy public policy approach is characterised by:

- a multisector approach, with an emphasis on seeing issues 'ecologically' so that social, economic and health policies are considered together and health moves higher up public policy agendas
- an emphasis on policy making for health at different levels, from local to global
- legislative and societal interventions to create supportive environments in which healthy choices are made easier for people
- a concern for equity within and between societies
- an emphasis on public accountability and the need for participation at an individual, group and community level in the policy-making process
- the emergence of new formal mechanisms to support policy change, such as interdepartmental committees, health impact analysis, action planning
- an orientation to northern hemisphere values, priorities and political traditions.

Influences on healthy public policy

The characteristics set out above highlight the breadth and ambition of the healthy public policy approach within health promotion. It is nothing less than the transformation of society through giving priority to a health agenda so that public policy changes also deliver greater equity and democracy. In the UK this has been expressed through the new public health movement but it builds on longer traditions within social welfare, public health and, most recently, health promotion.

The complex relationship between public health, social welfare, health promotion and healthy public policy is sketched in Figure 6.4. This plots the interdependent development of public health and health promotion (Macdonald and Bunton, 1993) but adds social welfare and environmental dimensions. It suggests that healthy public policy connects to social

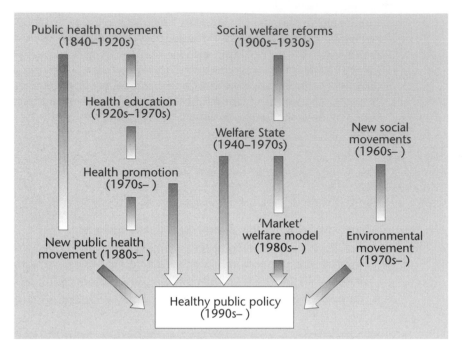

Figure 6.4   **The emergence of healthy public policy**

politics. The next three sections look at each of the influencing factors in turn.

6.4 The contribution of public health

Public health measures have been enacted against epidemic diseases, such as the plague, cholera and typhoid, by local and central governments in most Western countries since medieval times at least. The creation of statutory health services in most industrialised countries in the twentieth century and the growth of statutory social services, housing, planning and environmental control demonstrates the acceptance by legislators of the importance of primary, secondary and tertiary prevention, as well as disease treatment. In several European countries 'home visitors' or 'health visitors' were appointed specifically to protect and promote the health of 'healthy' children and families by instruction in hygiene, domestic and parenting skills (Davies, 1988; Jones, 1985).

The use of public policy measures to protect health became more widespread in the nineteenth century. Under the 1842 Public Health Act, for example, passed in response to a raging cholera epidemic, English local authorities were compelled to appoint a medical officer of health and enact protective sewage and drainage measures if the local death rate was above 40 per 1,000 inhabitants. Although the Board of Health, created to oversee the act, was violently attacked as a tyranny against the freedom of the individual and successfully closed down, by the 1880s all large towns had their own medical officer and public health team. Local authorities raised loans and by the turn of the century most had constructed complex sewage and drainage systems, piped water and, in many cases, gas lighting, municipal housing and tram systems as well.

The Victorian public health movement is probably the best known, but in many other European countries there were similar campaigns to improve public health in the eighteenth and nineteenth centuries (Riley, 1987). These were a response to rapidly growing migration into cities, which increased the pressure on already inadequate urban services and housing and sparked fears of social unrest. In addition, the effects of early industrialisation and mass production on the urban workforce were generally deleterious to health. Working hours were extremely long. Adults and children laboured in poor, cramped conditions for low wages and went home to housing that was frequently shoddily built, damp and overcrowded. The local environment in the poorer quarters of cities was filth-ridden and lacking in adequate pure water supply and hygienic sewage disposal. Such conditions left people unable to resist epidemic diseases such as cholera, typhoid and typhus. Box 6.1 focuses on one response to these health problems: that of nineteenth century France.

Box 6.1: The French public health movement: a case study

In France studies by Louis-Rene Villermé in the 1820s demonstrated that in some poor districts in Paris mortality rates were nearly double those in wealthy areas. 'In some rich departments the mortality rate for all deaths was as low as 1 in 50, whereas in the twelfth arrondissement of Paris the mortality rate was 1 in 24.21' (La Berge, 1992). Villermé attacked traditionalists who had been claiming that differences in death rates were caused by climate and topography. He also threw into question the widely held view, which Edwin Chadwick and other British public health campaigners held, that disease was caused by miasma (bad odours arising from putrefying matter and general filth). His studies indicated that low wages, appalling housing, overcrowding and malnutrition explained these markedly different rates. Above all, he noted the link between low wages and poor health (Coleman, 1982). In the 1830s Villermé turned his attention to industrialised workers in the French textile centres of Lille, Rouen, Lyon and Mulhouse. Cutting through claims and counter claims about industrialisation and harmful occupations his study concluded that poor living standards were the key to poor health. 'It is not the work of certain occupations which is harmful, but the profound misery of the workers.' He also drew attention to the exploitation of child labour, arguing that their use in factories 'is no longer work, it is torture'.

Until the late 1830s France was a European leader in public health theory and practice. Paris was an early magnet for migration and by the 1820s had an industrial working class of 400,000, the largest in Europe. On political as well as sanitary grounds, therefore, action on public health was important. There was a salaried health council in Paris as early as 1802, advising the prefect of police on matters such as public nuisances, waste regulation, epidemics and the treatment of foundling children (La Berge, 1992). By 1840 members had written 10,000 reports and had exerted considerable influence over public health policy; for example, guidelines for cleansing sewers, regulating slaughterhouses and dealing with cholera. In 1803, revolutionary France launched a national vaccination campaign against smallpox. By the 1830s health councils were being established all over France.

This long established tradition of state action on public health, dating back to before the French revolution but encouraged by revolutionary claims about people's rights to uniform disease prevention and health care, has been termed 'hygienism'. La Berge has called hygienism a 'secular religion' but there was no one central belief. Hygienism emphasised physical (or environmental) hygiene – preventing miasma by cleaning up filth, unhealthy dwellings, polluted rivers and so on – and personal and social hygiene – educating the poor to be clean and moral. Social hygiene involved denouncing debauchery and drunkenness, regulating prostitution, teaching morality and advancing social order. Beyond this, hygienists such as Villermé and Alexandre Parent-Duchatelet highlighted the central role of poverty in disease and death. Although they conflicted with each other, these different ideas existed side by side in the public health movement. But the view that carried most influence was that dirt caused disease and led to poverty, rather than the other way round. Personal and environmental cleanliness went hand in hand. This approach influenced British public health campaigners such as Edwin Chadwick and Southwood Smith. In his *Report on the Sanitary Condition of the Labouring Population Of England* (1842) Chadwick not only espoused miasmic theory but also commented on the close connection between cleanliness, morality and health.

By the early 1840s the leadership of the public health movement in Europe was firmly taken over by the UK, which brought in national legislation to force councils to take action. In France, many of the provincial health councils had declined in importance by the 1840s and even the Paris council was able only to influence and not legislate for change. Not until the later nineteenth century did France slowly take up ideas about piped water and waterborne sewage disposal, and begin to pass effective legislation which regulated unhealthy dwellings and limited hours of child labour. Evidently French public health campaigners were 'good on diagnosis, weak on therapy' (Coleman,1982). Ideas about the link between poverty and health, which litter French public health reports, were not acted on until after France's military defeat in the Franco-Prussian war of 1870–1 when broader public health measures were fuelled by a falling birth rate and concerns about national efficiency.

Note down the main conflicts within the French public health movement in the nineteenth century outlined in Box 6.1. Can you see any parallels between these conflicts and the different views expressed today about the causes of disease and death?

The main conflicts in the French public health movement were between a miasmic view, which sought to clean up the environment, a personal and social hygiene approach, which focused on cleanliness and morality, and a structural approach, which linked poverty and health. In the late twentieth century the main debate has been about the relative importance of individual lifestyle and broader structural influences on health.

Are there some parallels? In the UK, for example, there was a great reluctance on the part of governments in the 1980s to accept any connection between poverty and poor health. Instead, the main responsibility for ill health was seen to lie in personal lifestyle choices – to smoke, drink, practise unsafe sex. Official health policy was still to a great extent focused on modifying unhealthy lifestyles – the modern counterparts of dirt, drunkenness and debauchery. On the other hand, the interconnection of people's lifestyles and their material circumstances was highlighted with great regularity (Whitehead, 1987; Jacobson *et al.*, 1991; Benzeval *et al.*,1995) and subsequently acknowledged by government in the Health of the Nation Sub-Group Report on *Variations in Health* (DoH, 1995). Some earlier investigators also argued along such lines. Villermé, for example, suggested that the dehumanisation of industrialisation helped to demoralise workers and encourage drunkenness and debauchery (La Berge, 1992).

A renaissance for public health?

Some UK observers have attempted to create a 'grand tradition' in public health by linking together the work of the 'old' Victorian public health movement and the 'new' public health campaigns of the 1980s and 1990s (Ashton and Seymour, 1988). Certainly the newly industrialised cities with their densely packed streets, shoddily constructed housing, high levels of pollution and lack of sanitation offered opportunities for the spread of epidemic diseases on a much greater scale than in earlier centuries and thus prompted statutory intervention to avert potential disaster. One major incentive was the realisation that in crowded cities the middle and upper classes, not just ordinary working people, were vulnerable to such diseases. Concern for public order and for industrial productivity also encouraged limited intervention. But it is doubtful whether Victorian public health reformers would have recognised or endorsed the claim made by Ilona Kickbusch (1989) that 'public health is ecological in perspective, multisectoral in scope and collaborative in strategy', a comment that echoes Milio's claim about healthy public policy. While the ideas of a reformer such as Villermé might have fitted quite neatly into the revived public health movement traditional public health aims were much more restricted. Improved sanitation and slum clearance, rather than new housing, advice about hygiene and child rearing rather than anti-poverty programmes, were the focus for action (Jones, 1995a).

Public health traditions have undoubtedly provided an inspiration for healthy public policy (Milio, 1987). On the other hand, the healthy public policy focus in health promotion has provided a new justification for public health. As the major epidemics which had caused high mortality in nineteenth century industrial populations declined in importance the 'diseases of affluence', such as cancers and stroke, became more significant. The battle against these diseases centred on therapeutic advances in drug treatments and surgical procedures rather than preventive measures. Public health, with its strategy of preventing the onset of disease through sanitary engineering, health education, medical inspection and protective regulation, was thought to have reached the limits of its success. Its status declined in the twentieth century compared with other medical specialisms which concentrated on hospital treatment and crisis intervention. In the UK its responsibilities were fragmented, with environmental health functions remaining under local authority control while public health medicine, with responsibility for preventive strategies, became a rather narrowly focused health sector specialty.

Attempts to revive public health as a 'watchdog of the people's health' drew inspiration from the WHO's Health For All by the Year 2000 strategy with its emphasis on disease reduction, health education and health protection (WHO, 1985; Milio, 1987). In the UK in the mid-1980s, as we noted in Section 6.3, the 'new' public health movement was formed to broaden public health and act on the socio-economic determinants of health (White, 1996). The Acheson Report (1988) recommended the strengthening of public health medicine through government level interdepartmental committees and more effective monitoring and annual reporting of the health of local populations. More recently, the public health role of the nursing professions has been identified as:

> ...commissioning health services and providing professional care through organised collaboration in the NHS and society, to protect and promote health and well-being, prolong life and prevent ill-health in local communities, groups and populations.
>
> (Standing Nursing and Midwifery Advisory Committee, 1995: 5)

Public health has made a major intellectual contribution to the healthy public policy approach. It embraces a tradition of collective action at local and national level to protect health and deal with health problems, even if in the early twentieth century this approach was neglected as attention focused on biomedical advances. Public health medicine has recently sought to free itself from a medical model and recreate a broader role; on the other hand, its base in medical epidemiology and focus on medical risk have been questioned by new public health reformers.

6.5 Social policy and healthy public policy

A second major influence on healthy public policy has been the social welfare tradition. One reason for this has been the growing understanding of how health promotion, like social welfare, is embedded in a broader cultural politics. Health promotion analysts have drawn on social policy frameworks to explain the different and often conflicting accounts of 'what health promotion is' (see Chapter 9, Section 9.3).

Social policy has generally been used to describe any policy which is founded upon welfare principles and its main purpose has been seen as the promotion of individual welfare. It has also been seen as strongly integrative: that is, helping to bind society together. Marshall (1965) saw the eradication of poverty and the pursuit of equity as of central importance. Social policies, he argued, had welfare objectives – security, welfare and health – whereas economic policies were less altruistic. Yet for much of the history of welfare in Europe and North America social and economic objectives have been inextricably joined together. In the UK the setting up of the welfare state after the Second World War was advocated on grounds of promoting social solidarity and security for those who had 'risked their all' in the struggle against Hitler and Nazism. But it was also argued for on economic and political grounds. A state welfare system was seen as economically more efficient, drawing on the best elements of centralised state planning and reconciling the workforce to a capitalist economy by protecting it through full employment and 'cradle-to-grave' economic support (Beveridge, 1942).

In the UK social welfare policies had been enacted long before the 1940s but the Beveridge Report of 1942 opened an important new era in social policy analysis. The report argued that the giant evils of want, disease, ignorance, squalor and idleness would be vanquished by a welfare safety net for all citizens. For the first time piecemeal social legislation gave way to comprehensive welfare planning. Social security legislation insured the whole workforce against sickness and unemployment, housing and planning legislation created a public housing sector designed for all to participate in, education acts made schooling compulsory and free and the National Health Service provided free and comprehensive medical care. Underpinning all this, and defeating the fifth evil 'idleness', was the policy of 'full employment'. This was the keystone; only buoyant levels of economic growth could deliver the taxation receipts which would pay for social security and ensure that those out of work would not be so for long. The Beveridge scheme drew on the ideas of the economist, Maynard Keynes, who argued that governments could use their economic and political power to encourage growth, avoid recession and ensure low unemployment. Out of this would be born a 'welfare state' which gave its citizens 'cradle-to-grave' protection against unemployment, poverty and unnecessary sickness.

In what ways do the goals of social policy overlap with those of healthy public policy?

Many of the objectives of those engaged in promoting health through healthy public policy, whether in or outside the health sector, overlap with those of social policy. Health promotion also calls for strategies to maximise welfare, end poverty, create equity and increase efficiency. The Ottawa Charter (1986) contains the following pledge:

> To counteract the pressures towards harmful products, resources depletion, unhealthy living conditions and environments, and bad nutrition; and to focus attention on public health issues such as pollution, occupational hazards, housing and settlements.
>
> (WHO, 1986)

Beveridge's definition of unemployment as 'short intervals of standing by, with the certainty one will be wanted in one's old jobs again, or in a new job that is within one's power' (Beveridge, 1942) would be readily adopted by health promoters across the world, for whom long-term unemployment is a major health hazard. Research into possible links between income levels and health status has demonstrated across the world how health improves as income rises and income differentials narrow (Wilkinson, 1993). Without the framework of welfare policies to provide a minimum level of social security the health of the poorest groups in Europe would be even more at risk. The implications for health promotion of the UK's social welfare policies will be examined in Chapter 9.

6.6 The contribution of environmentalism

The third formative influence on healthy public policy has been environmentalism. During the 1980s 'green' politics moved from the political fringe in Europe to become a powerful political movement. In Germany, for example, the Green party became a significant force in national politics. Well-established political parties across Europe and in the United States have found it necessary to 'tag on' some 'green' rhetoric and even to make some modest political commitments to adopt 'green' policies such as cutting global atmospheric pollution. The Brundtland Report from the United Nations (1987) on global sustainability gave a new impetus to the environmental movement which increasingly looked to global action to solve global environmental problems. A series of global summits followed, resulting in Agenda 21 (UNCED, 1993) which called for action and set targets for reduction of pollution and environmental protection.

Agenda 21 was framed after the 'Earth Summit', The United Nations Conference on Environment and Development held in Rio de Janiero, Brazil in 1992. This created a practical agenda for change which was adopted readily by the 'green' movement and by many local authorities but more reluctantly by some national governments. At local level in the UK it linked to efforts already undertaken by some local councils to cut some of the causes of pollution and to introduce 'greener' policies on recycling, transport, energy conservation and wildlife protection. Local authorities now have a statutory duty to produce a local Agenda 21 plan (DoE, 1996b). Within national government it encouraged the development of policy appraisal guidelines which could assist in judging the health impact of policies in and outside the health sector (LGMB, 1995).

At the national policy-making level there are also signs that Agenda 21 has had some impact. The UK Environmental and Health Action Plan (DoE, 1996b), which went out for public consultation in 1995, was a response to the European Conference on Environment and Health held in Helsinki in 1994. It was a joint production by the Departments of Health and the Environment and built on environmental aspects of public health promotion as well as Environment White Papers such as *This Common Inheritance* (DoE, 1990). Agreement on priorities is clearly an important first step to getting an action plan which is realistic and costed.

There is now a growing linkage between healthy public policy, the new public health and environmentalism. The language of 'green' politics, with its talk of global crisis, the interconnectedness of global and local action, target-setting and the need for regulation, pervades the health promotion movement. Added to this is an emerging argument that environmental action is central to the protection and promotion of human health. As one leading radical public health analyst has commented:

> Closely linked to environmental concerns in relation to human health, Green politics has emerged in many countries as a minority but influential activity; but with the public's concern about the future of the human environment it has reached majority status, particularly since organisations like NASA (the US National Aeronautics and Space Administration) began to comment publicly on the reality of phenomena such as the destruction of the ozone layer and the greenhouse effect. The many connections between general environmental damage and hazards to human health have understandably fostered links between people in and around the new public health and people with Green sensitivities.
>
> (Draper, 1991)

A related aspect of the incorporation of an environmental agenda into health promotion and healthy public policy approaches in the UK has been the attempt to reclaim the role of the environmental health officer. The separation of environmental health and public health after 1974 has made it quite difficult for a common agenda to emerge. As public health became increasingly focused on medical approaches to prevention so environmental health became downgraded as 'refuse and pest control'. In fact, environmental health officers have a broad remit including housing standards, drinking water surveillance, environmental protection and health and safety at work. There are considerable opportunities for officers, employed by local authorities, to use their statutory powers to intervene in the name of health, but in many ways the regulatory powers they possess are too frail. Allen (1996) quotes the example of factory pollution where before a successful court action can be taken evidence is required to prove not only that pollution is emitted, but also that it damages local residents and that the factory is not taking the best practicable means to control it.

What evidence of environmental action exists in your own workplace or local area?

In recent years, some health and local authorities have become aware of the potential for linking to a wider health agenda through healthy cities initiatives and through Agenda 21, the execution of which in many cities has been spearheaded by environmental health departments (Allen, 1996). The Health Education Authority's Heartbeat Awards have provided incentives to establish 'healthy eating' and no-smoking areas. Many cities have now also established their own traffic-monitoring systems to supplement the government's inadequate monitoring stations and gain a clearer picture of local pollution incidence. Within the UK health sector there has also been some interest in becoming 'greener'. In late 1996 the Department of Health published a consultation paper in which it proposed that 'environment' should become a key target area in Health of the Nation (Dott, 1996).

6.7 Conclusion

Healthy public policy is underpinned by ideas drawn from the environmental movement, from social welfare policy and from the 'old' and 'new' public health. More than this, there is a convergence between their language and debates. Social policy, of course, is an academic discipline but one intensely concerned with individual and social welfare and therefore with the changing public policy agenda. For example, Townsend (1995) noted that the globalisation of poverty was a marked feature of the 1980s and 1990s as multinational enterprises shifted plant, bases and resources to maximise efficiency and governments could do very little to prevent this, even if the political will was there.

Healthy public policy has built in an ecletic way on social policy, the environmental movement and the public health tradition. The rest of this Part explores and develops aspects of this continuing legacy and discusses the implications of the convergence of environmental and health politics.

Opportunities for those with a remit for health promotion to make alliances with local statutory agencies are explored. In doing so, Part 2 demonstrates the importance of a public policy dimension in health promotion and discusses ways in which an understanding of public policy can assist those involved in promoting health work. But first, it is important to be clear about what policy is and how it is made and changed. Chapter 8 discusses the nature of policy and the implications of the policy-making process for health.

Chapter 7
Making and changing public policy

7.1 Introduction

What is public policy and why is it important for health promoters to understand how policy is made? Public policy is generally seen as the web of decisions made by international, national, regional and local government, and given expression in the form of legislation, regulation and guidance. In the health promotion field one of the most significant examples of policy making in recent decades has been the WHO's 1977 Health For All Strategy which set targets for the achievement of better health by the year 2000. Many countries signed up to the strategy, and this required them to demonstrate that action to attain the targets was being taken. England, Wales, Scotland and Northern Ireland each produced a national health strategy, with targets for health improvement.

There are probably few people involved in promoting health, whether professional or lay, in or outside the health sector, who have remained unaffected by these health promotion policies. They have helped to inform priority-setting, the flow of resources and ways of working in the health sector. Through national media campaigns and programmes they have played some part in shaping public ideas about health. Criticism of the strategies has spawned a lively debate about alternative priorities and health goals (see Bunton *et al.*, 1995). For all these reasons it is important not only to understand what the policy is (and is not) but to be aware of how and why it came into existence.

This chapter explores public policy and the policy-making process, using examples from the health field and beyond. It discusses how policies are made and why issues get onto the policy agenda. It briefly explores different models of policy making, and uses the case study of smoking to examine how conflicts of value and interest affect policy change. It suggests that health promoters can influence policy decisions directly, for example through lobbying and pressure group membership, and by the important role they play in policy implementation. But in order to do so they need to understand the nature of the policy-making process itself.

7.2 Understanding policy

It has been argued that a policy 'consists of a web of decisions and actions that allocate values' (Easton, 1953). In an influential work on policy making, Easton highlighted the central importance of values. Values are those aspects which people regard as important and may be reflected in physical or symbolic goods and services. Policy, he suggested, is about 'the authoritative allocation of values', in other words the ability of those in positions of influence at any level in or outside formal government to sanction or withhold approval in relation to particular goods and services. For example, many surveys have demonstrated that people in the UK attach great importance to retaining a national health service and, whatever health policies are enacted, politicians almost always make claims that they will make the NHS more effective and give better value for money.

Policy may be seen as 'the authoritative statements of intent about action', with the assumption that 'as government has the ultimate authority to act, it is their policies which become a focus for debate and action' (Allsop, 1995). Alternatively, and just as plausibly, it can be argued that policy is the consequence of the actions taken by individuals in the process of implementation (Barrett and Fudge, 1981). The first comment emphasises that policy is deliberate, systematic and usually government-led; the second highlights the potential for anyone at any level to be involved. It reminds us that policy doesn't just mean the latest government pronouncement but also how it is put into practice and its intended and unintended consequences.

Who makes policy?

In England, Ham (1992) has explored the relative influence of the Department of Health and the wider policy community in decision making. Although the organisational changes in health care have given more autonomy to hospital trusts and fund-holding general practitioners, the role of central government is a key one. But it is not a homogeneous body: (fairly) transient politicians, generalist career administrators and civil servants with a professional background may all have different interests to pursue. The Medical Division, headed by the Chief Medical Officer of Health for England, exerts considerable professional influence on policy making. Scotland, Wales and Northern Ireland have similar (but at crucial points distinctive) policy and organisational traditions.

Outside the national Departments of Health the wider policy community consists of the merged health authorities and Family Health Services Authorities (health boards in Scotland and combined health and care boards in Northern Ireland), trusts, advisory bodies, representative and powerful 'producer' groups (such as the British Medical Association), commissions and consumer groups. Standing commissions, such as Health Advisory Services which monitor local service developments and staffing standards, can have considerable influence. The influence of *ad hoc* bodies such as Royal Commissions which explore and report back on particular issues depends on political circumstances. Consumer groups, whether statutory (the Community Health Councils) or voluntary (such as Age Concern or MENCAP), can also wield some influence although this varies considerably. The policy-making community in health promotion is set out in Table 7.1.

Table 7.1 The 'policy-making' community in health promotion

	Statutory	Professional	Umbrella	Academic
International	World Health Organisation (WHO); European Union (EU); Organisation for Economic Co-operation and Development (OECD)		European Public Health Association (EUPHA); European Health For All Network (EURONET)	Association of Schools of Public Health in the European Region (ASPHER)
National	Department of Health NHS Management Executive and regional offices; Health Education Authority; Department of Environment Public Health Laboratory Service; Communicable Disease Surveillance Centre	Faculty of Public Health Medicine; British Medical Association and national 'craft committees', e.g. Committee for Public Health; Association of Directors of Public Health (ADPH); Other Royal Colleges and faculties, e.g. Faculty of Occupational Medicine, Royal College of Physicians, Royal College of General Practitioners Royal College of Nursing; Health Visitors' Association (HVA); Society of Health Education and Promotion Specialists (SHEPS); Institution of Environmental Health Officers	Chief Medical Officer's National Public Health Network; Standing Committee on Public Health (SCOPH); Association for Public Health; Public Health Alliance; Society for Public Health incorporating the Faculty of Community Health; Royal Institute of Public Health and Hygiene; Royal Society of Health; UK Health For All Network (UKHFAN)	Society for Social Medicine (SSM); Royal Statistical Society - Medical Section; Radical Statistics Health Group
Local	New health authorities (incorporating DHAs and FHSAs); General practices including fundholders; Community Health Councils; Local Councils (LAs)	BMA local 'craft committees', e.g. Committee for Public Health Medicine and Community Health Regional Specialist; Sub-Committees for Public Health Medicine (SSC-PHM) (sub-committee of the regional medial committee); Regional branches of SHEPS, HVA etc.	Regional public health associations, e.g. North West Public Health Association (NWPHA); Local health partnerships and joint advisory groups (linking statutory authorities); Regional Health For All networks; Local Health For All and Healthy City projects	Regional academic associations, e.g. Northern Epidemiology Group; Regional schools and institutes of public (and/or environmental) health; University departments of epidemiology, public health, health sciences, health promotion, health services research, primary healthcare etc.

(White, 1996)

Although governments make plans and state intentions in legislation or regulation this is only one part of the policy process. As they are implemented policies become adapted and transformed by the actions, inactions and priorities of other people into something rather different. Indeed, Allsop (1995) accepts that 'what policy is can only be seen in terms of outcomes'. In other words, both what governments decide to do and what actually gets done are important to study.

It could be claimed that policy is action and that decisions are not always the way in which policy comes into being. A particular set of actions may be taken at grass roots level to deal with a crisis, say excessive pressure on community nursing staff during an influenza epidemic, and these become the accepted way of working. Management, who can see the benefits of the change, might then ratify the actions through formal decision at a later stage or the actions might simply become a part of what new entrants learn from the old hands when coming into the area. 'Top-down' studies of decision making need to be balanced by 'bottom-up' research into actions (Ham, 1992).

There are several stages in the making of a policy and many opportunities for policy to change. A decision is not a policy, nor even an action, and the subsequent translation of a decision into action shifts the focus to other players. The people who make decisions in an attempt to create a policy are rarely the same as the people who will implement the decisions. Ham has commented that 'a decision network, often of considerable complexity, may therefore be involved in producing action'. Conversely, policy makers rarely operate with a blank sheet. They are influenced and constrained by earlier decisions from other policy sectors as well as their own (Walt, 1995).

One example of this would be the evolution of the United Kingdom National Environmental Action Plan, published in 1996. Significant actors in the initial creation of this policy were scientists who developed theories about ozone layer depletion and global warming, environmentalists who warned about deforestation and species depletion, civil servants, professionals, academics and politicians who wrote papers and attended conferences, climaxing in the Earth Summit in 1992, Agenda 21 and the Health Action Plan for Europe (1994). The plan was given a particular impetus because the UK was selected as one of six pilot countries to develop an action plan linking health and the environment. In 1995 a draft plan was issued for consultation and nearly 250 organisations and individuals responded, influencing the shape and wording of the final plan (DoE, 1996b). It commits a range of organisations from different sectors to meet a whole series of targets on pollution levels and other types of environmental protection. But the actual working out of this policy will depend crucially on the co-operation of people and agencies, such as environmental health officers, local authorities, health promoters, private sector businesses and the police. It will also depend on effective monitoring of targets, research to gather reliable information, effective training and outside scrutiny of progress, by pressure groups and independent auditors.

Policies almost always change over time as other policies impact upon them, as personnel change, as political developments require changes of direction. Consider the 'ring-fencing' of the mental health budget following the 1990 community care legislation. This meant that local authorities were given a specific budget by central government which they could only spend on mental health. This policy decision was not initially part of the Act. The government was pushed into action by a series of high profile cases involving psychiatric patients discharged into the community who attacked people and damaged themselves in spectacular ways. Pressure groups and the media were able to have a considerable influence in reshaping policy decisions.

Policy analysts have also highlighted the importance of studying non-decision making, inaction and resistance, arguing that a focus on decision making 'has ignored the importance of policy maintenance and even inertia' (Ham, 1992). For example, Family Health Services Authorities in the UK (formerly Family Practitioner Committees), who oversee the work of family doctors, began to appoint primary care facilitators in the 1980s to persuade doctors to engage in more active health education and promotion. This agency-level policy initiative was largely a failure because doctors did not see health promotion as a priority or were opposed in principle to introducing it into consultations with patients (Astrop and McWilliam, 1996). The introduction of the 1990 and the 1993 contracts had more success but the reluctance of GPs to become more involved was still evident (Calnan *et al.*, 1995). You may be able to think of policies which managers in your own organisation attempted to implement and which were effectively sabotaged by the refusal to respond of key, but perhaps quite junior members of the workforce. Or perhaps the outward form of the policy was implemented but the intention of the policy was undermined or ignored.

A role for health promoters

While policy might appear to many grass roots workers in the health and social services sector, in education, in statutory and voluntary agencies, or elsewhere, to be something that is imposed on them from above, in practice there are many possible ways in which their influence might count. From a health promotion viewpoint this means that those who seek to influence and change policy so that it puts a higher priority on health have several alternative strategies which they might adopt. They could attempt to influence initial decisions about health made at a national or local level, working through pressure groups, community groups and other voluntary agencies. Ewles and Simnett (1995) call this the 'societal change' approach, concerned with changing the attitude of society towards a behaviour through policy. The types of activities they envisage are characterised by the example of smoking:

> Aim – make smoking socially unacceptable, so it is easier not to smoke than to smoke.
>
> Activity – no-smoking policy in all public places. Cigarette sales less accessible, especially to children, promotion of non-smoking as a social norm. Limiting and challenging tobacco advertising and sports sponsorship.
>
> (Ewles and Simnett, 1995)

While most people involved in health promotion would probably welcome such changes the aim and activities might appear unrealistic, prompting a feeling of disempowerment or a judgement that involvement in policy change was a concern strictly for their managers or policy makers at national level. This reaction of 'What can I do anyway?' is highlighted in a study into the work of 65 practice nurses (Bradford and Winn, 1993). Only one practice nurse was using, in her own judgement, the 'social change' model, although 15 per cent of the over-40 age group and 29 per cent of the younger nurses, saw it as important. However, we have already noted that policies are made and influenced at a range of levels and that those who operationalise policy also play a part in making it.

Assess the range of professional and lay health promoters who might contribute to the changes in smoking policy called for by Ewles and Simnett (1995).

In order to work effectively a 'no-smoking' policy would need to be enforced and organisations would have to be willing to implement it. Occupational health workers, activists and anyone with an interest could have a role here, by building a consensus for change, gathering good practice on how to carry it through and helping to 'police' the policy. Although there are regulations about cigarette sales to children (see Table 7.2) these are sometimes ignored. One estimate by Action on Smoking and Health (ASH) is that illegal sales to children total £100 million a year in Britain and a 1995 survey indicated that 11 per cent of 11–15 year-olds smoke one or more cigarettes a week (HEA, 1995b; *Guardian*, 23.8.96). This offers a role to all those interested in promoting health to assist in implementing policy, for example by reporting retailers who break the law or by devising local programmes which might help to change attitudes towards under-age smoking. Being involved in a pressure group such as ASH which seeks to ban tobacco advertising and sports sponsorship would be another way in which anyone with an interest in changing smoking behaviour could help to influence policy change.

Thinking about policy as a web of decisions, at all levels and not just 'at the top', involving inaction and inertia and also individual or group action, can be quite an empowering approach. For example, getting together with other teachers to campaign for a smoke-free staff room or resisting the attempts of the catering manager in a hospital trust to maximise profits by concentrating on burgers and chips and cutting out salads both involve action on policy change. Seemingly small actions can make a difference. Protests at one Birmingham supermarket by parents and health professionals led to a change of policy by the management; sweets were no longer stacked appealingly by the exit tills to encourage children (and adults) into last minute buying. This has also happened elsewhere. Being alert in your own daily work to the potential for making and changing policy in order to promote health is a realistic way to start.

7.3 The policy-making process

There have been many attempts to describe policy making but most analysts use a process approach in which four main stages are delineated:

1 Agenda setting: problem identification and issues recognition.
2 Options development and appraisal: setting of alternatives, forecasting, cost benefit analysis.
3 Policy choice and implementation of this.
4 Evaluation and review.

A rational view

However, there is little agreement on how far this process is put into operation as a set of deliberate, systematic steps (Walt, 1995). A 'rational' model of policy making would suggest that policy makers start by identifying a problem and, using guiding objectives and values, analyse the various alternatives for dealing with it. Having assessed the various options and their relative political and resource costs, policy makers choose the option which maximises their objectives and values. But there is considerable scepticism about whether this approach is feasible. In the first place, problems are not discrete and cannot necessarily be dealt with in isolation. For example, securing better primary care services or more effective health promotion services is bound up with resource questions about secondary care.

Second, policy makers may be less concerned about finding a rational solution than a politically acceptable one. They are not likely to be wholly objective in their assessment. Ideological considerations, for example about the superiority of 'free market' solutions and the wisdom of deregulation, may mean that some policy options are ignored. Even if a problem is relatively uncontentious policy makers are unlikely to have the time to gather and weigh up all the evidence. In relation to some problems, for example global environmental concerns, conflicting evidence may mean that it may be impossible to be sure about what needs to be done. Finally, past decisions will influence the range of policy options available.

An incremental view

Incrementalists have criticised the rational model as unrealistic and have argued that most policy change happens in a much more disjointed and piecemeal way. Lindblom (1965) used the phrase 'incrementalism' (changing outcomes by minor adjustments) or 'muddling through' to describe much of policy analysis and change. He drew attention to incremental change, the inability to make clear decisions and the preference of most players to analyse policy problems one at a time and to make minor adjustments rather than explore the whole policy framework. The features of incrementalism can be defined as:

1 A blurring of the distinction between objectives and implementation, with objectives not clearly thought through.
2 Appraisal of only a limited range of policy options.
3 A restricted analysis of these options and their consequences.
4 Policy choice based on consensus rather than systematic cost-benefit analysis.
5 Acceptance of the remedial, incremental and temporary nature of any change.

This draws attention to the practical difficulties involved in any policy change: the weight of vested interests, organisational inertia and the problems of implementation that this raises. For example, Klein (1983) noted the policy inertia of the UK health service, which he argued arose from its occupational complexity and the distribution of power between the medical profession, the health authorities and the Department of Health. At times when more radical policy initiatives have been attempted the outcomes have not always been very lasting or substantial (Harrison *et al.*, 1990). Even in the late 1980s, when a radical analysis of UK health care resulted in attempts to carry through comprehensive rather than incremental policy change, the outcomes were not as dramatic as was expected. The projected working of the internal market in health care was initially undermined by long-standing relationships between hospitals, health authorities and family doctors.

Critics of incrementalism argue that it is at root a conservative analysis – suggesting that it is acceptable to make small adjustments. This may be appropriate in a society where there is a high degree of social stability, but it cannot adequately explain how more dramatic change can happen. Both models may be necessary. The rational model 'is really describing an ideal model of policy making (how it ought to be made)' whereas the incremental model is describing 'what actually happens in the policy process (how policy is made)' (Walt, 1995: 41).

7.4 Influences on policy making

We have noted that governments have considerable power to set agendas and create policies but also that incrementalism suggests there are effective boundaries on policy change, created by the implications of past decisions, political pressures and the complexities of policy making itself. In addition there is the question of how much influence can be exerted by the wider public, as opposed to the more influential members of the 'policy-making community'. An exploration of two models of policy making, pluralism and conflict, offers some answers to these questions.

A pluralist view

Figure 7.1 shows a simple model of policy making which begins to identify some of the main processes and stages. It is a systems theory or 'pluralist' approach; that is, it explores political activity as a series of processes which must be kept in balance and it draws on biology to furnish the idea of interaction and interdependence (Easton, 1965). It pays attention to some central aspects of the policy process: the pressures on the political system from the wider environment and the feedback loop from outputs to inputs. 'Resources' refer to natural, financial or human resources that enable governments to respond to demands. For example, a lack of people trained effectively in health promotion work may mean that health targets will not be met.

The 'demands' refer to pressures exerted by groups and individuals at all levels for some kind of change; for example, more resources for health, better services for AIDS/HIV sufferers, a ban on tobacco advertising and so on. 'Support' refers to the extent to which the political system counts on wider public support to sustain it. If demands for action are overwhelming or if support for politicians, the constitution or policies dwindles because of a failure to meet demands, then the system becomes unstable. If outputs are not acceptable this creates greater pressures at the 'inputs' end of the process. As a response, Easton argues, the political system will adapt and re-stabilise through policy or personnel changes. In the UK this is ultimately resolved by a general election, but before this happens governments with very slender majorities may change their policies in order to maximise support. In any case, a 'pluralist' view of policy making assumes that a balance is maintained between inputs and outputs in any political system (Walt, 1995).

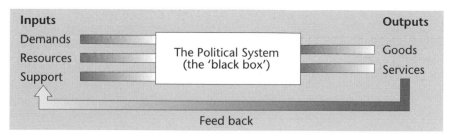

Figure 7.1   **A simple systems approach to policy making**   (adapted from Easton, 1965)

The limits of a pluralist analysis

On the other hand, it is clear that policy change is not that simple. Easton's analysis is underpinned by a 'pluralist', essentially consensual conception of policy making. In other words, it assumes that all the players in the policy making process are able to exert some influence and make their needs and demands felt. It assumes that the state is more or less even handed in the way it manages demands, balancing conflicting values and different interest groups. Others have drawn attention to the deficiencies in this analysis and argued that only some powerful or insider groups may influence policy making. Other groups may find their needs ignored.

Bradshaw (1980) distinguished between 'normative', 'felt' and 'expressed' needs and between whether those needs would or would not be met:

- Normative needs are defined by making judgements against set criteria or professional standards about what needs exist and whose needs are greatest. For example, professional judgement, perhaps of the 'comparative' needs of one group of clients or one individual as against another, is much more widely used to determine need than 'lay' judgement.

- Felt needs are what lay people themselves feel that they want, although these may not always be articulated or even really understood by them.

- Expressed needs are felt needs which are spoken about or acted upon, for example as requests for services, access, facilities and so on.

Not every group has the ability to articulate their needs; it is those groups better able to define their needs, express them in forms acceptable to professionals and then to muster support from influential groups to have those needs met that will be successful in changing policy.

Give an example of a group that currently finds it difficult to influence policy making.

Marginalised groups in current policy making would include those who are homeless or unemployed. Many are not on electoral rolls and cannot express their needs; coming together to press for change is very difficult. Governments can argue that there is no evidence of support for policy change and therefore no need to act or, as in the case of unemployed people, it may cut their benefit and entitlements. Some groups are unable to make their voice heard: those in prison, for example, or those with mental health problems.

A conflict analysis

A 'conflict' view of the policy process argues that many voices may never be heard. There will always be some more powerful groups who are able to influence policy unduly whereas others cannot ever get their concerns onto the policy agenda. For example, it has been argued that the Health of the Nation strategy in England (1992) was overwhelmingly influenced by a medical agenda. The targets set were therefore largely about disease reduction rather than the broader Health For All, although health promotion specialists and many in the new public health movement were very critical of this approach (see Chapter 8). Some of the 'community development' focus of contemporary health promotion, as we noted in Part 1, is aimed at assisting 'hard-to-reach' groups and enabling them to define their needs and seek change.

In the 1970s conflict theorists argued that 'corporatism' was a marked feature of policy making (Cawson, 1982). Corporatism highlighted the incorporation of the most powerful interest groups, such as trade unions and employers' groups, into the 'black box' of policy making. From being outsiders influencing policy and making demands, some groups become insiders, enmeshed in the policy process. In the UK health sector, for example, powerful professional groups such as the Royal Colleges or the British Medical Association have at times wielded considerable power over policy. Their key role in the provision of services has enabled them to ensure that they are protected in any policy change. Their influence in the setting up of the National Health Service ensured that hospital doctors received very generous contracts and that family doctors remained independent practitioners, subcontracted to the NHS. In comparison, the nursing professions have rarely been able to make their voice heard in health policy making (Dingwall et al., 1988).

In the 1980s, when managerialism became the vogue in the UK health sector, hospital doctors were generally successful at protecting their own conditions of service and privileges (Cox, 1991). Only in the 1990s, as the internal market system came more fully into effect via the purchaser-provider split and fund holding, did hospital doctors find their influence challenged to a greater extent by hospital managers and by general practitioners. Managers (and to some extent politicians) became more influential in health policy making and the health sector market signalled a change of priorities which reduced medical power. General practitioners who have become fund holders have seen their influence over patient services grow considerably and their contractor status as independent business people reinforced.

Conflict theorists draw attention to the 'closure' that can be effected by powerful insider groups. In other words, politicians and officials may create their own agenda and not respond to outside demands.

> Through the manipulation of language and the creation of crises, the authorities may impose their own definition of problems and help to frame the political agenda. Recognition of these processes is an important corrective to the naive assumptions found in some applications of systems theory.
>
> (Ham, 1992)

There is considerable evidence of this in relation to health policies. For example, there is not much evidence that the shift to a market system in the UK National Health Service was the result of demands for change coming from within the health sector itself or from the wider public in the late 1980s. Indeed, the 'crisis' of health care was seen by most as a cash crisis arising from underfunding not a management or organisational crisis. In 1990 the National Health Service legislation was not welcomed either by health sector workers or by the public. Policy was driven from within the 'black box' by the then prime minister Margaret Thatcher and Kenneth Clarke, the health minister (Clarke, 1996). What happens within the 'black box' part of the policy process may at times effectively recast or negate external demands.

The limits of a conflict analysis

The argument that only some powerful insider groups can influence policy making has been resisted on the grounds that it is ultimately too rigid and does not explain why policies do change, sometimes in quite radical ways (Walt, 1995). At the same time, it is evident that governments and their allies exercise a high degree of control over what can legitimately be considered to be within the national public policy domain. For example, in 1980 Sir Douglas Black's Report on Inequalities in Health was published with as little publicity as possible, instantly dismissed by health ministers, and in a political sense effectively 'buried'. It was not until 15 years later, in 1995, that inequalities in health – now termed 'variations' – made it back onto the national political agenda (DoH, 1995a). However, at regional and local levels, within academic research, national pressure groups and in public opinion evidence inequalities in health continued to be viewed as important throughout the 1980s and there was increasing evidence that inequalities themselves were growing (Whitehead, 1987; Townsend *et al.*, 1988).

It has been suggested that the notion of 'bounded pluralism' may best describe this conflict between policy-making levels and agendas (Hall *et al.*, 1975). Insider or elite groups may be able to screen out sensitive issues at national level and use the state to serve their own ideological interests, but this is compatible with accepting more open debate about less politically dangerous issues. Analysts have mainly identified economic issues as the 'high' politics over which the political elite keeps control whereas in particular policy fields there may be quite wide debate (Walt, 1995). This may explain why in the health field national policy debate on poverty and health inequalities was screened out but there was public debate about health care rationing, HIV/AIDS and other less potentially damaging concerns. A debate about poverty and inequality could not help but challenge tenets of economic liberalism espoused by the 'New Right' in the 1980s.

7.5 A case study of smoking policy

Smoking represents a useful example of policy change, highlighting conflicts of value over an issue of crucial interest to health promoters. The dangers of smoking have been known about for many years, since the pioneering work of Schrek and his colleagues in the United States and of Doll and Hill in the UK in the late 1940s and early 1950s (Schrek *et al.*, 1950; Doll and Hill, 1950, 1952). Together, these studies demonstrated a strong association between smoking and several major diseases, including lung cancer, coronary artery disease, chronic bronchitis and pulmonary tuberculosis. Longitudinal cohort studies, for example the Framingham cohort, were able to highlight the causative association between smoking and heart disease (Shurtleff, 1974). By the 1980s smoking was demonstrated to increase the risk of contracting a wide range of cancers, respiratory and cardiovascular diseases (RCP, 1992). In addition, the dangers of passive smoking began to be recognised, in particular the increased risk of lung cancer for non-smokers and of respiratory diseases in children (Wald *et al.*, 1991). By 1993 government figures suggested that 110,000 people were dying each year from smoking-related diseases (Hansard, 1993).

The tobacco companies' own research had highlighted an association between smoking and lung cancer by the 1960s and some cancer sufferers in the United States have taken out lawsuits, claiming that this information was illegally withheld from them and the tobacco companies were therefore liable to pay compensation. In August 1996 a Florida court awarded damages of £500,000 to a cancer victim who had sued British Associated Tobacco's (BAT) American subsidiary, Brown and Williamson, for withholding evidence about the health-damaging effects of smoking. Fourteen US states have launched legal actions against US tobacco manufacturers to recover the costs of medical treatment for smoking-related illnesses (*Guardian*, 23.8.96).

In public, tobacco companies have always sought to cast doubt on the evidence linking smoking and lung cancer and it proved difficult to demonstrate conclusively that a causal link existed. But by the 1960s medical evidence was sufficiently damning to persuade governments to take action. Aspects of the UK response, a mixture of voluntary agreement, government regulation and health warnings recently made more forceful by EC directives, are summarised in Table 7.2.

Table 7.2   UK government action on smoking and health: a summary

1965	television advertising of cigarettes banned
1971	first voluntary agreement with tobacco companies not to sponsor sports events aimed at under-18s
1971	requirement for cigarette packets and all advertising to carry health warnings
1977	government circular advising health authorities on tobacco control
1985	voluntary agreement on stopping advertising in teenage magazines
1986	poster advertisements visible from schools banned
1991	50 per cent voluntary reduction in shop front advertising
1991	shop front advertising to carry health warnings
1992	Health of the Nation sets target for one-third reduction in adult smoking by the year 2000
1992	European directive that all tobacco products must be labelled 'tobacco seriously damages your health'
1993	all NHS premises to introduce no-smoking policies
1993	revised GP contract targets health checks and support for those wishing to quit smoking
1996	voluntary ban on shop front advertising of tobacco products and requirement to display 'no sales to under 16s' in retail premises

The policy-making community at work

Smoking offers a good example of the complexity of the policy-making community. Politicians, health professionals, powerful producer groups (such as the British Medical Association) and 'insider' pressure groups with strong lobbying power (such as the tobacco companies) are all represented. Pressure and consumer-based groups, for example FOREST (Freedom Organisation for the Right to Enjoy Smoking Tobacco) and ASH (Action on Smoking and Health) are also influential and represent conflicting ideological and scientific interests. Perhaps most significant of all, smokers in the UK contribute many millions of pounds each year in tobacco taxes making it a major contributor to government revenue for any government and financially very damaging to tamper with. It also considerably outweighs the cost of treatment for those suffering from its effects, which is estimated at £893 million a year (TAC, 1992; HEA, 1993b).

The policy battle fought out in the 1980s and 1990s, as the evidence about smoking-linked diseases accumulated, demonstrates both the potential and the limitations of public policy action. In the first place, the role of ministers in setting agendas could be of central but not decisive importance. For example, between 1979 and 1981 there was ministerial interest in the Department of Health and Social Security in further restrictions on advertising and a willingness to use legislation to enforce this. However, evidence from the polling of Conservative back-benchers suggested that about a hundred would support a resolution against further limitation of tobacco advertising (Kinman and Vinten, 1996). A voluntary agreement with the industry on advertising was renegotiated in 1980 but ministerial attempts to introduce advertising restrictions in legislation failed when the Medicines Bill was pruned in 1983. After a cabinet reshuffle in 1981 pro-regulation ministers were moved elsewhere. For the rest of the 1980s no Secretary of State or Minister of Health was prepared to countenance legislation. Health minister Kenneth Clarke, for example, attacked what he claimed was 'the serious danger of grave damage being done to sport in this country purely in the interests of anti-smoking' (Hansard 1986: para. 860). Even in the 1990s, after the introduction of national targets for smoking reduction, ministers could not be persuaded that an outright ban on advertising or sports sponsorship was needed.

The power of back-bench MPs, even a small group, could be crucial in supporting the interests of the tobacco lobby. Between 1965 and 1981 private members' legislation against smoking had been attempted sixteen times and each one had been 'talked out', mainly by Conservative members of parliament. For example, a private member's bill was defeated in June 1981 when British Associated Tobacco's parliamentary consultant in the Commons, together with another MP, tabled 50 amendments on the previous bill to be presented, thus preventing the anti-smoking bill from gaining a first reading. Between 1990 and 1996 private members' bills have been no more successful, although it has been government opposition to legislation rather than 'talking out' tactics that has generally defeated them. In 1994, for example, a back-bench bill to make tobacco advertising a criminal offence was overwhelmingly supported on its first reading and opposed and defeated by the government on its second reading. Nearly a third of the House of Commons (227 MPs), voted to complete a full debate on the bill suggesting that support for legislation was growing (Kinman and Vinten, 1996).

Behind the overt political debate, and of key importance in gathering support and public campaigning, are influential lobbies for and against smoking. FOREST was formed in 1979 and immediately accepted funding from the large tobacco companies. It shifted from a freedom to smoke message to a more overtly anti-regulation and 'freedom lobby' campaigning theme. TAC (the Tobacco Advisory Council), the official organisation representing the tobacco companies, has argued strongly and successfully so far that a ban on advertising is not needed. In evidence to the House of Commons Select Committee on Health, TAC claimed that legislation was unnecessary since advertising did not cause people to take up smoking but only to change brands. Since UK consumption had fallen more sharply than in those countries which supported a ban, and since voluntary regulation had been in place since 1971, there was no need to take further action. An advertising ban, TAC argued, would simply damage health by preventing companies from advertising new 'safer' lower tar products. Another tactic has been to cast doubt on the evidence linking smoking and diseases. WCTR (the World Council for Tobacco Research) was still claiming in the mid-1990s that after extensive independent research, funded by WCTR, there was no conclusive scientific evidence to prove that cigarette smoking caused cancers or cardiovascular diseases (Sommers, 1993).

In contrast to this, the British Medical Association, ASH and other anti-smoking campaigners have claimed that the evidence linking smoking and a range of diseases is irrefutable and that advertising is crucial to the continued success of the tobacco industry. First, recruiting new young smokers is essential to replace older smokers who quit or die. Second, new low tar brands can actually increase profits because people smoke more of them. Third, voluntary regulation has been a failure because tobacco companies have evaded such agreements. In relation to advertising agreements for the teenage market in the 1980s, for example, while the level of advertising in teenage magazines fell the level of advertising in women's magazines, many of which were read by teenage girls, rose by 10 per cent between 1985 and 1988 (Amos *et al.*, 1991). Advertisers have sought to associate cigarettes with illicit pleasure, staying thin, initiation into adulthood, a lifestyle choice linked to alcohol and a successful social life.

The authoritative allocation of values

Earlier on we noted that policy decisions represent 'authoritative allocations of value'. For some critics the failure of governments to ban all advertising and deter smokers by increasing taxes on tobacco products demonstrates the power of the tobacco companies and smokers to influence government policy (Taylor, 1984; Jacobson, 1988; Raw 1990; Kinman and Vinten, 1996). In this interpretation government non-decisions – which as we noted earlier may be just as significant as decisions – were critically influenced by powerful lobbyists, assisted by insider politicians. On the other hand, liberals and libertarians have argued that in refusing to coerce people into giving up smoking through fiscal or other measures governments have reflected and respected dominant social values of individual free choice and autonomy. Smoking, they claim, should not be an area for public regulation but for private choice (FOREST, 1989).

A needs analysis

Using Bradshaw's typology on page 121 assess the conflicting definitions of 'needs' which this case study of smoking raises.

Part of this debate centres on definitions of need. Using Bradshaw's typology we might argue that calls for advertising bans and high tobacco taxes represent normative needs, as defined by researchers, health promoters and other professionals who offer conclusive evidence of the correlation between cigarette smoking and diseases such as lung cancer and stroke. A rival set of normative needs is represented by tobacco companies, some politicians and campaign groups such as FOREST who make powerful claims on moral (and practical and financial) grounds about people's rights to choose and government's lack of right to impose discriminatory legislation on private companies.

People's expressed needs, research has indicated, are not so clear cut. In a Health Education Authority survey 68 per cent of male and female smokers aged between 16 and 74 agreed that they would like to give up smoking, but 54 per cent of these men and 60 per cent of the women said that it would be fairly or very difficult to go without smoking for a day (HEA, 1996a). Another research report indicated that there was strong support for a ban on smoking in public buildings but not for banning smoking in places where people socialised, such as pubs and restaurants (HEA, 1995a).

In relation to felt needs there is considerable evidence to be picked up from surveys of people wanting to and trying to change. In the 1996 HEA survey, 43 per cent intended to give up within the next year but among these smokers 76 per cent of men and 77 per cent of women had already tried to quit on previous occasions, mainly on health grounds. Qualitative research with young mothers who smoked indicated that they were aware of the health dangers of smoking but saw it as a liberating and relaxing activity in an isolated and stressful situation where they had no time for themselves (Graham, 1993).

There are considerable tensions between these definitions of need. The Health of the Nation strategic target for smoking, set in 1992, was to reduce the number of cigarettes sold by 40 per cent by the year 2000 (DoH, 1992). Much of the work of health promoters on smoking issues will be focused on offering support and encouragement for people to quit, either through mass media messages or individual-based interventions. This will have the effect of working to support (or modify) people's felt and expressed needs so that increasing numbers of people give up or cut down their smoking. As the evidence of public distaste for smoking increases so it will be easier for proponents to persuade government that there is a moral consensus in favour of further restrictions on smoking. In a similar way, the tobacco companies will be trying to persuade the public through advertising that smoking is 'cool', 'sexy', 'grown up', 'safe' or 'risky, but worth it'. They will be trying to attract new, young smokers and persuade existing smokers to smoke more and try new brands (Chapman and Eggar, 1993).

A conflict or pluralist view?

Smoking policy also highlights the complexity of decision making and the unpredictability of outcomes. Debates about tobacco taxation have focused on how it might act as a deterrent to smokers, but supporters of a progressive tax rise have also been concerned that it will not affect all smokers equally. In addition, it is unlikely be price alone that will bring smoking rates down. One of the reasons for the rise in smoking among some groups of young women may be the 'hard selling' of the product to women by tobacco companies (Jacobson, 1988). Smoking has declined in higher social groups much faster than among unskilled and semi-skilled manual workers (social classes IIIa, IV and V) and among young women in these groups rates are slightly increasing in spite of rises in price (HEA, 1995b). Poorer smokers, who for social and environmental reasons might find it harder to quit, are therefore more likely to be penalised financially than better-off groups, without any benefit to their health. On the other hand, evidence from Australia suggests that a really sharp rise in taxation levels will result in much higher levels of smoking cessation among lower social class groups (HEA, 1996b).

7.6 Conclusion

Health promotion policy is not only about decision taking and policy enactment. It is also about making change and this involves policy implementation. Health promoters can play a significant part in the policy process through joining pressure groups and campaigns, through their membership of professional bodies which educate policy making, help to set agendas and lobby for change and through exercising their rights as citizens.

Health promoters, whether they are professional or lay, and whether they work in or outside the health sector, can have considerable influence on the later stages of the policy-making process: in particular implementation, evaluation and policy review. The enactment of policy does not mean that it is necessarily translated into action. Quite often this requires the commitment of people in the organisation to push the policy through and make it work. Looking for opportunities to endorse and support health promoting policies, and to modify policies which might damage health, can be part of any health promoter's role. Making healthy alliances and collaborating with other health promoters to achieve change can further extend success. Chapter 8 will look at the politics of health promotion in more depth, and at the opportunities for building a healthier public policy.

Chapter 8
The politics of health promotion

8.1 Introduction

In Chapter 6 we noted how building healthy public policy had become a central concern of health promotion at international level (WHO, 1986; 1988; 1992) and how it connected to a longer tradition in the UK of using public policy to protect and enhance health. This chapter explores initiatives within the UK health sector in the 1990s and assesses their impact on health promotion. It looks at some of the political struggles over healthy public policy, in particular those relating to the restructuring of health care and creation of national health strategies. It asks what opportunities for health promoters are offered by recent policy changes and what constraints are evident, and highlights the changing role of health promotion specialists and public health specialists within the health care market.

One major feature of the Health For All strategy (WHO, 1977; 1985) and subsequent international initiatives has been an emphasis on intersectoral collaboration. In the UK this has been characterised as 'healthy alliances' – a partnership of individuals and organisations working to promote health. The chapter assesses the impact of the healthy alliance approach within and outside the health sector. It notes current workplace health strategies developed both by the NHS itself and through health alliances with employer initiatives, asking what lessons health promoters can learn from these initiatives and how far tensions and contradictions between local projects and national strategies still exist. In doing so, it raises questions about future directions for health promotion in the UK.

8.2 The influence of the international agenda

There has been a considerable tradition of using legislation, regulation and fiscal measures to protect health, dating back to before the onset of industrialisation in Western Europe. As the health promotion movement gathered pace in the 1970s attention was again drawn to the scope for promoting health through public policy. In the European Health For All strategy 'legislative, administrative and economic mechanisms to provide broad intersectoral support and resources for the promotion of healthy lifestyles' are specifically targeted, along with 'multi-sectoral policies that effectively protect the environment from health hazards' and 'health policies and strategies in line with health for all principles' (WHO, 1985, targets 13,18, 33). In addition, member states were urged by 1990 to have 'developed health care systems that are based on primary health care', with resources distributed 'according to need' and a wide range of health-promotive, supportive and rehabilitative as well as curative services (targets 26–8). These targets all carried significant public policy implications.

The Health For All strategy drew on evidence of public health successes, both in the reduction of diseases such as smallpox (Strassburg, 1984) and in legislation for health protection and promotion. For example, in *A New Perspective on the Health of Canadians* (1974), Marc Lalonde, the Canadian Minister of Welfare, highlighted the public health implications of seat-belt use. The use of legislation to restrain drivers and passengers is now widespread. In the UK, seat-belt legislation for drivers and front seat passengers passed in 1981 resulted in reductions in fatal and serious accidents of about 30 per cent for passengers and 25 per cent for drivers over the next three years (Ashton *et al.*, 1985). There was some criticism of its consequences: namely that seat-belts encouraged drivers to behave more recklessly (Adams, 1981). However, the weight of evidence indicated the effectiveness of seat-belts in saving driver and passenger lives. Compliance levels are around 95 per cent and, following motorway accidents involving school minibuses and coaches, it is likely that the compulsory fitting and wearing of seat-belts in all motor vehicles except short-haul buses will soon become a statutory requirement. Seat-belt legislation stands as an example of a success story in prevention.

Suggest other 'success stories' where legislation has protected or promoted health.

Other examples of health promoting legislation at national level are the factory acts of the nineteenth century which limited the hours that children, women and men could work, the public health legislation which required towns to take steps to improve sanitary conditions and the clean air acts of the 1950s which reduced city 'smogs' (pollution-laden fogs) considerably. The Water (Fluoridation) Act of 1985 enabled health authorities to ask water companies to add fluoride to drinking water to cut dental decay.

In other cases legislation has been harder to enact. Where a strong link is established so that a health hazard is proved 'beyond reasonable doubt' there is a good case for state intervention (Weale, 1988). If a strong association exists, Weale argued, evaluative work should be done. But the type of response made is strongly linked to political and ideological factors and not just to the quality of research evidence. For example, tobacco demonstrably kills more people than all the 'soft' and 'hard' drugs that are illegal to trade in, purchase or consume, such as marijuana or heroin (RCP, 1983; Jacobson *et al.*, 1991). Yet it can still be bought freely over the counter, the government makes a huge amount of money out of the trade and manufacturers spend millions advertising the product, particularly to catch young smokers (Taylor, 1984). There is still reluctance to legislate or use pricing strategies to deter smokers, although some deterrent measures have been taken. These include controls on advertising which have gradually been tightened, government health warnings and recent budget tax increases above the level of inflation.

Policy change as a contested concept

The development of the World Health Organisation targets, important though they were, was only a first stage in the creation of legislative, administrative and economic mechanisms to enable people to live healthier lives and multi-sectoral policies to protect the environment. Even when member states had signed up to the strategy there still remained highly contentious issues about interpretation and implementation. For example, it has been argued that in some cases legislation or regulation can be less effective than using voluntary agreements. We noted this argument earlier in relation to smoking policy. In the United States, where seat-belt legislation was pushed through quickly in the 1970s, public resistance resulted in some states repealing such laws. This suggests that careful preparation of the climate for policy change is critical (Jacobson *et al.*, 1991).

One central debate within public health medicine about regulation and legislation for health is whether a population strategy or a high risk strategy is more appropriate, effective and ethical. The population strategy involves interventions at the level of the whole community as, for example, seat-belt legislation, pricing policies for tobacco or public health legislation. The key feature of the whole population approach is that measures apply across the population rather than to particular sections of it.

In contrast to this, the high risk strategy, as the phrase suggests, involves targeting sections of the community who have been identified as being at greatest risk of developing a disease or health problem. This might include identifying those with raised blood pressure who are then offered advice sessions, relaxation classes and medical treatment or offering support and advice for smokers. The high risk strategy focuses on targeted individuals or selected groups, whereas the whole population approach works at a general, non-selective level.

Assess what you see as the advantages and drawbacks of high risk and whole population strategies for health promotion.

The new public health movement and many specialist health promoters have been concerned that the high risk approach associated with traditional health education might turn into unethical 'victim blaming' and be used to distract attention from the social, economic and legislative influences on health and disease (Hart, 1986; Benzeval *et al.*, 1995). This argues for a whole population strategy in which fiscal or legislative measures are used to discourage harmful behaviours and support health by redistributing resources. On the other hand, some would see the whole population approach as unethical because people are targeted by health messages or have their freedom of action curtailed by legislation whether or not they choose it. In the high risk approach, by contrast, people can be selected on high risk grounds but left with a choice of whether or not to take up the offer of advice or treatment (Lewis *et al.*, 1986).

Both strategies have advantages and drawbacks and they are interdependent rather than mutually exclusive (Jacobson *et al.*, 1991). Researchers have pointed to a 'prevention paradox' in the whole population strategy; that is, the overall benefits for the population arising from this approach will be greater but the individual benefits may be very small indeed. In the high risk approach, however, the benefits are likely to be quite significant for the individual treated but non-existent for those not identified as being at high risk (Rose, 1981; 1985).

The debate about high risk and whole population is one important aspect of the growth of health promotion in the 1980s and 1990s. In the WHO Health For All strategies (WHO, 1977; 1985) there was implicitly a place for both approaches since calls for legislation and regulation (the whole population strategy) were set down beside specific disease reduction targets. Such targets could have been tackled either by targeting high risk individuals or by a mass media and regulatory approach which aimed to influence public attitudes and behaviour.

Implicit in the debate about high risk and whole population are even more contentious issues. How legitimate is it for health promoters to target individual lifestyle as opposed to modifying the environment within which individuals live their lives? Is there still a role for individual-focused health education in health promotion? In what circumstances should governments employ legislation and fiscal policies to promote health? What are the proper limits of health policy? Are poverty, unemployment and inadequate housing issues for the health sector or not? In the national UK health strategies that emerged in the early 1990s in response to Health For All, significantly different answers were given to these questions. These are examined below.

8.3 UK strategies for promoting health

There was considerable resistance to the development of a national health strategy in England but this was not experienced to a similar degree elsewhere in the UK, for example in Wales. In part this was because their populations were much smaller. Much prominence has been given to the English Health of the Nation strategy and, in spite of what the other UK countries might have wanted, it has tended to be seen as the UK policy. In fact, the other countries have guarded their right to set an independent policy fiercely. In Wales this produced a much earlier and in some ways pathbreaking and innovative approach to promoting health. In this section we'll consider Wales, Scotland and Northern Ireland first, before assessing strategic development in England.

Wales: the strategic intent and direction

In 1989 the Welsh Office produced an important paper: *The Strategic Intent and Direction for the NHS in Wales*. It had been produced by the Welsh Health Planning Forum – a sub-group of the Executive Committee of the Health Policy Board of the NHS. This paper had health promotion as a key aim and stated that:

> The NHS in Wales aims to add years to life and life to years... The NHS is at the forefront of the drive for better health in Wales and should be committed to the pursuit of excellence in all its activities... Working with others, the NHS should aim to take the people of Wales into the 21st Century with a level of health on course to compare with the best in Europe.
>
> (Welsh Office, 1989: 1)

The strategy was 'health gain focused', 'people centred' and 'resource effective'. It was designed to be challenging to the health service. The areas where significant gains in health could be made were seen as maternal and child health, mental handicap, emotional health and relationships, mental disease and illness, respiratory diseases, cardiovascular services, cancers, physical disability and discomfort and healthy environments. It also emphasised 'participation in planning', introduced the notion of community participation and encouraged all NHS staff to engage in health promotion.

Although this was clearly a strategy for the NHS, health promotion was a key feature. The notions of well-being, of people-centredness and participation were new and innovative concepts at the time in terms of UK health services, as were notions of emotional health and concern for healthy environments. The Welsh strategy drew strongly on the WHO Health For All approach and the health promotion conference resolutions of the later 1980s.

In 1994, the NHS in Wales published *Caring for the Future* (Welsh Office, 1994: 64). In some ways this narrowed the focus and concentrated more on health sector work. In the foreword, the paper was described as a quality initiative and was very care focused. Key priorities were mainly service focused and concerned with effectiveness, efficiency and communications and complaints, but it did include 'increasing well targeted health promotion and disease prevention measures'. Ten content areas were delineated as in the 1989 strategy, but some changes of focus were evident. Healthy living was introduced as a category: that is, helping people look after themselves. Emotional health and relationships were deleted and healthy environments were described as 'encompassing good health at home and at work' whereas the initial definition was broader in emphasis.

In addition, 'lifestyle' issues were highlighted for action – smoking, drug and alcohol misuse, obesity and inactivity. There were process priorities, e.g. 'the GP's role in health promotion is to advise patients to stop smoking and promote sensible eating, drinking and exercise', a Healthy Hospital award scheme and health promotion advice for schools. Most of the actions suggested were care and NHS focused and within a fairly traditional medical model approach. In short, the paper could be seen as a more narrowly focused account of priorities and actions, influenced perhaps by its English counterpart. The National Audit Office, however, commented in its review of the implementation of health promotion policies that targets helped to translate theoretical analysis into local policy and practice (National Audit Office, 1996).

Scotland

In Scotland the tradition of health education has always been strong and this has been a major focus in health promotion policy development. In March 1991 a national health education policy statement identified priority areas for improving health, set a number of national targets for health improvement and created a new Health Education Board for Scotland. To some extent the priority areas and targets were similar to those in England and included coronary heart disease, cancer, HIV/AIDS and accidents. Targets were set for smoking reduction and alcohol misuse which reflected the higher levels of smoking and alcohol consumption in Scotland. In addition, dental and oral health were included and this was a response to the very high rate of tooth loss and decay, even in young children.

In 1992 the Scottish Office produced *Scotland's Health: A Challenge to Us All* which had disease reduction as its main focus. Coronary heart disease continued to be a major concern, since mortality rates in Scotland were among the highest in Europe. Diet and oral health initiatives were also developed and additional funding was provided to combat rising smoking levels among young people, particularly young women. The concern about smoking rates, in particular, resulted in a new intiative to create a smoke-free health service and the wider adoption of no-smoking policies.

Behaviour change, as in the strategy for England, was seen as the ultimate route to health improvement.

> Targets and initiatives are important but ultimately the improvements we all seek will only be brought about by the determination of each one of us to give effect to necessary changes in our lifestyles and habits. The forms of personal behaviour which most contribute to ill-health are

smoking, poor diet, excessive use of alcohol, and lack of physical exercise.

(Scottish Office, 1992: 12)

There was a tentative acknowledgement that 'health varies according to socio-economic standing and wealth' although the strategy did not pronounce upon this except to say that this relationship is 'complex' and 'there is no general agreement on what are the most important factors'. What was drawn out of this debate was a health education message of behavioural change for those in manual occupations who smoked more and had a less healthy diet.

At the same time, there was an acknowledgement of the importance of government initiatives to encourage structural changes, for example in the organisation of food processing and distribution industries. 'No substantial change in consumption patterns can occur without matching changes by these bodies' (Scottish Office, 1992: 14). There was also awareness of environmental influences on health. The part that could be played by healthy alliances in improving health was also given more prominence, with schools and workplaces singled out as the settings 'which offer the greatest potential impact' on health. The collaborative work of the WHO Healthy Cities project in Glasgow and Urban Partnership initiatives in improving health were acknowledged. The leadership role of the health service, however, was given far more prominence than the roles of other statutory and voluntary sector organisations.

In many ways the development of health strategy in Scotland follows the pattern of England and reflects the political priorities of the early 1990s. Personal behaviour gets far more discussion than any other factor. Poverty and unemployment levels are not mentioned. The 1993 strategy has a much stronger focus on diseases and disease targets than does the earlier Welsh Strategic Intent and Direction. It includes some discussion of the settings approach, healthy alliances and environmental measures but overall the plans for policy change are tentative.

Northern Ireland

A Strategy for Health in Northern Ireland was produced in 1995 and builds on three earlier ones. In some ways the Northern Ireland strategy has had a different trajectory, beginning as a narrower strategy but becoming by the mid-1990s broader in intent. Wales, by contrast, was a pioneer in the late 1980s but, perhaps largely because of the political shifts in the Welsh Office in the early 1990s, became more cautious and focused. Contrasting the two demonstrates the difference that political leadership can have on health decision making. It also highlights the significance of health service organisation. In Northern Ireland boards are responsible for purchasing (and, until 1995, providing) health and social services, and have therefore been able to make links between health and social care needs more easily.

The 1995 strategy discussed the need to pursue 'health and social gain'. It sees priorities, objectives and targets for eight years hence to 'promote the physical and mental health and social well-being of the population'. 'The strategy emphasised those working within the health and personal social services will be champions for health and social gain' (DHSS, NI, 1994). It highlighted the importance of health promotion within health and social services and emphasised the 'central position of health promotion'. Health for All is not encompassed as a theme within the strategy but a number of elements are. For example, there was reference to inequity and an emphasis on the link between health and poverty.

It had four key themes: promoting health and social welfare, targeting health and social need, improving care in the community and improving acute care. The underlying principles were about encouraging public policy to support health and social welfare, enhancing the role of PHC, placing increased emphasis on prevention and measuring outcomes. There were many key areas for action, such as accidents, cancers and CHD, but there were also ones for air quality and physical activity. In addition, there was an emphasis on involving people, healthy alliances, assessing needs, targeting resources and services, research and development and tackling inequalities. It was the only national strategy to advocate community development.

The Northern Ireland strategy was the most comprehensive of the UK strategies, perhaps because it followed rather than led the field, and although it did not address Health For All directly, it contained a number of its elements. In 1996, when the next five year strategy *Health and Wellbeing: Into the Next Millenium* was produced (DHSS, NI, 1996), the language of Health For All and healthy public policy became more noticeable. The importance of 'social well-being', 'informed choice' and 'social support' was highlighted, for example for families and children, people with disabilities and those in need of community care. The central themes did not change but there was a greater emphasis on 'encouraging public policy which supports health and well-being' and 'supporting community development'.

> The Department Boards, Trusts and the Health Promotion Agency must seek to influence the co-ordination of public policies at all levels which have a direct bearing on health and social well-being, so that supportive environments are created.
>
> (DHSS, NI, 1996:13)

The strategy also benefited from the shift in priorities in England, where in 1995 health inequalities had come back onto the health agenda as 'health variations' and the need for an effective approach to tackle these was at last accepted (DoH, 1995). Acknowledging that there was considerable evidence of the extent of inequalities, the Northern Ireland strategy highlighted the need for research into their causes and into finding effective ways to address them. Its language was very similar to that of the 1995 Department of Health report. The three ways identified to address health inequalities were 'intersectoral co-operation', the 'involvement of local people in the decision-making process' and 'equitable and cost-effective allocation of resources through soundly based estimates of need'.

England: the Health of the Nation

In England, public health policy making was heavily overlaid with political tensions. The 1992 Health of the Nation strategy reads like an attempt to steer a delicate path between political liberalism and WHO-style interventionism. The strategy was dismissed by some as an old-fashioned medical model approach (Tones, interview, 1996). Others, while recognising its limitations, applauded its appearance and saw it as an essential building block of a revived public health. Political liberals denounced it as further evidence of unneccessary government inter-ference in health matters – a green light for the 'health police' (Green, 1992). Many on the political left, in the new public health movement and the environmental movement, wanted it to be much bolder in its use of regulation, legislation and fiscal measures to control pollution, combat health inequalities and counter the impact of poverty on health. Whereas political liberals saw this as 'nannying', collectivists saw it as promoting greater equity.

When the Department of Health launched the Green Paper for consultation in 1991 it was a major landmark in public health history: the first time a national strategy for health in England had been attempted. It was also the first concerted response to the WHO Health For All strategy, even though the UK government had been a Health For All signatory since the mid-1980s. Initially it had been argued that Health For All should be a matter for local health authority action rather than national government intervention (Parish, 1995). The 1980s represented a period of struggle within the Cabinet and government between those who supported the idea of a national strategy and those, including the Prime Minister, who rejected it. Only after a government reshuffle in 1990 was such a strategy launched. The reluctance of the government in England to develop a national health strategy has been commented on elsewhere (Jacobson *et al.*, 1991; Scott-Samuel, 1991; Parish, 1995).

In general, the 1991 Green Paper was welcomed as an opportunity to put public heath and health promotion policy on the national agenda, alongside treatment and care services (Ewles, 1996). Around 2,000 individuals and organisations responded in this consultation stage. It was seen as a constructive response to the WHO's call for governments to develop 'healthy public policies' and 'supportive environments'. There were, however, criticisms of the scope and focus of the proposals (Public Health Alliance, 1991). In particular, doubts were raised about resourcing the strategy, about the commitment of government departments other than health, and the range of targets and target areas.

In 1992 the government issued *The Health of the Nation – A Strategy for Health in England*. Its key goal was to 'add years to life' through an increase in life expectancy and reduction in premature death, and to 'add life to years' by increasing years lived free from ill health, reducing or minimising the adverse effects of illness and disability, promoting healthy lifestyle, physical and social environments, and overall improving the quality of life (DoH, 1992).

Evaluating the strategy

How adequate a strategy was the 'Health of the Nation' for improving health in England? In terms of action, it was helpful in outlining the responsibilities of government for health promotion in five key areas (see Box 8.1). It acknowledged that government did have a role in legislation and regulation for health, in allocating resources and in facilitating and encouraging action for health at all levels of society. In addition, it accepted the central importance of providing reliable information on which individuals could base their decisions about health and its key responsibility to monitor and assess changes in health. Other positive elements were the establishment of a ministerial Cabinet committee to move the strategy forward and of interdepartmental government working groups for a number of issues, such as nutrition, health at work and physical activity. A range of strategic supporting papers was subsequently developed, although the working groups have in some cases been slow to develop action plans and a lack of co-operation and joint working exists among government departments. It also had a huge impact within the health sector, emphasising the importance of health promotion to health authorities and prompting them to require action.

Box 8.1: The Health of the Nation five key areas

Coronary heart disease and stroke

To reduce death rates for both CHD and stroke in people under 65 by at least 40 per cent by the year 2000 (Baseline, 1990).

To reduce the death rate for CHD in people aged 65–74 by at least 30 per cent by the year 2000 (Baseline, 1990).

To reduce the death rate for stroke in people aged 65–74 by at least 40 per cent by the year 2000 (Baseline, 1990).

Cancers

To reduce the death rate for breast cancer in the population invited for screening by at least 25 per cent by the year 2000 (Baseline, 1990).

To reduce the incidence of invasive cervical cancer by at least 20 per cent by the year 2000 (Baseline, 1986).

To reduce the death rate for lung cancer under the age of 75 by at least 30 per cent in men and by at least 15 per cent in women by 2010 (Baseline,1990).

To halt the year-on-year increase in the incidence of skin cancer by 2005.

Mental illness

To improve significantly the health and social functioning of mentally ill people.

To reduce the overall suicide rate by at least 15 per cent by the year 2000 (Baseline, 1990).

To reduce the suicide rate of severely mentally ill people by at least 33 per cent by the year 2000 (Baseline, 1990).

HIV/AIDS and sexual health

To reduce the icidence of gonorrhoea by at least 20 per cent by 1995 (Baseline, 1990), as an indicator of HIV/AIDS trends.

To reduce by at least 50 per cent the rate of conceptions amongst the under 16s by the year 2000 (Baseline, 1989).

Accidents

To reduce the death rate for accidents among children aged under 15 by at least 33 per cent by 2005 (Baseline, 1990).

To reduce the death rate for accidents among young people aged 15–24 by at least 25 per cent by 2005 (Baseline, 1990).

To reduce the death rate for accidents among people aged 65 and over by at least 33 per cent by 2005 (Baseline, 1990).

The 1990 baseline for all mortality targets represents an average of three years centred around 1990.

The strategy also incorporated some features of Health For All such as a concern for community participation. It mentioned, briefly, environmental measures to improve health such as monitoring air quality, and accepted government responsibity for ensuring a healthy environment. Intersectoral working through 'healthy alliances' was encouraged at all levels. A number of settings for action were identified, including schools, homes, workplaces, hospitals and cities (where Health For All-inspired Healthy Cities projects had already been underway since the later 1980s). Important work has developed in hospital settings, such as staff health projects, patient education and 'Greening the NHS' schemes, such as recycling.

There was little acknowledgement of poverty and inequalities, however, or of the economic basis of much ill health in the 1992 strategy (Benzeval *et al.*, 1995). The main issue highlighted in relation to inequality was the behaviour of people, especially those in manual groups. Sheffield health promotion specialists, who set up a process of local consultation on the strategy in four city wards with high deprivation rates, commented that 'people were amazed to find that poverty was omitted from the key areas as this was thought to be most essential, affecting all aspects of physical and mental health' (Healthy Sheffield, 1991). Some critics have argued that the settings focus has shifted attention from programmes focusing on population groups and may not always be the best use of scarce resources. A settings-based approach may not enable underlying influences on health, such as poverty, housing and unemployment, to be easily tackled (Thomas, 1993).

The main agents of action proposed in the strategy are people themselves and changes in health status are strongly linked to people changing their behaviour:

> The way in which people live and the lifestyles they adopt can have a profound effect on subsequent health. Health education initiatives should continue to ensure that individuals are able to experience informed choice when selecting the lifestyles they adopt.
>
> (DoH, 1992: 11)

This is more aligned to a medical model approach and contrasts strongly with the social and ecological model of Health For All (Katz and Peberdy, 1997).

There was some concern about the heavy emphasis on the National Health Service as the organisation 'uniquely placed' to 'deliver' the strategy (DoH, 1992). Critics questioned whether the NHS, with its focus on presented sickness, was well placed to deliver the strategy in many areas (Adams, 1996). Some targets and objectives were outside its sphere of influence: for example, the reduction of teenage pregnancy. This might be helped by ensuring good contraceptive services are available, but much also depends on schools-based work, family support, youth work and so on. It also depends on effective intersectoral collaboration. The potential for such work exists but, despite the 'healthy alliances' message, the strategic emphasis on health sector issues has resulted in more work with health sector colleagues than with other agencies.

Opinion was also divided on whether the key areas and targets represented a realistic or an over cautious approach to health policy. The document concentrated on five key areas: cancers, sexual health, accident prevention, mental illness and coronary heart disease and stroke (oral health was added in 1995). In some areas wider work has had to be narrowed to concentrate on these national strategic areas. For example, where specialist health promoters may have formerly developed broad women's health promotion programmes focusing on local needs, the focus narrowed down to breast and cervical cancer. The 1996 arrangements for health promotion in general practice, discussed in Chapter 1, responded to those criticisms to some extent.

The key areas represented a considerable narrowing from the Green Paper, which had discussed 16 possible areas for action, and a strong contrast with the Welsh programme which had 26 areas for concerted action (Welsh Office, 1989). There was concern about the gap between Health For All as expressed in the Healthy Cities projects and the Health of the Nation approach (Thomas, 1993). Key areas were linked to a number of important population groups, such as infants and young people, elderly people, women, black and minority ethnic people and people with disabilities. This suggested that the 'normal citizen' projected in the strategy was a white, middle-aged and middle-class male.

Within these areas many of the targets could be met relatively easily. For example, the long-term decline in adult smoking indicated that the targets would very probably be met without any new action (Jacobson *et al.*, 1991). In some cases where targets were more difficult to set or to meet, areas of importance were excluded: for example physical activity, food safety or older adults' (over 65s) health. On the other hand, the area of mental illness was included because of its importance to health even though baseline information against which to measure progress was not at first available.

The monitoring of targets indicates that significant progress has been made. The second progress report on Health of the Nation published in 1995 noted that the gonorrhoea target had been met, suicide rates had fallen and mortality from stroke, cervical cancer and accidents was reduced. Health Education Authority monitoring suggested that the proportion of smokers trying to quit increased by 1996, salt and whole milk consumption had fallen whereas low fat spread consumption was rising (HEA, 1996b). In the 1996 progress report three areas of concern were highlighted: smoking among school children, drinking by women and increasing levels of obesity among men and women. Recent HEA monitoring has confirmed these trends and highlighted others, including rising breast cancer deaths in younger women, a rising incidence of malignant melanoma and as yet tentative evidence that heavy drinking among women is on the increase (HEA, 1996b). The progress on targets is highlighted in Table 8.1.

Table 8.1   **Progress towards Health of the Nation targets**

Code	Target	Progress towards target?
A1	CHD under 65 years	✔
A2	CHD 65–74 years	✔
A3	Stroke under 65 years	✔
A4	Stroke 65–74 years	✔
B1	Breast cancer 50–69 years	✔
B4	Lung cancer, men under 75 years	✔
C2	Suicide	✔
D1	Gonorrhoea	✔
E1	Accidents under 15 years	✔
E2	Accidents 15–24 years	✔
E3	Accidents 65 years and over	✔
A5/B6	Cigarette smoking – males	?✔
A5/B6	Cigarette smoking – females	?✔
A8	Energy from saturated fat	?✔
A9	Energy from total fat	?✔
B8	Cigarette consumption	?✔
D3	Conceptions under 16 years	?✔
A7	Obesity	✘
A10	Drinking – females	✘
B9	Smoking 11–15 years	✘
A6	Blood pressure	?
B2	Cervical cancer	?
B3	Skin cancer	?
B7	Giving up smoking in preganancy	?
B5	Lung cancer in females under 75	★
A10	Drinking – males	★
C1	Mental illnes	–
C3	Mental illness – suicide	–
D2	Drug misuers sharing needles	–

Key

✔   Making substantial progress towards target
✘   Moving in opposite direction to target
?✔ Making some progress towards target
?   Not yet possible to assess progress in either direction
★   No significant change from baseline or no clear trend
–   No monitoring data consistent with baseline yet available nationally,
    so no assessment practicable.

(National Audit Office analysis, reproduced in *Health of the Nation, Progresss Report*,
1996)

Review the Health of the Nation strategy. Would it be more appropriate to characterise it as a 'high risk' or a 'population' approach?

There is evidence of both approaches in the Health of the Nation strategy. On the one hand, there is discussion of strategic interventions, inter-departmental committees, the role of government regulation and of healthy alliances. On the other hand, the areas and the targets are very much disease focused and there is considerable discussion of targeting individuals and changing individual behaviour. This comes across as the predominant feature of the 1992 strategy. Population approaches aimed to reduce health inequalities or combat poverty, which were called for by many health authorities and by organisations such as the Public Health Alliance, are conspicuous by their absence (PHA, 1994).

The re-emergence of inequalities on the health agenda

In spite of the invisibility of health inequalities in the 1992 strategy, their extent and significance continued to be highlighted by health researchers (Whitehead and Dahlgren, 1991; Wilkinson, 1993; Phillimore and Beattie, 1994; Benzeval *et al.*, 1995). Then in 1995 the Department of Health published *Variations in Health,* a report prepared by a sub-group of the Chief Medical Officer of Health's Working Group on Health of the Nation (DoH, 1995a). This gathered together and summarised current epidemiological evidence about health inequalities or 'variations' as they are termed in the report. Noting the marked differences in life expectancy, healthy life expectancy, and incidence of and survival from a range of diseases, the report concluded that:

> While socio-economic, gender, regional and ethnic differences are widespread, and are observable in all countries, the magnitude of these differences is not fixed; differences are recorded within and between countries and over different time periods. It is likely that cumulative differential exposure to health-damaging or health-promoting physical and social environments is the main explanation for observed variations in health and life expectancy, with health-related social mobility, health-damaging or health-promoting behaviours, use of health services, and genetic or biological factors also contributing.
>
> (DoH, 1995: 1)

The report went on to specify a number of areas in which the health service should take action. It responded to the evidence that the effectiveness of previous interventions to reduce variations was disappointing by arguing that better research and more evaluation of interventions were needed. It called on health authorities and GP purchasers to develop plans 'for identifying and tackling variations, and for evaluating interventions' and 'working in alliance with other relevant bodies'. It set out recommendations about the role of the Department of Health in monitoring the implementation of these policies, providing supportive research to inform interventions and working actively 'in alliance with other government departments and other bodies to encourage social policies which promote health' (DoH, 1995a: 2).

The report also acknowledged that particular health promotion projects and initiatives, important though they may be, needed to be set in a longer-term programme of development and supported strategically. Commenting that in relation to tackling variations there was interest but that 'much of the activity is on a small scale' and 'on the margins of health authority business', the report argued that it was not another new initiative that was needed 'but a much more explicit targeting of the issue within existing policies and activities' (DoH, 1995a: 76). This notion of, as it were, writing action on health inequalities into mainstream health sector work responded not only to the original criticisms of the 1992 strategy but acknowledged the importance of principles that had been marginalised for some considerable time: those of equity and social justice.

8.4 The impact of health restructuring

In 1990 the National Health Service and Community Care Act introduced dramatic changes into the health sector in the UK. In both health and community care the purchaser-provider split was created, with fund-holding general practitioners, health authorities and social services departments as 'purchasers' and hospital and community trusts, general practices and public and private sector agencies as 'providers'. In the health sector, the creation of the quasi market (Ranade, 1994) was seen as a way of controlling costs and professionals through managed competition. Health authorities (or in some cases general practice fund holders), with their purchasing role, would assess their local population's health needs and commission services from the public and private sector to meet those needs. Health trusts would become self-managing agencies which concentrated on providing services in the most efficient and cost-effective way. The result, it was claimed, would be less bureaucracy, greater efficiency, more choice for patients and better patient care (DoH, 1989).

The reforms developed within a context of consumerism and market competition. There was a heavy emphasis on health care as an 'industry' and on the patient as a health 'consumer'. As in other industries, competition, although very sluggish at first, did 'shake out' some trusts, and mergers became commonplace as did provision of some local community services by new, private or non-local providers. Health authorities also began to merge, creating significantly bigger purchasing units. In 1996, following the logic of the health market approach, regional health authorities disappeared and became much reduced regional offices of the NHS Executive. In addition, health authorities and family health services authorities, which had been establishing informal joint commissioning arrangements, were allowed to merge and form unified health authorities. Their core functions were to establish health care needs, establish and implement an appropriate health care strategy to meet national priorities and local needs through the commissioning process, purchase existing services, and monitor and evaluate service delivery and changing needs (Ham, 1996). At the same time the growth of GP fund holding meant that for an increasing proportion of the population many of their treatment needs would be purchased by individual general practices.

Purchasing and commissioning for health promotion

This restructuring has had a profound effect on specialist health promotion functions and, more generally, on contracting for health promotion work. Health promotion and public health became implicit in all of the functions of the new health authorities, with their responsibility for health needs assessment, purchasing and monitoring (see Table 8.2).

Table 8.2   **Health authority functions, post-1990**

Health needs assessment/epidemiology
Contracting/purchasing with, or on behalf of, GPs
Research
Strategic planning and development
Provider development
Networking/healthy alliances
Community participation
Community development
Quality monitoring
Public health advocacy/lobbying/campaigning
Information development and dissemination
Public relations
Organisation development
Education and training
Staff welfare and development

However, health promotion specialists, the 1,000 or so professionals with responsibility for specialist health promotion services in the health sector, faced an initial fragmentation of their work and a consequent lessening of their influence. The health promotion specialist is essentially a worker to stimulate, co-ordinate and develop strategically activities to promote health. The majority work in the NHS but others work in local government, the voluntary sector, prisons and a few in industry. Some of these specialists were moved into purchasing, others into provider services and yet others were split or retained a purchaser and provider role

(Linney, 1993). If they were moved into provider units their relationships with public health medicine were dissipated (Ewles, 1996).

In spite of these constraints, the restructuring has provided new opportunities for health promotion to be written into contracts. Ewles (1996) has suggested three ways in which this can usefully be done. Contracts can have a general requirement that NHS services should promote the health of staff and patients, for example through promoting healthy eating options. Second, requirements can be attached to specific contracts, for example requiring smoking cessation support in a maternity services contract. Third, health promotion specialists can be contracted to provide specialist services, such as training, or work in particular settings or programmes.

Putting clauses in contracts does not guarantee action where health promotion is part of a general contract and no specific finance is accorded to it. Agreement to action is by goodwill on the trust's behalf and issues of reward and few sanctions can be linked to delivery or non-delivery. A lack of adequate training may mean that the in-house health promotion delivered by the trust is of poorer quality. Work on effectiveness of services is meant to enable decisions to be made to stop purchasing ineffective services. However, the reality is that such information is a long way from being available to health authorities. The claims for health services are often in excess of the proven efficiency and contribution to improved health status (Adams, 1994a). Some health authorities are now spending less time on constructing contracts because of the time-scale and lack of effectiveness, and more time in working jointly with providers and communities to commission services and activities that are effective and delivered in a principled way. The contracting process is one part of a range of activities in which a health authority needs to be engaged and it has resulted in the request for much tighter definitions of success in health promotion, in particular quantitive measures of outcomes, targets and quality standards which are not always easy to provide (Tolley, 1994).

Are there contradictions between NHS restructuring objectives and health promotion goals? Notions of markets and competition sit uneasily with collaboration, principles of equity and empowerment. On the other hand, the emphasis on listening to local voices and on consumer rights could be seen as compatible with those goals. NHS restructuring has reinforced the targets approach, with assumptions that disease reduction can be easily measured and that specialists, fund holders and health authorities should concentrate their efforts on this. There may be an inbuilt resistance to longer-term and more indirect health promotion work which may raise critical consciousness and empower communities but does not offer a clear balance sheet of outcomes. In addition:

> Health promotion can be seen as unwelcome 'nannying', coming from do-gooding spoilsports with negative messages, wasting public money because people don't respond anyway, and curbing the freedom of the individual.
>
> (Ewles, 1996: 71)

NHS restructuring emphasised health promotion as an aim of health authorities. They have also focused on effectiveness and quality issues. Some of the advantages of the purchaser/provider split for health promotion are that health promotion can be specified in a contract for a provider to deliver. It can highlight the importance of health promotion for providers but also for purchasers, the health promotion potential of all contracts can be considered and it can focus the attention of traditional NHS providers, for example hospitals, on their health promotion role. This may result in 'health gain', although it can be difficult to quantify (Scott-Samuel, 1992).

Future directions for health promotion?

The future also remains uncertain. The drive towards total fund holding may mean that the purchasing role of health authorities dwindles away and general practitioners take the lead. This may radically alter the focus of health promotion activities in the future. A related issue concerns the emergence of a primary health care-led NHS, a welcome step but one which is defined very much in medical terms. Government policy in the 1980s and early 1990s emphasised health promotion in primary health care and this was endorsed by health promotion specialists:

> Disease prevention, health promotion and health education are as much public concerns as medical matters. Much of what is involved (a sensible diet, moderate alcohol, more exercise) takes place where people live and work or spend their leisure time. That is why the health professionals who work in the community – whether in the home, the surgery, pharmacy, consulting room or clinic – are among the 'key players' in the government's health strategy.
>
> (Adams, 1994b: 354)

In recent years government has produced a number of new health promotion contracts for general practice. However, many general practitioners have been dissatisfied and critics have argued that the contracts are not always addressing real health needs. Much bureaucracy is involved, such as counting of smokers advised and so on, and it is a system of very selective prevention activity (Le Touze, 1996; Russell, 1995).

There is a real interest in health promotion in general practice, particularly among practice nurses. Health visitors, whose remit is to search out health needs, have called for a wider health promotion role (Caraher and MacNab, 1996). If there was some flexibility to use funds creatively and encourage locality-focused commissioning by health authorities, public health and health promotion specialists and the broadly defined primary health care team working together, then the prospects for health promotion could be transformed (Armstrong and Adams, 1995). The encouragement of general practices to formulate their own plans for health promotion may be one way forward here.

At present the future for health promotion specialists also looks unclear. At national level the statutory health promotion agencies of England, Wales, Scotland and Northern Ireland have all undergone reviews and have re-emerged as part of the contract culture. The Health Education Authority for England, for example, now has to bid for contracts from the Department of Health. It was successful in gaining the contract for work with children and young people but the £3 million smoking and young people contract went to a commercial public relations firm. To encourage young people to write in with details of their smoking experience the firm offered tokens for chocolate and trainers.

A 1993 Society of Health Education/Promotion Specialists (SHEPS) survey indicated that a significant number of health promotion specialist departments felt that their general managers did not understand their role, that they were undervalued, and their resources and budgets were poor. Since the reforms health promotion was being viewed more narrowly: health promoters were being expected to focus on the health service, especially those in provider trusts, and not so much on alliance working. In 1994, SHEPS issued a paper laying out roles for health promotion specialists in purchasing and providing in the NHS (see Table 8.3). This demonstrated not only the broad and comprehensive nature of their role but also their vulnerability; most of the roles were shared with others.

Table 8.3 **SHEPS definition of specialist health promoters' roles**

Commissioning/purchasing	Providing
Health needs assessment	Providing advice and action re health promotion
Multi-agency strategy development	Advising commissioners
Setting local targets	Strategic health promotion at provider/locality level
Defining specifications for programmes and services	Co-ordinating health promotion programmes
Developing contracts, monitoring and evaluation	Supporting other providers
Developing local alliances and networking	Identifying operational needs
Provider development	Developing measures of effectiveness
Developing measures of effectiveness/health promotion, agreeing these and monitoring effectiveness and quality	Research
	Support policy development
	Networking and alliance work
Promoting public understanding of health issues	Developing materials
	Local media work
Supporting and developing community participation	Disseminating good practice
Commissioning health information and materials	

Using the list of specialist health promotion roles in Table 8.3, consider what specialist support and help would be valuable in generalist health promotion.

Whether you work in or outside the health sector, as a lay or professional health promoter, the wide-ranging nature of specialist health promotion means that it can be a vital resource. Expertise in developing local projects and alliances, in networking, working with mass media and researching the health needs of local populations, are all aspects of specialists' work. Workers often view the specialist service mainly as a resource for leaflets and information about national campaigns but there is an opportunity for specialists to become a much richer resource for wider health promoting work.

From the perspective of health promotion specialists their expertise is essential if health authorities are to fulfil their functions in health promotion and public health and be champions of the people's health. Those working from health service trusts cannot easily lead healthy alliance work at a strategic level, nor manage district-wide programmes negotiating policy and strategic change. It has been argued that health authorities really need to shift their focus in future much more towards strategy development for health improvement and protection – that is, health promotion – as GPs take on more of the contracting responsibilities (Hanson et al., 1991).

From the national and health market perspective, however, the majority of the NHS budget is already tied up on contracts for the acute and community care services and the possibility for shifting the budget towards health promoting activity is severely limited. In such circumstances health promotion may not be seen as a legitimate activity. In Scotland, the Shields Report (1996) recommended that health boards should divest themselves of direct responsibility for health promotion services and a management executive letter to the General Managers of Health Boards required them to implement this recommendation. On the other hand, it seems that some health authorities are recognising that health promotion really needs to be central to their activities and have brought back specialists centrally into purchasing. A network of health authorities who value health promotion as part of their function, and have a strong health promotion specialist presence, has begun to meet for mutual support, and to influence the health service and government (Armstrong and Adams, 1995).

8.5 The 'local' politics of health promotion

The endorsement of co-operation and collaboration sets challenges for health promoters working at a local level, as we noted in Part 1. It is important to be aware of the politics of local and organisational health initiatives because they can influence the success of health promotion. The national health strategies of the UK and the purchaser-provider health care market were characterised by a belief in the value of local action through joint planning and 'healthy alliances'. The Department of Health adopted a definition of a healthy alliance as:

> a partnership of individuals and organisations... to enable people to influence the factors that affect their health and well-being, physically, mentally, socially and environmentally.
>
> (OPM, 1993: 4)

As we noted earlier, the definition of healthy alliances has much in common with the WHO idea of intersectoral collaboration, which is seen as fundamental to achieving health for all (WHO, 1986). In the UK context, healthy alliances fitted in well with a notion of 'health pluralism': that is, of responsibility for health as shared between a variety of organisations and individuals rather than just with national government. It also conveyed the idea that the 'consumer' was important in health promotion and that health purchasers should pay attention to 'local voices'. Finally, it linked to the idea of the 'health setting' in which a range of measures and organisational alliances could be undertaken to improve health (Scriven and Orme, 1996). Unlike the focus on a particular disease or the focus on a programme aimed at a high-risk group, such as smokers, the settings approach was claimed as a means of developing a more holistic way of working. The whole range of health needs of an organisation, school, hospital, business or even a city could be assessed and appropriate strategies based on alliances between different groups could be developed (Tannahill, 1994; Scriven and Orme, 1996).

The adoption of healthy alliances, as was probably intended, initially caused some confusion among those who called for a larger role for state action on health. The approach effectively defused calls for government action by emphasising that local control, through community participation and collaboration, was all important rather than central direction (Mawhinney, speech, 1993). The future for health promotion lay in effective local consultation and purchasing which alone could respond to local needs.

In the longer term, however, the strategic thrust of healthy alliances has been questioned. There is an inherent difficulty in building healthy alliances when the incentive to do so is lacking. Moreover, in conditions of deprivation, where unemployment, poverty and a hostile environment may be combined, the ingredients for an effective healthy alliance may be missing. While many self-help projects have eased conditions and given people hope, the possibility of curing unemployment or poverty remains very small. In such a situation a healthy alliance may become untenable and even unethical, critics have argued, unless macro-economic policies are also deployed to help improve the local labour market and raise income levels (Benzeval *et al.*, 1995). It is assumed that organisations will want to engage in healthy alliances, and that having done so they will be willing to share power, redefine their priorities in favour of health and accommodate their ways of working to other organisations (Delaney, 1996). But even within the NHS, for example in primary health care, the process of building alliances has been extremely slow (Orme and Wright, 1996).

Similar criticisms have also been made of the settings approach, which is based on a competitive ethos and is often management-led (Jones, 1996). Healthy Settings Awards take no account of the fact that some types of organisations and some sectors will find it easier to become involved in health promotion than others. This raises questions of equity and participation. Within organisations the assumption that people have interests in common and that partnerships can be developed is also open to question. In some organisational settings, for example the workplace, alliance building depends initially on establishing partnerships between employers and employees. Yet their interests may be very different and the notion of healthier workplace policies may be interpreted in several ways. The following discussion of three workplace health initiatives highlights some of the issues.

Workplace health: three types of health initiatives

The workplace is a prime site for health promotion. Over 700 people die each year in workplace accidents, 170,000 sustain major injuries and an estimated 10,000 die of work-related health damage (Beishon and Veale, 1996). The Health and Safety Executive has a statutory remit to inspect all work premises and enforce health and safety legislation. However, since 1980 the number of inspectors has been reduced by one-third. At the same time, trade union membership has declined so that it only covers about 35 per cent of the workforce and the percentage of workers who are part-time or are employed by small non-unionised businesses has grown (TUC, 1994). In this situation effective health initiatives can have a great impact. But what characterises effective workplace health?

The three examples that follow try to answer this question. The first initiative pre-dates healthy alliances and is a trade union-financed health and safety advice centre which works with union officials, employers and shop floor workers to improve working conditions. Tommy Harte, an adviser at the Health and Safety Advice Centre (HSAC) in Birmingham, commented in an interview in 1991 that the real threats to health were work-based rather than lifestyle-based. Chemicals, noise, dust and dangerous practices were the killers, not individual habits and behaviour. His job was to monitor factory conditions and ensure that workers knew about potential hazards to health, and then to help them work together to negotiate for improvements. It was in employers' interests, he argued, to overlook health problems where possible. For example, noise-induced loss of hearing and repetitive strain injury (RSI) were often not identified by workers as job related or such a link was denied by employers.

> We've interviewed people that have had to give up their jobs because
> they can't actually do the job anymore, because their wrists or their
> elbows have been damaged through repetitive work. Women can't turn
> the tap on, can't open a bottle of pop for the kids, can't drive a car, can't
> carry the shopping any more because they've been made ill by work, not
> because they don't eat properly. It's work that makes people ill.
> (Tommy Harte, interviewed in 1991, reported in Open University, 1992: K258,
> Workbook 2: 97–8)

The HSAC approach, while not necessarily confrontational, is based on
the assumption that working conditions are potentially dangerous, that
most employers do not give health and safety great priority and that
policing by trade union safety representatives is vital to safeguard workers'
interests. There is considerable evidence to support this view of work-
based threats to health (Jacobsen *et al.*, 1991).

The second initiative is one awarded a Working For Health Award by
the Wellness Forum, a body established to share best practice between
member companies. Its own research suggests that 'wellness' programmes
for staff benefit organisations by reducing absenteeism, creating better
morale and improving staff retention. 'A healthy workforce means a
healthy business' and 'healthy people for healthy profits' are two
comments in its briefing material. It believes in local decision making
and local alliances between companies (Wellness Forum, n.d.).

Aberthaw power station in Barry, South Glamorgan employs 323 people
and won first prize in the small business category.

> Its main wellness initiative is its voluntary health screening programme,
> Get Healthy, Stay Healthy. These screenings not only measure the
> participant's health but include a discussion on the client's lifestyle and
> medical history. There is access to specialist psychiatric counselling in
> particular circumstances and courses on stress management are now
> available from the occupational health department.
> (Wellness Forum, n.d.)

Other award winners include Scottish Nuclear, East Suffolk Local Health
Services (NHS Trust) and Rover in Birmingham. All these companies had
screening programmes and links with sports facilities. Stress, smoking,
strain, heart-related problems and alcohol abuse are seen as major targets
for action by the Wellness Forum. Many healthy hospital initiatives have
similar priorities, with smoking, dietary change and stress reduction being
targeted (NHSE, 1994).

The final example is the Health Credit Scheme piloted within the
Northern General Hospital Trust in 1994. This was proposed by a health
promotion officer who was engaged in developing workplace health
demonstration projects for Healthy Sheffield 2000, and was based on a
similar scheme run in 1986 in north Manchester. The scheme set up a
Health Credit system in which full-time staff were allowed 20 credits paid
time off work to look after their own health (each credit represented half
an hour). Staff could spend the time as they chose and the evaluation
study indicated that 57 per cent of staff spent the time resting and 26 per

cent in 'doing nothing', 11 per cent attended a fitness centre and 23 per cent visited health practitioners (Staff questionnaire, May, 1995).

Sickness rates on the wards involved fell in comparison with those in the hospital generally. In occupational therapy they nearly halved. This represented a significant saving but it was offset by the need to provide extra cover while staff involved used their credits. The hospital board was sceptical of the benefits and concerned about the costs. Even though 89 per cent of the staff involved thought that the scheme should be extended to the whole hospital, the Board decided to not to extend it (Northern General Hospital NHS Trust, n.d.).

Assess the main differences in focus and aims between the three health initiatives reported above and suggest why it is important to understand such differences.

The initiatives highlight the contentious nature of workplace health. The HSAC initiative targeted workplace health and safety issues, whereas the Wellness Forum approach focused mainly on lifestyle issues in a work context – smoking, alcohol, fitness, stress   rather than the impact of work itself on health. The hospital trust initiative allowed employees to choose how to spend their credits and, in this sense, encouraged them to identify their own health needs. Each had a different view of health promotion. In HSAC the focus was on reducing health hazards and disease identification, whereas the Wellness Forum focused on behaviour change. The trust initiative aimed to promote health in a broad sense, but its main justification from the hospital's point of view was its success in reducing sickness (and therefore costs). The Wellness Forum also linked success to reduced absenteeism and higher productivity.

What significance do these examples have for would-be health promoters? They suggest that as a health promoter it is important to understand the local politics of organisations and of local communities. Co-operation and collaboration to improve health will not proceed if people do not have some shared understanding of health promotion goals. In the workplace examples there are different political agendas and, underlying these, conflicting views about health priorities. For example, HSAC focused mainly on the work environment whereas the Wellness Forum targeted the worker.

Research into health promotion in small workplaces in Canada has indicated the barriers to workplace health, particularly in small businesses. Although many businesses had an interest in promoting health they did not see it as a high priority and lacked the resources to pursue it. It indicated that the most common attitude of the small employer was to see health and safety issues as the responsibility of the employee (Eakin, 1992; Eakin and Weir, 1995). When they did become involved it was mainly in lifestyle-led initiatives that ignored the workplace as a determinant of health. On the other hand, occupational health programmes tended to ignore non-work factors, such as the impact of family stress. Eakin suggests that lifestyle and occupational approaches need to be brought together:

> Lifestyle health promotion programs do not appear to address the etiological role of work and the workplace; and there is equally little evidence of occupational health promotion addressing the intersection between non-work health behaviour and the health effects of work... The theory and practice of the new health promotion movement, with its focus on the social determinants of health, individual and community empowerment, collective change, and intersectoral collaboration, would, if it were to penetrate the workplace health arena, be a compelling force for integration
>
> (Eakin and Weir, 1995: 113)

Looking back at the three examples, these may be interpreted as differences of emphasis and not mutually exclusive positions. Some Wellness Forum initiatives explored work-related stress and occupational strain. HSAC taught workers about protecting their hearing by wearing safety equipment. This suggests that success in workplace health promotion might come from identifying the common ground that exists between groups and advancing by small steps to tackle more contentious issues.

8.6 Conclusion

The politics of health promotion are complex and contradictory. On the one hand the national health strategies have 'mainstreamed' health promotion as the major way forward to better health. Prevention, health protection and health enhancement, as well as disease reduction, have come to be seen as health sector priorities. Health inequalities have come back onto the health service agenda, with a call to address these as a main part of the work of purchasers and providers.

On the other hand, the fragmentation of the specialist health promotion service and the creation of an internal health market which encourages competition and the play of market forces suggest that health promotion is viewed by government in rather narrow and prescribed ways. The broader strategic thrust of Health For All and the Ottawa Charter is in danger of being marginalised. The types of health promotion being introduced into primary health care, for example, sit uneasily with government support for healthy alliances with their emphasis on collaboration, work across different agencies and community participation. There is a sense in which the rhetoric of health promotion has been accepted but the implications in terms of ways of working have not. In particular, there has been a too-ready assumption that agencies and organisations at all levels and in all sectors would work for health even if there was no incentive to do so. Evidence from workplace health initiatives indicates that in many cases groups have different and contradictory agendas to pursue and patient, tactical work is needed to move health up the list of priorities.

The messages for generalist health promoters, whether lay or professional, are that it has never been more important to be clear, well focused and tactical. 'Wooliness' in health promotion will not win it any friends. A comment made about specialist health promotion is relevant also to the broader community of health promoters within the health sector and beyond. 'Traditionally, the emphasis has been on describing activity, perhaps with an underlying assumption that people will unquestioningly accept that such activity is a good thing. Often they do not... This has pointed up a need to learn how to present health promotion in terms of outcomes rather than activities, with much clearer rationale' (Ewles, 1996: 71). The current political struggles over health promotion point to the continued importance of rigorous and self-critical planning, implementation and evaluation.

Chapter 9
The social policy contribution to health promotion

9.1 Introduction

This chapter demonstrates the contribution that a social policy analysis can make to health promotion. It examines how health promotion has been influenced by welfare theories and how many of the central ideas of health promotion – concern for equity, the idea of community, the promotion of social welfare and security – draw on broader social policy traditions. As we noted in Chapter 6, health promotion shares many of the objectives of social policy as it was conceputalised in the UK in the 1940s. But the fragile consensus on which post-war social policy was built did not survive sluggish economic growth and creeping inflation –'stagflation' as it was termed. The welfare state came under attack as a 'nanny state', which, rather than curing poverty, had created an underclass of welfare dependants (Murray, 1994).

This chapter begins by sketching the growth of welfare policy in the UK and the major debates about the nature and extent of the welfare state that have characterised recent decades. A case study of poverty is included both to highlight these debates and to provide a deeper understanding of social policy change. Health promoters, it is argued, need to understand such debates in welfare in order to set priorities in health promotion and influence policy change. The chapter concludes by examining the relationship between poverty and health, and considers the potential for health promoters to give anti-poverty work a higher priority.

9.2 The welfare state in the UK

Social policies have welfare objectives but they have also been argued for on political and economic grounds. Such policies have been seen as binding society together and creating a more efficient workforce. The roots of modern social policy can be traced to the policies carried through in Germany after unification in 1871 by Chancellor Bismarck. Bismarck's concern was to underpin social solidarity rather than to carry through social reforms for their own sake, and the welfare policies of Germany provided a model for other European countries in the early twentieth century. In the UK this found expression in the Liberal government reforms before the First World War. Old age pensions and insurance legislation were created to cover the most vulnerable groups of workers.

Although these were designed to meet bare subsistence needs rather than to eradicate poverty, they created foundations on which later welfare policies were built.

Only after 1945 were these modest initiatives translated into the 'welfare state' although mass unemployment and unrest in the 1920s and 1930s had encouraged the extension of the means-tested 'dole'. A general National Insurance Act was passed which aimed to provide a 'safety net' of standard individual contributions and benefits for sickness, old age and unemployment. In *Full Employment in a Free Society* (1942), Beveridge argued that the post-war objective should be a determination to 'free Britain from Idleness, Want, Disease, Ignorance and Squalor' because they were 'common enemies of us all, not... enemies with whom each individual may seek a separate peace, escaping himself to personal prosperity while leaving his fellow in their clutches'.

The contemporary welfare system in the UK is complex, showing all the signs of incremental change (Lindblom, 1965). Box 9.1 (overleaf) gives some major features of the benefits system.

In addition to the benefits system, most of the services we use today were established in the 1940s. These included a national health service, needs-related and free at the point of use, a reformed national education system, and a broader role for public sector council housing and social services. Legislation aimed to underpin voluntary services and the private sector which were seen as no longer able to provide adequate, equitable or efficient services.

The end of consensus

Many of the prerequisites called for in Health For All Europe 40 years later were explicit goals for social policy in the UK in the 1940s. These included the satisfaction of basic needs, such as adequate food and income, basic education, safe water and sanitation, decent housing, secure work and a satisfying role in society, peace, and freedom from the fear of war. In the first decades after the Second World War there was a considerable degree of political agreement that the cost of the welfare state was compensated for by increased efficiency, political stability and economic growth. But as 'stagflation' took root, debates about the cost and effectiveness of the welfare state developed. Criticisms were made by politicians on both the Right and the Left of its mounting bureaucracy, inefficiency and failure to solve the problem of poverty. By the 1970s there was a considerable political momentum from economic liberals – the so-called 'New Right'– to roll back the welfare state. From being an arena characterised by a high degree of consensus in policy and theory, social policy became a political and intellectual battlefield. The next section examines some major debates in social policy.

Box 9.1: Main benefits of the 1990s welfare state in the UK

National Insurance is still paid by almost every worker, but contributions are graduated according to earnings. National Health Service treatment does not depend upon insurance contributions, but state old age pensions and unemployment benefit depend on a sufficient contribution record and provide a standard benefit.

Child benefit was developed in the 1970s to replace child tax allowances and give all families with children, in particular the prime carer, usually the mother, a small income which was independent of the breadwinner wage, and thus combat child poverty.

Family Credit is a means-tested benefit which was developed in the 1970s for low-earning families with children. It was designed to combat family poverty by supplementing family income.

Income Support has replaced National Assistance and is still available as a range of means-tested benefits to non-earners, not only the long-term unemployed but also pensioners and others. It has expanded massively, far outstripping the residual role envisaged for it in 1945, partly because of the growth of long-term unemployment and the large number of poor elderly people.

Housing Benefit was developed as a separate means-tested system to provide support for council and private tenants, but it also indirectly supports many elderly people in private and local authority residential and nursing homes. The government also gives tax relief on private house mortgages, although this was cut back in the late 1980s.

There are several important additional allowances and pensions available for disabled and chronically sick people, designed to provide help for them and their carers. Examples are:

- Community Care allowance, paid to people with disabilities to enable them to live independently in the community.

- Independent Living Fund, which enables dependent people to adapt their homes and purchase special equipment.

Most carers are women and a 1986 European Court ruling enabled them to claim care allowances even if they are 'housewives'.

9.3 Social policy theories and health promotion

Social policy as a discipline offers theories and models of distinctive welfare approaches which can be valuable to those engaged in working for health. Health promotion, as we noted in Chapter 7, does not happen in a vacuum but within a dynamic and complex set of social structures and forces. Health promoters seeking to understand and influence policy change have looked to social policy to provide a critical analysis. The discussion that follows suggests that there are many parallels between the different strands in social policy and distinctive approaches to health promotion.

These interconnections have been highlighted by several health promotion theorists, who have argued that real progress cannot be made without a clear understanding of how health promotion is embedded in society and influenced by wider economic, social-cultural and political change (Beattie, 1991; Caplan, 1993; Collins, 1995). For example, critics of health promotion have drawn heavily upon the 'New Right' arguments of economic liberals, who argued the case for 'rolling back the welfare state' in the 1970s (Anderson, 1986). They see health promotion as a similar type of health nannying which infringes the freedom of the individual. Instead, economic liberals endorse the right of the health consumer to make a free choice (about lifestyle as well as health care).

In contrast to this, a more traditional Conservative position (the 'Old Right', as it were) has been generally to support the post-1945 welfare structures but to resist extending them and to deplore the notion of creating an 'equal society' through state welfare as naive and unrealisable. In health promotion this links to a health education approach which seeks to persuade people to change their behaviour and supports them in doing so. It does not see extensive state action to remove health inequalities or poverty as appropriate or realistic since there will always be differences between people.

A 'conflict' model of health promotion tends to align with a collective approach to welfare, emphasising the necessity for structural change and harnessing the power of the state to promote equality and social justice (Walker, 1984). The Health For All approach in health promotion is probably nearest to this, at least in the sense that this strategy envisages a considerable role for government in developing healthy public policies, creating supportive environments and reshaping health services to promote health more effectively.

The other strand in Health For All and in the health promotion conference statements of the 1980s and early 1990s is community empowerment and participation. The new social and political movements of the 1960s and 1970s, foremost among them the women's movement, the community health movement and the environmental movement, emphasised community self-help and direct action. They were more sceptical about the role of the state, although the mobilisation of popular pressure was designed to force environmental problems, equality of opportunity issues and other concerns onto the national political agenda. It is this strong strand of community action that is reflected in contemporary health promotion.

Some health promotion models have made explicit use of social policy analysis. Beattie (1991) embedded his four approaches to health promotion in a social and cultural analysis which drew on the work of George

(1981) and Lee and Raban (1983). Starting from an account of different perspectives on welfare developed through the years by social policy analysts, Lee and Raban argued that the key conflicts in social policy had been the debates about equality and the role of the state. In the equality debate, some theorists claimed that social welfare cannot and should not strive for equality but should focus its sights on minimum standards and ending gross inequality, whereas others saw equality as the key objective.

The second debate was about the role and power of the state. To some, the state is the guarantor of individual freedom through its power to create social conditions in which ordinary citizens can enjoy security and participate fully in society. Social planning is thus seen as the safeguarding feature incorporated into the welfare state system. For others, and in particular the 'New Right' which became politically more powerful in the late 1970s with the rise of Thatcherism, the state is essentially restricting the freedom of the individual. It is only the strict limitation and diminution of state intervention or the complete retreat of the state from welfare (in a more radical view) that can free people to become sovereign consumers.

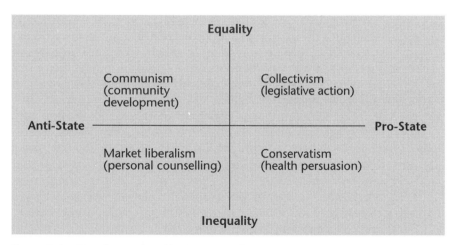

Figure 9.1 **Typology of welfare approaches** (adapted from Lee and Raban, 1983; Beattie; 1991)

By juxtaposing the axis of 'equality/inequality' and that of 'pro-state/anti-state' George created a four-fold typology which was plotted by Lee and Raban to identify distinctive approaches to social policy. Beattie (1991) adapted this to analyse different approaches to health promotion, where he saw the main tensions as being between 'authoritarian' and 'negotiated' approaches and an 'individual' or 'collective' focus. All the authors noted the complexity of the politics of welfare and how political parties may shift over time between quadrants. Figure 9.1 plots:

● 'Conservatism' – characterised by a strong reluctance to embrace state planning but an acceptance at certain times of the need to provide minimum social policies and security. An example would be the acceptance of the welfare state by the Conservatives after the Second World War. Beattie's health promotion approach, characterised by an authoritarian and individual focus, is 'health persuasion'.

- 'Collectivism' – characterised by a readiness to embrace state planning and to endorse a full welfare state system. An example would be the support for extending the welfare state shown by the more radical wing of Labour policy in the 1940s and after. The authoritarian and collective health promotion approach here is 'legislative action'.

- 'Market liberalism', 'New Right' – characterised by a distrust of the state, heavy emphasis on 'freedom of the individual' and a readiness to use market mechanisms to provide welfare through individual insurance and choice. The New Right policies of the 1980s are an example of this thinking at work. The individualist, negotiated health promotion approach is 'personal counselling' or 'libertarianism'.

- 'Communism' – characterised by a rejection of the state as oppressive but a high commitment to creating equality through community action and common ownership. This is more difficult to pin down, but community-based action would espouse many of these principles. The setting up of 'communes' and the character of the kibbutz in its early days are possible examples. Beattie's term for this in health promotion is 'community action', which is collective but negotiated.

What are the advantages and drawbacks of this type of diagrammatic representation of debates?

By no means every policy approach would fit neatly into one of these quadrants, as Lee and Raban themselves acknowledged. Some approaches would shift between a more and less ready adoption of state intervention. Looking back on the 1980s, for example, it is clear that although Thatcherism adopted 'market liberalism' in rhetoric it was much more difficult to sweep away the decades of 'collectivism'. In a similar way, the left of the Labour party was never able to get the full commitment of the party to state social planning. Within health promotion similar shifts and imprecisions are apparent. For example, the health persuaders (Old Right conservatism) endorsed some aspects of community action through their early 1990s health strategies. In a similar way collectivists have acknowledged the importance of involving local people in the policy process.

On the other hand, there are sometimes sharp divisions between different approaches and the prospects for progress in health promotion practice are poor if these are not acknowledged and acted upon. One of the criticisms made of the Ottawa Charter has been that it is fundamentally conservative as a health strategy because it attempts to accommodate structural change, community action, health education and self-help without fully acknowledging the tensions between these approaches (Caplan, 1993). In the 1990s the tensions between the Health For All emphasis on equity, empowerment and social justice and the disease reduction focus of the UK national health strategies was very evident, though each group also made increasing acknowledgement of the relevance of the other's position.

9.4 Social policies for health

Social welfare approaches have also influenced health promoters in their everyday work by offering accounts and interpretations of key issues and drawing attention to the significance of policy shifts. For example, the importance of housing to health was carefully documented in the 1990s (Ineichen, 1993: Burridge and Ormandy, 1993; Arblaster and Hawtin, 1993). The link between health and housing was first made explicit in the nineteenth century when local authorities took action to clear slums and then to build municipal housing for the working classes. In the 1940s the expansion of the public and private house-building programme was a main priority. But by the end of the 1970s, with general housing and living standards much improved, and economic liberals dominating the political scene, it was argued that housing was no longer a social issue. In the early 1980s the government required local authorities to increase rents substantially and to sell off much of public sector housing (Malpass, 1985).

However, the evidence that housing poverty still exists and that bad housing affects health is now strong. Homelessness among single people and families has grown since the end of the 1970s and housing quality and quantity has continued to be a problem (Whitehead and Kleinman, 1992; Best, 1995). The impact of damp and cold homes on health has been demonstrated by several studies (Strachan, 1989; Platt *et al.*, 1989). In particular, children were recorded as having much higher levels of wheezing and chesty coughs than those living in warm and dry homes. Overcrowding has been linked to higher levels of stress (Hunt, 1990) and homelessness to a greater incidence of chronic chest complaints and higher accident rates (Bines, 1994).

Such research has helped to place housing on the health promotion agenda and the UK national strategies for health acknowledged the importance of adequate housing in improving health. For example, the Northern Ireland strategy for 1997–2002 commented that 'although major improvements have been made in tackling unfit and substandard housing... problems remain in terms of high levels of unfitness in certain localities and in ensuring that the needs of special groups and those in acute need are met' (DHSS, NI, 1996).

The scope for policy change to improve health, it has been argued, is much greater than this (Best, 1995). A substantial shift in housing subsidies from owner occupiers in general to poor homeowners (for example older people), together with reinvestment in public sector housing, is necessary. In addition, investment in community development, particularly in disadvantaged neighbourhoods and isolated estates, can help to combat insecurity and deteriorating quality of life.

> Tackling inequalities in housing also addresses health inequalities. National investment in new and improved housing, and in improving disadvantaged neighbourhoods, also has important impacts on the wider issues of health and well-being. Thus, heavy expenditure on reducing cold and damp conditions on a council estate will not only reduce illness among the residents but can also be the catalyst for community development – the involvement of residents in the whole process – as well as bringing the opportunity for jobs and skill-building to the estate, with spin-offs in reduced crime and stress associated with poverty.
>
> (Best, 1995: 68)

The significance of this comment for health promoters is that it links together policy change and community action, suggesting that both are important. Action to influence policy change might be taken, as we noted in Chapter 7, through a professional association, pressure group or campaign, but intervening in the downward spiral of illness and decay might very well be achievable within the remit of everyday practice.

Outreach work by a psychiatric hospital in South Wales, for example, focused on an isolated council estate where unemployment and poverty were high and the housing quality was poor. Health professionals worked through the local school to provide a 'winter survival kit' of cash, food and clothing to vulnerable older people and establish a befriending scheme in which the children were involved (interview, Tregoran Hospital, 1996).

A broader social policy analysis of other issues, such as unemployment and poverty, can also contribute to a more holistic approach to health promotion. It can direct attention to the political and socio-economic roots of health problems (Jones, 1994). An acknowledgement of the external influences on an identified 'problem' can alter the priorities of health promotion work. For example, if a particular family is identified only in terms of normatively defined problems – 'poor dietary habits' or 'poor parenting' – the interventions will probably focus on modifying the behaviour of the family through giving health advice and support for change. If the external influences on family life, such as poverty, local unemployment levels or lack of access to good shops, are also brought into the picture the interpretation of the 'problem' and the type of intervention (and evaluation) can be extended. The health promotion action will not just include health advice and family support but perhaps planning a local 'take-up' campaign on benefit entitlement or working with local people to set up a food co-operative. So direct work to support the family becomes linked to work outside the family to influence policy change.

9.5 A case study of poverty

Poverty is a 'relative' concept, measured in terms of people's ability to sustain a basic lifestyle in accordance with the norms and standards of their own society. Although world indicators of poverty exist, most debates are about the relative positions of different groups within a particular society or across a range of countries with similar economic and social characteristics. The most brutal way of thinking about poverty is in terms of life and death, of not having enough nourishment, warmth or shelter to survive. In the rich countries of the world very few people are in this state of absolute poverty whereas in the poorest countries many people live under its threat.

Defining and measuring poverty

The most influential modern definition of poverty has been 'subsistence', which is defined as the level at which an individual or household has just enough income or resources to meet a minimum number of basic needs (for food, clothing and shelter).

The scientific surveys of poverty carried out at the end of the nineteenth century in Britain defined poverty in terms of subsistence (Booth, 1891; Rowntree, 1901). These have had a considerable impact on policy makers because they established the concept of a poverty threshold and of a basket of goods and services necessary to maintain health at a minimum level. It began the involvement of experts, researchers, and the general public to some degree, in the business of defining and measuring poverty: to determine what an adequate dietary intake was, what minimum necessities were and when income was deemed to be too low.

The unofficial subsistence 'poverty line' in the UK today is the income support level, but there are clearly problems with measuring the extent of poverty by using a scale benefit which is designed to 'solve' poverty through provision of an adequate income for all those that need it. As benefit levels rise, so inevitably do the numbers in and at the margins of poverty. Measuring poverty by numbers of claimants doesn't reveal much about levels of household income or real standards of living.

Townsend (1979) challenged the subsistence approach and put forward the concept of relative poverty as 'relative deprivation' within a society. He sought to establish as far as possible an objective measure of poverty, a threshold below which families or groups in the population were clearly excluded, materially and socially, from the society in which they lived.

> Poverty can be defined objectively and applied consistently only in terms of the concept of relative deprivation ... Individuals, families and groups in the population can be said to be in poverty when they lack the resources to obtain the types of diets, participate in the activities and have the living conditions and amenities which are customary, or are at

least widely encouraged and approved, in the societies to which they belong. Their resources are so seriously below those commanded by the average individual or family that they are, in effect, excluded from ordinary living patterns, customs and activities.

(Townsend, 1979: 31)

His research was conducted by means of a representative sample of 2,000 households and a complex questionnaire containing 167 questions which covered income (earnings, savings, and state and 'fringe' benefits), employment, health, and style of living. Levels of social participation were measured using 60 indicators of style of living, including diet, health, education, working conditions and so on. Among his indicators of deprivation for children were not having a birthday party and not having a friend to play or to tea in the last four weeks. Those for houshods included not having a refrigerator, not having a weekly Sunday joint and not having had an afternoon or evening out with friends in the last two weeks. As a result, the poverty or 'deprivation' threshold suggested by Townsend (1979) was 150 per cent of the income support level. Below this, he claimed, there was a sharp decrease in people's ability to participate. Using this definition, 22.9 per cent were judged to be in poverty.

Other researchers have favoured a more cautious 'social coping' model, in which people are deemed to be in poverty if they are unable to sustain a modest working-class style of living (Piachaud, 1981; George and Howards, 1991). They have seen this as a more realistic approach in terms of influencing public policy and of advancing conceptual understanding since the poor are, on the whole, part of the working class. This still raises questions about the threshold at which individuals and households are deemed not to have the necessary resources for social coping and become isolated and marginalised.

Another approach to defining poverty, which avoids fixing on a single, contentious poverty line, has been to assess the numbers of people below average income (*Social Trends*, 1994). This is currently measured through calculations about households and is therefore not sensitive to possible variations in living standards between members of the same household (Graham, 1984). However, it can show the relationship between the poorest groups and the rest of society. In 1991–2, for example, 5.2 million of a total of 21.6 million couples with children, 2.1 million of a total of 3.6 million lone parents with children and 3.2 million of a total of 9.7 million pensioners had less than 50 per cent of average income (Benzeval and Webb, 1995).

There have also been efforts to discover how far there is agreement on the basket of goods and services necessary to maintain health (Mack and Lansley, 1991). A 1992 study defined and priced a basket of goods and services selected to represent 'low cost' and 'modest-but-adequate' living standards (Bradshaw et. al., 1992). The low-cost budget included essential, basic food, basic clothing, public transport and hair cuts but excluded cigarettes, alcohol, cosmetics, a freezer and an annual holiday. Even so, 50 per cent of lone mothers and single pensioners had too little income to afford it. Around 70 per cent of people in these two groups failed to achieve the 'modest-but-adequate' standard, which would have enabled them to afford a five-year-old car and a one week annual holiday. In a large-scale representative survey of public attitudes to poverty in Britain in 1991 there was a high level of consensus about items regarded as necessities (Table 9.1).

Table 9.1 **Items regarded as necessities by at least two-thirds of British adults**

Self-contained, damp-free accommodation with an indoor toilet and bath

A weekly roast joint for the family and three daily meals for each child

Two pairs of all-weather shoes and a warm waterproof coat

Sufficient money for public transport

Adequate bedrooms and beds

Heating and carpeting

A refrigerator and washing machine

Enough money for special occasions like Christmas

Toys for the children

(Frayman, 1991)

What does Table 9.1 suggest about the general public's perception of poverty?

Respondents to this survey went considerably beyond a subsistence approach in their view of poverty. They certainly endorsed a notion of social coping and to some extent supported Townsend's idea of social participation. They considered a reasonably comfortable furnished home, with modern amenities, as necessities. Some of the items seen as necessities are similar to Townsend's indicators, for example the weekly joint and refrigerator. Inclusion of birthday and Christmas celebrations (in Townsend's case measured by children's birthdays and the giving and receiving of hospitality) suggests that not just coping but wider participation is accepted as necessary.

Who are the poor?

The groups in the population most likely to find themselves in poverty are not dissimilar to those identified by Rowntree in his 1901 study of poverty in York. They are older people, the low-paid, unemployed people, lone-parent families and people with disabilities. Large families are more at risk of poverty, but not by any means to the same extent as in 1901. Researchers have commented on the increasing visibility of women among those in poverty, and there is some evidence that the 'feminisation of poverty', while not new, has been increasing (Glendinning and Millar, 1987). Another significant change by the mid-twentieth century was the evidence of poverty among black and minority ethnic groups, much of it due to discrimination and racism in the job market; occupational class, average wages, and employment levels are all markedly lower for black workers (Cook and Watt, 1987).

There is some evidence that the risks of poverty do not vary greatly across the generations. Nevertheless there have been significant changes in the proportions in poverty in each of the groups mentioned above, due to changes in levels of benefit and changing economic circumstances. For example, unemployed people were a very small proportion of those in poverty until the return of high unemployment in the early 1980s. The low paid, on the other hand, have benefited from Family Income Support which was introduced in the 1970s.

Older people, particularly those living alone, are still at greatest risk of being in poverty. If poverty is defined as below 140 per cent of benefit level then well over half of all pensioners were in poverty in the late 1980s (George and Howards, 1991). As we noted earlier, if the measure used is households below average income then 30 per cent have less than half of UK average income (Benzeval *et al.*, 1995). While most pensioners have been helped out of official poverty by welfare benefits and occupational pensions, the very elderly who were in low paid jobs – and elderly women in particular, who live longer, have generally earned less and are least likely to have pension rights – are still highly vulnerable. Also at risk are the one million or so lone-parent families, 90 per cent of which are headed by women, and the long-term sick and disabled, especially elderly women with severe disabilities and unmarried and married disabled people with dependent children. Martin and White's study (1988) of the financial circumstances of disabled adults found that, whether measured in terms of income (earnings and benefits), consumer goods, diet or basic social needs, these two groups were especially vulnerable to poverty.

Debates about poverty

The debate about poverty in social policy is illuminating, partly because poverty has been a reliable barometer of shifts in thinking about welfare (Jones, 1994). In the late 1960s, when it was thought that the UK welfare state had abolished poverty, it was 're-discovered' by social policy researchers and increasingly strong claims were made about its impact on health status (Townsend, 1979). Pressure groups such as the Child Poverty Action Group provided documentary evidence of family poverty which helped to persuade the government to bring in child benefit and family income support (see Box 9.1). In the 1980s, with economic liberalism in the ascendency, it was insisted that 'real' poverty had disappeared and the debate about poverty had re-emerged in the 1960s for political reasons rather than because poverty was a problem:

By the 1960s the gulf in living standards between countries under
socialist governments and those with capitalist systems had become
glaringly apparent to everyone... free enterprise capitalism, so vilified by
socialists for creating poverty, was in fact having substantial success in
relieving it. Socialism... was in danger of being dismissed as serious
political ideology. At this point academics came to the rescue.

(Moore, 1989: 7)

The New Right argued that 'monetarism', by stimulating risk-taking and
wealth creation through market deregulation and a stable money supply,
had delivered growth and signalled the 'death' of Keynesianism.
Monetarist policy was also seen as the best anti-poverty strategy. Increased
wealth and rising incomes, aided by better-targeted benefits which
reinforced the incentive to work, would cause a 'trickle-down effect', so
that the poor also shared in the growing prosperity (Jones, 1994).

Claims about the trickle-down effect were given substance by evidence
from the 1989 statistical series we noted earlier, 'Households Below
Average Income', which used the household as the unit of measurement of
income, rather than the individual or family units receiving benefit. The
new series replaced the 'Low Income Family' statistical series, which since
the mid-1970s had assessed the numbers of individuals and family units
living at or just above income support level. It initially seemed to show
that between 1981 and 1985 the real income of the bottom 10 per cent of
the population (that is, of over 5 million people) had risen by 8.4 per cent,
nearly twice as much as for the population as a whole (Timmins, 1990).

For economic liberals the figures proved the efficacy of trickle-down.
Compared to overall average household income, which 'rose between
1970 and 1985 by more than a quarter over and above price increases...
families on income support did even better than the population as a whole
with an increase of 28 per cent. Incomes of pensioners increased still more
by 31 per cent' (Moore, 1989). This indicated that not only were the poor
not getting poorer, Moore argued: 'they are substantially better off than
they have ever been before'. What was called 'poverty' was in reality
merely unavoidable 'inequality'; for poverty itself and the poverty lobby it
was 'the end of the line'.

The new figures were greeted with considerable suspicion, not least by
the all-party social services committee of the House of Commons, which
commissioned its own, independent survey of poverty from the Institute
of Fiscal Studies using the format of the 'Low Income Family' statistical
series. On this basis the Institute found that the real income of the bottom
10 per cent was growing at a slower rate than that of the population as a
whole. Government statisticians had made errors in calculating the new
figures and between 1981 and 1985 real incomes for the population as a
whole had grown by only 5.4 per cent and the income of the bottom
decile by only 2.6 per cent – barely more than a quarter of the
government's proclaimed rise (Johnson and Webb, 1993). As the social
services committee commented, the revised figures 'change completely
the picture of what has been happening to the position of people living in

the poorest households'. The poorest tenth had not benefited from a trickle-down effect at all (Table 9.2).

Table 9.2   **Distribution of disposable household income in the UK (percentages)**

	Bottom fifth	Next fifth	Middle fifth	Next fifth	Top fifth	Total
Net income before housing costs						
1979	10	14	18	23	35	100
1981	10	14	18	23	36	100
1987	9	13	17	23	39	100
1988–89	8	12	17	23	41	100
1990–91	7	12	17	23	41	100
Net income after housing costs						
1979	10	14	18	23	35	100
1981	9	14	18	23	36	100
1987	8	12	17	23	40	100
1988–89	7	12	17	23	41	100
1990–91	6	12	17	23	43	100

Quintile groups of individuals

The unit of analysis is the individual and the income measure is net equivalent household income.

(*Social Trends*, 1994)

In the 1990s several influential reports attempted to put poverty back on the political agenda (Bradshaw *et al.*, 1992; Wilkinson, 1994; Rowntree Foundation, 1995). The 1995 Rowntree inquiry on 'Income and Wealth' concluded that 'the bottom 20–30 per cent in terms of their income are not better off than the equivalent people were 20 years ago' (Lipsey, 1995: 1). It called for a strategy for equality which included tax cuts for low earners, better child care provision, increases in social security benefits and greater investment in education, retraining and regional regeneration (Table 9.3). It rested its case on practical not moral grounds:

> Just as in the last century it was in the interests of all to introduce public health measures to combat the spread of infectious physical disease fostered by poverty, so in this century it is in the interests of all to remove the factors which are fostering the social diseases of drugs, crime, political extremism and social unrest.
>
> (Rowntree Foundation, 1995: 2)

The study was undertaken by a broad group drawn from business, journalism, trade unionism, the voluntary sector and social policy research, a factor which ensured that it was given considerable media attention and not immediately dismissed. However, its agenda was not accepted by the government which sought to discredit it through ridicule and allegations of political bias. The fierce exchanges in the House of Commons and the press in the days following its publication highlighted the intensely political nature of the poverty debate (Beresford and Green, 1996).

Table 9.3   **A strategy for equality**

---

1 More investment in education and training to improve employability.

2 More opportunities for the long-term jobless on community and environmental improvement projects.

3 Better child care provision, and other initiatives to make work opportunities.

4 Benefit changes to make it easier for those on benefits to take jobs.

5 Any real tax cuts to be targeted towards low earners.

6 Real increases in social security benefits.

7 More regional regeneration initiatives and action on problem council estates.

(Rowntree Report, 1995: 3)

A study of poverty, therefore, brings into sharp focus the debates that we noted in Section 9.4 about whether social policies can and should help to create equality and about the relative merits of state and market approaches to welfare. Such debates are not merely academic but are reflected in everyday policy decisions and outcomes. Poverty has moved up the agenda within health promotion, for example, partly because of the increasingly compelling evidence that social researchers have produced of the impact of poverty on health.

9.6 Poverty and the health promotion movement

Poverty has been an explicit concern for the health promotion movement, although it has been couched not in terms of abolishing poverty but of meeting basic needs. The Health For All prerequisites, for example, called for 'satisfaction of basic needs' among which are listed 'adequate food and income', 'decent housing', 'secure work' and 'a satisfying role in society' (WHO, 1977). Among the 38 targets for health in the European region were ones which called for all people to 'have the basic opportunity to develop and use their health potential to live socially and economically useful lives' and to 'have a better opportunity of living in houses... which provide a healthy and safe environment' (Targets 2, 24, WHO, 1985). The Adelaide Conference (WHO, 1988) was more explicit about the need for 'ensuring an equitable distribution of resources even in adverse economic circumstances' and several speeches mentioned poverty and disadvantage as major factors in limiting the success of other health measures, in particular attempts to change behaviour.

Look back at the definitions of poverty in Section 9.4. Which of these definitions of poverty is being used by the WHO and why?

The concerns expressed in the WHO prerequisites are very much about meeting basic needs and in this sense are most closely linked to a 'subsistence' or 'social coping' view of poverty. Since the WHO statements have to be acceptable to all signatory countries it is not surprising that the view of poverty as relative deprivation does not feature, although it is implicit. 'Adequate', 'decent' and even 'basic' are bound to relate to the society to which the terms are applied and will have very different meanings in rich and poor countries.

Poverty and health inequalities

In the UK health promoters have extended the social policy analysis by linking it more explicitly to health. A range of national and local reports have discussed poverty and health within a wider framework of concern for welfare needs. The most prominent and enduring has been The Black Report which commented in 1980 that:

> There are marked inequalities in health between the social classes in Britain.... Mortality tends to rise inversely with falling occupational rank or status, for both sexes and at all ages. At birth and in the first month of life twice as many babies of unskilled manual parents as of professional parents die, and in the next eleven months of life nearly three times as many boys and more than three times as many girls, respectively, die. In later years of childhood the ratio of deaths in the poorest class falls to between one and a half and two times that of the wealthiest class, but increases again in early adulthood before falling again in middle and old age.
>
> (Townsend *et al.*, 1988: 55–56)

The Black Report detailed the growing social class gradient in mortality and morbidity from all the major diseases. In particular, the presence of a universal health service had not ameliorated the health of the poorest groups. Between the 1950s and the 1970s the mortality rates for both men and women aged 35 and over in occupational classes I and II had steadily declined, whereas those in classes IV and V were the same or marginally worse. It called for increased spending outside the health service, based on a recognition that social and economic factors like income levels, work, environment, housing, transport, education and 'lifestyle' choices influenced health. It suggested that universalist benefits such as Child

Benefit were most effective means of fighting health inequalities. It argued that an intersectoral approach, and a greater concentration upon vital areas such as child health services were needed. A main feature of its recommendations was a series of measures to end child poverty (Townsend *et al.*, 1988).

But the recommendations were decisively rejected by economic liberals who saw the application of free market principles as the way to solve poverty. Through the 1980s, there were several local studies of health and socio-economic groupings and evidence from a number of longitudinal datasets (Marmot *et al.*, 1984; Goldblatt, 1990; Fox *et al.*, 1990). Two broadly-based research reports, for the Health Education Council (1987) and for the King's Fund, concluded that the link between income levels and health status remained strong (Whitehead, 1987; Smith and Jacobson, 1988). The issue hardly figured on the national political agenda despite these heavyweight and hard-hitting reports with their clear and well evidenced message about the impact of poverty:

> While we may still lack knowledge of the exact mechanisms through which [risk] factors operate, this does not put their contributory role in doubt... Income is clearly associated with health. The evidence is clear that the death rates of old people are affected by changes in the real value of state pensions, and also that as occupations move up or down the occupational earnings rankings they show a corresponding and opposite movement in the occupational mortality rate. The implication is that income – perhaps the major determinant of standard of living and of life-style – has a direct effect on health. It is also clear that health is more sensitive to small changes in income at lower than at higher levels.
>
> (Smith and Jacobson, 1988: 114)

In 1992, as we noted in Chapter 8, the English national health strategy did not mention poverty and this fuelled another round of debate about the link between poverty and poor health which drew not just on UK data but on the more comprehensive international evidence that existed, including that from the USA, Canada and the rest of Europe (Benzeval and Webb, 1995). In the UK survey evidence was assembled to demonstrate a clear and consistent association between income and health (Blaxter, 1990) and a statistically significant negative relationship between income and age/sex-standardised morbidity (O'Donnell and Propper, 1991).

Wilkinson (1993, 1995) highlighted the health effects of widening income differences within a society. Beyond a certain level, he concluded, it was not the absolute but the relative living standard that influenced health. 'The scale of relative deprivation (as measured by income differences between people in the same society) continues to be a powerful determinant of health' (1993: 54). His evidence compared a range of data in which the statistical associations were striking, although it is less clear that a causal relationship exists. For example, in England and Wales the proportion of children living in households below half of the national average income (the current European relative poverty measure) had grown from 10 per cent in 1979 to 31 per cent in 1990. Infant mortality in England and Wales was strikingly higher than in Sweden, where income differences were not great and only 2 per cent of children in one-parent families were in relative poverty (Figure 9.2). Having mapped income differences against national standards of health, Wilkinson argued that the best way of improving health in developed countries 'would almost certainly be by reducing income differences. It was much more important than, for instance, smoking or other behavioural risk factors' (1995: 3).

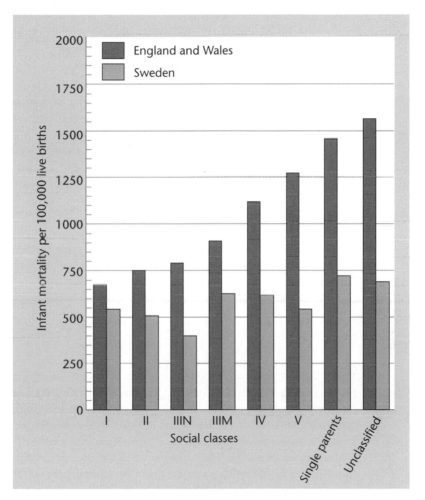

Figure 9.2   **Social class differences in mortality in Sweden compared to England and Wales**   (Wilkinson, 1995)

As we noted in Chapter 8, the Health of the Nation Sub-group on Health Variations set up by the Chief Medical Officer of Health in England brought issues about low income back onto the health agenda (DoH, 1995a). The *Variations in Health* Report commented on the marked differences by occupational class, as well as sex, ethnicity and region, in levels of mortality and morbidity. Comparing social class I (professionals such as doctors, lawyers and clergymen) with class IV (semi-skilled workers such as traffic wardens and telephonists) and V (unskilled manual workers such as labourers and cleaners), the report noted that:

> life expectancy at birth is currently around 7 years higher in the Registrar General's social class I than social class V;
>
> children in social class V are four times more likely to suffer accidental death than their peers in social class I;
>
> of the 66 major causes of death in men, 62 were more common among those in social classes IV and V combined than in other social classes;
>
> of the 70 major causes of death in women, 64 were more common in women married to men in social classes IV and V.
>
> (DoH, 1995a: 9)

The only contrary statistic was for breast cancer, where women in social class I had a higher incidence than those in class V. Although poverty was not specifically mentioned, material aspects of living conditions 'such as household income and wealth' were seen as a major factor in explaining these differences.

Health risks of poverty

People on low or very low incomes suffer more illness and die earlier than those in higher income groups, as successive health reports have demonstrated.

What do you think are likely to be the main health risks for the groups that are most prone to poverty?

Think back to the groups we noted were most likely to be poor. Lone mothers with children are more likely to live in sub-standard housing in a poor environment (Graham, 1993). People who are unemployed have a much higher rate of suicide (Platt, 1984). Older people are more at risk of hypothermia and malnutrition. People in social classes IV and V have a higher incidence of a whole range of diseases, including coronary heart disease, stroke, most cancers, respiratory and infectious diseases.

Blackburn (1991) suggested that in addition to the physiological effects of poverty, such as exposure to harmful environments, there are also psychological effects, such as added stresses and behavioural effects. Health-damaging behaviours like smoking may provide a way of coping with a stressful enviornment. For all groups in poverty inadequate nutrition is likely to be a feature of their style of life, although only about 2 per cent of older people suffer serious subnutrition (MacLennan, 1986). Poverty, as well as 'lifestyle' and cultural influences, plays an important part in determining eating patterns and preventing change.

Bradshaw *et al.* (1992) calculated that even if a family of four bought only essential food and other provisions it would cost 40 per cent more than was available in the £105.00 per week benefit scale. A 'healthy' diet was costed at 17 per cent more than an 'unhealthy' one (NCH, 1991).

There are about 500 deaths from hypothermia recorded each year, the vast majority of them of older people, and added to this is the much bigger problem of what is termed 'cold-associated disease'. From the figures of weekly death rates between 1974 and 1984 it has been estimated that there are about 40,000–50,000 cold-associated deaths in the UK every year (Smith and Jacobson, 1988). Older people are the most vulnerable, and in severe winters suffer up to 50 per cent excess mortality from respiratory disease and heart disease. Being in poverty or at the margins of poverty – with the fear of not being able to pay the heating bill and getting into debt – is the position in which many elderly people find themselves, and it has a direct impact on their health.

9.6 Poverty and health promotion practice

The survey of poverty connects directly to much of the work of health promotion and other workers in community, residential and hospital settings. Poverty not only increases the risks of sickness and disease but makes it more difficult for people to respond to health promotion advice (Blaxter, 1990). If this is accepted, combating poverty then comes into focus as a major element of health promotion work.

There are several implications for health promotion work in the analysis of poverty and health. The rising level of poverty, in particular the widening of differentials between rich and poor, is associated with increased morbidity and mortality. This will mean that health service costs rise more steeply as the service attempts to cope with the increased burden of poverty-related conditions which require medical treatment and nursing care. Health promoters are right to argue, therefore, that at least some of the money should be spent to lift individuals out of poverty rather than on treatment for them as they become sick. This 'prevention' argument is not new: as we noted earlier it was widely used in Victorian times to justify expenditure on public housing and sanitation; in the early twentieth century to justify old age pensions and maternity payments; and in the 1940s to justify the welfare state. It was restated in a different form in 1995 in the Rowntree Report on Income and Wealth, where the removal of poverty was seen as a practical policy step to avoid fostering 'the social diseases of drugs, crime, political extremism and social unrest'.

A second implication relates to the debate about high risk and whole population strategies in health promotion. The focus on specific diseases and on high risk individuals has often been at the expense of a whole population strategy which would have focused attention on why lower income groups experience more disease and premature mortality. While a high risk strategy may sometimes be appropriate, Rose (1992) argued that whenever risk is widely diffused through a population, for example in relation to blood pressure or cholesterol, a whole population approach is justifiable. This argument has also been applied to poverty (Watt, 1996). A focus on risk factors for mortality in the two Scottish cities of Edinburgh and Glasgow would encourage the targeting of coronary heart disease and prevention initiatives on smoking and diet but in Glasgow this would leave a major explanation and solution unexplored:

> The difference in coronary mortality is part of a difference in mortality from all causes of death. By focusing on specific diseases health policy does not address the fundamental question of why some groups of people die earlier from most major categories of death. It is age of death, not cause, that counts... The cities reflect greatly contrasting balances of affluence and poverty within their populations.
>
> (Watt, 1996: 1026–7)

This also relates to poverty, Watt argues, where health policy focuses on what individuals and communities should do and 'ignores actions which require the support and involvement of society as a whole'.

A third, related issue concerns what explanations are given for poverty. Individualist explanations draw attention to the characteristics of individuals and groups in poverty and tend to blame them for their situation. In this view poverty is mainly the consequence of individual lifestyle choices, low educational attainment or fecklessness. A broader interpretation would suggest that these behaviours partly reflect the range of options and constraints that exist in society. Blaxter's (1993) comment that 'there is no doubt that behaviour is implicated, but it is behaviour which is inevitable in certain environments' is relevant to poverty too.

Theories of poverty

Social policy provides an analysis of poverty and a framework for understanding how health promotion might challenge poverty and begin to improve health. This involves shifting from a pathogenic approach to health: that is, concentrating most efforts on care and treatment at an individual level. It also involves a shift from modifying individual or family behaviour. The pathogenic, behavioural focus can be seen as falling within an individualist theoretical framework, drawing upon the 'cycle of deprivation' model (Figure 9.3). It is the individual or family (or sub-culture) that is being targeted. Poverty – and poverty-related ill health and lack of response to health education – is seen as largely generated within these sub-systems, in dysfunctional families and communities. The practical steps taken are to modify and change behaviours by health advice and more effective education (Jones, 1994).

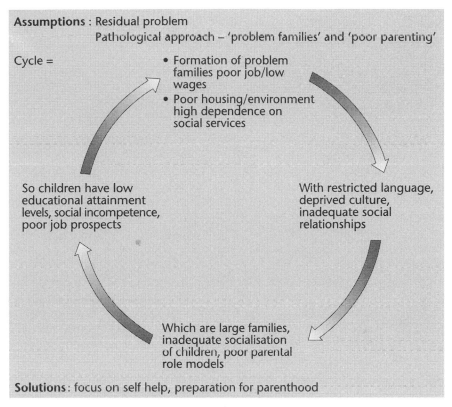

Figure 9.3 **Cycle of deprivation**   (Jones, 1994)

However, if the causes of poverty are seen to lie in wider social and economic structures of inequality then the potential focus of health promotion is much broader (Figure 9.4). A 'cycle of inequality' explanation of poverty points to disparities of wealth and income within society as a whole. Structural factors and a range of social divisions along the lines of class, race, gender, age and disability can be seen as playing a part in the cause and continuation of poverty and ill health. National and international economic policies, the decisions of multinational, national and local companies to invest or withdraw investment, welfare structures and policies all become important to consider. This is the characteristic approach of recent developments in health promotion which call for healthy public policies to enable people to live in supportive environments and give them the means to make healthy choices (WHO, 1986, 1992).

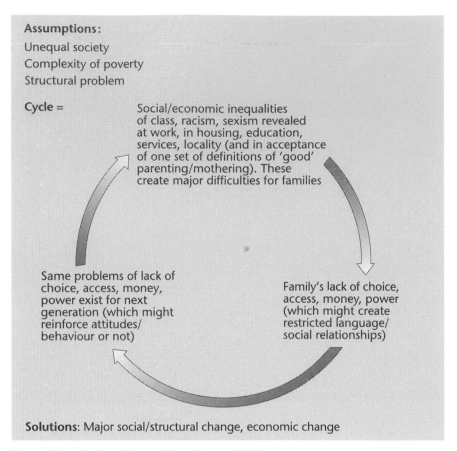

Figure 9.4 **Cycle of inequality** (Jones, 1994)

Anti-poverty action

In part, debates about poverty necessarily focus on influencing policy change at a national or international level. Calls to reform the benefits system and invest in education and retraining (Rowntree Foundation, 1995) or to create a more redistributive tax system (Benzeval and Webb, 1995) might be supported by health promoters but they do not easily translate into everyday health promotion work. There are also organisation-wide implications in a relative poverty analysis which need to be adopted by commissioners and providers (Blackburn, 1995).

But at 'grass-roots' level there is plenty of scope for action. Blackburn (1995) has commented of health services that when they are flexible and responsive they can help mitigate some of the effects of poverty, whereas insensitive or inappropriate services can make matters worse. This is not just the case within a health, local or voluntary agency but also at an individual level. Second, she has argued, 'putting a poverty component into health-needs assessments and information collection' can transform the priorities of a contract and the working of a primary health care team. Once again, it is not only at an organisation level that needs assessments are done. In their work at an individual, group or local population level health promoters could create many opportunities to assess needs more broadly, taking poverty into account. The collection of data about poverty in a household, group or organisation can provide the essential information on which to base a more realistic needs assessment.

In addition, as some of the discussion about working at a local level in Part 1 indicated, a community development approach can encourage local people to work together to mitigate the effects of poverty for themselves. A review of community regeneration projects in eight cities in Germany and the UK concluded that interventions stood a better chance of success if they incorporated particular elements. These included:

- promoting strong citizen groups
- co-ordinating and integrating programmes
- giving priority to creating employment opportunities and combating poverty
- establishing a sense of partnership between the participants
- giving long-term commitment
- allocating adequate and protected resources.

(reported in Whitehead, 1995: 37)

Whilst health and social care workers cannot eradicate poverty they can help families to cope and avoid 'blaming the victims' of poverty. Blackburn suggested that seven aspects are important in tackling poverty in households and these can all be related to health promotion work:

- non-victim-blaming advice and services
- realistic advice which focuses on the household's needs and prioirites
- help with the costs of caring, for example, through developing or utilising equipment loan schemes, co-ops to provide cheap food
- maximising income through sound, well informed advice on benefits
- advocacy, to help families gain access to services and help them to negotiate with professionals
- flexibility in services so that people can gain access rather than trying, and failing, to jump service barriers
- social support networks, to help households through the stigma and isolation that poverty brings.

Review the two lists above and consider which of the aspects are relevant to your situation as a health promoter.

Together these lists contain many practical ideas which are relevant to health promotion. Since so many groups, lay and professional, are involved in health promotion it is difficult to determine which aspects will be most useful. Those working in community settings might acknowledge the importance of promoting strong citizen groups and prioritising fundamentally important anti-poverty issues, such as helping people into work rather than anti-smoking campaigns which might seem irrelevant to local people. If you work with families, then the prioritising of effective well informed support as well as, rather than instead of, advocacy might well be an approach you would endorse. Both lists are underpinned by a cycle of inequality rather than a cycle of deprivation approach, in the sense that they do not blame the households or communities for their poverty but seek a non-judgemental route into a helping relationship.

9.7 Conclusion

Poverty is of fundamental importance in health promotion. There is now widespread acceptance of the damage done to people's health by inadequate income. Excess mortality and morbidity from a whole range of diseases has been demonstrated to be strongly associated with low income levels. Moreover, there is also evidence that it is the relative distribution of income in an affluent society such as the UK which is crucial. Since health promotion is about 'swimming upstream' to prevent people falling into the river of ill health the argument for combating poverty becomes a very strong one.

This chapter has argued that health promoters have much to learn from a social policy analysis and this has been demonstrated in relation to poverty. Although freedom from poverty or, to put it in health promotion language, the meeting of basic needs is seen as a prerequisite for health, the health sector has been generally very cautious about adopting an anti-poverty strategy. This is not surprising since such a strategy is overtly political in nature. However, as Rose (1992) commented, 'medicine and politics cannot and should not be kept apart'. International and national level policy change will be required to overcome poverty, and health promoters can help to create pressure for change as professional or concerned citizens. Understanding the origins and development of debates about poverty can be helpful in this process.

At the same time, it is important for health promoters to have a real commitment to reducing inequalities in their own practice and to have an informed understanding of the nature and extent of poverty. Building on such an understanding health promoters will be better able to create 'helping relationships' that do not blame the victims of poverty but assist individuals, households and communities in a realistic way to break out of a cycle of poverty.

Chapter 10
Health promotion and environmental politics

10.1 Introduction

This chapter explores how and why environmental objectives have moved higher up the health promotion agenda. First, it discusses the growth of the environmental movement in the 1960s and 1970s and the debates about economic growth and environmental degradation. It examines the concept of 'sustainable development', the principles underlying this and the attempts to ensure that sustainability policies are developed. In the UK, for example, the development of health appraisal and environmental health action planning has attempted to bring together health and environmental issues. This has involved political judgements about equity, quality of life and risk.

Attention is also focused on the increasing interest in sustainable development in the health promotion movement. In 1977 the Health For All strategy acknowledged the importance of a healthy environment and this was reinforced and extended in the Ottawa Charter and in the Sundsvall Statement on supportive environments. In the UK the new public health movement attempted to build on traditional public health concern for environmental intervention by highlighting how public policy interventions could improve public health. The chapter examines how far health and environmental principles share common ground and what tensions exist.

Most important, it considers the implications for health promotion practice of putting environmental principles into health promotion. How far should health promoters incorporate the messages of sustainability into everyday practice and how might this be done? What is the relevance of 'green consumerism'? At what level and to what extent can those working for health make new alliances which will deliver improved environmental health outcomes? What can health promoters learn from the successes and failures of the environmental movement? The chapter concludes by examining the evidence from current projects which are attempting to build a creative synergy between environmentalism and health promotion.

10.2 The rise of the environmental movement

In the 1970s and 1980s environmentalism, in the shape of the Green movement in particular, became more prominent (Dobson, 1991). Many would date the birth of 'green' politics as coinciding with the publication in 1962 of Rachel Carson's campaigning book *Silent Spring* which warned of the disastrous environmental consequences of indiscriminate use of pesticides, fungicides and herbicides on the land. As a powerful mix of prophecy and science, it both detailed the increasing use of chemicals in every aspect of daily life and characterised the future 'silent spring' in the following vision:

> There was once a town in the heart of America where all life seemed to live in harmony with its surroundings... The countryside was famous for the abundance and variety of its bird life [and for] the streams, which flowed clear and cold out of the hills and contained shady pools where trout lay... Then a strange blight crept over the area and everything began to change. Some evil spell had settled on the community: mysterious maladies swept the flocks of chickens; the cattle and sheep sickened and died. The farmers spoke of much illness among their families. In the town the doctors had become more and more puzzled by new kinds of sickness appearing amongst their patients... There was a strange stillness. The birds, for example, where had they gone? The few birds seen anywhere were moribund; they trembled violently and could not fly. It was a spring without voices... The roadsides, once so attractive, were now lined with browned and withered vegetation as though swept by fire... Even the streams were now lifeless... No witchcraft, no enemy action had silenced the rebirth of new life in this stricken world. The people had done it to themselves...
>
> (Carson, 1965 edn.: 25-27)

Carson commented that, while she knew of no community which had suffered all these environmental consequences, 'yet every one of these disasters has actually happened somewhere, and many real communities have already suffered a substantial number of them' (1965: 27).

This assault on the growing use of chemicals was part of a more general attack on what was seen by some critics as the abuse of scientific knowledge to drive unlimited economic growth. It was acknowledged that economic growth had delivered higher living standards and, from a health perspective, there was strong evidence that higher living standards had played the major part in improving health (McKeown, 1976). But a policy of untrammelled growth, it was argued, entailed the consumption of finite resources and in the longer term widespread pollution, the undermining of industrial capacity, global instability and population decline (Schumacher, 1974).

The Limits to Growth, produced by a group of industrialists, researchers and scientists in 1972, used computer modelling to demonstrate that infinite growth in a finite system was unsustainable. It argued that on current trends the limits to growth would be reached within 100 years; 'the most probable result will be a rather sudden and uncontrollable decline in population and industrial capacity' (Meadows *et. al.,* 1972: 23). The solution was seen as stability – no or low growth – which recognised the interdependence of all systems on a shared earth.

> It is possible to alter these growth trends and to establish a condition of ecological and economic stability that is sustainable far into the future. The state of global equilibrium could be designed so that the basic material needs of each person on earth are satisfied and each person has an equal opportunity to realize his [sic] individual potential.
>
> (Meadows *et al.,* 1972: 23–24)

Environmental capacity

The implication that 'no growth' was the most sensible way forward, in social or environmental terms, was subsequently challenged (Schumacher, 1974; Daly, 1977). The problem was redefined not as one of growth or no-growth, but of developing a better balance between environmental resources and industrial demands. This, it was argued, required the focus to shift to 'environmental capacity': that is, ensuring that current rates of use of resources did not exceed the ability of these resources to recover or be replaced (Jacobs, 1991).

Types of resources, it was claimed, needed to be treated differently (Lovins, 1977; Jacobs, 1991). For non-renewable resources such as metals or coal there was a finite supply, though it was not necessarily clear what that was. New extraction methods or recycling could extend their potential contribution but both activities used up new resource: for example, the energy required for the recycling process. On the other hand, renewable resources could continually be replaced, providing the rate of consumption did not exceed renewal. In theory reforestation could cancel out deforestation, although destruction of forests, especially the tropical rainforests, was exceeding the rate of replacement. Finally, continuing resources such as solar energy or wind power did not need replacement, although they might be affected by other environmental changes.

Modern industrial and distribution methods were also held up to scrutiny (Schumacher, 1974; Ekins, 1986) They were seen as very demanding in their use of finite resources and could have a detrimental impact on the environment. In contemporary system food distribution, for example, long hauls are made to carry foodstuffs to distributors, then to supermarkets and then (by use of the private car) from supermarkets to people's homes. This consumed large amounts of energy and created considerable pollution. Environmentalists called for food to be produced and sold locally. 'The two could have a similar effect on GNP but make vastly different use of resources and contributions to air pollution' (Crombie, 1995).

Critics questioned the whole approach of measuring growth in terms of changes in Gross National Product (GNP), a measure which calculates the amount of market-based economic activity within a country. Not only did it not count in informal exchange and subsistence, it assumed that an upward movement in GNP is inevitably of benefit to the country and its population. But:

> It is only by showing that the growth has taken place through the production of goods and services that are inherently beneficial; demonstrating that these goods and services have been widely distributed throughout society; and proving that these benefits outweigh any detrimental effects of the growth process on other parts of society, that one can arrive at any sort of assessment as to whether a particular instance of economic growth is in fact a good or bad thing.

> In time, perhaps certain patterns of economic growth might come to be recognized as benign and life-enhancing, while others are perceived as wasteful, polluting or inequitable, as the case my be. Conventional economic thinking makes little or no attempt to make this assessment.
> (Ekins, 1986: 9)

In GNP terms all measurable development was seen as progress irrespective of its quality or outcome. Hence excessive consumption of fossil fuels to create unneccessary products would be seen as productive whereas unpaid or informal work would not be included in the measurement at all (Popay *et al.*, 1993).

10.3 Sustainable development

Underpinning these concerns about environmental capacity and the questioning of GNP measurements of progress lies the concept of 'sustainable development'. This came into prominence in the later 1980s with the publication of The Brundtland Report by the United Nations World Commission on Environment and Development (1987). Sustainable development was defined as:

> Development that meets the needs of current generations without compromising the ability of future generations to meet their needs.
> (United Nations World Commission on Environment and Development, 1987: 8)

> Suggest what view of economic growth underpins the concept of sustainable development.

The concept of sustainable development carried with it the demand that economic growth should be balanced against resource depletion and the recognition of ultimate dependence on the natural environment. If growth outstripped resources then the ability of future generations to live in a similar way to the present generation would be compromised. Elsewhere in the Brundtland Report this was described as 'non-declining per capita utility (satisfaction or well-being)'. In other words, economic growth should be such that it could deliver to people similar levels of satisfaction/well-being in 2050 or 3000 as it delivered in the current year.

This raised issues about how sustainability and satisfaction were to be measured. The identification of reliable indicators of sustainability and the incorporation of these into the policy-making process became of critical importance. It has been argued that the undermining of sustainable development is not linear but that one fairly small, incremental change may tip the balance towards a catastrophic shift (Crombie, 1995). Munn (1992) identified three general types of indicators which might measure the degree to which environmental sustainability is being reached (see Table 10.1). The first type involved measures of the health of the natural world, such as species diversity. The second type included indicators that would require quite major policy changes to control effectively, such as controls on the rate of transportation growth, and on energy and water consumption. The third type, the indicators of improvement, also demanded substantial policy shifts. For example, to achieve declining sales of pesticides and herbicides there would have to be changes in land use and farming methods.

Table 10.1 **Indicators of sustainability**

A	**General indicators**
1	State of health of natural ecosystems (e.g. primary productivity, efficiency of nutrient recycling, species diversity, population fluctuations, prevalence of pests)
2	Resilience indicators (e.g. biodiversity, distribution of species)
B	**Indicators of threats to ecosystem integrity**
1	Increasing population (especially urbanisation)
2	Increasing energy consumption (e.g. type, per capita and total amounts, energy required to produce a unit of manufactured goods)
3	Increasing consumption of water (per capita and total)
4	Rates of depletion of renewable and non-renewable resources (e.g. forests, prime agricultural land, mineral reserves)
5	Increasing amounts of wastes
6	Transportation indicators (e.g. number of cars, kilometres of road, number of airline passengers)
C	**Indicators of improving ecosystem integrity**
1	Increasing output of production per unit of natural resources used (both renewable and non-renewable)
2	Increasing extent of recycling schemes
3	Conservation of scarce or highly valued resources (endangered species)
4	Declining sales of pesticides and herbicides
5	Declining economic and energy subsidies given to the natural resource sectors
6	The degree of citizen involvement in 'environmentally friendly' actions.

(Munn, 1992)

Sustainable development principles

The Brundtland Report stressed the importance of popular participation in decision making about development and sustainability. It also recognised that sustainable development might require social and economic change and argued that an:

> overriding priority should be given to the essential needs of the world's poor... Development involves a progressive transformation of economy and society... Even the narrow notion of physical sustainability implies a concern for social equity between generations that must logically be extended to equity within each generation.
>
> (United Nations World Commission on Environment and Development, 1987: 165–6)

This positioned sustainable development as a radical approach concerned with achieving greater equity between countries or within societies. For example, deforestation, acid rain or other pollution in one country might create an environmental risk for those in other parts of the world (Conroy and Litvinoff, 1988). Within a society, some social groups might have very high consumption rates and their use of finite resources might need to be sharply constrained in order to improve levels of satisfaction and well-being for the poorest groups. In the UK, where the poorest groups in the population have found their living standards falling in comparison with more affluent groups (Rowntree, 1995), this would suggest that the application of sustainability principles should assist in redressing inequalities. Otherwise the effect would be to create a type of sustainable development which locks people into current inequalities.

This point has been highlighted in the debate about transport policy. Higher socio-economic groups are statistically multiple car owners with high annual mileage rates, generating demand for more roads rather than public transport (Transport and Health Study Group, 1991). They are, directly and indirectly, large consumers of finite resources and producers of high levels of atmospheric pollution. The Department of the Environment has begun to acknowledge that the levels of consumption (and perhaps of satisfaction and well-being) of such groups might need to be constrained in order to protect environmental quality (DoE, 1995).

Since Brundtland, sustainable development has been fleshed out as a concept in various ways. One emphasis has been on 'internalising externalities': in other words, costing in natural resources, pollution and the costs of clearing up environmental damage (Elkin *et al.*, 1991). This has been seen as costs to be set against GNP rather than adding to it. Another has been on counting in quality so that measures of quality of the environment are seen as being central as well as material measures. This is sometimes called 'nurturing the intangibles' (Labonte, 1991): that is, things that cannot be easily quantified but are important sources of satisfaction and well-being. An example of this might be having local streets in inner city areas which are attractive rather than simply functional.

A third emphasis has been on the 'precautionary principle'. This was adopted by the 'Earth Summit', the 1992 United Nations Conference on Environment and Development (UNCED). Participants at the summit agreed that:

> Where there are threats of serious or irreversible damage, lack of full scientific certainty shall not be used as a reason for postponing cost-effective measures to prevent environmental degradation.
>
> (UNCED, 1993)

The concept of sustainable development, therefore, has raised important issues about equity, participation, quality of life and cost-benefit assessment. This has resonances with the concerns of those involved in promoting health and suggests that a sustainable development approach might offer a robust means of analysing environmental issues. The next section discusses the growing interest in sustainable development within the health sector.

10.4 Environmental concerns and public health

Concern about the environment has been an important feature of public health since the early nineteenth century. The work of Medical Officers of Health in improving sanitation, streets and housing in industrial cities has already been noted. One important consequence of the public health movement in the UK was the creation of local government responsibility for setting environmental standards and dealing with a range of issues, such as noise, inspection of food premises and refuse disposal (Allen, 1996). In the late nineteenth and early twentieth centuries the drive to clean up the environment led to some creative collaboration within local authorities. However, as public health developed it became a specialist branch of medicine inside the health service and the links with the environmental health function in local government became weaker.

The 'new' public health

The development of the 'New Public Health movement' in the UK in the mid-1980s was partly aimed at re-creating the link between environmental health and public health medicine. It had a strong concern for 'the effect of the total environment on health': that is, the effect of both the 'physical' and the 'socio-economic' environment (Nutbeam, 1986). The notion of creating healthy environments was noted in all the UK national public health strategies but in the new public health movement it was seen as a central objective. The Public Health Alliance, for example, set out a Charter for Public Health in which it listed goods and services which would secure 'every citizen's right to good health'. These included several with a focus on environmental change:

Homes that are warm, dry, secure and affordable.

Food that is safe, nourishing, widely available and affordable.

Transport that permits accessible, safe travel at reasonable cost and encourages fuel economy and a clean environment.

Work that is... free from hazards to health and safety.

Environments which are protected from dangerous pollution and radiation, and are planned to preserve and enhance our quality of life.

Public services which... provide clean, safe water and waste disposal.

(PHA, 1984)

The starting point for the revival of public health was a critique of the extent to which modern hospital-based medicine had dominated thinking about health, to the near exclusion of serious concern for prevention and the wider environment. The origins of this argument lay in claims that the decline of cholera, tuberculosis and typhoid in the nineteenth and early twentieth centuries owed little to clinical medicine and much to improvements in nutrition, hygiene and housing (McKeown, 1976). Mass immunisation, screening and antibiotics arrived after the main health improvements had been made. This suggested that living standards were critical to public health and prompted a focus on work, housing and income redistribution to raise those of the poorest groups.

The other implication of the critique of medicine was the need to focus on environmental protection. Nineteenth century hygienic measures carried out by local authorities and the Medical Officer of Health team had included slum clearance, street paving and lighting, control of nuisances and industrial emissions, provision of clean water and sewage disposal. Many of these environmental protection measures had been downgraded in importance by clinical medicine but the new public health movement argued that they were still central to the people's health. This is reflected, for example, in the Public Health Alliance Charter, by the inclusion of concern 'for a clean environment', 'clean, safe water and waste disposal' and protection from 'dangerous pollution and radiation'. Environmental protection was also emphasised in response to the growing evidence that some diseases might be amenable to a preventive approach rather than to an exclusive treatment focus. Airborne pollutants from motor vehicles, for example, have been implicated in the triggering of asthma attacks and critical episodes requiring hospitalisation in other respiratory diseases (Walters, 1994). Environmental hazards such as malignant skin melanoma from increased ultra-violet radiation and ill effects from chemical contamination of water or land again indicate a significant role for environmental protection (Brown et al., 1992).

The argument has been for an acknowledgement of the importance of environmental management and protection, and for a better balance to be struck between curative treatment and environmental assessment and prevention. Since the health professions are more expert at assessing existing disease states, they may miss emerging patterns of disease (Brown *et al.*, 1992). Highlighting such patterns by assembling the evidence on environmental hazards to health could be an important role for public health and health promotion (Labonte, 1991).

Another key aspect of the new public health analysis has been the claim that some aspects of current economic growth were health damaging and should not be seen as progressive. This built on the work of researchers at the Unit for the Study of Health Policy at Guy's Hospital in London in the late 1970s and early 1980s who argued that there was a 'need to look very seriously not so much at industrialisation *per se*, but at the largely indiscriminate nature of present economic growth – that is, at much of what is ironically termed wealth-creation' (Popay *et al.*, 1993). The increase in wealth in a society, they claimed, did not necessarily lead to better health for all. They suggested that anti-pollution activities, for example, were strikingly inappropriate for inclusion in the GNP. The actions associated with clearing up after oil spillages around the UK coastline formed part of growth statistics whereas preventing spillages in the first place, which would be a far greater contribution in resource and environmental terms, would make a less significant contribution to the GNP.

GNP measures tended to distort and marginalise non-measurable, informal or 'private' activities. In the food industry, for example, money spent on frozen vegetables has a positive effect on the GNP, whereas home-grown vegetables if consumed or exchanged informally do not enter the GNP. Unpaid child-rearing, housework and informal caring have been categorised as having no economic value and thus not contributing to economic welfare. These conflicts between health and wealth were identified at the level of production, consumption and distribution. For example:

> The higher the level of transport activity, the more fuel will be consumed and so in economic terms (at least on paper) things will be better: but other things being equal, the more transport, the more accident and emergency resources that will have to be devoted to traffic accidents. Similarly, cigarettes and alcohol production are 'wealth producing' from an economic perspective, but from a health perspective they are 'ill-health producing'.
>
> (Popay *et al.*,1993: 275)

In production terms, they acknowledged, there may be strong economic reasons for using chemicals and toxic materials but these can be health-destroying for individuals exposed to asbestos or radiation. People may be under strong pressure to consume harmful products, for example through advertising. Maldistribution, despite higher and higher levels of total output, may perpetuate inequalities, for example in housing provision and basic amenities (Popay *et al.*, 1993). Economic assumptions about what was valuable, progressive, beneficial and productive, it was claimed, served to marginalise some activities and outputs while endorsing other health-damaging ones.

How far do the ideas of the New Public Health build on those of the nineteenth century public health movement?

The nineteenth century public health movement also had a concern for environmental protection, in the sense of providing clean water, safe sewage disposal and a more hygienic environment, but the New Public Health agenda is far broader and more radical. The nineteenth century public health movement was more narrowly focused on disease prevention; the contemporary movement lays claim to intervene in all areas of public policy which may influence health. It has recast 'environment' to include the social, economic and psychological as well as the physical environment.

In the 1990s these claims were articulated forcefully by some supporters of the new public health movement (Draper, 1991). 'The core of public health action is avoiding or countering hazards in the environment' (Draper, 1991: 7). The result was a much more ambitious definition of public health which encompassed action to counter a range of 'hostile environments'. These included the 'ecological' environment, such as the thinning of the ozone layer, the greenhouse effect, deforestation and over-use of pesticides, the 'socio-economic environment', such as poverty, unemployment and inappropriate economic growth, the 'psycho-social environment' of social isolation and mental ill health, and the 'military environment' of nuclear threats and the arms trade. The analysis also drew on the work of the WHO in identifying the need for an intersectoral approach which operated at a range of levels from international to local.

10.5 Integrating health and sustainable development

This emphasis on protecting the total environment, equalising opportunities and meeting basic material needs had some parallels with moves in the health sector in the 1970s towards Health For All principles. While this had little immediate practical impact it did begin to link environment and health together. First, Health For All targets reflected contemporary concerns about environmental risks, such as air and water pollution, and recognised the role of sectors other than the health sector in contributing to health improvement. Second, the 1977 strategy put a greater emphasis on addressing the basic health needs of whole populations and, implicitly, criticised the over-concentration on high technology, high-cost, industrialised hospital-dominated medicine.

The Alma Ata Declaration of 1978 called for a shift of resources towards creating a sound system of primary health care which 'addresses the main health problems in the community'. This was recognised as involving all sectors 'of national and community development' and 'maximum community and individual self-reliance and participation' (WHO, 1978). The primary goals were: prevention, control and treatment of common diseases and injuries, immunisation, an adequate food supply, safe water and basic sanitation, family planning, maternal and child health care and provision of essential drugs. Such a shift towards primary health care would inevitably require countries to give less resource to secondary and tertiary care, in particular to the very expensive high technology hospitals which consumed large parts of the health budget.

Supportive environments for health

The Ottawa Charter (WHO, 1986) identified 'building healthy public policies' and 'creating sustainable environments' as key elements of its health promotion strategy. The first called for the creation of public policies which supported health and made 'healthy choices' easier for people. The second of these, as outlined in the Charter, had a close affinity with the concept of sustainability.

> Our societies are complex and interrelated. Health cannot be separated from other goals. The inextricable links between people and their environments constitutes the basis for a socio-ecological approach to health. The overall guiding principle for the world, nations, regions and communities alike, is the need to encourage reciprocal maintenance – to take care of each other, our communities and our natural environment. The conservation of natural resources throughout the world should be emphasized as a global responsibility.
>
> (WHO, 1986: 1)

To what extent does the concept of 'sustainable development' (the Brundtland Report) coincide with the approach of creating 'supportive environments', as stated in the Ottawa Charter?

Sustainable development, as conceived of in the Brundtland Report, emphasised resource conservation and interdependence across the generations as well as the need for participation and equity between and within societies. To that extent the approach is similar but the focus of sustainable development is on sustaining levels of satisfaction across generations, whereas in the Ottawa Charter supportive environments are framed to support health. However, it is notable that satisfaction and well-being as terms are closely connected to the WHO's broad view of health as a resource for living and a state of complete physical, social and mental well-being.

Health and sustainable development were linked explicitly in the WHO Charter on Environment and Health (1989) which began by claiming that every individual was entitled to:

an environment conducive to the highest attainable level of health and well-being;

information and consultation on the state of the environment, and on plans, decisions and activities likely to affect both the environment and health;

participation in the decision-making process.

(WHO, 1989:1)

The Charter emphasised the responsibility of government, all public and private organisations and agencies, the media and individuals to protect the environment and promote human health. It was symbolic of the increasing concern to integrate health and sustainable development. Within health promotion the Adelaide conference on healthy public policy (1988) and the Sundsvall conference on supportive environments (1991) helped to clarify how sustainable development could be translated into everyday health promoting action.

Although health had been implicit in the concept of sustainable development, this approach had largely been driven by economic and environmental concerns. The health sector has played little part in agenda setting or policy making for sustainability (Labonte, 1991). However, there are shared principles and objectives which suggest that health promotion and the environmental movement could strengthen each other's position by working together. The impact of transport on health, for example, has begun to be documented (Transport and Health Study Group, 1991; Hunt, 1993; Jones, 1995b). This has complemented and extended the environmental evidence about land take, environmental degradation, depletion of finite energy resources and rising levels of atmospheric pollution (Elkin et al., 1991). But there remains considerable scope for exploring the social impact of transport and linking this to levels of well-being, satisfaction or quality of life indicators.

How far can the mapping of environmental and health principles help to create a unified agenda and priorities? Comparing the priorities of Australian conservation groups with Canadian public health principles, Brown and colleagues (1992) noted the similarity between principles identified by environmentalists and those of public health practitioners, although they were from different continents and professions (see Table 10.2). The central concern of both of them with ecology, empowerment, intergenerational equity and quality is very evident and the convergence of language is striking. At this level of generalisation it is a fairly straightforward matter to see similarities. A more real test would be to decide on priorities for policy change and set key targets.

Table 10.2   **Principles of sustainable development produced by public
health practitioners and environmentalists**

Environmentalists	*Public health practitioners*
Ecological integrity and biodiversity	Ecological principles and sustaining diversity
Intergenerational equity	Planning across generations
Community participation	Sustaining communities
Social equity	Empowering equally
Natural capital with sustainable income	Producing fairly and healthily
Global perspectives	Shrinking global and national inequities
Limits on natural resource use	Repairing, recycling, replacing, reducing
Qualitative development	Nurturing the intangibles
Pricing environmental values and natural resources	Internalising all costs
Precautionary principles	Social health principles

(Brown *et al.*, 1992)

Agenda 21 – a turning point?

The 1992 Earth Summit developed a programme of action on sustainable
development: Agenda 21. In it, 27 principles were set out to guide and
underpin the action programme. Health and sustainability were viewed as
'intimately interconnected' and there was an explicit sense of political and
economic crisis.

> Humanity has reached a turning point. We can continue with present
> policies which are deepening economic divisions within and between
> countries – which increase poverty, hunger, sickness and illiteracy and
> cause the continuing deterioration of the ecosystem on which life on
> Earth depends. Or we can change course. We can act to improve the
> living standards of those who are in need. We can better manage and
> protect the ecosystem and bring about a more prosperous future for us
> all.
>
> (UNCED, 1993: 3)

In the section dealing with health, the six designated programme areas
reflected a 'Health For All' orientation with an emphasis on intersectoral
collaboration, prevention and community participation in the developing
world. The six areas were: meeting primary health care needs, controlling
communicable diseases, protecting vulnerable groups, meeting the urban

health challenge and reducing risk from environmental pollution. In particular, meeting primary health needs was seen as 'integral to the achievement of the goals of sustainable development and primary environmental care' (UNCED, 1993: 42).

Agenda 21 endorsed principles central to sustainable development: the precautionary principle, internalisation of environmental costs, equity in development, and eradication of poverty. It proclaimed the right of all people to a 'healthy and productive life in harmony with nature' (UNCED, 1993: 9). Perhaps its greatest achievement was in gaining agreement on environmental impact assessment in each case where proposed actions 'are likely to have a significant adverse impact on the environment'.

Agenda 21 explicitly called for change; for example, it commented that 'for hundreds of millions of people, the poor living conditions in urban and peri-urban areas are destroying lives, health, and social and moral values' (1993: 48). But the report was extremely inexplicit, perhaps not surprisingly, in commenting on the economic and political policies that gave rise to such conditions or on what particular policies would provide the solution. Among the 27 principles, for example, was one which called for 'sustainable development and a higher quality of life for all people' (1993: 10). Yet we have noted that sustainability, if it is to be implemented, is likely to require that some groups restrain their demands for resources and do not advance their quality of life.

In principle 12, states were called upon to co-operate 'to promote a supportive and open economic system that would lead to economic growth and sustainable development in all countries'. This raises a host of definitional problems. What constitutes an 'open' economic system? What should it support? How are economic growth and sustainable development to be held in balance? Even in relation to principle 17, which endorsed environmental impact assessment, it is clear that there is much room for debate about what constitutes a 'significant adverse impact'.

European-level initiatives

Within Europe the European Health For All targets (1985) have also influenced change. Two conferences on environment and health, held in Frankfurt in 1989 and in Helsinki in 1992, have focused on how European member states can reach the eight environmental health targets. These include targets on water, air and food quality, waste management and soil pollution, human ecology and health at work (targets 20–25). Target 19 emphasised the need for effective environmental management systems for monitoring and evaluation, and target 18 called for member states to have developed:

> ...policies on the environment and health that ensure ecologically sustainable development, effective prevention and control of environmental health risks and equitable access to healthy environments.
> (WHO, 1991)

These targets, whilst broadly supported, were seen as too generalised to become the basis for action. Instead the Helsinki Declaration of 1994 established Environmental Health Action Plan objectives for Europe (EHAPE) and member states were expected to develop national environmental health plans which specify the types of action to be taken to meet these objectives. They covered similar ground to the WHO targets but established much more precise requirements. These included the development of country-specific environmental health profiles as the basis for defining priorities for action and monitoring progress, regulatory control of hazardous activities, the use of fiscal measures to encourage investments in enviornmental health, public participation in planning, priority setting and implementation and a whole range of objectives for specific protection of water and air quality, noise levels, radiation, soil pollution and so on. Three levels of action were identified in the plan: basic requirements that needed to be met to secure environmental health, prevention and control of medium- and longer- term hazards, and promotion of well-being and mental health. In other words, there was a significant convergence between health and environmental aims.

The UK, which was selected as one of the countries to produce a pilot national environmental health action plan, published a consultation document in 1995 and the completed plan in July 1996. This was a joint publication of the Department of the Environment and the Department of Health. They set the plan within the existing framework of environmental protection, noting the role of local authorities, the Health and Safety Executive, the water and energy regulators and the range of government reports on the environment in the previous decade (DoE, 1990; DoE, 1994). One significant new initiative was to establish the Environment Agency with overall powers in relation to pollution, rivers, water and waste control.

The plan was widely welcomed by environmental groups, although it was questioned whether there there was enough commitment to regulation. The importance of partnership and 'education', as opposed to legislation and enforcement, features strongly in the plan where it is claimed that 'enforcement may lead to a minimum standard whereas partnership may lead to agreement on a better-than-minimum standard' (1996b: 30). One national pressure group, Friends of the Earth, argued that 'we are failing to meet most of our international commitments of health and the environment' and called for the government to take more practical measures (Friends of the Earth, 1996). There has been particular concern about lead and organic pollutants in water, the increase in microbiological food-borne disease, and the fact that air quality regularly exceeds WHO and DoE guidelines on sulphur dioxides, nitrogen oxides, particulates (PM10s) and ozone (South East Institute of Public Health, 1996).

10.6 Action on sustainable development

National and international initiatives have had a significant influence on the UK agenda on health and the environment. What should the response of health promoters be to this evidence of convergence between health and environmental action? Now that sustainable development is being taken more seriously, how can health promoters incorporate its principles into their everyday work? Table 10.3 considers action at a number of different levels.

Table 10.3   **Examples of the potential for environmental health promoting action at different levels**

Consumer action – 'green' purchasing, fitting double glazing

Citizen action – joining a pressure group, starting a local campaign, growing vegetables

Household action – recycling, monitoring and reducing energy use

Community action – setting up a recyling project, establishing a skills-exchange scheme

Professional action – giving greater priority to 'green' issues within health promotion work, supporting local 'green' initiatives, harnessing external resources from national or local campaigns

Local authority action – traffic restraint policies, energy-saving advice, setting and enforcing targets, enabling public participation in environmental priority setting

Organisational action – assessing the potential for energy saving in transport, cleaning, heating and lighting

National and international action – setting policy frameworks and targets, monitoring targets, enforcing regulations and inspection, providing resource to encourage change at lower levels

Perhaps the most obvious way in which health promoters can take action is as consumers and citizens. There has been a surge of public interest in purchasing 'green' products, from washing-up liquid and free-range eggs to catalytic converters and products grown in sustainable forests. Household and citizen action on 'green' issues is possible, for example through recycling bottles and paper, reusing materials, growing vegetables and saving energy. There has also been a rise in the membership of 'green' pressure groups and networks and a corresponding concern to incorporate 'green' policies into the agendas of the major political parties. In Germany the environmental movement broke into national politics through its capture of seats in regional legislatures and, although this has not happened in the UK, the Green Party does control some local council seats.

For health promoters environmental action can form part of working for health with families and communities. For example, the national Going For Green Campaign, launched in 1995, included a major public awareness campaign to encourage people to 'think green' in their daily lives and a 'Green Code' to help people follow a more sustainable lifestyle. It also developed six 'sustainable community' projects in England, Wales and Scotland to test out ideas about adapting ways of living in small, well defined communities. These resources and projects, or similar resources produced by pressure groups and campaigns, could be adapted for use with local communities.

Review the potential within your own health promotion work for environmental action.

Sustainability is a broad concept. It also seems an abstract one, and part of a health promoter's work is to turn it into a practical tool. Initiatives such as setting up a fruit and vegetable co-operative on a poor housing estate might be given a 'green' dimension if local people could be helped to gain access to allotments and contribute their own produce. An outreach project run by a hospital in mid-Wales supported local women in setting up a clothes exchange shop on a poor and isolated housing estate (interview, 1996). This had the effect of directly recycling goods and cutting out the 'middleman'. There can be a coincidence between action on national health targets and environmental gains. For example, supporting a local campaign for traffic calming which made an area safer for children to play in would also help to meet physical activity targets and might have a long-term effect on local rates of coronary heart disease. By discouraging through traffic it could also help to cut pollution levels and have an impact on levels of acute asthma episodes.

Local authority action

There is a key role for local authorities to play in environmental health promotion. Agenda 21 made a significant impact because those who signed up to it were required to inititiate immediate action to reduce carbon dioxide to 1990 levels and this involved measures to curtail motor vehicle emissions, the largest contributor. The Rio programme of action led to the establishment of a strong local Agenda 21 movement by local authorities in the UK who have been charged by government to develop new environmental initiatives. This has led to a systematic attempt to involve local people in defining the biggest threats to environmental health and in participating in the development of policies to bring about change. In Birmingham, for example, the environmental health and leisure services department has held a series of public consultative workshops on different environmental topics: energy saving, transport, urban conservation and so on. Representatives from a variety of business interests, local campaigns and pressure groups, such as Friends of the Earth, Transport 2000, the West Midlands Environmental Network, the Chamber of Commerce and Age Concern, have worked with officers to identify concerns and priorities.

This attempt to create an intersectoral consensus on environmental issues has been identified as a basic building block of success, but there are other barriers to overcome (Allen, 1992). Local government has a strong tradition of acting 'for the people' with some consultation but no real participation in decision making. It is often seen as remote and bureaucratic and there is difficulty in understanding how the system operates. Allen has argued that local authorities need to share power with local people since cutting pollution, saving energy and other environmental actions cannot be done unless public opinion is supportive. Change will also be difficult to achieve at a local level unless local authorities have enough autonomy to act for the public health. For example, much health, safety and environmental responsibility lies with the National Health and Safety Executive but staff cuts and pressures in the 1980s and early 1990s meant that the number of visits, inspections and prosecutions fell, while accident levels have risen. 'We have the wrong locus of power. It is central when it should be local' (Allen, 1992: 104).

Organisational action: 'greening' the National Health Service

Within organisations, action for environmental change is often difficult because it is bound up with ways of working which are hard to adapt. The Department of Health (1996) has responded to this by proposing that environment becomes a key area, arguing that this would focus attention on environmental improvements which would enhance 'well-being and quality of life.' The National Health Service, for example, is an enormous consumer of energy, spending over £225 million a year, and in 1991 the Department of Health set English health authorities a goal of a 25 per cent reduction in energy consumption over five years. The Audit Commission studied energy use in the NHS and suggested that inadequate energy management, monitoring and targeting and inappropriate technology were inhibiting progress, together with lack of investment and the incentive to change (Audit Commission, 1991). These recommendations were interesting because they identified that overcoming the barriers to change was not only about gathering the correct information, the right technology or the realistic targets but also about improving morale and providing incentives to change. The commitment of senior staff – the 'product champions' – was identified as critical.

One attempt to create product champions and incentives to change was the establishment of a 'Greening the NHS' project in 1994 with its own quarterly newsletter. The newsletter editorial board reflected a mini 'healthy alliance' between several trusts, health authorities and private companies. The focus was initially on energy, transport, land use and new building, waste disposal and resource consumption (Lowry, 1994; Hookham, 1995). 'Green' packaging, water management and air quality were introduced in later issues. It is unclear how far the project has been successful as no evaluation of its impact has been undertaken. It has gained the commitment of a number of prominent public health physicians and managers and is addressed mainly to purchasers of services, offering advice about strategies to reduce consumption and encourage 'good practice'.

Energy saving in transport services is one example of the type of intervention the newsletter suggested that managers can make (Lowry, 1994; Hookham, 1995). Ideas included providing shower facilties for staff who cycle, introducing driver training to help reduce fuel consumption, modernising vehicle fleets, reviewing the environmental policies of contractors when contracts are discussed, and encouraging car sharing. Some trusts have taken more radical measures, such as introducing cycle lease schemes, extending and subsidising bus access schemes and restricting staff living very near the hospital from using their cars (Jones, 1995b).

The Healthy Cities project

The Healthy Cities project, first established by the WHO in 1985, was seen as a 'test bed' for Health For All. In particular, it was thought that strategies for building supportive environments, combating health inequalities and developing healthy public policies could be created and evaluated at city level so that real change could take place (Tsouros, 1990). In an important sense it sought to combine many levels of action, to involve consumers, citizens, households, neighbourhoods and communities in creating supportive environments and healthier policies. Rather than experts applying scientific methods to effect change, the project tried to draw in lay people and experts to work together.

The project has been described as a 'post-modern' movement, which had its roots, not in the application of scientific rationality and a biological view of health, but in a 'post-modern aesthetic and moral view of health' which built on innovation and participation (Davies and Kelly, 1993). Central to the Healthy Cities project was the notion that 'health is created and lived by people in the settings of their everyday lives' (Tsouros, 1990). The project has demonstrated both the potential of a Health For All approach and the considerable limitations that exist in most cities for achieving these goals. In the first few years, Tsouros and Draper have commented, the project 'looked more promising as a concept than as a practical reality' (1993: 25).

One major issue which was not addressed initially was research and evaluation but the first five-year progress report attempted to measure change and explored the relative progress made by different cities. In particular, the review suggested that a range of factors influenced the degree of success that had been achieved (Tsouros and Draper, 1993). Among these were:

- structural features – political traditions, culture, size, strength and nature of the economy, level of community participation
- degree of political commitment – by politicians and through public awareness
- ability to innovate – more successful projects had developed new organisational strategies characterised by intersectoral action and decentralisation
- effective working methods – enabling different sectors to work together, plan, communicate and gain support
- functional project offices – to provide ideas, support, information and legitimacy
- support for community groups – strategies for developing community participation, giving financial help and technical advice
- effective political and managerial accountability of the projects.

The first of these factors may present the most important barrier to change. Many economic decisions which affect a city, such as the level of investment, are taken at national or international level. The political culture and degree of autonomy which exists in different countries will influence change. In Germany, for example, the tradition of political stability and consensus in local government and the relatively high degree of autonomy enjoyed by cities has enabled a steady pace of change.

In the UK, by contrast, many local authority functions are tightly controlled by national political priorities and allocations. Local authorities are not allowed to spend more than 20 per cent of the income from council rents on new building and this limits their housing policy response. Unlike their German counterparts they do not have control of transport policy for their areas; the strategic highway system and motorway building are determined at national level. As we noted earlier, although local authorities have considerable environmental health functions some key responsibilities for inspection rest with central government. If local authorities want to monitor air quality in a comprehensive way, for example, they have to undertake the work themselves because government monitoring is very patchy.

The Healthy Cities projects have not had a strong emphasis on environmental policy. They have been notable for their attempts to develop intersectoral collaboration between local authorities, health services, voluntary agencies and the private sector which has often been focused on particular programmes. Considerable activity took place in the early years of the UK projects on issues of health inequality and poverty and in community development. The national health strategies of the early 1990s encouraged the development of disease reduction strategies. However, in the mid-1990s cities like Liverpool and Sheffield responded to public concern about environmental issues. In both cities, for example, public opinion surveys revealed air pollution as a major concern for local people and both initiated work on transport policy. Concern about water quality and noise have also become more evident.

An environment action model

The Sundsvall Statement on supportive environments (WHO, 1992) presented a useful framework – the Supportive Environments Action Model (SESAME) – through which to develop the interventions needed to build supportive environments (Figure 10.1). It suggested, as had the analysis of healthy cities, that processes such as building alliances, mobilising resources, setting realistic targets, creating organisational structures and strategies that were flexible, monitoring and evaluating progress, were crucial. The assumption was that community and individual particpation were also critical. The messages were about trial and error and adaptation; for example, 'renew, reinforce and reorient' suggested that actions would be 'a dynamic and potentially never-ending process' (WHO, 1992 : 205).

The Sundsvall handbook lists a wide range of action projects. Story 87 concerns a Swedish community where skills and knowledge about gardening and food production was low and local diets were poor. In a 'learning-by-experience' approach local families were enabled to set up a demonstration garden, helped by experienced gardeners and nutritionists, which others living in the area could visit. A local gardening group and a heart association also formed part of the healthy alliance. The project was then adapted for use with school children.

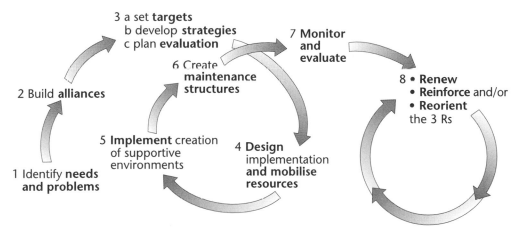

Figure 10.1 **The Supportive Environment Action Model**   (SESAME)

> **Choose an environmental problem from your health-promoting work and use SESAME to plan your response.**

We have discussed a number of environmental problems during the course of this chapter, for example air pollution, poor housing, traffic congestion and noise. Such problems are more likely to be encountered by some types of health promoters than others but most of us have probably encountered, directly or by proxy, the problem of living in a street made noisy and unpleasant by traffic. Following through the steps of the SESAME model we could:

- identify issues, needs, opportunities and problems – these would include an excess of traffic causing pollution and noise for people in the street. An obvious starting point would be to gather information about this and find out what powers the local authority has to effect change
- build alliances – contact local people, develop a shared agenda of concerns, work out a division of labour and roles so that everyone feels committed to action
- set targets, develop strategies and plan evaluation – a main target might be the introduction of traffic calming and to achieve this would require strategies to draw attention to the problem, to make it easier for the local council to take action and ensure that the outcomes can be evaluated
- design implementation and mobilise resources – this involves the concrete planning of action, for example planning direct action (sitting in the street to stop traffic, lobbying the local councillor, organising a petition, contacting the press and so on) and the building up of a budget to support such activities
- implement activities – experimenting to see what works; 'at some point you simply have to take the plunge' (WHO, 1992: 204)
- create maintenance structures – it may take a long time to convince the local council to take action; keeping the initiative going through skilling local people, extending involvement and media coverage is vital
- monitor and evaluate – this could apply to your own campaign for change as well as to the successful initiative
- renew, reinforce and reorient activities – adaptation is important if no change is forthcoming; review the chosen strategies and be flexible enough to change.

This discussion is based on a real incident where such a strategy was successful in obtaining traffic calming in a busy city street near a primary school. It suggests that environmental action does not have to be remote from local people or only initiated by government. It offers the prospect to health promoters of taking direct action on issues that are of concern to local people, a step that can promote the empowerment of local people (and of the health promoter).

10.7 Conclusion

The call to build supportive environments has become more prominent in the health promotion movement. At one level this requires action by international agencies and national governments to lay down a framework of guidance and regulation. To health promoters working at a local level it might seem that only through such a framework can environments be made more supportive and it is clear that effective regulation of air or water quality, waste disposal and environmental hazards are essential prerequisites for successful local work for health.

At the same time, local action is essential in identifying new problems, encouraging public participation and stimulating change. Health promoters have not usually seen environmental health as a major issue, except where it has been linked to disease reduction and lifestyle issues. The development of environmental health action plans for the UK and beyond has helped to change this focus, although there has been very little advice or support for health promoters in any of the national plans. The Healthy Cities projects offer useful, though limited, examples of environmental health action. Beyond this, health promoters need to review the potential for action in a flexible way, identifying and seizing opportunities as citizens, consumers and professionals. The rhetoric of supportive environments is loud and clear. What is still needed is much more evidence of how they can be created.

Part 3
Debates and dilemmas in promoting health

Introduction

This final part of the book focuses on a number of key debates and dilemmas about priorities, focus and legitimacy in health promotion practice. In doing so, it draws on and develops themes and issues that have been running through earlier parts, including concerns about equity, partnership, social justice and policy change. The contested nature of health promotion is evident both in the variety of perspectives represented in these chapters and in the critical approaches explored.

Chapters 11 and 12 each take one of the central values in contemporary health promotion – namely, equity and co-operation – and tease out what this means in practice and in a particular context. Chapter 11 addresses the topical issue of men's health. A comparison of male and female patterns of mortality, morbidity and lifestyles raises interesting questions for the planning of health promotion strategies. Graham Holroyd, Senior Lecturer in the Faculty of Health at the University of Central Lancashire, argues that there is a connection between men's lack of concern for their own health and relationships between men and women within the family and in the wider society as a whole. He explores ways of drawing men more fully into the whole project of health promotion.

In Chapter 12, Audrey Leathard, Professor in Interprofessional Studies at South Bank University, examines the concept of collaboration for health. Building on the discussion of 'healthy alliances' in Part 2 of this book, she traces the recent history of inter-agency collaboration. She looks in depth at a number of analytical models and teases out their usefulness for different aspects of practice. The chapter concludes that a realistic mix of collaboration and conflict offers a way forward.

Chapter 13 discusses fundamental questions about the nature and purpose of health promotion, maintaining that health promotion values and ethics are shaped by our vision of the kind of society we wish to see. Alan Cribb, Senior Lecturer in Ethics, King's College, London, distinguishes three main stances: 'health', 'welfare' and 'well-being' accounts of health promotion. The implications of each are explored both for work with individuals and for decisions relating to the provision of healthy public policy.

Developing further this more critical tone, Martin O'Brien, Lecturer in the Department of Environmental Studies at the University of Surrey, argues in Chapter 14 that health promotion is inescapably embroiled in the political projects of a diverse collection of social and institutional interests and that to promote health is to promote certain of these projects. He explores how two particular sociological critiques – surveillance and modernisation – illuminate these processes. The ever-extending scope of health screening and the development of 'risk consciousness' are scrutinised in relation to shifting power relationships.

In Chapter 15 Gareth Williams, Reader in Sociology of Health and Illness, and Jennie Popay, Professor of Community Health Studies, both at the University of Salford, also write about power and risk, although from a quite different standpoint. Their concern here is with the way population health research should develop to incorporate the societal, philosophical and health changes of the late twentieth century. In particular they argue for the importance of local and lay knowledge which allows research to engage with the realities of people's lives and acknowledges the role of politics in public health research.

The final chapter, which explores alternative futures, is written by a range of people engaged in health promotion at different levels. Jenny Douglas, a Lecturer in Health Education at the University of Birmingham, argues that health inequalities must be tackled as a major priority so that the targets proposed in Health For All and the Ottawa Charter can be reached. Sarah Nettleton, Lecturer in Social Policy at the University of York, also views poverty as the major challenge for health promotion. Two professionals working for Health Promotion Wales, Peter Farley, Director of Training and Education, and Chris Tudor-Smith, Director of Research and Development, call for a real shift from an illness to a wellness paradigm and a sound understanding of how globalisation, fragmentation and the information revolution can be harnessed in the drive for health improvement. Kathy Elliott, Director of the Health Education Authority for England argues that the future will require a greater focus on the impact of public policy and private sector decisions on health. At the same time critics of health promotion will continue to demand evidence of effectiveness. The book ends with the contribution of the Chief Medical Officer, Sir Kenneth Calman. He argues that health promoters will increasingly need to provide answers to research questions, to build research into practice and to evaluate health promotion rigorously. Using policy appraisal and audit can help to assess the health impact of policies, and collaborative working at all levels is central to this. Health alliances, he suggests, are essential to understand and reduce some of the variations in health between different populations.

Chapter 11
Men's health in perspective

11.1 Introduction

Men's health as a distinct area has been the focus of increasing interest during recent years. The importance of addressing men's health was raised by the Chief Medical Officer's report *The State of the Public Health 1992* (DoH, 1993a). 1995 saw the launch of two magazines dedicated to men and health, the first national conference in Britain on men's health, and a 'Men and Health' module included in at least one health studies undergraduate degree programme. There is now a Men's Health Helpline (Bradford, 1995). Health care workers and the general public are showing more interest in men's health, but why this explosion of concern *now*?

The origins of the current interest in men's health may be traced back to the 1960s, the decade in which the socio-cultural model of health was becoming increasingly important in helping people gain an understanding of health and illness. By the 1970s gender had joined other widely accepted variables such as race and ethnicity, socio-economic status, and geographical area to be considered when explaining health. At the same time there was also a growth in feminist research and the women's movement, both contributing directly to the growth of the women's health movement (Sabo and Gordon, 1995). Significantly, though, researchers and academics equated studies of gender and health almost exclusively with women and health. Only a minority were linking notions of masculinity and the male role with both physical and mental health issues (Farrell, 1974; Fasteau, 1974). The growth of interest in men's studies in the 1980s (Brod, 1987; Kimmel and Messner, 1993) has now brought into greater prominence questions about the relationship between concepts of health, masculinity, men's lives and their experience of illness. Before looking in more depth at these relationships, it may help to compare male and female patterns of mortality and morbidity.

11.2 The health career of men

In western industrialised societies today, men have a different health career to that of women. Men generally have a lower life expectancy than women (Nicholson, 1993): in Great Britain, women, on average, live to 78 years, men to 72 (DoH, 1993a). In every age group from birth to old age, male mortality rates are significantly higher than those for females

(Whitehead, 1988). In 1950, for example, women could expect to live five years longer than men; by 1981, however, women could expect to live 6.4 years longer (Whitehead, 1988). This difference in mortality rates can be observed across all contemporary industrialised societies (Renzetti and Curran, 1995; Moon and Gillespie, 1995). But now there are signs that the pattern is changing: the life expectancy of both men and women is rising and men's is rising faster than women's, so the gap between the two is closing.

Some 70 per cent of all male deaths in England in 1992 were caused by circulatory diseases and cancers and 13.1 per cent by suicides, injury and poisoning. By comparison, cancer accounted for 50 per cent of female mortality, circulatory diseases 24 per cent and suicides 6.8 per cent (DoH, 1993a). Men as a group are prone to heart disease, cancers and drug misuse, though the extent to which the first two of these are linked to lifestyle choices is an important question. Men's greater susceptibility to cardiovascular and respiratory diseases, some forms of cancer, and cirrhosis of the liver may be closely linked to the fact that men smoke and drink more than women do (Sarafino, 1990).

Over the past 15 years, suicide rates in the UK, whilst declining in women, have risen steadily in men. There are many possible explanations for this phenomenon: the threat of unemployment, the greater independence of women, the reluctance of men to seek help, and men's often inadequate social networks (Charlton et al., 1992).

There are also certain gender-specific male illnesses, for example testicular and prostate disease, that need to be considered. Testicular cancer is amongst the most common cancer in men aged 15–34 years, accounting for approximately 12 per cent of all cancer deaths in this age group. There are some 500 new cases of testicular cancer in the UK each year (Blandy, 1989) and testicular cancer is on the increase (Griffiths, 1992). Prostate cancer has doubled in the last 30 years, is presently the second biggest cancer killer in men, and accounts for four times as many deaths as cervical cancer (Sadler, 1992). Of the 8,000 new cases diagnosed in the United States each year, only one-third of men are alive five years later. Late diagnosis is apparent in up to 70 per cent of all newly diagnosed cases (Hamand, 1991). Men are dangerously ignorant about the growing menace of both prostate and testicular cancer, and in a recent study 84 per cent of men admitted knowing little or nothing about these two conditions (Gorman, 1995). In a different study 37 per cent of men could not indicate where the prostate gland is to be found in their body, or what function it performs (Jarvis, 1995).

Examining male lifestyles may give us some indication of the most appropriate ways of working with men on health-related issues. Men generally are much more likely than women to indulge in health-damaging or risk-taking behaviour, such as high alcohol consumption. In particular, young to middle-aged, separated, divorced, or widowed men are much more likely to engage in risky sexual activity, smoke more, and drink alcohol in excess, than other men (Wellings, 1993; DoH, 1993b).

11.3   Questions of lifestyle

Lifestyle is a popular, if somewhat nebulous concept. It may be described as a set of behaviours, undertaken by an individual or a group of people, which has a notable outcome. Similarly, lifestyles have been defined as patterns of behavioural choices made from the alternatives that are available to people according to their socio-economic circumstances, and to the ease with which they are able to choose certain ones over others. An individual's lifestyle is made up of the reactions and behaviour patterns that are learned through social interactions with parents, peers, siblings, or through the influence of schools, the mass media etc. (Mischel, 1968). The term 'lifestyle' is often only used to mean *voluntary* choices people make regarding alcohol consumption, their dietary intake and how they spend their leisure time. There is overwhelming evidence, however, of the need to acknowledge the importance of the economic and cultural dimensions that have a bearing on a person's lifestyle and over which the individual has little control (Blaxter, 1990; Renzetti and Curran, 1995).

Learned gender roles are one important area affecting lifestyle choices. But these need to be understood in the context of socio-economic differences, both within the male population and between men and women. Both men and women in the manual skilled and un-skilled socio-economic groups have a poorer health status and lower expectation of life than those in professional groups (McKie, 1994). Not only does health status alter with social class, but so too does health behaviour. Individuals with a lower socio-economic status tend to smoke more and participate less in exercise and any physical activity. In 1984, 36 per cent of men in employment were smokers, compared to 61 per cent of unemployed men. Men consume more alcohol than women do (Blaxter, 1990). For all ages, male alcohol consumption is approximately double that of women. Alcohol consumption also varies between social classes, with those from manual groups drinking more heavily than non-manual workers. Townsend *et al.* (1988) show that 26 per cent of unskilled manual working men were categorised as heavy drinkers, whereas only 8 per cent of professional men were found in the same category. Alcohol consumption by semi-skilled manual male workers increased by 30 per cent between 1987 and 1989, whilst consumption by all other male socio-economic groups fell (McKie, 1994) and, not surprisingly, unemployed men are more likely to drink than those in employment (Blaxter, 1990).

Diet is a significant factor in determining health status (Blaxter, 1990). Despite major health promotion campaigns demonstrating the link between inappropriate diet and most of the major diseases, for example cancers and heart disease, it is women who are making the most effort to change their diets. The Oxford Regional Health Authority Lifestyle Survey of 13,000 randomly selected adults living in Berkshire, Buckinghamshire and Northamptonshire provides helpful data relating to exercise, smoking, alcohol consumption and dietary habits (Roberts, 1992). More female than male respondents described their health status as poor, although they reported fewer examples of health-damaging behaviour.

The survey also indicated that women had healthier diets, and smoked and drank less than the men surveyed. Women were more likely than men to associate diet with health. For example, 65 per cent of women, compared with 53 per cent of men, agreed with the statement that the type of food that one consumes has an important effect on health. Women in the family are overwhelmingly responsible for food purchases and sometimes prepare different food for their husbands (Roberts, 1992). Red meat, for example, is considered to be masculine food, and is consumed more frequently by males than females. Diet and nutrition are influenced by economic status as well as by gender, with the highest income groups tending to have the healthier diets (Townsend *et al.*, 1988). In all age and gender groups, good dietary habits are influenced by income, but so-called healthy balanced diets are more common among women than men (Blaxter, 1990; Office for National Statistics/HEA, 1996).

11.4   What does it mean to be male?

Masculinity is determined by physical, psychological and emotional development interacting with societal and cultural expectations (Meth and Pasick, 1990). Unlike sex-roles, which are biologically determined and understood in terms of anatomy, physiology and hormones, gender roles are constructed through psychological, cultural and social means (Lorber and Farrell, 1991). From birth, as soon as biological sex is determined, a gender identity begins to take shape (Lloyd and Duvean, 1992) and expectations designed to outline appropriate behaviour for each sex begin to be expressed. Gender identity includes psycho-sexual development, learning social roles, and shaping sexual preferences. Social rearing, or socialisation, is a crucial element for gender identity (Gagnon and Henderson, 1985). Pressure to conform to prescribed roles comes first from the family and is later re-enforced by peers, school, work and society as a whole. A fear of what is regarded as femininity, feminine values and feminine traits is said to be a common result of male socialisation and may lead to self-destructive behaviour (Farrell, 1974). From the cradle, boys are generally expected to be competitive, autonomous, independent and to suppress their emotions (O'Neil, 1981). Social and economic status, race and ethnicity are all factors which affect the intensity of the messages from parents, and, for example, working-class fathers tend to be more insistent than middle-class fathers that their sons should adhere to sex-stereotyped roles (Chodorow, 1978).

It is widely agreed that men in contemporary western societies find it difficult to express their emotions adequately. This emotional illiteracy, or failure to express emotions, in addition to the urge to be independent, could significantly influence men's health-related behaviour and ultimately their health status. I would therefore suggest that men become good at 'non-speak' with regard to important emotional issues, and that it is a positive attribute to be emotionally invulnerable. Part of men's resistance to acknowledging illness may be due to a fear of the dependence on women as carers. Contradicting the received wisdom that women are dependent on men, Millet (1969) argues that it is women who are brought up to provide for the dependency needs of children, husbands and so on. Eichenbaum and Orbach (1984) contrast the myth of men's independence with their actual reliance on women:

> Boys can live with the expectation of continued maternal nurturance, first from mother and later from wife. At the same time as men acquire power in the outside world – by being born male in a patriarchal culture – they continue to be looked after (as children are) at home.
>
> (Eichenbaum and Orbach, 1984)

Married males have lower death rates than those who have never married, and married men report better health than do single men. This may be due to the presence or absence of a significant female carer encouraging her male partner to seek help when needed and setting the tone for a healthy life (Miles, 1991). The idea that failing health signifies vulnerability may explain why some men will not admit to illness until it is too late. Men's denial of illness is so strong, argues Goldberg (1976), that it is one reason their average life span is considerably shorter than women's. Even pain as strong as a heart attack has been ignored, so that the victim would not be seen as weak or effeminate (Solomon, 1981).

Being in employment will obviously affect health status. This is true for both women and men, though it may be that factors associated with paid employment and roles within the sphere of work, the public arena, are of special importance to men because of their socialisation to place a high value on success in work (Thompson and Pleck, 1988). An increasing volume of research has drawn attention to the numerous physical and emotional health problems, such as depression, irritability and insomnia, that can be attributed to loss of work (Fryer and Payne, 1986; Banks and Ullah, 1988). Over and above the direct effects of loss of income, unemployment in men can reduce self-esteem, autonomy, identity, self-confidence and may produce an inability to cope with everyday problems (Berryman, 1984).

During adolescence, boys tend to put their health at risk by indulging in dangerous behaviour in keeping with their supposed machismo image. Boys have a higher rate of injury than girls from sports-related activities. Deaths from car accidents is proportionately higher amongst young adult males than in other groups of people (Sarafino, 1990) and motor vehicle accidents are a leading cause of death for young males aged between 14–24 years (Freud and Meredith, 1991). Over two-thirds of victims of violent crimes are male, of whom 43 per cent are assaulted on the street or in pubs (DoH, 1993b). It can be argued that men's life expectancy is shortened because of self-destructive tendencies developed at an early age. Men respond differently to stress and change than do women. This is partly reflected in recent suicide trends. Suicide rates for males, both during adolescence and adulthood, are higher than those of females which are steadily decreasing (Charlton, 1993). There is a worrying increase in suicide rates amongst young men (DoH, 1993b). This may be a reflection of men's unwillingness to solicit help when it is needed (Meth and Pasick, 1990).

11.5   Health promotion services for men

Historically, men were lucky to get even their blood pressure measured when they visited their GP. Generally speaking, men make little use of primary care services and Well Men Centres, where they exist, are limited in their success (Trevelyan, 1989). First envisaged as providing for all problems associated with men's health (Moffat, 1980), in practice they focus in the main on screening for specific illnesses such as heart disease, hypertension management, diabetes, alcohol and smoking-related advice, measuring performance, and offering advice on family planning.

Well Women Centres have existed in the UK since the beginning of the 1970s. Thornley (1987) suggests that Well Women Centres grew as a result of the women's health movement and criticism of the type, quality and choice of health care that was available to women. Initially, Well Women Centres concentrated on screening services for breast and cervical cancer, rather than the 'whole woman' (Deans, 1988). Well Women Centres developed in tandem with the Women's Movement in the 1960s, which questioned traditional power structures in society, and ultimately, services provided for and available to women. The women's health movement argued that an exploration of gender roles, sexual harassment, imbalances in power and violence were as important to women's health and well-being as was advice on breast examination, diet or exercise (Ashley, 1986). The women's health-care movement, at grass-roots community level at least, relies very much on the principles of self-help and the concept of responsiveness to need.

In contrast, a men's health movement does not at present exist and the approach to health promotion for men has been somewhat sporadic (Fareed, 1994). Some attempt has been made at a settings approach (Kickbusch, 1989). For example, the advertising of safer-sex messages at football grounds and leisure centres is advocated (Jackson, 1993). A workplace initiative that involved a mobile health promotion unit being placed at a factory for a short while is also another example of targeting men collectively (Jackson, 1993). Accessible health information in the workplace is a valuable part of the role of occupational health, and preventive advice in this setting is likely to be listened to (Cox *et al.*, 1995). Such approaches recognise the lack in effectiveness for traditional health services for men, and take health messages to arenas where men congregate and socialise.

In *The Health of the Nation* (DoH, 1992) there is a suggestion that women should take more responsibility for men's health, though it might well be argued that this simply perpetuates gender stereotypes and increases the guilt that women may already feel within families. Men's health as a distinct area is not considered a priority for Directors of Public Health (Royal College of Nursing, 1995). Indeed, when Directors of Public Health were prompted with a list of discrete groups of people to be targeted, men, as a distinct group, failed to be described as critical importance for specific work (Royal College of Nursing, 1995). Most of the risk factors associated with men's health are preventable (DoH, 1993a). Bruckenwall (1995) suggests that men should take a more positive and proactive approach to their own health care, but there remains the question of how this can be achieved.

Men generally use health care services far less than women do, both in terms of frequency and absolute totals (HMSO, 1991). Men make fewer visits to their GPs and often delay seeking help when they are ill (Perelberg and Miller, 1990; DoH, 1993a). Why is this, when men are more susceptible to fatal infections and diseases (Nicholson, 1993)? One answer may be that illness and health are interpreted differently by men and women, identical states might have typically masculine and feminine interpretations (Perelberg and Miller, 1990; Roberts, 1992). The issue of how to motivate men to take an interest in their health is a difficult one. Getting men to turn up for health checks, men's reluctance to talk about their health, the lack of availability of men during the day to attend clinics, all contribute to this problem (Royal College of Nursing, 1995).

How far are men actively interested in protecting and promoting their own health? A qualitative study of men between the ages of 16–75 (HEA, 1995c) indicated that concern about health tends to be simply a reaction to an experience of ill-health:

> When you are in your teens and 20s you think you'll live for ever. It's only when you get ill unexpectedly or someone in your family gets something serious that you get pulled up short and realise you *are* at risk.
>
> (HEA, 1995c: 1)

Few men under the age of 59 take steps to monitor their health and the general view is that only hypochondriacs would check their own bodies or attend a clinic for a check up if there was no particular reason for doing so.

Men do not perceive women to be any more seriously interested in health issues than they are in their early years, and their concern about weight and diet tends to be regarded as simply to do with appearance: 'The shops are full of magazines about women's health, but it's really all slimming isn't it. Diet and skincare. That's not about health. It's about vanity.' (HEA, 1995c: 2). The fact that women are drawn into the health service from an early age for regular check-ups to do with contraception, pregnancy and so on and are therefore regularly monitored is seen by men to have both advantages and disadvantages. As one younger man put it:

> I'd hate to be a woman because they have so much that can go wrong, but it does mean they're in touch with their doctor... They have their blood pressure checked and their breasts checked and all the scrapes and smears and all that. It must be horrible for them, but at least they know when they're not healthy. No one ever checks us.
>
> (HEA, 1995c: 2)

11.6   Strategies for health promoters

So what is the future for men's health and, in particular, what are the most appropriate approaches to work with men's health? A starting place for health promoters in their own work could be to try to make men's health issues more visible.

What are the most appropriate ways in which you might make issues to do with men's health more prominent in your professional and personal capacity?

You might begin by considering existing initiatives to improve men's health. One of the first initiatives was in the Castlemilk area of Glasgow. The setting up of a Well Man Clinic was initiated by two male health visitors. The emphasis was on basic health education, information giving, and primary prevention. Other examples of this type of service exist, staffed by health care workers, and offering an essentially bio-medical approach. Brent Health Authority set up a Well Man Clinic in 1985, offering men family planning and health screening services. The aim of this service was to encourage men to take responsibility for contraception and to think about their own health needs (Pownall, 1985). The service was staffed entirely by men as it was thought men might find it more acceptable to speak to male health workers than women (Lamond, 1985). There is some evidence that male patients show a preference for a same-sex physician, especially when consulting for a sexual or otherwise 'embarrassing' condition (Ackerman-Ross and Sochat, 1980; Kelly, 1980). But more recent qualitative research into awareness of men's cancers (HEA, 1995c) has indicated that most young men are happier with the thought of being examined by a woman than a man. Some dreaded the thought of their male GP handling their testicles and penis, and possibly conducting a rectal investigation. One young man summed up this feeling: 'Some man looking around there doesn't appeal to me at all. The idea of a man doctor... I think a female nurse would be better.' (HEA, 1995c: 9).

Other suggestions of what men would find helpful in relation to preventing men's cancers include: more Well Man Clinics, more emphasis in the workplace on raising awareness of men's cancers, special late-night or weekend appointments so time isn't taken from work, greater provision of leaflets on men's cancers and more incentives to GPs to provide screening facilities (HEA, 1995c: 11).

Another possibility is to encourage men to visit and use local health projects. Throughout the UK there are examples of locally-based health projects, where men are encouraged to seek help with their physical, mental and emotional problems in a user-friendly setting. Perhaps more examples of these community-based approaches are needed, focusing on specific groups of men. For example, gay or bisexual men's health, such as the MESMAC Project mentioned in Chapter 5. One of the initiatives of the Health Education Authority's HIV/AIDs and sexual health programme, the MESMAC Project is an HIV prevention project which works within a community development framework, involving men in both formal and informal networks.

11.7 Conclusion

There is still much work to be done to make men's health issues more 'visible'. The most pressing health issue for gay men is HIV/AIDS (Hart *et al.*, 1990, 1993). Other areas of work may include the health of men in mid-life. This period may be one of contentment and consolidation, but equally it could be a time of crisis. Mid-life can bring with it loss of various kinds. Loss of parents, partners and also children leaving home; it may even mean loss of a job or what was considered a life-long role. There is also generally a recognition by men of a decline in energy and physical fitness (Kruger, 1994; Stansfield *et al.*, 1991). Men's mental well-being could also offer some possibilities of areas of work and initiatives around the effects of unemployment and poverty on men may also prove useful (Benzeval *et al.*, 1995).

Awareness of the health needs of men from different ethnic back-grounds and of their differing cultural expectations and concerns is another dimension to consider. This is particularly pertinent in inner city areas, where, generally speaking, housing is poorest, unemployment highest and the population has disproportionately higher numbers of men from ethnic minority backgrounds (Smaje, 1995; Rudat, 1994).

Work needs to be fostered and developed in these areas, not just around the health needs of the dominant group within society: white, middle-aged, middle-class, heterosexual men. One of the main problems facing people working in the field of health, is that demands to orientate health education towards specific groups, for example men, is increasingly having to compete with arguments in favour of focusing on topics or targets. But perhaps both group- and topic-oriented needs can be addressed in an integrated way, through the settings approach (Kickbusch, 1989b; Tannahill, 1994). More innovative approaches to address the health needs of men may be the most appropriate way forward. There is a wealth of knowledge and experience within communities, and the success and failures of the community health movement are well documented (Watt and Rodmell, 1988; Community Projects Foundation, 1988). These innovative approaches could take the form of being community based. They should be socially and culturally specific, designed for and by the men themselves, in partnership with health care workers. Examples of these do exist, and more initiatives at local level are developing, such as the Glasgow Drumchapel Men's Health Project, and Signpost Multi Agency Resource Centre – Men's Health Initiative, based in Morecambe. Community Health UK, based in Bath, is also facilitating the growth of local men's health initiatives, such as the Men's Health Awareness Project (Community Health UK, 1995), which examines the current crisis in men's health from a lay perspective.

Such initiatives have demonstrated that health alliances, working collaboratively across professional boundaries and encouraging lay voices to be heard, are an effective way of working (DoH, 1993c). Working with and through men in local settings is a positive way forward. Men's unwillingness to consider their health needs has been attributed to fear, ignorance, complacency and machismo. The danger is to ignore men's health needs; the challenge is to acknowledge them and give them a higher priority.

Chapter 12
Collaboration: united we stand, divided we fall?

12.1 Introduction

Collaborative working between professions, agencies and sectors became significant not only in health promotion but throughout the health and community care services in Britain in the 1990s. In this chapter we ask what a united stand might mean and whether divisions between professions, agencies and individuals imply the failure of collaborative policies?

To tease out some answers the following route will be taken so that the territory can be clarified. Some key words need closer inspection; then the policy context of collaboration will be outlined; followed by three key arenas of collaboration at work and their outcomes. Models will be used to show a range of options in collaborative working within health and social care provision. Three major issues overall have been selected for further review: interprofessional education, the place of users, and tension between personal care and teamwork.

12.2 The meaning of 'collaboration'

The Oxford English dictionary defines collaboration as 'co-operating treacherously with the enemy; working in combination with; moving from the former towards the latter'. The danger implied within the definition captures the essence of risk involved for professionals and individuals who may perceive that collaborative working threatens their identity and professional territory. The second element in the definition shows a way forward: the potential of inter-professional action (Shaw, 1994).

Inter-professional, inter-agency approaches are riddled with different meanings, interpretations and traditions. The wide range of health and welfare professionals involved speak different languages which influence their thinking and identity (Pietroni, 1992). For simplification, the arena of collaboration can be divided into three main categories:

- concept-based (e.g. multi-professional, holistic, generic)
- agency-based (e.g. inter-sectoral, consortium, healthy alliances)
- process-based (e.g. partnership, co-ordination, integration, teamwork, collaboration, joint planning).

(Leathard, 1994)

Whether in education or in practice, the numerous terms involved are basically concerned with learning together and working together.

Why collaborate?

What is it that predisposes agencies to work together? Hudson (1987) lists five factors: similar values and cultures; agreement on roles and responsibilities; network awareness; all parties gaining from working together; and an absence of alternative resources. Where trust is at a low ebb between agencies, collaborative endeavours should be modest, low risk and easy to achieve. Positive ways forward have repeatedly emphasised the need for clearly stated and agreed principles and objectives for joint working; the sharing of information between agencies; the need to publicise good practice examples of working together; and for staff to share in the decision making (Haggard and Ormiston, 1993; West and Anderson, 1994).

How can inter-professional relationships be effectively undertaken? Haggard and Ormiston (1993) suggest that staff need regular mechanisms to see ways of resolving problems and to develop respect for one another – a view shared by Smith *et al.* (1993) from extensive research into community care projects involved in working together. Smith *et al.* also go on to recommend the use of financial resources to create incentives for joint working as well as to engage facilitators.

This leads us on to consider the main disadvantages of collaborative working. These have been widely documented to include: the costs of time-consuming administration and communication; the professional concerns over differing leadership styles, language, values, training, status, pay and tribal instincts over professional boundaries and identity (Marshall *et al.*, 1979; Leathard; 1994; Ovretveit, 1990); and the personal anxieties expressed through coping defence mechanisms (Woodhouse and Pengelly, 1991). McGrath (1991) has outlined further drawbacks to include dual loyalty and dual accountability situations, and ineffective teamwork due to professional conflict and role confusion.

There are many positive aspects of collaboration at work. Most commentators, from studies and observations, would include the more efficient use of staff resources, the more effective provision of services, the more satisfying work environment, and the greater possibility of professional and lay people being able to achieve their objectives more fully and economically (McGrath, 1991; Pritchards, 1992). The balance, arguably, would appear to lie in favour of collaboration (Leathard, 1994).

Of particular relevance to health promotion is the assessment of strengths and weaknesses in the work undertaken with community mental handicap teams in Wales. McGrath (1991) describes the achievements of the teams in their collaborative work with the voluntary sector, with private sector links and liaison with para-professionals. Interaction between structural, process and individual factors similarly reflects organisational and operational approaches in health promotion.

12.3 The policy context of collaboration in health and community care

Before the 1990s there were several attempts at collaboration, including hospital surgical teams (Marshall *et al.*, 1979) and primary health care teams, of general practitioners, nurses and sometimes health visitors or social workers, (Pietroni, 1994). Joint planning and joint consultative committees had also been set up, to try to overcome the pre-war legacy of a deep administrative divide between local government, responsible for care in the community, and the NHS, responsible for health care provision across the country. The record on joint planning was generally regarded as disappointing (Lewis, 1993).

Three major developments placed collaborative working on a new footing: the 1989 Children Act, the 1990 National Health Service and Community Care Act and the 1992 Health of the Nation (DoH, 1992) policy on health alliances. We will now briefly review these three areas before looking in more detail at collaborative working in health promotion and health and community care.

The 1989 Children Act

The lack of co-ordination amongst groups involved in child protection (such as doctors, health visitors, nurses, social workers, the police, the courts, school welfare officers, teachers, parents and relatives, amongst others) had been reflected, over the previous 20 years, in a series of reports and investigations which culminated in the major *Report of the Inquiry into Child Abuse in Cleveland* (Butler Sloss, 1988) and led directly to the Children Act of 1989. The immediate impact on collaboration was reflected in the subsequent Department of Health policy guidance in which a high priority was given, as its title indicates, to *Working Together: A Guide to Arrangements for Inter-Agency Co-operation for the Protection of Children from Abuse* (DoH, 1991). Nevertheless it has proved difficult to establish effective collaborative practice across administrative divisions between the police, NHS professionals, local authority social workers and local schools, partly because of the fundamentally differing perspectives, training, traditions and values held by those involved in child protection.

Considerable progress was made through the DoH (1991) guidelines, but the 1995 West case – concerning both sexual abuse and serial killing – highlighted that there was still a long way to go. 'Once again it was as though the agencies were operating in separate, hermetically sealed compartments' (*Guardian*, 1995).

The 1990 National Health Service and Community Care Act

The NHS and community care reforms under the 1990 legislation made a most significant impact on collaborative development. Their central feature was the purchaser/provider split through which health and social care managers would assess the needs of their population and purchase contracted services from the providers to meet those needs. Managed care through an internal market was intended to curb costs through assessing budgeted need in contrast to the previous system largely based on a demand-led process. Hospitals and community health units who satisfied specified management criteria could apply for self-governing status independent of health authority control to become the 'providers' of health care. By 1995, nearly all units had achieved trust status but NHS providers then found themselves having to compete with the independent hospitals for contracts.

In one sense, therefore, competition has been the focus but the reforms have also produced new types of collaboration as Section 12.4 demonstrates.

The 1992 Health of the Nation policy on health alliances

The aim of the Health of the Nation policy (DoH, 1992) was to secure a significant improvement in the nation's health. Five priority areas were targeted as noted in Chapter 8. In seeking to develop preventive health strategies, the government emphasised inter-sectoral initiatives through 'healthy alliances'.

Collaborative arrangements were envisaged on two levels. A Ministerial Cabinet Committee, drawn from eleven government departments, was established to oversee health strategies. At a more local level, a range of organisations and agencies was expected to take part in healthy alliances: for example the NHS, the HEA, local authorities, voluntary organisations, the media, schools, cities, the working environment and homes.

By 1993 the Department of Health was promoting a positive view of *Working Together for Better Health* (Secretary of State for Health 1993) in order to meet the 'challenging' targets set by the Health of the Nation programme. Healthy alliances were seen by the government as a vehicle to secure more effective use of resources, to broaden responsibility for health, to break down barriers between partners in the alliance, to promote better knowledge and understanding of partners, to improve the exchange of information, to generate networks and the opportunity to develop accessible seamless services. Section 12.5 assesses some outcomes of healthy alliances by the mid-1990s.

Why do you think inter-professional, inter-agency work came into the foreground of British policy in the 1990s?

Structural changes spurred on competition but also provided incentives for collaboration in the form of mergers between trusts, alliances between GP fund holders, and the emergence of combined FHSA/health authority boards. Within health promotion the national health strategies put a new emphasis on health alliances and this linked to existing inter-agency initiatives.

12.4 Collaboration in the health and care sector

Since the 1990 NHS and Community Care Act a variety of collaborative initiatives have been developed:

- *District Health Authorities* (DHAs) (concerned with purchasing hospital and community health services) started to work together informally which escalated to 'merger mania', as Harrison's (1992) continuum of purchasing shows: the move has been, in general, from individual DHAs purchasing to informal joint purchasing to formal joint purchasing to consortia or agencies to DHA mergers.

- *City Health Conglomerations*, which merge health authorities across a major city – as in Birmingham – have produced single city amalgamations to cover some 200,000 people (Millar, 1995).

- *Family Health Service Authorities* (responsible for services provided by GPs, pharmacists, dentists and opticians) and District Health Authorities started to collaborate informally, but warily. Integrated purchasing began to emerge on the NHS agenda (Ham and Shapiro, 1995) when the government stepped in to speed up the process which required integration by 1996.

- *GP fund holders*. By 1995, 40 per cent of GPs had joined the fund-holding scheme which gave them limited powers to purchase certain services direct from hospitals (Moore 1994/5). Within the framework of fund holding more ambitious patterns of collaboration are now emerging. New types of fund holding have enabled single-handed practitioners to co-operate, as in multi and total fund holding. Consortium practices and district health authorities have linked together, as in Berkshire (Smith, 1994) and in West Yorkshire (Hunter and O'Toole, 1995).

It has been suggested that GPs might be put in charge of all health care purchasing which would leave health authorities a diminished and difficult supervisory role (Moore, 1994/5). While rationalisation has secured collaborative purchasing outcomes, so contracts are a crucial mechanism through which purchasers influence providers of health care. Most attention has been given to the commissioning and contracting process in acute hospital services. However, the somewhat neglected element of the specification and implementation of community health services has more recently been shown to militate against provider competition. Community health services have been found to be intrinsically problematical in an internal or 'quasi' market. It has been argued that community health services have more in common with networks than markets and require collaborative rather than adversarial relationships between purchasers and providers (Flynn *et al.*, 1995).

Collaboration between the NHS and Community Care Services

A second major disjunction remains within the delivery system of the health and welfare services, namely the continuing administrative gulf between a National Health Service and local authority community care services. Without co-operation between hospitals and community health trusts, a seamless service remains impossible and the emphasis remains on competition for contracts rather than on working for collaborative care (Paton, 1995b).

Hospital discharge tests inter-agency and inter-professional arrangements at their most vulnerable point. Hospital discharge, managed by no one group in particular, remains a negotiated area determined by perceived resource availability. However, long-term care has traditionally been vested in the NHS, either in the acute sector or in the community health services.

Amidst the mounting costs of long-term care, the NHS executives produced revised guidelines on continuing care of elderly people, but this failed to clarify at a national level where health care ends and social care begins (DoH, 1995a). The guidance proposed that individual health authorities, together with care providers and local authorities, should decide who is eligible for NHS-funded long-term care. It exhorted health and social services to work collaboratively to devise agreements and local eligibility criteria for continuing care but critics commented that it would not prevent those agencies 'pulling in opposite directions when it comes to the question of what is best for elderly patients and who should pick up the tab for their care' (Cervi, 1995). This debate has put the spotlight on the inter-agency divisions between health and community care services.

As a result at an interprofessional level, it has not been easy for GPs and social workers to work together effectively to assess the social care needs in their locality. General practice and social work differ in philosophy, training, agenda, language and ways of working. The potential for misunderstanding is accentuated by differences in status, professional autonomy and organisational arrangements (Hudson, 1994). However, surveys are beginning to show that in some areas GPs are working quietly and gradually with social services to 'bridge the cultural gap' (e.g. Elkind, 1995). In Kent the Medway Project was funded and co-ordinated by the Department of Health working together with the local health and social services managers, to form an inter-agency working group. This 'Core Group' has become involved with training needs and joint care management and, as an inter-agency development, has effectively harnessed 'power' which includes power based on status, knowledge, connections and time. The structure was strengthened by a clear definition of task, responsibilities and communication systems (Carpenter, 1995). Overlapping health and social services imply that professionals can share their skills. Such an inter-professional approach can only be achieved when morale is high and different professions do not feel threatened by others (Wilson and Dockrell, 1995).

12.5 Health alliances and their collaborative outcomes

The government's *Health of the Nation* white paper on a *Strategy for Health* highlighted the importance of healthy alliances which were described as 'active partnerships between the many organisations and individuals who can come together to help improve health' (DoH, 1992). Early on, one leading health education commentator foresaw that the key issue was the likelihood that multi-disciplinary collaboration within healthy alliances would bump into the social divisions in the British health and welfare planning system and the fragmented nature of services (Beattie, 1994). This led him to question whether healthy alliances might not become dangerous liaisons. He also noted a serious shortage of research on the new alliances for health. Some of this research has now been undertaken and the assessed outcomes suggest a far more fundamental problem: whether healthy alliances can ever be meaningfully evaluated.

In one sense the progress towards health targets might indicate that healthy alliances are having some effect. There have been some imaginative responses such as the collaboration between the NHS, city council and health promotion services in Oxford (Allen, 1992). But as the former health promotion liaison officer at Oxford City Council has pointed out, the Health of the Nation targets do not address key issues which also have an immense bearing on health, such as poverty, racism, sexism and class inequalities (Root, 1995).

Where the healthy alliances approach extends to the media, outcomes become even more problematic. As Tones and Tilford (1994) have shown, mass media campaigns do not easily change people's behaviour unless an individual is already motivated. Specific targets are much more easily assessed, but even the present known outcomes of national average targets do not tell us how far multi-disiplinary collaboration has contributed towards positive outcomes or impeded them.

The Department of Health and the NHS as a whole have taken a lead role in nurturing and sustaining the alliances at all levels to underline their importance. The Department of Health's (1995c) *Variations in Health* establishes that the differentials in mortality and morbidity rates between socio-economic groups continue. It accepts that variations in health may prove a barrier to the achievement of the *Health of the Nation* targets and that alliances and collaboration could help redress variations.

Specific, committed, community involvement programmes have shown positive outcomes across the country. In London, for example, the Camden and Islington family health services authority works together with the Camden health and race group in order to involve the views of their local black and minority ethnic groups in commissioning and in setting their own agenda (Pratten and Choudbury, 1995). A small, rural district near Rugby has developed an effective health promotion approach through healthy alliances with GPs, schools and even the local prison (Dix, 1995). But the problem of assessing healthy outcomes, based on health alliances and targeted programmes remains considerable, particularly in relation to poverty.

12.6 Interprofessional collaboration models in health and social care

Having looked at some issues in collaboration, the models that follow set out possible options for collaborative practice. The examples given so far have shown that working together has taken place and continues to do so but that this is by no means straightforward. The models presented therefore offer options for the future. Some models provide theoretical possibilities, and others are based on researched studies. So far these perspectives have not been gathered together before – which means the debate is wide open for new ideas, the realigning of old ones and for encouraging participants to construct their own models. A selection of models focusing on interprofessional working is presented first, followed by those models which are more related to inter-agency working.

Two distinct versions of inter-professional practice have been identified: the additive and the multiplicitive approach. (Rawson, 1994). The Additive Effects version proposes that each profession adds its own particular contribution. The practice field is defined by the added sum (2 + 2 + 2 + 2 = 8) of its professional parts. No one group controls the area overall. The best achievement is to work together with no overlap, no gaps. More negatively, when there is no collaboration, conflicting duplication can occur between professionals. Multiplicitive Effects are more powerful in that where professional efforts are combined effectively they can produce a multiple effect (2 x 2 x 2 x 2 = 16) which can achieve more than by simply adding contributions together. Inter-professional work can thus generate new potential and enhance professional input. On the negative side, without working together, the effects can be divisive and fragmented.

One of the most contentious areas of collaborative work concerns boundaries and their overlap. Slightly modifying Rawson's (1994) 'sets' one can see at least two models which can be readily applied for action in the field of health promotion. In the first instance, an example is constructed from the HEA's 'Helping people change' project for primary health care professionals (Wyman, 1994).

Figure 12.1 shows three different professionals whose work overlaps; the overlap is clearly defined to be manageable in one section but the boundary line may be more fluid in another (the dotted line). The three professional groupings are placed, in this instance, with the health promotion officers in the centre seeking to train the trainers, but such a placing does not preclude overlapping boundaries – whether permeable or impermeable – between the two professional groupings placed either side of the centre set. However, where the boundary line is less intact, less firm, hypothetically one section may more readily be eclipsed by another or even potentially be taken over and assimilated (Rawson, 1994).

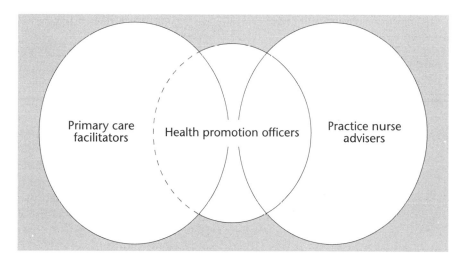

Figure 12.1 **Overlapping sets for differing professional groupings**
(adapted from Rawson, 1994)

Figure 12.2 shows a second model, again applied to a primary health care setting, but this time of four different professionals who work together alongside each other but retain their own area of identity.

General Practitioner	Practice Manager
Nurse	Health Visitor

Figure 12.2   **Sets alongside each other for different professional groups** (adapted from Rawson, 1994)

Review Figures 12.1 and 12.2 in the light of your own professional or lay experience of working with others.

Depending on your experience, one or other of the models may be more familiar to you. You may also be aware of the difficulties in trying to move from boundaried working as shown in Figure 12.2 to the more fluid shown in Figure 12.1. Underlying the boundary divisions, the use of differing languages pervade. The concept of seamless services between professionals suggests the dissolution of boundaries (Rawson, 1994). However, boundary disputes still remain, in particular between health and social services over continuing long-term care for elderly people. Where boundaries have dissolved, this has been largely due to economic pressures.

Collaborative approaches

One of the first researched studies on collaboration in primary health care (Gregson *et al.*, 1991) sought to develop indices of the degree of collaboration between district nurses, general practitioners and health visitors. The results showed that only 27 per cent of GPs and district nurses with patients in common collaborated; and that only 11 per cent of GPs and health visitors collaborated. This study was one of the first to ask the crucial question: why collaborate? The study concluded that it was a generally held belief that collaboration was 'a good thing'.

Building on previous work Gregson (1991) set about constructing a taxonomy of collaboration. He suggested that the level of collaboration might vary from being formal and brief, to 'regular communication and consultation', a 'high level of joint working' and finally 'multi-disciplinary working'. In addition, the nature of collaboration will vary, depending on its primary purpose. Reviewing user-focused initiatives in collaborative care, Hornby (1993) identified primary, secondary and participatory collaboration.

Primary collaboration, he suggested, was when user and face worker started working together on presenting situations. Secondary collaboration described the relationships between several helpers working together for the benefit of the user without the latter present. Participatory collaboration described the complexity of individual and group relationships when the user is present and taking part, even minimally. The rating of collaborative achievement lies on a continuum, between maximum effectiveness at one end to total breakdown at the other. Most fall between, he suggested, between 'fit' and 'friction'.

In order to move towards collaboration the roles of the individual, the group and the organisation need to be reviewed, and problems of inter-agency collaboration and inter-professional communication must be identified (Hornby, 1993). The inescapable conclusion is that the intention to collaborate is not enough. Trust, commitment, resources, a shared identity and common objectives are needed to achieve the main purpose of collaboration: that is, to provide maximum help to the user. Drawing on practice-based experience, the building up of defences and barriers between professionals are recognised and ways to increase role security are discussed.

Team working in primary care

Primary health care team working is important for health promotion but inter-professional work presents some peculiar methodological challenges (Engel, 1994). Reconciling different methods and states of evidence particular to each professional group can lead to potential difficulties. Furthermore, teamwork is perceived as lacking a coherent definition, although in primary health care it is usually associated with formally identified groups of professionals: doctors, nurses, practice managers, health visitors, receptionists, and sometimes social workers.

Several models of primary health care team working have been noted (Styles, 1994). The notion of a 'string quartet model' has been proposed drawing an analogy with string quartets and the internal dynamics between team members which affect joint performance, and their inherent paradoxes. Styles has argued that democratic decision making is embraced by most successful primary care teams in the same way as successful string quartets. A paradox then arises: to work together effectively, if all members are to contribute fully, some form of leadership is needed. 'Flying second fiddle' represents those players in string quartets who echo the first violin's tune and play a less prominent role. These are people who present a difficult issue for quartets: people who feel the most put upon and the most likely to leave. Similar dilemmas occur in primary care where all members are critical to the group's success but there remains fear of medical power domination, compounded by the role of the GP as the employer. 'Confrontation verses compromise' highlights a third paradox for string quartets and, by analogy, for primary care teams. How should disputes be resolved within the team: by strong leadership or by democratic decision making?

Some of the essentials for creating an effective basis for teamwork, which Styles suggested, include:

- a clarity of purpose and objectives
- a shared vision for the future
- each team member having a clear understanding of his or her roles and responsibilities and those of other team members
- all team members sharing in the outcome of their work
- the recognition of the internal dynamics between team members.

Inter-agency models

Underpinning inter-professional work is the organisational basis across which collaboration can occur. Two models have been selected to demonstrate how shared working between agencies can be approached. Figure 12.3, the 'calibration model' is drawn from the Audit Commission's 1993 report on joint working between health authorities. It identifies the steady steps that can be taken to enable liaison between neighbouring District Health Authorities and to develop closer working relationships with other bodies. The process is approached on a clearly defined task basis

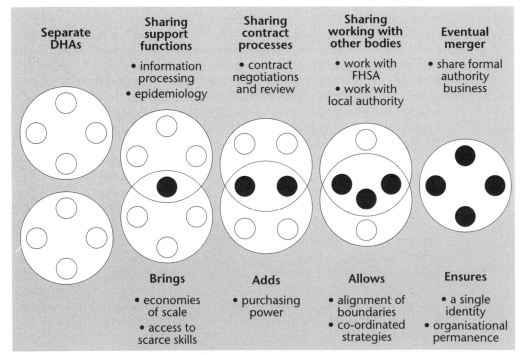

Figure 12.3 **The Calibration Model** (Audit Commission, 1993)

and the ensuing benefits are itemised. Some health care practitioners have found this model useful as way of thinking about changing their own practice.

A rather different inter-agency model is drawn from the field of mental health (Figure 12.4). On this occasion, the Audit Commission (1994) set out a visual plan of how District Health Authority (DHA) purchasers should be developing their strategic role to link with primary care, social services (SSD), and Family Health Authorities (FHSA), amongst other agencies, to set contracts for providers; to share information on co-ordination and joint planning; and to avoid working in isolation. Strategic planning across the various parts of the interlocking jigsaw was seen as a means to determine the level and balance of resources, the priorities for those resources and the means of co-ordination between them.

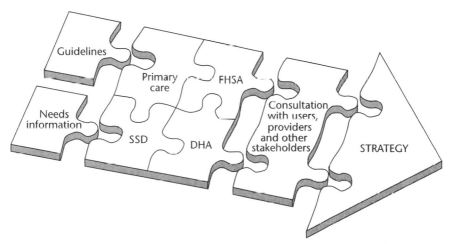

Figure 12.4   **The jigsaw model; developing a strategy for mental health** (Audit Commission, 1994)

12.7 Ways forward for collaboration in health promotion

Another way of thinking about practice and collaboration is to ask the question: how can working together in health and social care be best managed? This approaches inter-professional and inter-agency work from another angle altogether. Table 12.1 identifies five distinctive approaches to the management of collaborative work between professionals and across agencies.

Table 12.1   **Models for the management of interprofessional inter-agency work**

The Structural Model	Working together is enabled by the structure provided albeit facilitating specialist teams. This model is concerned with inter-organisational relationships.
The Professional Leadership Model	One professional leads a team of health and social workers (e.g. GPs have traditionally lead primary health care teams). This model is based on inter-professional relationships.
The Egalitarian Team Model	The team exists by definition of a group who have to collaborate to undertake their work (e.g. child protection). Without a leader necessarily, the context enables a more egalitarian team approach.
The Managerial Model	The manager is the co-ordinator to enable inter-professional teams to collaborate across boundaries. Interface management is concerned more with a corporate form of organisation.
The User-centred Model	The views and participation of the user lead the needs-based approach to which professions and agencies respond. Hornby's (1993) work comes the nearest to this challenging concept.

(Adapted from Leathard, 1994)

> **Review Table 12.1 in the light of your own experience of collaborative working. Which model of management offers the maximum benefit to you?**

Your answer will depend on your area of work but it is likely that health promoters and agencies may make use of more than one of these models. In relation to more structured aspects of practice a professional leadership approach might be employed, for example; but in more indeterminate areas such as working with local communities to identify needs a user-centred model would be more useful.

Training and education issues

There are major issues that need to be addressed in order to improve the potential for collaboration in health promotion work. One key factor concerns training for health promotion/health education. A basic tension exists between tailoring training to the work of specific professional groups and training that deliberately sets out to look at and to cross the boundaries between the different professions. Until recently, it would appear that health promotion has focused on only the former (Beattie, 1994) but, if collaborative working is to be advanced, we need to come to terms with 'inter-professional' education. The first study in primary health and community care, commissioned by CAIPE (the UK Centre for the Advancement of Inter-professional Education) in 1988 identified inter-professional education as education which involved participants from two or more selected professional groups who were learning together within a multidisciplinary context. The survey showed that there were in all 695 valid examples of inter-professional education (albeit of somewhat short interventions) involving 466 organising agencies amongst health visitors, district nurses, social workers, general practitioners and community midwives (Shakespeare *et al.*, 1989).

Developments have moved apace – often because of the initiatives of individuals. Professional bodies and the government have also increasingly sought to encourage joint and collaborative training initiatives. The HEA projects are one example. This approach is well exemplified by the HEA's 'Train the Trainers' courses in the West Midlands, Yorkshire, the North West, Oxfordshire and North West Thames, amongst other areas. Joint training is achieved by bringing together a range of primary care professionals to train to deliver HPC (Help People Change – their lifestyles) courses locally. Courses last for some 28 hours on four specialist modules which cover smoking, alcohol, eating and physical activity (Wyman, 1994). Most participants are nurses, others include primary care facilitators, occupational health specialists, dieticians, counsellors and social workers. The implications from the user and personal perspectives of this type of educational approach will be touched on shortly.

A further example has been the joint practice teaching initiatives for nurses and social workers, set up by the English National Board and the Central Council for the Education and Training of Social Workers, more particularly for those who planned to work with people with learning disabilities. Other joint courses with the Mental Handicap branch of Project 2000 followed but there have been reservations about the schemes (Weinstein, 1994). Joint training for child protection has revealed the underlying anxiety about the topic amongst nurses and social workers which led to shared attributes used to cover up fundamental professional differences. The development of joint training between social workers and the police, despite their different value systems, has led to an increase in respect for and understanding of each other's roles and values (Weinstein, 1994).

CAIPE has also commissioned further research into shared learning. Amongst a wide-ranging investigation which covered three different papers, the researchers Barr and Shaw (1995) concluded from an ever-increasing number of interactive shared learning initiatives that reciprocal perceptions between professions had largely improved as a result of college-based shared learning. By inference, shared learning predisposed participants towards collaborative practice. However, Shaw (1994) followed up participants only to find that these improvements in perception of other professions were reversed when the course was completed.

One of the key questions for the future of inter-professional education, therefore, is how to ensure that shared learning influences practice. Another is to evaluate outcomes both in learning and subsequent practice. What should be assessed for whom and for what purpose, and what methodology is appropriate? Educators, practitioners and professional bodies are now trying to grapple with these questions (Vanclay, 1995).

The user perspective and collaboration

A third key issue concerns the user. Just where does the patient, client consumer or user come into the inter-professional picture? One question might be: does collaborative care make any improved difference as to how the user sees need being met? It could be argued that, from a user perspective, hospital waiting lists are of far greater concern than how many professionals are working together on patient care. Within community care, the major preoccupation for elderly people is to have access to sufficient resources to lead independent lives or to secure care and support when needed. Whether this requires a team of professionals or one support worker might be a more marginal issue for the user. Confusion can quickly arise for clients if collaboration is complex. When Kingston upon Thames surveyed 23 users and fifteen carers, following an assessment of need, the findings showed that users were confused between their community care assessment and earlier assessments undertaken by other health and social services professionals (Sone, 1993).

For the user, a further significant factor is the emphasis which the government has placed on choice accorded to the user for access to the health and social care services (DoH, 1989a; DoH, 1989b). This is very limited for users, apart from consumers who can afford to pay for services to meet their own needs. As Klein (1995) has pointed out, choice is largely determined by resource availability and resides with health and social care commissioners and GP fund holders. In areas where health and social care professionals are involved in determining choice, however, it is vital that users' veiws are heard and responded to. After all, they are 'experts' too. Evers and colleagues (1994) have suggested that in collaborative care, where elderly and disabled people have long experience of their health needs all the workers involved, including service users and carers, should be described as 'experts'.

From a health promotion perspective paying attention to the views of users is of central importance. First, meanings surrounding health and illness vary between cultures and between users' perceptions of need, for example between white, black and minority ethnic groups in the general population (Rehman and Walker, 1995). Secondly, as we have noted already in Parts 1 and 2, the overall relationship between health and housing, employment, income, politics and culture is crucial in assessing users' health needs, and health promoters need to address health change in this context. Networking and joint working has been seen as imperative in order to find common solutions (Solanke, 1996).

Personal care versus teamwork

A fourth and final issue, which is particularly relevant to collaborative care, is whether inter-professional work underestimates the importance of personal caring? Is the difference between personal care and teamwork significant and are these care values incompatible?

In the context of health promotion, respect for the personal views of individuals can lead into dilemmas. Health promoters may provide information, support and facilitation to help people give up smoking, for example, or promote a healthy diet, but despite being well informed about the official messages conveyed, many people reject the idea of healthy eating or stopping smoking (Goode, 1996; Cole, 1996). The dilemma for health promotion is how to confront 'unacceptable' behaviour or the rejection of the message which could also be described as the wielding of user choice. Health promoters will need to decide how to reconcile official messages with the need to support and empower users to make their own health promotion choices.

12.8 Conclusion

Collaboration is an increasingly complex area. A united stand on collaborative practice appears to run counter to the structures of competition between the providers and purchasers in health care. Yet at the same time, there is evidence of growing collaboration between providers and purchasers. Could it be that the 1990 NHS reforms will lead round full circle to a newly unified National Health Service? What meaning does collaboration have for those working to promote health? 'Health alliances', so favoured by national health strategists, are beginning to show results but are still dispersed and difficult to evaluate.

So if it is too complex to stand united on collaboration, will divisions and conflict accelerate a decline in collaborative working? The answer is no. We only have to turn to Handy's (1994) guidance from the Sigmoid Curve to comprehend the nature of successful organisations. Conflict, divisions, renewal, reorganisation, even turmoil are needed to uphold the vibrancy of an organisation. Organisations have to address the future – even when they are at their most seemingly successful point, otherwise they atrophy and wither away. For collaboration to succeed, it has to be achieved the hard way – by people working together beyond divisions.

Chapter 13
Ethics: from health care to public policy

13.1   The scope of health promotion ethics

An adequate ethics of health promotion would have to address a very broad range of practical and theoretical concerns. Some of these concerns will be relatively familiar to students of professional ethics or health care ethics, others raise more fundamental questions of moral and political philosophy. This range and complexity is, in large part, a result of the open-ended and contestable nature of health promotion itself. Indeed it is impossible to reflect on the ethics of health promotion without also giving thought to other conceptual and philosophical questions raised by health promotion, and I will begin with a few summary remarks about the nature of health promotion as a 'subject matter' for ethics.

Anyone who has thought about it knows that the expression 'health promotion' can be used to refer to different sorts of things. It sometimes refers to an occupation or self-conscious activity, i.e. something someone or some group deliberately *does* most typically – but not necessarily – as part of their professional life. But it can also refer to a process, i.e. something that happens or *gets done* as a result or side-effect of other activities or processes. This is, perhaps, more of a spectrum than a clear-cut distinction because health is promoted with varying degrees of professional commitment, self-consciousness and deliberateness, and of course one of the aims of the health promotion movement is to increase awareness of the health effects of everything that goes on. But, roughly speaking, we can make a distinction between *health promotion as a specialist activity* and *health promotion as a process* – where the latter encompasses an indefinite number of social, political and environmental processes, activities and agencies, many of which are not primarily focused on health.

The former would include things like health education campaigns, or the organisation of immunisation and screening programmes. The latter forms the thrust of the healthy public policy and supportive environments approach of the 1980s and 1990s (see Chapter 8 for a fuller discussion of this). It would include things like changes in transport or housing policies, or even peace negotiations, where health may be favourably (or adversely) affected but where it may or may not figure very much on the agenda of decision makers.

An ethics of health promotion has, therefore, to consider both professional activities relating to specific interventions and very general socio-political processes, including the public policy context as a whole. Some themes will run right across the range but there are also some important and difficult questions raised by the latter which can be obscured if only the former are considered. At the 'activity' end of the spectrum we are dealing with a more or less circumscribed field. The 'health promoters' and the intended beneficiaries tend to be identifiable, the lines of responsibility and accountability tend to be clear, and the intended benefits or outcomes tend to be specifiable. All of this helps us to get a purchase on the nonetheless demanding ethical issues raised. The situation is in many ways analogous to professional–client relationships in clinical or therapeutic health care, and in some instances of one-to-one health promotion it will overlap completely. In this regard health promotion ethics can be viewed merely as another sub-domain of health care ethics – one in which the same ideas are applied, albeit to some rather different and arguably more complex problems (some of these differences are discussed in the next section).

At the 'process' end of the spectrum all clarity and specificity is lost and instead there is almost total indeterminacy. It is far from clear who should and should not take responsibility for health promotion; neither is it clear who 'they' should see as the beneficiaries of their efforts; nor is it clear in what respects or to what degree 'they' should seek to improve health. There may be some value in saying 'everyone should promote everyone's health as much as possible' but it doesn't really help. For we can perfectly well ask, 'Is everyone *equally* responsible? Is everyone *equally* in need of health promotion? Is every type of benefit *equally* worthwhile? Is every intervention in the name of health *equally* legitimate?' Unless we, somewhat perversely, answer 'yes' to all of these questions we are still left with complete indeterminacy and a considerable set of ethical puzzles. These puzzles are interlocked and cannot be translated into a set of discrete ethical dilemmas which might be analysed and resolved separately. Their resolution depends upon developing a general view about the nature of 'the good society', about what ends are worth pursuing and what forms of influence it is legitimate for people to exercise over one another.

I will continue to operate with this rough distinction between health care professional ethics and what might be called 'public policy ethics' in order to explore the territory. I would argue that the former cannot be divorced from the latter with all of its difficulties. (This is true for all health care ethics, not just for health promotion ethics – one of the virtues of the idea of health promotion is that it makes these connections more visible.) But there is an important job of 'ethical evaluation' to be done with respect to the most circumscribed and routinely recognised health promotion interventions such as those associated with health education, public health and preventive medicine. In the first section of this chapter I will consider the sort of ethical evaluation which is linked to specific interventions and sketch out the key issues which it raises. All of these issues are also relevant to public policy ethics and in subsequent sections I will move into this broader arena by discussing a few of these issues in more depth.

13.2 The distinctive challenge of health promotion ethics

There are a number of factors which appear to make the ethical evaluation of health promotion interventions different, and often more problematic, than the evaluation of therapeutic interventions. It is important to state that some of these differences are more apparent than real, or are differences in degree rather than differences in kind, but together they form a distinctive combination. It is worth summarising these factors so as to give a feel for the challenge of health promotion ethics.

Drawing on your own experience, whether lay or professional, what would you identify as forming the main differences between health promotion and therapeutic interventions?

First, health promotion interventions are frequently initiated by professionals rather than clients. The professional is not only 'interfering' in the lives of people but is doing so without the initial 'invitation' that typically precedes therapeutic interventions and which suggests an 'implied contract' between the patient and the health professional.

Second, health promotion may be aimed at local and national populations and not simply at specific individuals. This has several important implications:

- the overall effects for good or ill can be so much greater (a misjudgement can affect the lives of thousands or millions of people)
- health promoters are more likely to have to think about 'abstract' or 'statistical' people rather than identifiable people (this matters because we tend to take the needs of people we relate to directly more seriously)
- health promoters will routinely have to weigh together the different needs and priorities of different groups and individuals
- health promotion is more likely to consist of 'many-to-many' rather than one-to-one relationships – this is critical because group relationships bring to light different forms of power, and the need for different forms of agreement and legitimacy.

Third, the overall aims, or the 'ends', of health promotion are innately problematic and contested – questions about ends tend to be marginalised or obscured in therapeutic ethics but here they become salient:

- as we have already noted there are questions about the targeting of efforts and the distribution of benefits (questions about distributive justice)
- there are also questions about *what* is to be promoted – issues around the meaning, and the different dimensions, of health
- there are difficult questions about the short-term versus the long-term consequences of interventions – e.g. is it acceptable for health promotion to have no measurable 'health' impact if it contributes

towards changes in the climate for the long term? How much should concern for the health of future generations be allowed to shape current policies?

Fourth, health promotion interventions work on and 'through' human beings in a variety of ways and cannot be as easily isolated from their cultural, economic and social contexts as can most therapeutic interventions. Of course the latter take place in a social context but they work through physical and biological processes. Health promotion interventions work through both physical and social processes – that is to say, 'culture' is frequently not only a context but also a working medium of health promotion (for example, sex education, tobacco pricing). This raises two corresponding difficulties for the ethics of health promotion:

- how ought we to assess the ethical acceptability of what is sometimes called social or cultural engineering (that is, interventions through public policy aimed at changing people's behaviour)?
- how far is it possible to evaluate ethically health promotion interventions in isolation from a consideration of their contribution to the broader social climate (for example whether they contribute to a more medicalised and/or less democratic society)?

This last factor highlights another feature of health promotion which it is important to mention. At every stage including the characterisation of 'health problems', evidence assessment, the construction of explanations, the formulation of 'solutions' and their evaluation, health promotion relies upon social scientific forms of knowledge. It is thus subject to all of the doubts and controversies which dog these sorts of knowledge claims. Given the other complicating factors listed above this is not a minor matter. In short it means that anyone who is in the business of justifying a health promotion intervention is constantly in danger of having the rug pulled out from under their feet by someone arguing that in some small or profound manner they have misconstrued the whole situation. The rest of this chapter provides a survey of some of these central issues.

13.3 Key issues in health promotion ethics

In the health promotion literature a few key value questions receive widespread attention. There is the question of how far it is acceptable to be persuasive, prescriptive, or 'pressurising' in order to promote health; or how far health promotion should be relatively 'pressure free' and work essentially for informed choice or empowerment? Closely related to this is the question of how we assess the effectiveness of health promotion. Whether, for example, 'health gain' or informed choice should be seen as primary. And there is the pervasive debate about the extent to which health promotion should be directed at changing the structures of society rather than at changing individuals and individual lifestyles; and in particular how far it should address the profound inequalities in health that exist between different social groups.

These questions map fairly closely on to those which are often presented as central to health care ethics: does a particular approach respect *autonomy*? Does it bring about some *benefit*, and does it *avoid harm* – and what combinations of benefit and harm does it produce? What about *justice*? Does it take into account the way in which benefits and harms, including the benefits of being respected, are distributed in society? Finally, when these values come into conflict, how can we resolve the resulting dilemmas? These are the questions lying behind the famous 'four principles' approach to health care ethics (Beauchamp and Childress, 1995). Hence we can see that the basic issues raised by ethical evaluation correspond with those already well rehearsed in the wider health promotion literature.

The ethical concerns most commonly associated with health promotion interventions can be quickly stated. The prize of improved health and the population focus tend to encourage crude forms of *utilitarianism*: that is, a cost-benefit mentality in which overall population benefits are achieved perhaps at the cost of significant harms or risks to individuals and/or of sustaining social inequalities or injustice. This raises the problem of *the individual versus the community* – to what extent should the wants and needs of individuals be respected if to do so entails the wider community paying a price. Are some types of *coercion* sometimes justified for the greater good or alternatively as an exercise in *paternalism* (in other words the overriding or constraining of people's autonomous choices 'for their own sake'). Behind all of this is the problem of what becomes of 'respect for autonomy' and 'informed consent' in health promotion, especially where large numbers of people are involved and even were they to be consulted they would disagree.

It is worth noting in passing that the dangers of narrow utilitarianism, paternalism and the overriding of individual wishes and interests exist equally for 'bottom-up' or community-initiated approaches. In both instances there are problems of establishing the legitimacy of interventions, not only because consent or agreement is unlikely to be universal but also because even where agreement appears to exist it is often not entirely voluntary given the power imbalances that exist between professions and clients or between different sections of a community.

For all of these reasons it would be no exaggeration to say that health promotion is inherently contentious, and that ethical dilemmas are the norm rather than the exception. Two central points stand out and are worth reiterating: neither the worthwhileness of the 'ends' nor the legitimacy of the 'means' of health promotion interventions can be defended without controversy. Indeed, if it was necessary to demonstrate conclusively the ethical acceptability of health promotion interventions before implementing them then none, or very few, would ever be implemented. This is partly because of the fallibility and contestability of the knowledge claims which underpin health promotion; but it is largely because there are very different views about the ethical accept-ability of health promoters setting out to 'interfere in' and change a local or national population's lives or life circumstances. Here our fundamental but divergent moral and political beliefs come into play. This is why the dilemmas in health promotion ethics ultimately turn upon an under-standing of public policy ethics and political philosophy. In the remaining part of the chapter I will turn to these broader questions and look in a little more depth at some questions about the ends and the legitimacy of health promotion. However, before broadening the focus, I want to stress that the ethical evaluation of specific interventions should not be seen as an all-or-nothing affair.

The practical issue is not whether a specific health promotion intervention can be uncontroversially defended but whether we are better off with it or without it:

- ought it to be implemented bearing in mind the consequences of both implementation and non-implementation?
- given that it exists is it being conducted in an (or the most) ethically defensible manner?

As policy makers we may see the first of these two related questions as the more important but it is essential to treat the second with great seriousness. For example, we may – rightly or wrongly – have grave doubts about whether a national breast screening programme ought to exist (Dines, 1997), but if a programme does exist then this should make us attach even more attention to those aspects of the programme which we believe would optimise its ethical acceptability – such as more emphasis on education or informed choice, or ethnic minority needs and perceptions, or more openness about programme successes and failures. This sort of attention may in itself, on occasions, tip the balance in favour of controversial interventions.

13.4   What is health promotion for?

In order to explore questions about ends I will play down the problem of who counts as a health promoter and who has responsibility for health promotion. Let us stick with people who have 'health promotion' as part of their job description, and let's agree that they are health promoters. What is health promotion for? This is a question about health promoters' priorities, but it is also a question about their vision of the good society. What sort of society do health promoters see themselves as working towards?

What is your own response to questions about the purpose of health promotion and the sort of society you want to work towards?

Of course this is where disagreement and debate arise. Health promoters may have very different pictures of an 'ideal' society, and some of these pictures may be more negative than positive. I will just sketch out three possibilities corresponding to three conceptions of health. These possibilities carry with them very different ideas about health promotion roles and responsibilities.

First, heath promoters may be interested primarily in a society in which the morbidity and mortality indices are as low as possible. Thereafter they may be largely agnostic about how society should be organised, perhaps believing that this falls outside the sphere of health promotion. A second possibility is that they have a rather 'thicker' picture of an ideal society as one in which everyone has their basic needs met, and the rights and opportunities to achieve a meaningful and worthwhile life, whilst remaining agnostic about what ways of life are worthwhile – perhaps believing that this is a matter for individual choice. The third possibility is that they have a more comprehensive picture of the ideal society which not only embraces welfare rights and equal opportunities but which also includes some positive conception of how people might live, of what sorts of lives are valuable.

Just for convenience I will label these three positions as a concern for 'health' (in a narrow sense), 'welfare', and 'well-being' respectively. Of course these positions are not entirely discrete and will tend to merge into one another in theory and in practice. Typically someone who wishes to promote health will develop an interest in 'welfare promotion' because they will come to see the connection between such things as housing, education, and employment on the one hand and disease and death on the other. Similarly someone who wishes to promote welfare is likely to adopt (although not necessarily self-consciously) some picture of well-being. Otherwise how can they determine what kinds of rights and opportunities should be fostered by a society? At the very least – if they are operating in the modern world – they are likely to see individual autonomy as a fundamental component of well-being.

Now it may be that some health promoters have a clear conception of well-being but see their own professional role as more restricted. There are two plausible justifications for such an attitude. First, they might regard their conception of the good society and valuable lives as their personal but not their professional business. Just as a plumber may have a picture of the ideal society but regard it as outside of the scope of plumbing (although plumbing would make a contribution!), so a professional 'health promoter' may see a restricted scope for health promotion. Second, even if they see a very broad scope for health promotion in general they may still believe in the 'division of labour' and see much of this scope as beyond their own professional remit which they may prefer to define narrowly according to their experience, expertise and job description. But, leaving these complications aside, we can see that the scope of interest, and sphere of responsibility, of a team of health promoters can extend more or less widely. This can be further illustrated by an example.

Practical priorities and philosophical problems

Imagine that a team of health promoters are asked to promote the health of a group of 16 to 18-year-olds who have left school, are unemployed, and spend much of their time watching television, hanging out together, smoking, drinking and playing slot machines. We can assume that the team will want to consult the young people about their needs and personal priorities. But consultation alone cannot set the agenda; the team will also need some sense of the focus, boundaries and rationale of their role. Should they see their priority as reducing (or alternatively providing informed choice about) tobacco and alcohol use? Should they try to help with employment opportunities, either because employment may lead to a healthier lifestyle or because it is a valuable source of independence and psychological well-being? Should they worry about the continued use of slot machines providing the young people have enough money left for their necessities? Are activities like watching television or playing slot machines any of their business?

If you were a member of such a health promotion team what would you say about each of these issues? It is not simply a matter of deciding whether or not certain things might or might not fall outside your legitimate concerns, but of deciding *why* they might – what makes something a legitimate concern of health promoters? Unless we can answer this question we cannot make much progress with the ethics of health promotion – but, unfortunately, it is a very difficult question indeed. The danger is not so much one of superficial disagreement but one of superficial agreement obscuring really substantial differences.

> **How might someone respond differently to these young people depending on whether a well-being, welfare or health approach to health promotion is being pursued?**

Someone with a focus on health is likely to see tobacco and alcohol use as a real concern, but they may also be at least as concerned about the ill effects of unemployment and what they may regard as an 'unhealthy lifestyle'.

Someone with a focus on welfare is going to be concerned primarily with whether these young people have the basic resources to pursue their chosen lifestyle. To the extent that these young people are relatively poor and lacking in independence and economic and physical security they will be concerned to provide greater opportunities for them. This sort of 'health promoter' may also have doubts about the extent to which the group's current lifestyle is actually freely chosen rather than 'forced' on them, and to that extent they may be concerned with their lifestyle-related health risks.

Someone with a focus on well-being will certainly wish to secure the basic welfare of the group but, in addition, they may question the value of even the autonomous choices of the young people, arguing that their lifestyle, even if it is freely chosen, does not provide the highest likelihood of a meaningful and worthwhile existence. This sort of 'health promoter' (just like the other two types) would not necessarily want to interfere directly in the lives of these young people. Rather they may want to work towards building a community with what they saw as richer and more rewarding social and cultural opportunities, (making 'well-being-conducive choices' easier choices). Finally, someone with a focus on well-being may regard the use of alcohol and tobacco as a possible indicator of an unrewarding existence, but as a relatively insignificant factor overall.

Hence all these 'health promoters' will be interested in the same range of factors for different reasons. But the underlying differences are more important than the superficial similarities. Differences in emphasis paper over the cracks caused by serious philosophical and ethical disagreements. What really matters? How much does 'health' matter in relation to other aspects of welfare and well-being? These disagreements can be subject to careful analysis and debate, and this is the task which moral and political philosophy sets itself, but it should be clear that there is no simple resolution to them, and that merely invoking a framework of values or principles will not do the job.

This is because what is at stake in the health promotion debates is broadly the same as what is at stake in the ethical debates. We can only interpret 'values' like benefit or justice, and we can only decide what to do when they come into conflict, in the light of some picture of what sort of human life and society is possible, desirable or worthwhile – and this is also what health promoters are trying to work out. The disagreements are deep because they are not only about what is desirable in the abstract but what sorts of measures are desirable to achieve these abstract ends.

Thus, to return to the example, there is disagreement about how far slot machines or teenage drug-use are features of the kind of society we want to live in but this disagreement multiplies if we ask whether and how these things should be controlled. Do we, for example, want to live in a society which bans these things, or one which places no restrictions upon them? Of course there are many intermediate possibilities but they all raise ethical issues. One of the benefits of health promotion ethics is that it raises fundamental questions about the acceptability of the various personal and social 'forms of influence' which we exert upon one another. Influence is rarely, if ever, either entirely voluntary or entirely coercive. Peer pressure, social pressure, advertising, incentives, professional persuasion, taxation and so on are all morally ambiguous and are all possible instruments of health promotion. Which combinations of ends and means are compatible with a good society?

As well as questions about ends and means, health promotion ethics raises fundamental questions about agency and responsibility. Who can and should take responsibility for health promotion? I have already referred to the extreme indeterminacy generated by this question, but the discussion of different ends highlights it further.

Clearly if we include 'welfare promotion' or 'well-being promotion' in our consideration then the distribution of possible roles and responsibilities becomes even more complex and contestable. In the following and final section I will raise a few questions about the role of the state as the ultimate health promotion agency. For reasons of space I will say relatively little – except by implication – about an alternative, and complementary, view: that individuals, either as private citizens working alone or in voluntary communities, ought to shoulder the burden of responsibility for one another's health.

13.5   The state and public policy

The same questions about purpose arise at the level of the state as arise for individuals in a health promotion team. Is it the role of the state and public policy to promote health, welfare or well-being? This echoes questions at the heart of political philosophy. What is the proper scope for the exercise of state power? How should responsibility be divided between individuals and the state? These are not only questions about the legitimate scope of government policy but also about the legitimacy of the agencies and individuals (including health professionals) whose authority and influence is underpinned by the state.

As we noted in Part 2, it is characteristic of modern liberal political philosophies to emphasise what I have called welfare. That is, to stress the role of the state in underpinning economic and physical security, and securing basic freedoms for individuals. But there is considerable disagreement about the extent to which the state should actively intervene to promote, rather than merely to protect, welfare. And, of course, there is disagreement about appropriate measures for securing welfare, but welfare tends to be treated as the appropriate 'end' for the state's activities, and the yardstick against which other ends are assessed.

Promoting health is thus acceptable insofar as securing the population's health is one of the functions of 'the welfare state'. People need health just as they need education if they are to have a chance of a tolerable life and are to participate in society economically and socially. However, health promotion has to be circumscribed by a regard for other values, including the personal and economic freedoms which contribute to individual and social welfare. This gives rise to clashes on those occasions where 'more health' can apparently be obtained only at the expense of other elements of welfare. According to this perspective, therefore, health is not pursued as an end in itself but as part of a package of values, in which economic

welfare and individual autonomy, including freedom from 'state interference', play a large part.

You will recall from Chapter 7 that another characteristic of modern
liberal political philosophy is the view that the state should be *neutral* with
regard to conceptions of well-being. It is the job of individuals and
voluntary communities to decide how they ought to live, and against
what standards to evaluate the worthwhileness of their lives. Hence,
according to this model, the state (or its policies or agents) should have
regard to the basic conditions for well-being but should in no way
promote 'well-being' according to any particular conception.

These liberal views represent a central strand in the underlying political
philosophy and overt political culture of a society like ours. But they have
to compete, philosophically and in practical politics, with other strands.
There is, by contrast, the view that we put too much emphasis on securing
welfare, either (from the political right) because this undermines the
enterprise, competitiveness, and individual thriving which would result
from a less 'protective' society, or (from the left) because the concentration
on welfare is too minimal, and detracts from the need to secure much
greater equality and social justice – including the need to close 'the health
divide'.

Similarly, there are those, from across the political spectrum, who take
the view that the state does and must have some role in promoting
broader conceptions of well-being, and that this is not necessarily
incompatible with a largely liberal culture. Legislation or other policies
on the control and use of the media, on the family and sexuality, on the
sale of drugs, or on religious education, for example, can reflect concerns
to support certain ways of life as worthwhile ones. Of course, in reality,
debates about the role of the state (or about conceptions of well-being) are
not only 'philosophical', and not only about ideals, but are also informed
by custom, tradition, prejudice, vested interests, self-interest, and all the
other ingredients of practical politics.

All public policy, including policy explicitly aimed at health promotion, is constructed as part of these value debates. Public policy has,
therefore, to be understood and interpreted in the light of the ideological
and moral framework it embodies. The government's 'Health of the
Nation' strategy is a good example. This strategy – which is discussed in
greater depth in earlier chapters – is built around narrow 'health' targets.
In the main it incorporates health promotion into a revised conception of
'the welfare state', which places increasing responsibility on individuals to
look after themselves. Health promotion is seen largely as an extension of
and complementary to (or even a replacement for) health care. This is
shown not only by the stress the strategy places upon the NHS but also –
and more importantly – by its neglect of poverty, and of economic,
environmental and social change as an instrument of health promotion.
The near assimilation of health promotion to health care serves at least
two vital policy functions. First, it helps to 'rein in' the more open-ended
and radical conceptions of health promotion. Second, it lends 'population

medicine' some of the considerable legitimacy of the NHS and personal health care services. No doubt a strategy which was aimed only at effective health promotion would have a different emphasis but, as we have noted, this sort of policy has to balance together a number of aims, interests and values.

Those governments responsible for the Health of the Nation strategy would defend what others might see as its relatively modest conception of health promotion. For them a more radical approach to promoting health would only serve to undermine other, more important, aspects of welfare and well-being and might also be self-defeating. First and foremost, they would reject the extensive use of public policy for the 'engineering of health' as incompatible – in principle – with respect for individual freedom. But in addition they would see a risk to 'free enterprise' and material prosperity which arguably not only protect and promote health in themselves, but which also allow people to choose and work for lives which they regard as worthwhile and fulfilling. (Both proponents and critics might thus agree that other facets of public policy are more important determinants of health and more central to understanding health promotion.) Many people would be sympathetic up to a point with this sort of argument, and it is too easy just to dismiss it as self-serving ideological dogma. Anyone who is committed to a less modest conception of health promotion must be prepared to show how their vision takes account of other aspects of welfare and well-being, and is not counter-productive. It is no good simply being in favour of 'more health'.

Which components of what I have called health, welfare, or well-being are central to health promotion and which are central to achieving a good society? As health promoters we need to answer this at a number of levels – in relation to the state, in relation to the organisations we work for, and in relation to our own roles. Along with this we have to decide what 'trade-offs' between these components are acceptable and in particular what justifies intervening in people's lives. Without some such view – whatever it is – fundamental ethical evaluation is impossible.

13.7 Conclusion

Health promotion is thoroughly value laden. The rhetoric of health promotion has succeeded in large part because it has coincided with the advocacy of value reform in health care. Health promotion has been associated with more empowerment, more equity, more participation, more respect for individuals and communities and so on. On the other hand, there have been numerous critics of health promotion who see it as another form of social control – a means of exploiting health to, for example, manipulate, judge and moralise about lifestyle. Some of the more recent forms of sociological critique are sophisticated and subtle – exposing the connections between empowering people and exercising power over them – and pose an important challenge for health promotion ethics.

It is obviously inadequate to wrap oneself in the sometimes near Utopian rhetoric of health promotion, but neither is it acceptable to 'bash' health promotion indiscriminately. I have tried to suggest that two related tasks have to be attempted: first, it is essential to openly and systematically subject specific interventions to ethical evaluation. This process can draw upon the literature of health-care ethics but should be seen as a normal part of public debate about the legitimacy of measures. Second, these specific debates should in turn be seen as part of a larger process of debating the appropriate contribution of public policy to health promotion. Ultimately this rests upon achieving some measure of agreement about the meaning and relative importance of health and health promotion in the good society.

Chapter 14
Health promotion and society: critical perspectives

14.1   Introduction

The purpose of this chapter is to encourage the development of critical, sociological perspectives on health promotion. The value of sociological perspectives to the practice of health promotion lies in encouraging health promoters to be self-reflective in their practice and to try to make sense of the relationships between that practice and the wider social and political contexts in which it occurs. To be critical, in the sociological sense of the term, means to grasp and to work through key connections between contexts and practices, social forces and personal endeavours. It means becoming aware of the relationship between the institutional and political structures of contemporary societies and the experiences, routines and strategies of both providers and recipients of resources for health. In short, a critical perspective on health promotion involves challenging common understandings and questioning accepted ideologies.

Health promotion is embroiled in the political projects of a diverse collection of social and institutional interests: to promote health is to promote certain of those projects, whether the practitioner wishes to do so or not. A basic understanding of how and why this is the case is therefore a necessary requirement for any would-be health promoter. This chapter explores and evaluates two accounts that have been influential in recent sociologies of health promotion. First we consider the surveillance critique derived largely from the work of Michel Foucault (1973, 1977), and then the modernisation critique associated with the work of Anthony Giddens (1990a, 1991) and Ulrich Beck (1992).

14.2   The surveillance critique

The origin of the surveillance critique lies in the claim that what is crucial to a *health system* is not the existence or absence of particular diseases but the organisation and control of the technologies of health and illness. The implication of this claim is that health and disease states only become visible and comprehensible under certain political and social conditions, when specific relationships between knowledge and power exist. In Foucault's work, the birth of clinical medicine is tied to a shift in the organisation of power and authority over individuals and populations. Specifically, Foucault argues that modern societies are dominated by a form of 'capillary' power. By this term, Foucault means that control over everyday life – over behaviours, attitudes, beliefs, habits and norms – is dispersed throughout a wide range of decentralised authorities, rather than being concentrated or unified in the institution of a monarch or sovereign state. Everyday life is regulated (in the name of health, welfare, well-being or order, for example) by a plurality of expert or otherwise exclusive institutions and their personnel. In this perspective, doctors, teachers, social workers, psychiatrists, counsellors, nurses and others, are viewed as nodal points in a vast and continuous network of power relations.

Armstrong (1983, 1993, 1995) has written extensively on these connections, arguing that, increasingly, a 'hospital model' of medical practice – characteristic of the nineteenth century – has been displaced during the twentieth century by a 'surveillance model'. The difference, according to Armstrong, is that the former implied a three-dimensional, spatial, model of disease: illness and health were located in the (three-dimensional) body of the patient and the hospital or clinic was the (three-dimensional) structure for their maintenance and/or treatment. The surveillance model, in contrast, implies a four-dimensional perspective which addresses health and illness temporally as well as spatially. What distinguishes the second from the first perspective is the finding that 'normal' health is a mirage whilst chronic or potential illness is the 'norm':

> The techniques of Surveillance Medicine – screening, surveys, and public health campaigns – would all address this problem [of 'potential' and 'chronic' illness] in terms of searching for temporal regularities, offering anticipatory care, and attempting to transform the future by changing the health attitudes and health behaviours of the present.
>
> (Armstrong, 1995: 402)

It is not necessary to accept uncritically Armstrong's historical division between the 'hospital' and 'surveillance' models to see the significance of his analysis. Treatment in a hospital implies that a person temporarily gives up control of his or her own health maintenance: professionals and quasi-professionals are charged with providing treatments and cures for the time that the patient is hospitalised. In contrast, screening populations, redirecting attitudes and behaviours, changing the content of school lessons or banning smoking in the workplace, and so on, in the name of health implies that people give up this control permanently, at least in certain dimensions of their lives. This observation is not a moral argument at this stage: people give up and take back control of their lives in countless everyday encounters with the social institutions of health care. The significant issue is that the impacts of and responses to particular states of health and illness are inescapably linked to socially organised relations of power and authority – in the 'clinic' and in the 'community'.

It is these relations, rather than disease states as such, which determine how individual and/or collective health is administered and experienced.

In this context, health promotion is sometimes seen more as a shift in terminology from health education than a true shift in the philosophy and delivery of health care (Lupton, 1995; Rawson, 1992). This is partly because explicit health promotion models propose a view of the social actor that parallels the rational, choice-making individual of health education, and partly because health promotion schemes continue to implement professional interpretations of the causes and treatments of ill-health. From her study of community health action, Farrant (1991: 425) concluded that:

> Health promotion priorities continued to be professionally, specifically medically, defined, with 'community participation' being used to describe what often amounted more to community manipulation.
>
> (cited in Lupton, 1995: 60)

In the surveillance critique, such prioritisations and 'manipulations' are not understood as the conscious actions of imperialist or megalomaniac professionals. Rather, they conform to deeply entrenched procedures embedded in the structures and relationships characteristic of modern institutions. A good example of this procedural embedding is found in the extension of health screening to cover more and more of the numerical population and more and more of each individual person's characteristics.

In what ways might the extension of health screening into more and more areas of life be regarded as a means of social and political control?

Three versions of health screening in particular give substance to this claim: population screening, personal check-ups and genetic screening.

Population health screening

The first version of health screening we consider here is the epidemiological survey or population health screening which, according to Lupton (1995: 67),

> ...acts as a technique of normalisation, focused as it is on measuring the continuum of bodily states evident in populations, as well as a device for individualisation, through measuring the differences between people.
>
> (see also Armstrong, 1983: 51–3)

The epidemiological survey – or population health screening – encourages the development of social regulation because it offers a form of 'damage control' against epidemics (Singer, 1993). Social interventions, behavioural management and infringements of personal liberty, which might seem morally unacceptable can all be justified on the grounds of pre-emptive or preventive health care. Such controls are often targeted at particular social groups – the poor, gay, non-white, and so on – who are seen as more health-threatening than the 'norm'. By targeting specific types of (ostensibly) health information, the epidemiological survey functions also as a form of political screening, legitimising interventions in some people's lives in the name of health. Armstrong (1983: 84) writes that the epidemiological survey served to establish:

> ...a domain of medical reality and with it the surveillance apparatus of support groups and social networks which act both to sustain and monitor the new temporally ordered medical space [of every day life].

Personal health check-ups

The second version of screening comprises the plethora of personal health check-ups and wellness screening programmes that have been adopted by the health services, and employers in particular. Here, what are being screened are personal beliefs, attitudes and behaviours as much as symptoms of physical or mental illness. (For a discussion of the general features of these programmes see O'Brien 1994, 1995.) Here, I want to draw attention to the social relations involved in screening for cervical cancer. McKie (1995) observes that cervical screening procedures reproduce wider patriarchal controls around women's bodies, identities and behaviours. These controls apply both to women themselves but also to organisations and personnel responsible for their (cervical) health. For example, the cervical screening clinic reinforces divisions between 'experts' and 'lay people' around the most intimate dimensions of bodily experience. Women attending such clinics often feel demeaned by the experience and are required to divulge beliefs and accounts about their own and others' sexual experiences. McKie (ibid, p.453) writes:

> Tests are taken in medical environments which are regulated by unequal power relations between the professional and female patient. Women may have to outline their sexual activity. Many health care professionals assume that women are heterosexual without any experience of sexual abuse or trauma concerning such conversations and internal examinations. All this happens to women who may be considered at risk but are largely without symptoms and thus would consider themselves normal.
>
> (McKie, 1995: 453)

At the same time, the 'encouragement' to women to attend for smear tests every three to five years comprises a mechanism for monitoring the attainment of health promotion targets (defined in terms of numbers of women attending for tests) by medical institutions. Such self-monitoring by the professionals fulfils contractual obligations through which incomes for completing requisite test-rates are derived.

Genetic screening

Finally, genetic screening raises similarly controversial political questions around the issue of surveillance. Genetic screening has been likened to 'the new eugenics', proposing to distinguish between 'healthy' (read 'fit') and 'abnormal' (read 'defective') individuals and groups. Genetic screening appears at first as a powerful tool for addressing inherited disorders, yet its organisation signals a problematic arrangement of social controls around individual and group rights. For example, 'negative' genetic tests lead to loss of life-insurance cover, employment and other social and economic opportunities, and may lead to termination of foetuses on social and cultural rather than strictly medical grounds. US employers already use genetic testing procedures and the results lead to exclusionary or intrusive policies towards their workforces. Nelkin and Tancredi (1989: 176) warn of the risk of creating a 'biological underclass'. Commenting on Nelkin's and Tancredi's and other related research, Lupton observes that:

> The technology of genetic screening, therefore, acts as a highly individualised strategy of normalisation, in which previously invisible aspects of people's genetic make-up are singled out and constructed as problems and certain groups are identified as deviating from the norm and rendered subject to intervention on the part of the medical and allied professionals.
>
> (Lupton, 1995: 104)

It should be noted here, contra Lupton, that it is precisely the fact that medical professionals are *only one of the many* constituencies to make use of, control or base decisions on such sophisticated medical technologies that makes screening an issue of particular note. The surveillance critique points to the ways that social and cultural pressures intersect around (actual or potential) health and illness and shows how, in the name of health promotion, patriarchal, economic and political interests and priorities are embedded in the regulation of both the most banal and the most intimate details of people's everyday lives.

14.3   The modernisation critique

The modernisation critique similarly points to the dependencies between knowledge about health and the control of health and illness. It differs in its insistence that the connections between health knowledge and power are not the sole province of experts or exclusive institutions. The modernisation critique views health knowledge and action as an arena of contested social relations in which health promotion strategies shape new correlations between personal identity and institutional resources. The basis of the modernisation critique is the claim that both individual identities and institutional strategies are 'reflexively organised'. There is some confusion over the meaning and implications of this concept (see Hay *et al.*,1994) but in debates about health promotion it is usually taken to indicate the ability of both individuals and institutions fundamentally to reorient their behaviours, beliefs and organisation in the face of new information. Given this analytical focus, the modernisation critique of health promotion turns most commonly on a consideration of the development and distribution of information and knowledge (or 'discourses') about health and on the processes by which such knowledge and information is assimilated and used.

The modernisation critique begins from the observation that modern (or 'late modern') societies such as our own betray a number of key characteristics that distinguishes them from earlier (and other) forms of social organisation. These characteristics include:

- an unprecedented range of technological and social changes occurring at an unprecedented rate of change
- a widespread cultural perception of uncertainty and risk associated with human interventions into nature and with human technological progress
- the rise of a politics of lifestyle and consumption, displacing a politics of class and production
- a bewildering diffusion of 'expertise' about everything from sex to shopping (and often the two combined) and including health and illness. (See Giddens, 1990a, 1991; Castel, 1991; Beck, 1992; Shilling, 1993.)

Contrasting the classic 'sick role' with recent philosophies of health and well-being, Bunton and Burrows observe that:

> The contemporary citizen is increasingly attributed with responsibilities to ceaselessly maintain and improve his or her own health by using a whole range of measures. To do this she or he is increasingly expected to take note of and act upon the recommendations of a whole range of 'experts' and 'advisers' located in a range of *diffuse* institutional and cultural sites:

> The duties that health promotion invokes have thus been added to those of the sick role.
>
> (Bunton and Burrows, 1995: 208)

The changes noted by Bunton and Burrows comprise the emergence of new social roles against which behaviours, beliefs and attitudes are assessed: that is,'health roles'. The latter represent the cultural embodiments of health promotion discourses which, in turn, represent 'commodified spaces' for the consumption of health. The modernisation critique of health promotion construes health as a set of socially embedded roles and relationships whose cultural meanings are shaped by a 'consumption calculus':

> Health is idealised as self-governed lifestyle choice. Health promotion and the new public health attempt to cultivate consumption preferences

driven by the reflexive calculation, monitoring and re-calibration of commodity inputs in the pursuit of health.

(Bunton and Burrows, 1995: 210)

How might an emphasis on lifestyles and the active pursuit of health contribute to a growing consciousness of risk?

The 'pursuit of health' is an indefinite project: cultural meanings of health range through ideals of ecological balance, capacities to function physically, levels of vigour and stamina to states of happiness. The pursuit of health is thus a potentially endless activity, comprising a continuous review of behaviours, beliefs, feelings, abilities, environments and relationships. It is also an extremely ambiguous activity. No one can be certain, under these conditions, that they are in fact 'healthy', even less that they are healthy *enough*. An individual may live to the letter of a recommended healthy life and still feel their health threatened or undermined by inherited, environmental or technological forces.

Risk consciousness

The consequence of these uncertainties is the development of a 'risk consciousness' (Beck, 1992) in which both individuals and institutions continuously monitor their activities in order to avoid and/or offset threats which appear, in part, as products of their own making. A good example of this consciousness can be found in the widespread and uncertain debate about the relationships between heart disease and lifestyle.

Heart disease, along with some cancers, has been labelled a disease of 'civilisation' and a disease of 'maladaptation' (see Bryant, 1988: 293). Its causes are said to lie in a combination of genetic and environmental factors whose relationships are themselves highly ambiguous. Nonetheless, in spite of a genetic component in the aetiology of such diseases, they are still seen as amenable to manipulation and evasion and are said to be largely preventable. Heart disease, in particular, has been the subject of an extended lifestyle education and then promotion campaign revolving around a set of contributory behavioural and attitudinal factors. These are said to arise from the unique character of modern, 'developed' societies and consist of the five risk factors of diet, alcohol consumption (as a category separate to diet) exercise, smoking and stress. The health promotion campaigns around heart disease, backed by governments but developed in a number of key professional and international organisations, have paralleled and contributed to wider changes in people's behaviours and roles and in relationships between people and social institutions. The campaigns have served as media or vehicles for changes in institutional strategies and in cultural identities.

For example, the factor of 'diet' has figured in cardio-vascular health promotion as a concern over bodily levels of specific 'risk' substances, notably cholesterol, and the correlation between these and the intake of specific foods, notably saturated fats. Campaigns to influence the national diet – by education about foodstuffs, by persuading retailers to provide nutritional information on products, or by convincing producers to supply 'healthier' products (such as low fat milk) – have reinforced changes in the structures of food retailing. The campaign has relied on the underlying idea that controlled diversity ('a little bit of what you fancy', 'moderation in all things', 'a healthy diet is a balanced diet', etc.) provides the surest (but not certain) and most practical route to continued cardiac health. At the same time, the food retail industry has grown into an international niche-marketing operation and diversity of product lines has been seen as the key to competitive edge. Large retailers like Tesco, Sainsbury and Asda have been keen to develop a total shopping experience where every portion of a meal – pre-prepared, pre-packed or 'fresh' – together with the implements for its preparation, the accoutrements for its presentation and the materials for its expurgation – can be found under one hypermarket roof. The interests of the retail section in encouraging controlled consumption diversity coincide with the interests of the health promotion sector in encouraging controlled behavioural diversity. An interesting example of the ways that the institutions of the retail sector and the institutions of health maintenance intersect is the parallel increase in the availability of low fat milk which is marketed aggressively by both manufacturers and retailers. Where there was one product there are now several from which more 'choices' can be made: the more controlled diversity the better!

Reflexivity

The modernisation critique accounts for this coincidence of interests as an example of the reflexive organisation of social life: the institutions of both the health and retail sectors face environmental challenges – the prominence of particular diseases, changes in supply and demand chains – which are seen to result partly from earlier patterns of consumption and behaviour, and must respond in ways that maintain the integrity and coherence of the institutions. Each set of institutions draws on resources that are unique – the social status of its professional representatives or the 'reputation' of the institution, the validity of its scientific knowledge-base, the capacity to assimilate new production chains, storage or transport technologies and systems, and so on – and resources that are shared – televisual and printed media, cultural aspirations towards youth and fitness, the increasing cosmopolitanism of European societies, and so on. Each set of institutions incorporates elements of the other's knowledge and practice – the marketability of 'healthy' lifestyles, for example, has been a key feature of both the change in retail organisation and practice and the change in ideologies of health maintenance that accompany the health promotion movement. At least in these senses, modern institutions are said to be 'reflexive'.

At a different level, as Lupton and Chapman observe:

> The contemporary cultural meanings around food are replete with paradoxes. Food occupies the dual and conflicting roles of potential pathogen, source of disease and death, versus those of the giver of life, nourishment and emotional comfort.
>
> (1995: 478)

Paradox

The idea of paradox – the co-existence of contrary realities – is central to the modernisation critique and to the claim that health promotion represents a medium for shifts in cultural identities (Nettleton and Bunton, 1995: 50–2; Lupton, 1995: 142–9). The idea underpins Giddens's (1991) account of the biographic basis of modern identities: individuals undertake 'projects of the self' in the face of contradictory and competing information, incorporating and rejecting beliefs and behaviours according to their success in maintaining personal biographical coherence. As in the account of institutional change, individuals are said to organise their lives 'reflexively'. Stocks of knowledge comprising 'expertise' about health, for example, are derived from a wide range of sources (newspapers, magazines, television, radio and oral traditions as well as retailers and public institutions) and are subject both to translation and recomposition in the contexts of learned experiences, and to assessments about their value or validity. Knowledges about health – such as the relationships between cholesterol, food intake and heart disease, for example – circulate through both formal and informal media within the routines of daily life and are subject to challenges and redirections on the basis of those routines and knowledges (Lupton and Chapman, 1995: 491). In part, such challenges – like changes in demand for products – influence institutions into procedural and/or structural changes and the cycle of knowledge-development, distribution, challenge, change and redistribution continues. Individuals, like institutions, are working or striving to maintain coherence in contradictory and rapidly-changing environments. This applies both at the level of society as a whole and at the level of specific social locations. The identities of both the provider and the recipient of health services are shaped through their respective and interacting projects, but the shaping takes very different forms. The move from patient to consumer to customer, for example, is not the same as the move from nurse to health adviser to wellness practitioner, for example, even though both changes are inextricably connected.

14.4 Conclusions

There are some significant sociological problems with both of the perspectives outlined here. The surveillance critique faces the challenge of accounting for the persistence of the inequalities that the critique unpacks: the 'particular groups' who are always singled out for special attention. 'Particular' groups are formed through struggle and resistance with other 'particular' groups, not primarily or even necessarily through the minutiae of health projects. Some of the particular groups that are singled out for special surveillance (for example, women) are also vitally important actors in maintaining the coherence of such projects, for example in their role as health workers (O'Brien, 1994). The coincidences and contradictions between these social locations may be influenced by surveillance systems but the 'upstream' sociological processes that generate them remain obscure. The modernisation critique faces this same challenge – why do rapid change and reflexivity cause the persistence of specific iniquities? – and also a related problem of definition. It is possible to point to examples of 'reflexivity' and 'risk consciousness', as I have indicated above, but these are often at a very generalised and usually abstract level, making it difficult to identify which groups and individuals are doing what to whom.

Nonetheless, both critiques contain valuable insights into the processes and practices of health promotion. The surveillance critique draws attention to power and its application through institutional procedures. The operation of programmes and projects aimed at alleviating distress or at improving health states is entangled in political relations which establish and govern 'expertise', 'authority' and 'participation' in the institutions of health and outside them. The interests and priorities of different groups are assimilated into health promotion programmes through unequal rewards, structures and expectations. The surveillance critique thus emphasises the connections between structural or institutional features and the practices of institutional actors.

The modernisation critique draws attention to the active construction of both social contexts and cultural identities by exposing the interaction between individual and institutional projects. Health promotion programmes embody a series of logics and strategies that draw resources from and also provide resources for parallel social institutions – such as those of the retail sector, for example. At the same time, the knowledges and practices incited by health promotion projects are challenged and retranslated in the context of competing knowledge claims and practical priorities. The modernisation critique thus emphasises the connections between social change and personal action and knowledge.

Health promotion is bound to widen social forces that both support and undermine its philosophies, policies and practices. The practice of health promotion – the delivery of services, the provision of information, the persuasions and coercions, the administration and regulation of its resources – is always inescapably political. Sociological perspectives, like the surveillance and modernisation critiques, provide frameworks for making sense of these political relations and the ways that professionals and non-professionals are embroiled in them: the different ways that challenges to individuals and institutions generate sometimes reciprocal and sometimes oppositional alliances. Health promotion is an element of wider social processes that give shape to the experience of health but at the same time it is also shaped by those same forces.

Chapter 15
Social science and the future of population health research

15.1 Introduction

In this chapter we define our area of concern as the future of research concerned with the health of populations. There are four main reasons for this emphasis. First, as we are not epidemiologists – not even 'social' ones – it seems inappropriate for us to address the likely developments in a discipline that is not our own and which has its own very complex and particular history and culture. Secondly, in our writing on different aspects of public health and health research, we have always argued that the enquiry into the health of populations should be both multi- and inter-disciplinary (Popay and Williams, 1994, 1996).

The third reason for a broad focus is that epidemiology – particularly in its most modern forms – is a militantly quantitive, empiricist discipline. In contrast, developments now taking place in population health research are increasingly indicating the need for methods of, and approaches to, research which are 'appropriate' (McKinlay, 1993) and informed by an understanding of the 'theoretical domains' in which they are situated (Dean *et al.*, 1993; Dean and Hunter, 1996). This means taking seriously the contribution to be made by qualitative research. The final reason for concerning ourselves with population health research, rather than with epidemiology more narrowly conceived, is that in spite of its practical origins in public health, the latter has come to operate increasingly in a 'context of discovery' rather than a 'context of application'. This seems to us to contrast with the challenges facing research on the health of populations in coming decades, which will require at the very least a movement from the former to the latter and ideally an obliteration of the distinction between pure and applied research.

In the future, whatever the discipline, research concerned with understanding the health of populations will need take account of wider developments taking place in theory, culture and society. At present the conventional view is that:

> ...the aim of epidemiology is to decipher nature with respect to human health and disease...'
>
> (Trichopoulos, 1996: 436)

However, in population health research, as in other areas of human inquiry, the challenge that human knowledge cannot be a 'mirror of nature' has to be faced (Rorty, 1980). If knowledge is constructed through dialogue and engagement (Bryant, 1995), this is as relevant to population health research as to any other area of human enquiry. If epidemiologists and other scientists fail to take seriously the assumptions and implications of this view, they are going to find themselves increasingly irrelevant to the problems and concerns facing societies – both globally and locally – in the years to come. In this chapter we elaborate on what we perceive to be the main limitations of much current population health research, and consider the ways in which we believe population health research might move hopefully and constructively into the future.

15.2   The limits of current population health research

Although at its best the epidemiological imagination is informed by an ethical and political response to the existence of public health problems – using whatever methods, biographical, sociological or biological, it has at its disposal (Ashton, 1994) – the development of epidemiology in particular and population health research in general in the twentieth century is marked by a growing domination of quasi-experimental designs, notwithstanding that it is 'non-experimental' (Trichopoulos, 1996) and an increasing isolation of scientific developments in epidemiology from the political context of public health. In the nineteenth century public health enquiry was strongly linked to social reform and was dominated by concerns over clean water and sanitary housing. This was transformed by the rise of bacteriology, with the work of Koch and Pasteur in the late nineteenth century which provided the biological foundations for the development of a 'new' epidemiology oriented to the control of specific diseases such as tuberculosis, diphtheria and syphilis. In some ways you could say that the rise of bacteriology made modern epidemiology possible and this, in turn, made public health more a medical than a social science. Public health became medicalised and medicine began to dominate for the first time the 'untrained amateurs' in the field of public health, such as engineers, biologists and social scientists (Acheson, 1990).

In some ways this was progress, because it made possible the development of specific interventions against particular infectious diseases. However, there is a sense in which the ascension of bio-scientific methods in public health was a mixed blessing. For all their explanatory power, these methods also had the consequence of moderating and sometimes replacing the political commitment to social improvements for the poor characteristic of early public health (Fee and Porter, 1992; Armstrong, 1993). Some commentators have suggested that medical public health focused downstream to such an extent that it lost sight of what was going on up the river (*The Lancet*, 1994). Moreover, epidemiological public health increasingly excluded from its microscopic attention the voices of the people who inhabited the 'ruinous and filthy districts' within which the stuff of bacteriology's interest was festering (Engels, 1969).

With the decline of infectious and the rise of chronic disease the attention of epidemiologists has shifted from germs to behaviours. However, the quasi-experimental model which came to define scientific public health during the rise of bacteriology has continued to dominate: variables are specified and controlled and complex statistical analyses are undertaken to explore their interrelationships. What this approach excludes are those 'contextual factors', such as class or power, which cannot easily be reduced to a set of unambiguous variables, and those 'subjective factors' – unhappiness, discontent, alienation – which cannot be transformed into measures that are operational for the researcher and meaningful for the researched. In recent years, however:

> There [has been] a growing disquiet among population health reseachers that something has not been quite right about the way in which research on health has been conducted. It appears that much health research is driven by a need to satisfy fairly rigid research criteria established much earlier by methodologists concerned with a classical view of science.
>
> (Dean *et al.*, 1993: 227)

This quotation reflects the considered view of a growing number of people involved in population health research. However, it is in some ways peculiar that this disquiet has emerged. After all, as one prominent public health practitioner has noted in the preface to a collection of classical epidemiological studies:

> ...social science and the epidemiological method are part and parcel of the same culture of enquiry and understanding aimed at improving the human condition.
>
> (Ashton, 1994: ix)

However, closer examination of this statement suggests a number of ways in which the epidemiological method may be in need of an overhaul. It suggests little appreciation of the philosophical contextualisation of science that is already under way (Bryant, 1995); and the professed desire for intellectual unity sits uneasily with the multidisciplinary developments taking place within population health research. 'Social science', 'epidemiological method', 'culture of enquiry', and 'human condition' are all phrases which suggest a misplaced search for singularity at a time when there is growing pressure for greater plurality in method and discipline, and more heterodoxy in epistemology.

These pressures derive from a number of sources. For example: the recognition of both change and continuity in patterns of ill-health in contemporary societies; increasing demands for evaluation within health care systems; changing discourses on the nature of 'risk' in modern societies; and changing attitudes towards 'expert knowledge'. Against this background, we suggest, population health research in the future must reinstate a political dimension to intellectual enquiry, and develop more sensitive methods for exploring and understanding the social context of people's lives.

Contemporary patterns of ill-health: change and continuity

What are the new challenges facing population health research and practice?

We are now faced with new times and new situations in population health research and practice (Ashton and Seymour, 1988). Coronary heart disease and cancer have replaced cholera and syphilis at the centre of public health's concerns (*The Lancet,* 1993). The considerable burden of chronic illness also means that population health concerns must move beyond disease to disability – a phenomenon which inevitably includes a complex mixture of biological, behavioural, social and political aspects or dimensions (Barnes and Mercer, 1996). There is also a profusion of new anxieties about the effects of the physical and social environment on human health.

Alongside growing recognition of the profound changes taking place in the nature of ill health in the late twentieth century, old issues persist. Infectious diseases still represent major threats to the health of many populations, within and outside the poorer nations, as evidenced by the prominence of HIV and AIDS as global public health concerns and the growing incidence of tuberculosis in western societies. There is also an appreciation that the distributional aspects of ill health – locally, nationally and globally – have remained unchanged. Continuing debate over inequalities, or variations, in health has shown that something more than the continuing refinement of the statistical analysis of epidemiological data is required in order to explain inequalities in morbidity and mortality; particularly in the context of continuing disagreement over the relative contribution of 'behaviour' and 'material circumstances' (Wilkinson, 1996).

The juxtaposition of change and continuity in population health – the recognition of new problems and the persistence of old concerns – has created an urgent need to think again about the nature of the connection between the biological, historical, social, economic and political dimensions of human health.

Evaluation and the nature of evidence

The growing interest in the need to demonstrate the effectiveness of health (and increasingly, social) care has highlighted a further important limitation of much current population health research. The holy grail of 'evidence-based medicine' has encouraged a plethora of related missions, notably the international Cochrane collaboration (Abramson, 1997), national health technology assessment programmes, and sophisticated methodologies for systematic reviewing, meta-analysis and dissemination and development activities.

The gauntlet thrown down by Archie Cochrane a quarter of a century ago has at last been taken up within modern health care systems, and the pursuit of effectiveness consumes the time and energies of an increasing number of health researchers and practitioners. In this endeavour, however, a hierarchy of research methods has been created with the randomised control trial (RCT) accepted by many health researchers and practitioners as the 'gold standard' against which all other research methods are to be compared. However, while health services continue to provide both therapies of various kinds and 'board and lodging and tender loving care' (Cochrane, 1972: 3), the idea that the evaluation of the former requires 'science' in the form of the RCT while methods needed to evaluate the latter are 'unscientific' is no longer tenable.

> **Why do you think that it is no longer tenable to assume that methods evaluating therapies and tender loving care are unscientific?**

All aspects of health services require evaluation, and many aspects of health service work cannot be evaluated within the epistemological context of the RCT.

Diverging discourses on 'risk'

A further difficulty with current research into the people's health is that it fails to engage with and critically analyse new conceptions of 'risk' being developed particularly by social theorists (Beck, 1992; Giddens, 1990b). Within the health field, the growing emphasis on prevention of disease and promotion of health has meant that the notion of populations 'at risk' is much broader than it was. There are a number of risk perceptions with which both lay and professional epidemiological expertise operate. However, in broad terms, our understanding of risk is now framed by a discourse of behaviour on one side and the environment on the other. These have very different implications for policy and practice in the health field and beyond (Lupton,1995).

Epidemiology in particular and population health research in general are increasingly concerned about the distribution of risks of morbidity and mortality. These are seen for the most part in terms of individual, behavioural and genetic risks of specific causes of morbidity and mortality. However, this approach to risk assessment is flawed because the risks are often part of cultural universes of pleasure or enjoyment – alcohol, sex or food – and because the definition of those risks in terms of behaviour overlooks the extent to which they are part of a material world which defines the distribution of those risks. The risks attached to the consumption of high fat foods, for example, are typically discussed without reference to either the material possibilities an individual or household may have of re-orientating expenditure from high to low fat products, or the cultural desire to eliminate pleasurable eating experiences from the diet.

The argument raised in the previous chapter that late modern society is a 'risk society' (Beck, 1992) is an important one. This notion, of individuals and whole populations being 'at risk', is partly a reflection of the development of the concept of risk as 'a fundamental parameter of life in late modernity, structuring the way in which experts and lay people alike organise their social worlds' (Williams and Calnan, 1996: 1614). However, there is also a sense in which much of the post-empiricist work on risk allows the real material differences which provide the conditions in which risks are distributed and perceived to disappear within some global theory of manufactured risk in a homogenised society. While (in some meaningless theoretical sense) we may all be equally at risk of acid rain, those risks which have a direct bearing on the day-to-day reality of people's lives are clearly not equally distributed.

Not the least of the dangers involved in the apocalyptic play with imponderables that many theorists of risk now enjoy, is the imperious distancing of the analysis from the social and material conditions experienced by children, women and men living in poor material circumstances on low incomes. If the populations of late modernity feel chronically insecure and 'at risk' it is because they are: at risk in terms of their employment status, their housing, their personal safety, and their health. A worker struggling to bring up young children, with neither a permanent contract nor union representation in a volatile sector of the economy, saddled with a large mortgage in a stagnant housing market, can hardly be expected to feel comfortable and secure (Hutton, 1995).

However, the material circumstances experienced by the insecure citizen will provide the material for the development of understanding rooted in personal experience. Between the 'abstracted empiricism' of epidemiologists and the 'Grand Theory' of sociologists lies a form of knowledge that is empirical without being empiricist and theoretical but not irrelevant. This is the knowledge developed by lay people to understand and act upon the conditions of risk in which they find themselves. This knowledge is critical (in the best traditions of the Frankfurt School), and it is most certainly reflexive in the sense of being 'subject to ... revision in the light of changing circumstances' (Williams and Calnan, 1996: 1612). There is also a growing confidence amongst the lay public about the 'expertise' they gain from their personal experience (Popay and Williams, 1994). This reflects, in part, a wider public scepticism of 'professional expertise' that will be an important context for population health research in the future – an issue to which we return at the end of the chapter.

Public scepticism of professional expertise

Changing public attitudes towards the status of professional expert knowledge is another aspect of the 'new times' that commentators have discerned (Gabe *et al.*, 1994; Williams and Calnan, 1996). This is evident in the way people understand the nature of scientific knowledge, the relationships between different scientific disciplines and between the knowledge of professional experts and of lay people. Together these trends should also herald new times for researching the people's health. To date, however, research in this field has largely failed to recognise and respond to the profound implications of these trends.

Desire for scientific certainty co-exists with the recognition that this is not possible. The British Government, dealing with the many implications of the crisis over beef, draws upon the rhetoric of scientific neutrality and the importance of 'evidence' as opposed to 'gossip' (*Guardian*, 1996). However, it is perfectly plain to the man and woman in the butcher's shop, the farm and the abattoir that professional experts 'disagree', and the nature of that disagreement often goes beyond any simple accumulation of epidemiological or other factual evidence. Expert knowledge is essentially contested, and experts are increasingly seen as integral to the world of politics and power which makes public opinion more suspicious of the quality of their judgements. In a world of epistemological uncertainty and 'competing rationalities' there is no universal map to guide us, only a number of alternative projections (Curry, 1996). Local knowledge – in the sense of knowledge that lay people obtain in the daily routine of their lives – is seen by some as a failed or flawed form of scientific knowledge, or as something other than knowledge altogether. However, stimulated by developments in anthropology (Geertz, 1973), lay knowledge derived from the particular – the particular locality, biography and body – is increasingly recognised as very rich and directed at different ends. Local knowledge as material knowledge provides understanding which is 'emplaced' (Curry, 1996).

While this may raise for some the prospect of a post-modern maelstrom of perspectivism, subjectivism, and relativism, we would see it as something different: an opportunity for the development of dialogue across areas of expertise, lay and professional, and for exploring the understanding developed within different discourses. What is the point of searching for the most perfect universal map if it has no meaning for the individuals and communities located on it? If epidemiology or population health research were 'emplaced' and reflexive, then practitioners would be able to take account of the socio-economic and historical dimensions of particularistic knowledge in framing research questions, designing projects, collecting and analysing data, interpreting and disseminating.

Lay knowledge: essential datum in population health research

We have so far been considering the limitations of much existing population health research. But what of the way forward? How is this field of research to go forward to address the key issues of the next century? We would suggest that if public health research is to develop more robust and holistic explanations for patterns of health and illness in contemporary society, and contribute to more appropriate and effective preventive policies, then the key is to utilise and build on lay knowledge – the knowledge that lay people have about illness, health, risk, disability and death.

The pressure to treat lay knowledge as 'an essential datum' in public health, is raised by the severe limits attaching to the contemporary practice of much public health research reviewed above. While research in the social sciences and humanities has given more attention to the meaning of health and illness in people's lives, much of this work too fails to recognise the full contribution lay knowledge can make to our understanding of the determinants of the public health. As the research briefly discussed in the next section illustrates, however, the insights to be gained if we can access and use such knowledge are many and diverse.

15.3   Lay knowledge about health in populations: an illustrative case

In 1993 Salford Health Authority commissioned a small-scale qualitative study in an inner city area. The aim was to enable people to talk widely about what it was like living in the area and to explore their perceptions of the health-related risks they faced within the context of their daily lives (Bissell, 1993).

Salford is a city of contrasts, with areas of relative affluence lying adjacent to areas of extreme social deprivation. Its mortality rate is amongst the worst in England and Wales. Standardised Mortality Ratios (SMRs) show that for every 100 deaths in England and Wales, there are 123 recorded in Salford (OPCS, 1990). In Blackfriars 80 per cent of households have no car, compared to the city average of 54.3 per cent. 22.7 per cent of the male population were officially unemployed in March 1992, and of these 47 per cent were classified as long-term unemployed. Respondents were selected from a number of sampling points including public houses, tenants associations, community drug team offices, social services departments, youth clubs, schools, along with 'snowballing' from other respondents. All in all, in-depth interviews were carried out with 69 men and women ranging in age from teenagers to people in their fifties.

Living in the material world

Although aware of the effects of individual/behavioural factors, such as smoking, drugs, drinking, diet and exercise, on their health status, respondents emphasised structural, socio-economic factors as the most powerful influences on their health. In some accounts a range of specific problems was identified. People living in high-rise accommodation stressed the practical and psychological difficulties of bringing up children in this environment – feeling depressed and isolated, being unable physically to get in and out of the area because of faulty lifts, trying to negotiate the area with prams and shopping. Some respondents had found it difficult to obtain any stable and secure accommodation in the first place, being subject to numerous moves around the locality over relatively short periods of time.

Unemployment, poverty, economic decline and the experience of crime were frequently mentioned as having severe and debilitating effects on people's health. Some people found it difficult to identify specific factors damaging their health, but feeling generally 'stressed' was central to their experience. As one woman commented:

> I think the biggest health risk is mentally... 'cause it's a lot of pressure and there's nothing really for you to do. You're sort of segregated all of the time.

There was also a concern amongst some of the people interviewed that this area had inherited a legacy of pollution from the heavy industry that used to be widespread in the area, permeating their environment:

> Up here we are lucky... but at Greengage [an adjacent area in the valley]... and over the years, how much of the pollution has gone into the pipes and the buildings still there? It's a big problem.

Some of the people interviewed presented a sophisticated understanding of the network of factors which may structure perceptions of health-related risks and associated behaviour:

> ...there are reasons why people are smoking. If they don't have a smoke then they are going round the twist and ending up going to the doctor for their nerves or having a drink. I put it down to the environment... you'll find that in areas where people are poor. ... What happens to these people when they are going on the dole is that they are living on nothing until their giro arrives and they are so depressed that they are going straight to the pub when the giro arrives and living on nothing until the next one arrives... then they are back to being depressed afterwards.

Health related risk: who knows best?

Although the understanding of their situation had not led the residents of this area into protest or revolt, there was a recognition among them of a gap between the origin and extent of the problems they faced and the public response to them. There were amongst this group of inner city residents, for example, many ways in which the knowledge and activities of 'professionals' were viewed with some scepticism. The expertise of individual professionals was questioned. Doctors were challenged by a number of respondents, with accounts of misdiagnosis being prominent themes in some interviews. As one woman noted: 'I've got no faith in the medical profession'. Beyond criticism of individual professionals, public agency responses to the problems identified in the interviews were often considered to be inadequate:

> You can have all the community workers under the sun... but that's no good, neither are youth centres. People want work, that's what they want...

In other instances these agencies were described in stronger terms. Several respondents reported thinking about or actually instituting legal proceedings against the housing department for poor maintenance or for unfair eviction. Similarly, one angry respondent commenting on the poor health of people in the local area noted that '...to me it is sheer bloody neglect by social services, the council, the police, and everybody'.

The criticisms were not confined to the action of officials, but also represented a challenge to the official definition of the problems people faced. This was most evident in relation to accounts of damp problems in houses.

> Do you mean my place? It's a nightmare... it's just literally damp everywhere. We keep getting told that it is just condensation by the Council... but we've had other people round who have verified that it is damp.

A similar challenge was apparent with regard to interpretations about the health risks associated with the legacy of the industrial past. One resident suggested that whilst 'the Council seemed to think it was nothing... over the years how many people... have died of so many diseases which is never brought forward?'

Knowledge and action: a tenuous link

In an important sense the people interviewed in inner city Salford were 'going down together'. Amongst this small sample of people there was a considerable shared understanding of the problems they faced in their everyday lives of the harm that it could and was doing to their health and that of their children and neighbours, and of their lack of power to change things. But a sense of powerlessness and the burden of simply coping with the social and material difficulties they faced were starkly evident in many people's accounts. The common ground shared, and also the factors that mitigate collective action to change things, is illustrated in accounts of an industrial accident which occurred in the area some ten years previously.

Talking about the potential harm arising from this accident, one young man noted:

> ...that was a worry and when Vicki got pregnant we thought, well, could it be airborne? But then we fairly quickly forgot about it... we have to live and work, so...

The Silk Street Chemical Explosion

On the 25th September 1982, an explosion occurred at a factory in Silk Street, in the centre of the Blackfriars area. The blast was heard 15 miles away and over 700 residents were evacuated from their homes on the evening of the explosion. Nobody was killed, though 60 people were treated in hospital. This event received national and local newspaper coverage for a number of days and it emerged that the warehouse in question had contained over 2,000 tons of flammable and explosive substances, including over 25 tons of sodium nitrate – a toxic chemical.

Dust from the blast was carried as far north as Bury and Radcliffe, and the *Salford City Reporter* (the local newspaper) of 30 September 1982 noted that '...people were warned not to touch the ash but to sweep it off cars and to wash their cars or any part of their body on which ash may have fallen'. The immediate area, as noted by the then Labour MP Frank Allaun, was one of the most densely populated in Europe and was surrounded by 15–20 storey tower blocks. Although there was considerable local and national media coverage of the event, the explosion does not seem to have given rise to any concerted form of protest. Residents in the area certainly link it to a range of health problems. As one respondent noted:

> I remember having a sore throat and running eyes for weeks after it... and it completely destroyed my garden – killed everything in it.

Another couple, drinking in a local pub on the evening of the blast, remember how dust from the blast settled on their car, destroying the chrome and some of the paint work.

> If it was doing that to cars, it makes you wonder what it was doing to your lungs doesn't it?

Alongside the view that it represented a substantial threat to health, there was, however, also scepticism about the feasibility of establishing whether there were any long-term health effects resulting from the explosion, given the diverse nature of the environmental risks in the area – in any event what could be done about it anyway?

> We were told it was alright to move back after one night, even though there was all this dust around, for weeks afterwards. But what with all the old factories and chemical works that used to be around here, you'll never really know if it caused any real harm. There's so much else around here that's bad for you...

The silencing of doubt, or the inability to express concern, could be seen as acceptance of expert authority or apathy about health damage. However, as Irwin (1996) has argued, for unprepared citizens it is very difficult to challenge the authority of experts directly, especially where the realistic view is that a connection would be very difficult to prove in any case. Whatever anxieties may exist, the exigencies of daily life crowd them out:

> I know two lads who went on to get cancer – they both moved out though, after it happened. I know a lot of people at the time were worried about it, but you can't just sit around worrying about it can you?

Embedded in these accounts is perhaps a partial explanation for the lack of local political action following the explosion. Although residents felt that there was likely to have been negative health effects as a result of the blast, life demanded their full attention – and in any event where would people go and how would they survive if they left the area?

15.4   The politics of population health research

Our guiding assumptions in this chapter have been anti-foundationalist and post-empiricist (Bryant, 1995): there is no sure foundation to our knowledge, and knowledge is not determined by the painstaking accumulation of empirical information. These assumptions inform our central contention that individuals are human agents who are knowledgeable about their society and capable of acting in it (Giddens, 1979, 1982). The research we have drawn upon above should have served as an illustration of this view.

How might such 'local knowledge' – the personal knowledge of particular circumstances revealed in the Salford study – have relevance beyond that local research area?

This small study points in a modest and very provisional way to the 'political' dimensions of population health, the complex and sophisticated knowledge that local populations hold, and the way in which individual behaviour is embedded in the social relationships and circumstances in which people conduct their lives. These accounts show us not just that individuals experience society in interesting ways, but that the knowledge people have of the impact of social forces upon them contains an understanding of the complex interplay of biography, history, locality, and the broader social divisions of class and gender. Contrary to what some professional experts may believe (Trichopoulos, 1996), sceptical and critical thinking are alive and well amongst 'the general public', whether or not they have benefited from exposure through the media to the latest epidemiological findings. In an important sense, the empirical work we have presented serves as a pointer to the 'embedded' and 'emplaced' population health research that we would wish to see developed.

In order for population health research to move in this direction it will have to draw widely on the social sciences, focusing less on the abstract relativities of behavioural risk in individuals or environmental risk to communities, and more on the dynamics of biographies, social relationships, and socio-economic conditions – within an historical context (Abrams, 1982). Social relationships, for example, need exploration that goes beyond the quantitive work on social support and networks. There needs to be a focus on individual and group relationships, both informally and with organisations and institutions, including the agencies of the state. Social relationships need to be studied as a 'site' for structures of power and control to be played out, as in gender relationships, and as the location for contemporary forms of social resistance, such as women's changing relationships with men, both within households and in the public domain.

Epidemiology describes and explains the influences on human health: why do some people die earlier than others? Why does this group have higher mortality from coronary heart disease than that group? Why does this population with rheumatoid arthritis suffer higher levels of disability than that population with the same disease? While these kinds of questions will need to remain part of population health research, they are not necessarily the most important, nor are professional epidemiologists the sole proprietors of the answers to them. As Irving Zola argued a long time ago, even if medicine and health care were able to add six inches to our heights, 30 years to our lives, and generally expand our potentialities,

> we should still be able to ask, what do six inches matter, in what kind of environment will the additional 30 years be spent, or who will decide what potentialities and potencies will be expanded and what curbed?
>
> (Zola, 1972: 504)

With the rise of evidence-based health care, it is all the more important that such questions are asked by people in a range of disciplines, and that we listen to the answers provided by both lay and professional experts.

15.5   Conclusion

We would argue that the future for population health research is not the ever more detailed, objective representation of reality but rather an engagement with it and, in conclusion, we would suggest six main areas of development for the new population health research:

1 The development of contexts for facilitating multi- and inter-disciplinary population health research. Seminars and forums are required in which scientists share information, not just on methods, but on

perspectives, interpretations and theories, including theories about theories.

2 Beyond the conference hall and the seminar room, there is a need to take lay knowledge seriously as an equal partner in developing personal and public understanding of health problems. This will involve continual involvement of lay people in different facets of research and health policy and practice.

3 The need to develop knowledge that is both epistemologically and ontologically sound. That is, recognising the value of knowledge both for its explanatory capacity and for its power to orientate people – individually and collectively – in the meaningful conduct of their everyday lives.

4 Recognising the importance of a sociological as opposed to a social epidemiology which focuses on and theorises boldly about the meaning and dynamics of social relationships and their effects on health in the manner of Durkheim in *Suicide*.

5 Notwithstanding the post-Marxist times in which we live, recognising the need for a historical materialism which grounds our analysis of health and risk within localities which have their own histories, and in which individual people live day to day in circumstances not of their own choosing.

6 The need for a reinsertion of politics into public health research, with researchers working at the interface of research, policy and practice and developing interpretations across many discourses or bodies of knowledge.

The future of population health research requires attention to the politics of public health issues, from the multiple causes of inequalities in health to the complex issues of global economics involved in environmental pollution; and doing so through exploration of the many discourses which may have a contribution to make. For social, biological and health scientists working in the population health field the challenge is the same: how to move from being, in Bauman's (1987) terms, 'legislators' in search of universal laws, to being 'interpreters' facilitating the exchange of knowledge and understanding between disciplines and social and other scientists, and between professional experts and those lay experts whose own knowledge is so often overlooked.

Chapter 16
The future of health promotion

16.1 Introduction

What is the future of health promotion? Will it become a mainstream activity within the health sector and across other areas of public policy? What are the priorities for action in health promotion? What should be our vision as we move into the twenty-first century? This final chapter brings together different visions of the future for health promotion for the UK and internationally. We asked a range of people, some working at the 'grassroots' level and others in key health policy arenas, to discuss their priorities for action. The authors weigh up the successes and failures to date of different visions of health promotion, and contemplate how some of the successes can be sustained within a changing economic climate.

16.2 Jenny Douglas

The first contributor is Jenny Douglas, who until recently was Director of Health Promotion for Sandwell, one of the most deprived areas of the UK with high rates of unemployment and poverty. She now works as a Lecturer in Health Education at the University of Birmingham. Not surprisingly, she sees the redress of health inequalities as a key priority and building health alliances and community-based action as crucial mechanisms to achieve change.

The definition of health promotion used in the Ottawa Charter: 'health promotion is the process of enabling people to increase control over and thereby improve their health', is the definition that appeals to me most. Thus the main principles underlying health promotion as I see it are those described by the WHO Health For All Charter:

...equity, community participation, multi-sectoral and international co-operation, a focus on primary health care and sustainable development.

The Ottawa Charter called for action in five areas:

- Build healthy public policy
- Create supportive environments
- Strengthen community action
- Develop personal skills
- Reorient health services.

My vision of health promotion in the future is one which holds true to the Health For All and Ottawa Charter. However this is very difficult to achieve without a political commitment to health promotion in the form of a national strategy for health. At present our national strategy 'The Health of the Nation' is focused on disease prevention, not health promotion, and takes little account of health inequalities and determinants of health.

Health promotion strategies must be developed which address inequalities, particularly those due to income, social and economic disadvantage and racial disadvantage. The development of such strategies requires the concerted efforts of a range of organisations and at all levels: international, national, regional and local. Health promotion strategies developed in one country (e.g. reduction in tobacco sales) should not put people in other less developed countries at risk (e.g. tobacco manufacturers looking for new markets in developing countries).

Health promotion must involve local people and communities in assessing health promotion needs and setting priorities for health promotion. This means there needs to be collaboration between voluntary organisations and community groups, statutory organisations and research establishments and academic organisations. Research should involve local people in assessing health promotion needs and evaluating the effectiveness of health promotion programmes and policies.

With the NHS and Community Care Act and the split between purchasers and providers, the role and function of health promotion units at an operational level in the UK is unclear. Some health promotion units are in provider organisations, while in other districts health promotion is within purchaser organisations. In addition the focus on key areas of the health of the nation and the turmoil in the organisational situation and context of most health promotion units nationally has meant that the emphasis has shifted to focusing on individual behaviour change and enabling individuals to make 'healthy choices'.

This shift has also meant that the focus of health promotion has been on professionals delivering health promotion and hence a move away from community development approaches to health promotion and health promotion strategies which truly involve local people and local communities.

Although primary care should be the cornerstone of health promotion, this too has placed emphasis on disease prevention rather than on important prerequisites like building community support and strengthening community organisations. Overall, anti-oppressive strategies promoting equality in health do not currently feature as a legitimate and valid part of the work of many health promotion units.

Although Health of the Nation places emphasis on developing healthy alliances the lead has been taken by health services. The demise of local authority health strategy units has meant that few local authorities now have healthy cities or healthy towns offices or borough-wide health strategies. As the key determinants of health fall outside the remit of national health authorities and trusts, local authorities and voluntary organisations have a major role to play in health promotion.

My vision for health promotion in the future is not optimistic. We need a clear national strategy for health which places at the centre the need to reduce inequalities in health through a range of statutory and voluntary organisations concerned with developing appropriate social and organisational policies to improve and promote health. The academic base for health promotion needs further development to provide a link between research and health promotion policy and practice. Research to support health promotion must include a range of disciplines and approaches including organisational development, and must address the social and economic causes of poor health and document the health experiences and health beliefs of local people and communities.

16.3   Sarah Nettleton

This concern to address issues of poverty and inequality is echoed by our next contributor, Sarah Nettleton, a researcher in health promotion and contemporary health services policy. She is concerned in particular about the social and economic causes of poverty and emphasises that action outside the health sector is crucial for promoting health.

It seems to me that if we want to promote health effectively the two most important things that we need to do are work towards the elimination of poverty and the reduction of social inequalities. The impact of material deprivation, social exclusion, bad housing and poor environments on health are well documented, and their effect on health and well-being are more profound than the so-called 'unhealthy' behaviours. Any genuine attempt to prevent disease and to promote health and well-being must address structural factors such as the distribution of resources throughout societies. This is not just my view, it is the view of many people working within a whole range of settings and represents a perspective that has been articulated for many decades.

Those working to promote health may acknowledge these issues and develop sensitive, community-based and non-judgemental strategies and methods which avoid victim blaming. However, people working to improve health within health and welfare settings cannot be expected to do much more than compensate for the impact of wider social and economic forces. An analogy can be drawn here with crime and policing. Whilst the police deal with the consequences of crime, and may make suggestions about how crime levels may be reduced, they cannot be expected, in their routine work, to address the causes of crime which are rooted in far wider social structures. Ironically, health is a product of factors which are not explicitly concerned with health. For example, within the arena of social policy if we want to promote health it is to policies on education, housing, employment, transport, the environment and social security that we should be turning our attention. The promotion of health requires a more profound transformation at the level of national politics and it must not remain within the sole province of health policy.

Such a view may be shared by many but it may also be castigated as being mere 'pie in the sky'. The 'new consensus politics' appears to be that economic well-being must take priority over all else so that Britain can become an economically 'robust' and 'competitive' nation. Anti-inflation policies are prioritised over unemployment; a radical restructuring of welfare provision is required to ensure that resources are not 'wasted' on those who least need them; and the rise of flexible employment practices are accepted as being inevitable within a globalised economy. Such priorities do not bode well for those who are committed to the promotion of health and who want to see a more equitable distribution of resources. Far from it, the consequences are likely to be greater social polarisation, and insecurity is likely to become endemic.

An understanding of these social processes is fundamental to the promotion of health. Matters such as globalisation, the emergence of post-industrial societies, the transformation of the nature of work, the casualisation of labour and flexible working practices, the restructuring and marketisation of welfare are not remote from health. Indeed, the extent of unemployment, the insecure nature of contemporary employ-ment and the social and geographical exclusion and marginalisation of certain social groups impact on the health of *all of us* in different ways. The material impact on health of such social polarisation on those who are worse off is obvious, but research also tells us that such inequalities are detrimental even to those who are 'better off'. This is the case because living in an unequal society which places a high value on competitiveness but which largely disregards those who are 'losing out', is ultimately unlikely to be a happy one. Such matters must not remain the province of politicians, economists, political scientists, and social policy analysts who have little explicit interest in health. An understanding of these issues by those seeking to promote health is a fundamental prerequisite to the promotion of health in the future. And those involved in the policy processes must be made to reflect upon the health consequences of their actions.

The promotion of health, therefore, requires change at three levels: cultural, economic and social. At a cultural level health is on the popular and political agenda. The media currently has an insatiable appetite for health issues and politicians are keen to demonstrate that they are committed to it. In contemporary discourse the term 'health' conjures up images of lifestyles and 'healthy' or 'unhealthy' behaviours. This does not have to be so. Health needs to be re-articulated in terms of notions of well-being, self-esteem, security, social citizenship, social participation, free-dom from fear and vulnerability, social inclusion and equity. Questions about health therefore might ask: What type of society do we want to live in? Such a question begs a collective and not an individual response.

The political assumptions and priorities of today are very different to those of the post-war years. Economic success is now seen as the precursor of health and welfare, and this is justified through recourse to matters such as the changing nature of global markets and national competitiveness – what has been regarded by some as 'unhealthy' economics. However, such arguments are not simply based on rational and objective analyses; they are also imbued with values. It may be possible therefore to shift the dialogue to one which includes a wider set of values such as equity and social inclusion. Decisions must take health consequences and costs into account and those economic analyses which fail to include social and health costs must be shown to be counterproductive. Health needs to become a prerequisite of wealth rather than the unfettered creation of wealth being a prerequisite for health.

Sound social policies are a prerequisite to a 'healthy' economy and society. We must discount the notion that they can only be implemented effectively when we have established economic competitiveness. We need to ensure that the objectives of social policy are congruent with the promotion of health. For example, social security policies should be about just that – social security. The objectives should not be to provide a safety net as a last resort, or to contribute to the perpetuation of the distinction between the deserving and undeserving poor.

Ideally, in the future the promotion of health will involve less and less emphasis on 'health promotion' within the sphere of health work. The development of healthy social and public policies which make health, defined in terms of social well-being, their prime objective would make many health promotion activities redundant. Surely the goal of health promotion is to eliminate the need for its existence?

16.4   Chris Tudor-Smith and Peter Farley

The national health promotion agencies have a particular interest, as might be expected, in the future of health promotion. What do they see as the main challenges? We hear from Chris Tudor-Smith, Director of Research and Development, and Peter Farley, Director of Training and Education from Health Promotion Wales, who look at some of the structural issues that health policy makers need to consider when contemplating how to promote health.

In developed countries the cost of health care and the demands placed on providers of health care, or rather illness, services continues to cause concern. At the same time as the technical revolution in medicine is calling for more resources, we are relying on fewer people of working age to support the health costs of an expanding elderly population. Alongside this, expectations are rising about what illness care services can achieve.

One approach to challenging this relentless shift of health and social care towards unaffordability is to more comprehensively address the issues of wellness – the more we can keep people out of the illness care system, the better we can deal with those people who unavoidably fall into it. Although there is little new in this, the time seems right for a real paradigm shift to wellness and to the vehicle for this change, health promotion.

To take up this challenge effectively, health promotion will need to cross national and organisational boundaries to deliver holistic solutions during a time of great change. It is beyond the scope of this article to consider all the pertinent changes, but three – globalisation, fragmentation and the information revolution – seem of such importance as to deserve comment.

The world is increasingly becoming a global village. For example, we will not reduce the health damage from smoking if we shift the focus of the tobacco industry from the developed to the developing world – nor will we solve the problem of air pollution if only a handful of nation states reduce harmful emissions from transport and industry. Health promoters in the future will increasingly need the advocacy skills to argue the case for health with international organisations and multinational corporations, and the facilitation skills to establish partnerships for mobilising people and material resources for health at the international level. They will also need to work with an increasing number of players on the international scene. For example, following the Maastrich Treaty, the European Union is becoming a major force in public health.

At the same time as the world appears to be becoming smaller, it also appears to be fragmenting. Nation states, large industrial units and centralised bodies for the delivery of public services all appear to be handing over responsibility to smaller-scale units. In the UK, this development is being reinforced by the purchaser/provider split with, for example, emphasis shifting from core-funded national health promotion agencies, education and health authorities to independent contractors, schools and general practitioners. This makes it even more likely that campaigns and projects will be delivered by a variety of provider organisations, public and private. We can expect less synergy between projects and less emphasis on integrated programmes, both nationally and locally. The challenge here for health promotion is that we will have to deal with an increasing number of often specialised partners, thus increasing the difficulty of offering a holistic approach to health.

Fragmentation should also enhance opportunities for local democracy and opportunities for working with communities to identify and act upon common concerns. Such development is likely to lead to even greater emphasis on settings amenable to local influence and this will be reinforced by evidence from effectiveness reviews which are very likely to continue to show the importance of complementary interventions with focal points such as schools, health services and workplaces. So in addition to skills for operating at the macro level, future health promoters will need the skills to really understand the communities they serve, to provide those communities with appropriate technical assistance and to connect them to the sources of support necessary to take effective action for health.

Parallel to these developments are the increasing availability of information and the growing variety of information sources. This may assist in developing a well-informed population and in targeting some groups who are currently regarded as hard to reach, such as young men. But, the dangers of information overload and inequality of access to information will be ever present. Again there is a challenge here for health promotion to work with those developing the new information technologies to ensure that the messages are consistent across information channels and form part of a multi-faceted approach to health. Validation schemes, similar to those that have been developed for health education leaflets, may also need to be developed for electronically-derived data to avoid potentially biased or misleading information. So future health promoters are likely to need another dimension to their skill base – a touch of technological wizardry.

In sum, the future should look bright for health promotion, providing it can establish a central role in shifting health care from an illness to wellness paradigm. This will require vision, intellectual creativity and practical ability, along with modesty, in both gaining acceptance for this change from those with a vested interest in the illness paradigm, and in realistically responding to such issues as globalisation, fragmentation and information technology. Clearly, this is an ambitious and demanding future for health promotion – would all superhumans kindly step forward!

16.5   Kathy Elliott

Kathy Elliott, a Director of the Health Education Authority for England moves the discussion into the area of debate about the value placed on positive health by policy makers and others. She sees the need for health promotion to develop new skills in evaluation and an enhanced understanding of how decisions are made and influenced.

Individual and public perceptions of health are changing. Access to health care and information, improving standards of living and other factors are having an impact on understanding and expectations in relation to health. Ways of capturing and interpreting public perceptions of health have begun to be developed: for example, surveys of health knowledge, attitudes and behaviour, focus groups, and in-depth investigations of health in the lives of individuals and families. These changes will influence the future of health promotion. They will have an impact on our understanding about health, the focus for action to improve health, the range of organisations and sectors that will be involved in action and the public's expectations about the types of action that will be taken. A health focus will take its place alongside the measurements of disease and death that have previously shaped health promotion. There will be tensions between the developing perceptions about health by individuals, the media, and the public and private sectors.

The future will bring renewed debate and action on the focus of health promotion – on the individual or the community and society? With significant exceptions, the past decades have seen a focus on the individual. Developing the tools to measure health, increasing commitment to a health focus and increasing investment, and implementing action to demonstrate effectiveness have often meant a focus on individuals rather than families, communities or nations. Caring about relevance to individual's circumstances and opinions is vital for effective health action, but if the focus on health is to grow, the contexts within which people's lives are shaped will also need to take into account an understanding of their impact on health.

Is health promotion an idea which stimulates debate or do we want to build investment for action? Forging the action has meant pioneering work, for it has meant responding to current investment patterns, and understanding about health and prevention. The future must bring more bridges between those building a theoretical understanding of health and interventions to improve health and those building investment and implementing action.

Investment and action will continue to grow, with a more realistic and informed understanding of purpose and outcomes. There will need to be public and media support, understanding and interest in the action. Public policy shaped with health improvement as a focus will continue to be essential, as will a growing sophistication about the resources needed for effective action. The future will bring opportunities to learn from the research, campaigns and other action which has focused on individual health behaviours, diseases or settings. Our understanding and experience has grown and will mean it is possible to develop further our understanding of investment options for action to improve health within a strategic framework. In the past, models of health promotion have rarely caught the imagination of investors, policy makers or politicians. A strategic framework which responds to and takes forward a publicly supported vision of health and cross-sector options for action which can demonstrate impact are needed to respond to current and future health challenges. Will they also respond to the needs of specific population groups, such as young people, older people, and deprived communities?

The future will demand an increasing focus on the impact of public policy and private sector decisions on health. Health promotion will need to develop new skills and an understanding of how decisions are made and influenced. As public and civic perceptions of health are strengthening, the number and range of situations where policy impacts on health is becoming evident. Greater use and respect for the formal mechanisms of influence and the creative ways health can be debated with opinion formers will be added to the important traditions of voluntary sector work and public health advocacy.

Communications about health have and will continue to be an important force. Public expectations of their right to information from the medical profession, media and business responses to public interest in health, an increasing educational base for individuals to learn about health, and the range of new methods of communication are all having an impact. We are all affected as individuals, within our families, at work and in communities. In the future the increased access to information about health, which could be empowering, will bring ethical dilemmas. Is access equitable? Does increasing information lead to abuse and confusion?

Health promotion will continue to be challenged to provide evidence of effectiveness. The media, public, investors in all sectors, and health professionals will continue to want to explore the value and impact of health promotion. Does it result in health gain? Does it respond to all groups, particularly those with limited resources? Does it increase equity? Our research, experience and understanding will enable those involved in health promotion to respond to these challenges.

16.6   Sir Kenneth Calman

The final contributor is the Chief Medical Officer of Health for England, a man with a strong interest in health promotion. He explores how politicians' concern for the health of the population appears to be replacing their pre-occupation with illness. He is, however, not at all complacent about what has been achieved so far and sets out some additional challenges to be faced if health is to be enhanced in the future.

A concern with health, as distinct from the treatment of illness, has taken on a higher profile in recent years. The introduction of the Health of the Nation White Paper, the first government-wide strategy to improve health in England; the creation of health authorities which have an explicit remit to identify and act upon the health needs of local populations; these developments provide a strong grounding for the practice of health promotion and a stimulus for national and local action.

Nonetheless, looking ahead, those of us who see health promotion as central to our responsibilities face a number of challenges.

Just as in clinical medicine, we need to become better at questioning practice, evaluating effectiveness, and learning from the findings of others. I do not underestimate the difficulties of research in this area – assessing the specific outcome of a single health promotion measure has been memorably described by one academic as 'like disentangling gossamer with boxing gloves'. Sometimes there is a need to educate those who are looking unrealistically for quick, cheap and unequivocal answers to complex questions. But I do see a pressing need within health promotion to extend the skills, or access to the skills, of framing testable questions; identifying sound and appropriate research techniques; building evaluation into health promotion practice; disseminating findings in accessible and useful ways; and using research findings to influence practice.

I am heartened by the way in which people are increasingly working together for better health across professional and organisational boundaries. At one end of the spectrum, national policies such as the promotion of cycling by the Department of Transport, and locally-led policies such as major urban regeneration initiatives are taking explicit account of health factors in their planning and development. The publication of *Policy Appraisal and Health* by the Department of Health (1996) provides a valuable tool for policy makers in taking account of the health impact of their policies. At the other end of the spectrum, a multitude of small initiatives brings together individuals, statutory and non-statutory organisations to promote health. The challenge for the future is to build on these relationships, demonstrate their effectiveness, and make them enduring and productive.

This means identifying the opportunities for joint working to improve health and taking a leadership role in making it happen. It can also mean having to confront, and finding ways to overcome, occasional funding and organisational inflexibilities, and reconciling differences in priorities, perspectives and responsibilities.

Given the many factors which influence health, health alliance working is likely to be essential to help reduce avoidable variations in health between different population groups, another key challenge for health promotion. The ways in which health varies across the developed world between different groups – men and women, socio-economic groups, ethnic groups, regional populations – have been well-documented. However, we are much less clear about the steps which might deliver significant reductions in those variations, over what time-scale they might have an impact, and how the scale of investment needed might relate to the scale of the benefits achieved. Health promotion in the future has an important role in helping us better understand variations in health; identifying the scope for workable measures to help reduce variations and acting as their advocate, and improving our knowledge about the effectiveness of different approaches to reducing variations.

We are faced with a number of challenges in the field of communications and ways of working. Increasingly, health promotion is seeking to be receptive to the concerns and priorities of individuals and communities themselves, and to encourage change to come from within those communities. There is still a good deal to learn about how to engage with people most successfully for this process to bear fruit, and many groups who remain hard to reach or influence, or whose needs are simply overlooked.

Finally, relations with the media remain key, not only in terms of paid-for communications, but in trying to influence the way in which health issues are presented as part of mainstream reporting, programming and advertising. We need to keep up to date with new developments in communications, and harness them for health promotion.

References

Abrams, P. (1982) *Historical Sociology*, Open Books.

Abramson, J.H. (1997) 'Epidemiology: to be taken with care', in Sidell, M. *et al.* (eds) *Debates and Dilemmas in Promoting Health: A Reader*, Macmillan, pp. 143–55.

Acheson, D. (1988) *Public Health in England*, HMSO

Acheson, R. (1990) 'The medicalisation of public health: the United Kingdom and the United States contrasted', *Journal of Public Health Medicine*, 12: 31–36.

Ackerman-Ross, F. and Sochat, N. (1980) in Miles, A. (ed.) (1991) *Women Health and Medicine*, The Open University Press.

Adams, J. (1981) *The Efficiency of Seat Belt Legislation*, University College, London, occasional paper.

Adams, L. (1989) 'Healthy cities, healthy participation', *Health Education Journal*, Vol. 48, No. 4: 179–82.

Adams, L. (1994a) 'A challenge to prevailing theory and practice', *Critical Public Health*, 5 (20): 17–29.

Adams, L. (1994b) 'Heath promotion in crisis', *Health Educational Journal*, 55: 32–33.

Adams, L. (1996) 'The role of health authorities in the promotion of health' in Scriven, A. and Orme, J. (eds) *Health Promotion: Professional Perspectives*, Macmillan, pp. 35–43.

Adams, L. quoted in Cox, R. and Findlay, G. (1990) *Community Development Health Project: A Review of Achievements So Far* , Health Promotion Service, Cambridge.

Aggleton, P. (1990) *Health: Society Now*, Routledge.

Allen, P. (1992) *Off the Rocking Horse; How Local Councils Can Promote Your Health and Environment*, Green Print.

Allen, P. (1996) 'Health promotion, environmental health and the local authority' in Scriven, A. and Orme, J. (eds) (1996) *Health Promotion: Professional Perspectives*, Macmillan, pp. 89-94.

Allsop, J. (1995) *Health Policy and the NHS, Towards 2000*, Longman.

Amos, A., Jacobson, B. and White, P. (1991) 'Cigarette advertising policy and coverage of smoking and health in British women's magazines', *Lancet*, 337: 93–96.

Anderson, D. (1986) *A Diet of Reason*, Social Affairs Unit.

Anderson, P. (1993) 'Resources for prevention and health promotion', in Fowler, G., Gray, M. and Anderson, P. (eds) *Prevention in General Practice* (2nd edn) Oxford University Press.

Arblaster, L. and Hawtin, M. (1993) *Health, Housing and Social Policy*, Socialist Health Association.

Armstrong, D. (1983) *Political Anatomy of the Body: Medical Knowledge in Britain in the Twentieth Century*, Cambridge University Press.

Armstrong, D. (1993) 'Public health spaces and the fabrication of identity', *Sociology*, 27: 3: 393–410.

Armstrong, D. (1995) 'The rise of surveillance medicine', *Sociology of Health and Illness*, 17; 3: 393–404.

Armstrong, E. and Adams, L. (1995) 'Penrith paradox', report of Symposium, forthcoming in *Journal of Health Care Analysis*.

Ashley, Y. (1986) 'Promoting positive health in women' *Focus* (3).

Ashton, J. (ed.) (1994) *The Epidemiological Imagination*, Open University Press.

Ashton, J. and Seymour, H. (1988) *The New Public Health*, Open University Press.

Ashton, J. (1993) *Healthy Cities*, Open University Press.

Ashton, S.J. *et al.* (1985) 'The effects of mandatory seat belt use in Great Britain' presented at the 10th Annual Conference of Experimental Safety Vehicles, July, Transport Road Research Laboratory.

Astrop, P. and McWilliam, J. (1996) 'The role of the Family Health Services Authorities in promoting health', Scriven, A. and Orme, J. (eds) *Health Promotion: Professional Perspectives*, Macmillan

Atkin, K., Lunt, N., Parker, G. and Hirst, M. (1993) *Nurses Count: A National Census of Practice Nurses*, Social Policy Research Unit, University of York.

Audit Commission (1991) *Saving Energy in the NHS*, No. 2, March, HMSO.

Audit Commission (1993) *Their Health, Your Business: The New Role of the District Health Authority*, HMSO.

Audit Commission (1994) *Finding Place: A Review of Mental Health Services for Adults*, HMSO.

Backett, K., Davison, C. and Mullen, K. (1994) 'Lay evaluation of health and healthy lifestyles: evidence from three studies', *British Journal of General Practice* 44: 277–80.

Bailey, L. (1991) *Roots and Branches*, Papers from the OU/HEA Winter School on Community Development and Health, The Open University.

Banks, M.H. and Ullah, P. (1988) *Youth Unemployment in the 1980s... ICS Psychological Effects*, Croom Helm.

Barnes, C. and Mercer, G. (1996) *Exploring the Divide: Illness and Disability*, The Disability Press.

Barr, H. and Shaw, I. (1995) *Shared Learning: Selected Examples from the Literature*, CAIPE.

Barrett, S. and Fudge, C. (1981) *Policy and Action: Essays on the Implementation of Public Policy*, Methuen.

Baum, F. (1992) 'Moving targets: evaluation community development', Paper presented at the 4th National Health Promotion Conference, Adelaide, Australia.

Bauman, Z. (1987) *Legislators and Interpreters: on Modernity, Postmodernity and Intellectuals*, Polity.

Beattie, A. (1991) 'Knowledge and control in health promotion: a test case for social policy and social theory' in Gabe, J., Calnan, M. and Bury, M. (eds) *The Sociology of the Health Service*, Routledge.

Beattie, A. (1991) [Chapter 5 of this text refers] 'The evaluation of community development initiatives in health promotion: a review of current strategies', *Roots and Branches*, Papers from the OU/HEA Winter School on Community Development and Health, The Open University.

Beattie, A. (1994) 'Health alliances or dangerous liaisons?', in Leathard A. (ed.) *Going Inter-Professional: Working Together for Health and Welfare*, Routledge.

Beauchamp, T.L. and Childress, J.F. (1995) *Principles of Biomedical Ethics*, Oxford University Press.

Beck, U. (1992) *Risk Society: Towards a New Modernity*, Sage.

Beck, U. (1995) *Ecological Enlightenment*, Humanities Press.

Bedford, B. (1996) Letter to *Health Services Journal*, 25th April.

Beishon, M. and Veale, S. (1996) 'Trade unions and health promotion' in Scriven, A. and Orme, J. (eds) *Health Promotion: Professional Perspectives*, Macmillan, pp. 220–7.

Benzeval, M. and Webb, S. (1995) 'Family poverty and poor health', Benzeval, M., Judge, K. and Whitehead, M. (eds) *Tackling Inequalities in Health: An Agenda for Action*, Kings Fund.

Benzeval, M., Judge, K. and Whitehead, M. (1995) *Tackling Inequalities in Health: An Agenda for Action*, Kings Fund.

Beresford, P. and Green, D. (1996) 'Income and wealth: an opportunity to reassess the poverty debate', Critical Social Policy, 16 (1): 95–109.

Berryman, J. (1984) *The Psychological Effects of Unemployment*, University of Lancaster.

Best, R. (1995) 'The housing dimension', Benzeval, M., Judge, K. and Whitehead, M. (eds) *Tackling Inequalities in Health: An Agenda for Action*, Kings Fund.

Beveridge, W. (1942) *Full Employment in a Free Society*, George Allen and Unwin.

Bines, W. (1994) *The Health of Single, Homeless People*, Housing Research Finding No. 128, Joseph Rowntree Foundation.

Bissell, P. (1993) *Risk: An Exploration of Styles of Life and Structural Context. A Locality Study*. A Report to the Department of Health Promotion, Salford Health Authority.

Blackburn, C. (1991) *Poverty and Health, Working with Families*, Open University Press.

Blackburn, C. (1995) *Poverty and Health: Tools For Change*, Public Health Alliance.

Blandy, J. (1989) *Lecture Notes on Urology*, Blackwell Scientific Publications.

Blaxter, M. (1983) 'The causes of disease: women talking' *Social Science and Medicine*, Vol. 17, No. 2: 59–69.

Blaxter, M. (1990) *Health and Lifestyles*, Routledge.

Blennerhassett, S., Farrant, W. and Jones, J. (1989) 'Support for community health projects in the UK: a role for the National Health Service', *Health Promotion International*, Vol. 4, No. 3: 198–206.

Booth, C. (1891) *Life and Labour of the London Poor*, Macmillan.

Bracht, N. and Tsouros, A. (1990) 'Principles and strategies of effective community participation', *Health Promotion International*, 5: 199–208.

Bradford, M. and Winn, S. (1993) 'Practice nursing and health promotion: a case study' in Wilson-Barnett, J. and Macleod Clark, J. (eds) *Research in Health Promotion and Nursing*: 119–31, Macmillan.

Bradford, N. (1995) *Men's Health Matters*, Vermillion.

Bradshaw, J. (1980) 'An end to differentials?', *New Society*, 9 October.

Bradshaw, J. *et al.*, (1992) *Household Budgets and Living Standards – Findings*, Joseph Rowntree Foundation.

British Medical Journal (1991) Editorial, BMJ 303: 1547–8.

British Medical Journal (1996) 'British GPs take charge of health promotion', *BMJ* 312: 1058.

Brod, H. (ed.) (1987) *The Making of Masculinities: The New Men's Studies*, Allen and Unwin.

Brown, I. and Lunt, F. (1992) Evaluating a Well Man Clinic, *Health Visitor*, Vol. 65, No. 1.

Brown, V., Ritchie, J. and Rotem, A. (1992) 'Health promotion and environmental management: a partnership for the future', *Health Promotion International*, 7 (3): 219–30.

Bruce, N., Springett, J., Hotchkiss, J. and Scott-Samuel, A. (1995) *Research and Change in Urban Community Health*, Avebury.

Bruckenwell, P. (1995) *The Crisis in Men's Health*, Community Health UK.

Bryant, C. (1995) *Practical Sociology: Post-Empiricism and the Reconstruction of Theory and Application,* Polity.

Bryant, J.H. (1988) 'Health for All: the dream and the reality', *World Health Forum*, Vol. 9.

Bunton, R. and Burrows, R. (1995) 'Consumption and health in the "epidemiological clinic" of late modern medicine', in Bunton, R., Nettleton S. and Burrows, R. (eds) *The Sociology of Health Promotion and the New Public Health*, Routledge.

Bunton, R. in Bunton, R. and Macdonald, G. (eds) (1993) *Health Promotion: Disciplines and Diversity*, London, Routledge.

Bunton, R., Nettleton, S. and Burrows, R. (eds) (1995) *The Sociology of Health Promotion*, Routledge.

Burridge, R. and Ormandy, D. (eds) (1993) *Unhealthy Housing: Research, Remedies and Reform*, E. and F.N. Spon.

Butler Sloss, E. (1988) *Report of the Inquiry into Child Abuse in Cleveland 1987* Cm 413, HMSO.

Calnan, M. *et al.* (1994) 'Involvement of the primary health care team in coronary heart disease prevention', *British Journal of General Practice*, 44: 224–8.

CAOT (1996) 'Position statement on primary health care' in *Canadian Journal of Occupational Therapy* Vol. 63, No. 2: 143–4.

Caplan, R. (1993) 'The importance of social theory for health promotion: from description to reflexity' *Health Promotion International*, Vol. 8, No. 2: 147–57.

Capra, F. (1982) *The Turning Point,* Wellwood House.

Caraher, M. and McNab, M. (1997) 'Public health nursing. Challenging the challenge: an alternative viewpoint' in *Health Visitor* (forthcoming).

Carson, R. (1965) *Silent Spring*, Penguin.

Castel, R. (1991) 'From dangerousness to risk' in Burchell, G., Gordon, G. and Miller, P. (eds) *The Foucault Effect: Studies in Governmentality*, Harvester Wheatsheaf.

Catford, J. and Parish, R. (1989) 'Heartbeat Wales: New horizons for health promotion in the community – the philosophy of Heartbeat Wales', in Seedhouse, D. and Cribb, A. (eds) *Changing Ideas in Health Care*, John Wiley & Sons Ltd.

Cawson, A. (1982) *Corporatism and Welfare: Social Policy and State Intervention in Britain*, Macmillan.

Cervi, B. (1995) 'Is our starting point all wrong?', *IHSM Network* Vol. 2, Number 9, 9 May: 4.

Chadwick, E. (1842) *Report of the Sanitary Condition of the Labouring Population of England*, Vol. 26, HMSO.

Chapman, S. and Eggar, G. (1993) 'Myth in cigarette advertising and health promotion' in Beattie, A. *et al.* (eds) *Health and Wellbeing: A Reader*, Macmillan.

Charlton, J. (1993) 'Suicide trends in England and Wales: trends in factors associated with suicide deaths', *Population Trends* (71).

Charlton, J., Kelly, S., Dunnell, K., Evans, B., Jenkins, R. and Wallis, R. (1992) 'Trends in suicide death in England and Wales', *Population Trends* (69).

Chodorow, N. (1978) *The Reproduction of Mothering: Psychoanalysis and the Sociology of Gender*, University of California Press.

Clarke, K. (1996) television interview, BBC2, September 1996

Cochrane, A. (1972) *Effectiveness and Efficiency: Random Reflections on Health Services*, The Nuffield Provincial Hospitals Trust.

COHP (1993) *Annual Report*, Camden Occupational Health Project.

Coke, J. (1991) 'Building alliances: but on whose terms? Some reflections on a Black woman's experiences', *Roots and Branches*, Papers from the OU/HEA Winter School on Community Development and Health, The Open University.

Cole, A. (1995/1986) 'The persuaders', *Health Lines*, December/January: 17–19.

Coleman, F. (1982) *Death is a Social Disease*, University of Wisconsin.

Colin-Thomé, D. (1993) 'The public health nurse: a new model for health visiting?', *Primary Care Management* 3, 5: 4–6.

Collins, T. (1997) 'Models of health: pervasive, persuasive and politically charged', in Sidell, M. *et al.* (eds) *Debates and Dilemmas in Promoting Health: A Reader*, Macmillan, pp. 54–64.

Community Health UK (1995) *The Crisis in Men's Health*, Community Health UK, Bath.

Community Projects Foundation (1988) *Action for Health: Initiatives in Local Communities*, Community Projects Foundation.

Conroy, C. and Litvinoff, M. (1988) *The Greening of Aid*, Earthscan.

Cook, J. and Watt, S. (1987) 'Racism, women and poverty', Glendinning, C. and Millar, J. (eds) (1987) *Women and Poverty in Britain*, Harvester.

Coulter, A. (1993) 'Socio-economic influences on health' in Fowler, G., Gray, M. and Anderson, P. (eds) *Prevention in General Practice* (2nd edn) Oxford University Press.

Cowley, S. (1995) 'Health Visitors' Association response to the OXCHECK study and the British Family Heart Study' in National Heart Forum *Preventing Coronary Heart Disease in Primary Care: The Way Forward*, HMSO.

Cox, D. (1991) 'Health service management – a sociological view: Griffiths and the non-negotiated order of the hospital' in Gabe, J., Calnan, M. and Bury, M. (eds) *The Sociology of the Health Service*, Routledge.

Cox, R. and Findlay, G. (1990) Community Development Health Project: A Review of Achievements So Far, Health Promotion Service, Cambridge.

Cox, R.A.F., Edwards, F.C., McCallum R.I. (1995), *Fitness for Work*, Oxford University Press.

Croft, S. and Beresford, P. (1992) 'The politics of participation', *Critical Social Policy,* Vol. 12, No. 2: 20–44.

Crombie, H. (1995) *Sustainable Development and Health*, Public Health Alliance.

Curry, R. (1996) 'Space and place in geographic decision-making', *Technical Expertise and Public Decisions* (Proceedings of the 1996 International Symposium on Technology and Society), IEEE and Princeton University, NJ, USA.

Curtice, J. (1991) 'Can participation achieve changes in health?', in *Roots and Branches*, Papers from OU/HEA Winter School on Community Development and Health, The Open University.

Daly, H. (1977) 'The steady state economy: what, why and how?', Pirages, D. (ed.) *The Sustainable Society: Implications for Limited Growth*, Praeger.

Dalziel, Y. (1994) 'Integrating a community development approach with mainstream health visiting', *Health Visitor*, Vol. 67, No. 10: 355–6.

Davidson, N. (1987) *A Question of Care*, Michael Joseph.

Davies, C. (1988) 'The health visitor as mother's friend', *Journal of the Society for the Study of the Social History of Medicine*, Vol. 1: 1–25

Davies, J.K. and Kelly, M. (1993) *Healthy Cities, Research and Practice*, Routledge.

Davis, A. and Jones, L.J. (1996) Health and environmental constraints: listening to children's views' in *Health Education Journal*, Dec.

Daykin, N., Naidoo, J. and Wilson, N. (1995) *Effective Health Promotion in Primary Care: A Resource for Primary Health Care Workers*, University of the West of England.

De Leeuw, R. and Polman, S. (1995) 'Policy making for health: the Dutch experience' *Health Promotion International* No. 3: 105–17.

Dean, K. and Hunter, D. (1996) 'New directions for health: towards a knowledge base for public health action' *Social Science and Medicine*, 42: 745–50.

Dean, K., Kreiner, S. and McQueen, D. (1993) 'Researching population health: new directions' in Dean, K. (ed.) *Population Health Research: Linking Theory and Methods*, Sage.

Deans, W. (1988) 'Well Man Clinics' *Nursing*, 26: 975–8.

Delaney, F. (1996) 'Theoretical issues in intersectoral collaboration' in Scriven, A. and Orme, J. (eds) *Health Promotion: Professional Perspectives*, Macmillan, pp. 22–32.

Department of Health (DoH) (1987) *Healthy Cities Initiative,* HMSO.

Department of Health (DoH) (1989a) *Working for Patients: The Health Service: Caring for the 1990s*, Cm 489, HMSO.

Department of Health (DoH) (1989b) *Caring for People: Community care in the next decade and beyond: Policy Guidance*, HMSO.

Department of Health (DoH) (1990) *General Practice in the NHS. The 1990 Contract*, HMSO.

Department of Health (DoH) (1991) *Working together: A guide to arrangements for inter-agency cooperation for the protection of children from abuse*, HMSO.

Department of Health (DoH) (1992) *The 'Health of the Nation'. A Strategy for Health in England*, HMSO.

Department of Health (DoH) (1993a) *The State of Public Health 1992,* HMSO.

Department of Health (DoH) (1993b) *The Health of the Nation – One Year On: A Report on the Progress of the Health of the Nation*, HMSO.

Department of Health (DoH) (1993c) *Working Together for Better Health,* HMSO.

Department of Health (DoH) (1993d) *Better Living, Better Life,* HMSO.

Department of Health (DoH) (1995a) *Variations in Health, What can the Department of Health and the NHS do?,* Report of the Variations Sub-Group of the Chief Medical Officer's Health of the Nation Working Group, HMSO.

Department of Health (DoH) (1995b) *Policy Appraisal and Health,* HMSO.

Department of Health (DoH) (1995c) *Making it Happen,* Report of Standing Nursing and Midwifery Administration Committee (SNMAC).

Department of Health (DoH) (1996) The Health of the Nation Consultative Document: *The Environment and Health,* HMSO.

Department of Health for Northern Ireland (DHSS, NI) (1995) *A Strategy for Health in Northern Ireland,* HMSO.

Department of Health for Northern Ireland (DHSS, NI) (1996) *Health and Wellbeing: Into the Next Millenium,* HMSO.

Department of the Environment (DoE) (1990) *This Common Inheritance: Britain's Environmental Strategy,* HMSO.

Department of the Environment (DoE) (1994) *Sustainable Development – The UK Strategy,* Cmnd 2426, HMSO.

Department of the Environment (DoE) (1995) *Policy and Planning Guidance Paper 13,* HMSO.

Department of the Environment (DoE) (1996a) *Indicators of Sustainable Development for the United Kingdom,* HMSO.

Department of the Environment (DoE) (1996b) *The United Kingdom National Environmental Action Plan,* HMSO.

Dines, A. (1997) 'A case study of the ethical issues in health promotion – mammography screening: the nurse's position', in Sidell, M. *et al.* (eds) *Debates and Dilemmas in Promoting Health: A Reader,* Macmillan, pp. 114–27.

Dingwall, R., Rafferty, A.M. and Webster, C. (1988) *An Introduction to the Social History of Nursing,* Routledge.

Dix, A. (1995) 'Promotional tactics', *Health Service Journal* 23 November: 37.

Dobson, A. (ed.) (1991) *The Green Reader,* André Deutsch.

Doherty, J.W. and Campbell, L.T. (1988) *Families and Health,* Sage.

Doll, R. and Hill, A.B. (1950) 'Smoking and carcinoma of the lung: preliminary report' in *British Medical Journal,* 2: 739–48.

Doll, R. and Hill, A.B. (1952) 'A study of the aetiology of carcinoma of the lung' in *British Medical Journal,* 2: 1271–86.

Douglas, J. (1991) 'Influences on the community development and health movement – a personal view' in *Roots and Branches,* Papers from the OU/ HEA Winter School on Community Development and Health, The Open University.

Douglas, J. (1996) 'Developing health promotion strategies with Black and minority ethnic communities which address social inequalities' in Bywaters, P. and McLeod, E. (eds) *Working for Equality in Health,* Routledge.

Draper, P. (ed.) (1991) *Health Through Public Policy,* Green Print.

Draper, R. (1992) *Reflections on Progress – Health for All 2000,* WHO, European Region.

Dubos, R. (1959) *Mirage of Health,* Doubleday.

Eakin, J. (1992) 'Leaving it up to the workers: sociological perspectives on the management of health and safety in small workplaces' *International Journal of Health Services*, Vol. 22, No. 4: 689–704.

Eakin, J.M. and Weir, N. (1995) 'Canadian approaches to the promotion of health in small workplaces', *Canadian Journal of Public Health*, March–April: 109–13.

Easton, D. (1965) *A Systems Analysis of Political Life,* Wiley.

Eichenbaum, L. and Orbach, S. (1984), *What do Women Want?* Fontana.

Ekins, P. (1986) *The Living Economy*, Routledge and Kegan Paul.

Ekins, P. (1993) *Trading Off the Future*, New Economic Foundation.

Elkin, T., McLaren, D. with Hillman, M. (1991) *Reviving the City: Towards Sustainable Urban Development*, Friends of the Earth.

Elkind, A. (1995) 'Pass Notes', *Health Service Journal*, 4 May: 30–31.

Engel, C. (1994) 'A functional anatomy of teamwork', in Leathard A. (ed.) *Going Inter-Professional: Working Together for Health and Welfare*, Routledge.

Engels, F. (1969) *The Condition of the Working Class in England: from Personal Observation and Authentic Sources*, Panther.

EURO/WHO (1994) *The Environmental Health Action Plan for Europe*, WHO/EURO

Evers, H., Cameron, C., Badger, F. (1994) 'Inter-professional work with old and disabled people', in Leathard A. (ed.) *Going Inter-Professional: Working Together for Health and Welfare*, Routledge.

Ewles, L. (1996) 'The impact of the NHS reforms on specialist health promotion in the NHS' in Scriven, A. and Orme, J. (eds) *Health Promotion: Professional Perspectives*, Macmillan, pp. 66–74.

Ewles, L. and Simnett, I. (1995) *Promoting Health* (3rd edn), Scutari Press.

Family Heart Study Group (1994) 'Randomised control trial evaluating cardiovascular screening and intervention in general practice: principal results of British family heart study', *British Medical Journal* 308: 313–20.

Fareed, A. (1994) 'Equal rights for men', *Nursing Times*. Vol. 90, No. 5.

Farrant, W. (1991) 'Addressing the contradictions: health promotion and community health action in the United Kingdom', *International Journal of Health Services*, 21; 3: 423–39.

Farrant, W. (1994) 'Addressing the contradictions: health promotion and community health action in the United Kingdom', *Critical Public Health*, Vol. 5, No.1: 5–19.

Farrell, W. (1974) *The Liberated Man,* Bantam.

Fasteau, M.F. (1974) *The Male Machine,* McGraw-Hall.

Fee, E. and Porter, D. (1992) 'Public health, preventive medicine, and professionalisation', Wear, A. (ed.) *Medicine in Society: Historical Essays*, Cambridge University Press.

Fisher, B. (1994) 'The Wells Park Health Project', in Heritage, Z. (ed.) *Community Participation in Primary Care*, Occasional Paper 64, Royal College of General Practitioners.

Flynn, R., Pickard, S. and Williams, G. (1995) 'Contracts and the quasi market in community health services', *Journal of Social Policy*, Vol. 24, Part 4, October: 529–50.

FOREST (Freedom Organisation for the Right to Enjoy Smoking Tobacco) (1989) *Newsletter*, No. 1, June.

Foucault, M. (1973) *The Birth of the Clinic: An Archaeology of Medical Perception*, Tavistock.

Foucault, M. (1977) *Discipline and Punishment: The Birth of the Prison*, Penguin.

Foucault, M. (1980) *Power/Knowledge: Selected Interviews and Other Writings, 1972-1977*, Gordon, C. (ed.), Harvester Press.

Fowler, G. and Mant, D. (1990) 'Health checks for adults', *British Medical Journal* 300: 1318–20.

Fox, J., Goldblatt, P. and Jones, D. (1990) 'Social class mortality differentials: artefact, selection or life circumstances', Goldblatt, P. (ed.) *Longitudinal Study: Mortality and Social Organisation 1971-1981*, OPCS series LS No. 6, HMSO.

Frayman, H. (1991) *Breadline Britain 1990s*, Domino Films/London Weekend Television.

Freire, P. (1972) *Pedagogy of the Oppressed*, Sheed Ward.

French, J. (1990) 'Boundaries and horizons, the role of health education within health promotion', *Health Education Journal*, 49, 1: 7–10.

Freud, P. and Meredith, B. (1991) *Health Illness and the Social Body*, Prentice Hall.

Friends of the Earth (1996) Press release: 'FoE says UK will fail to meet 7 out of 9 targets on health and the environment', FoE, July 8.

Fryer, D.M. and Payne, R.L. (1986) 'Being unemployed: A review of the literature and the psychological experience of unemployment', in Coopy, C.L. and Robertson, I. (eds) *Review of Industrial and Organisational Psychology*, Wiley.

Funnell, R., Oldfield, K. and Speller, V. (1995) *Towards Healthier Alliances*, HEA.

Gabe, J., Kelleher, D. and Williams, G. (eds) (1994) *Challenging Medicine*, Routledge.

Gagnon, J. and Henderson, B. (1985) 'The social psychology of sexual development', in Henslin, J.M. (ed.) *Marriage and Family in a Changing Society*, Free Press.

Geertz, C. (1973) *The Interpretation of Cultures*, Basic Books, New York.

General Services Medical Committee (1992) *The New Health Promotion Package*, British Medical Association.

George, V. (1981) 'Ideology and the welfare state', unpublished paper given to Social Administration Annual Conference, Leeds, July 1981.

George, V. and Howards, I. (1991) *Poverty Amidst Affluence*, Edward Elgar.

Gerhardt, U. (1989) *Ideas about Illness: An Intellectual and Political History of Medical Sociology*, Macmillan.

Giddens, A. (1979) *Central Problems in Social Theory: Action, Structure and Contradiction in Social Analysis*, Macmillan.

Giddens, A. (1982) *Profiles and Critiques in Social Theory*, Macmillan.

Giddens, A. (1990a) *The Consequences of Modernity*, Polity.

Giddens, A. (1990b) *Modernity and Self-identity*, Polity.

Giddens, A. (1991) *Modernity and Self-identity: Self and Society in the Late Modern Age*, Polity.

Gillam, S. (1992) 'Provision of health promotion clinics in relation to population need: another example of the inverse care law?', *British Journal of General Practice*. 42: 54–56.

Gillam, S., Pampling, D., McClenahan, J., Harries, J. and Epstein, L. (1994) *Community Oriented Primary Care*, King's Fund.

GLACHC (Greater London Association of Community Health Councils) (1995) *A Review of Health Promotion in Primary Care: From the GP Health Promotion Contract to Promoting Health with Local Communities*, GLACHC, London.

Glan y Mor NHS Trust (undated) *Healthy Hospitals Initiative Projects, Cefn Coed Hospital 1993-1998*, bound with *A Strategy for Health in West Glamorgan 1993-1998*, District Services Unit, Glan y Mor NHS Trust.

Glendinning, C. and Millar, J. (eds) (1987) *Women and Poverty in Britain*, Harvester.

Goldberg, H. (1976) *The Hazards of Being Male*, New American Library.

Goldblatt, P. (ed.) (1990) *Longitudinal Study: Mortality and Social Organisation 1971-1981*, OPCS series LS, No. 6, HMSO.

Goode, J. (1995/1996) 'Nutritional guidelines: constructing a variable menu', *Health Line*, December/January: 6–7.

Gorman, E. (1995) 'Men are complacent about their health', *The Times*, 20 March 1995.

Gosling, A. (1992) 'Wells Park Health Project: joy, caring and better health', *Community Health Action*, 23: 12–13.

Grace, V.M. (1991) 'The marketing of empowerment and the construction of the health consumer: a critique of health promotion', *International Journal of Health Services*, 21: 329–43.

Graham, H. (1984) *Women, Health and the Family*, Health Education Council/ Harvester Wheatsheaf.

Graham, H. (1993) *Health and Hardship in Women's Lives*, Harvester Wheatsheaf.

Green, D. (1992) *Equalising People*, Institute of Economic Affairs, Health and Welfare Unit.

Green, J. (1994) *Talking with Children*, Report to the City Advising Board, Newcastle-upon-Tyne Social Welfare Research Unit, University of Northumria at Newcastle.

Gregson, B., Cartlidge, A. and Bond, J. (1991) *Interprofessional Collaboration in Primary Health Care Organisations*, Occasional Paper 52, Royal College of General Practitioners.

Griffiths, J. (1990) 'A new GP contract for health promotion', *Primary Health Care Management* 1: 8–10.

Griffiths, S. (1992) 'The neglected male', *British Journal of Hospital Medicine*. 48 (10): 627–9.

Griffiths, S. (1993) *Through Health Workers to Welfare Rights. A Report on the Health and Benefits Pilot in Goodinge and Finsbury Health Centres*, Camden and Islington FHSA.

Gruber, J. and Tricket, E.J. (1987) 'Can we empower others? The paradox of empowerment in the governing of an alternative public school', *American Journal of Community Psychology*, 15: 353–72.

Guardian (1995) 'Depravity beyond words. The West trial has left many questions unanswered', 23 November.

Guardian (1996) 'Hiding behind experts' (editorial), *Guardian*, 26 March.

Guardian, 23 August 1996, p.3.

Haggard, L. and Ormiston, H. (1993) 'A long road ahead', *Community Care* 17 June: 16–17.

Hall, P. (ed.) (1975) *Change, Choice and Conflict in Social Policy*, Methuen.

Ham, C. (1992) *Health policy in the UK*, Macmillan.

Ham, C. (1996) 'The organisation of the NHS', *Health Service Yearbook*, NAHAT, pp. 27–40.

Ham, C. and Shapiro, J. (1995) 'The alliance of scions', *Health Service Journal*, 18 May: 22–23.

Hamand, J. (1991) *Prostate Problems,* Thorsens.

Hancock, T. (1993) 'Health, human development and the community ecosystem: three ecological models', *Health Promotion International* Vol. 8, No. 1.

Handy, C. (1994) *The Empty Raincoat: Making Sense of the Future*, Hutchinson.

Hansard (House of Commons) (1986, 1993) reported in Kinman, B.F. and Vinten, G. (1996) 'The role of UK tobacco advertising: no effect on the nation's health?' in *Journal of the Royal Society of Health*, Vol. 116 (1) February: 21–26.

Hanson, S. *et al.* (1991) *Health Before Health Care*, Social Policy Paper No. 4, Institute for Public Policy Research.

Harris, V. (ed.) (1994) *Community Work Skills Manual,* Association of Community Workers.

Harrison, A. (ed.) (1992) *Health Care UK 1991*, King's Fund Institute.

Harrison, S., Hunter, D. and Pollitt, C. (1990) *The Dynamics of British Health Policy*, Unwin.

Hart, G., Fitzpatrick, R., McLean, J., Dawson, J., Boulton, M. (1990) 'Gay men, social support and HIV disease: a study of social integration in the gay community', *AIDS Care,* No. 2.

Hart, G., Fitzpatrick, R., McLean, J., Dawson, J., Boulton, M. (1993) 'Risk behaviour, anti-HIV and anti-HBc prevalence in clinic and non-clinic samples of gay men in England 1991–2', *AIDS Care*, No. 7.

Hart, N. (1986) 'Inequalities in health: The individual versus the environment' *in Journal of the Royal Statistical Society* (series A), Vol. 149, Pt. 3: 228–46.

Hawe, P. (1994) 'Capturing the meaning of "community" in community intervention evaluation: some contributions from community psychology', *Health Promotion International*, Vol. 9, No. 3: 199–208.

Hay, C., O'Brien, M. and Penna, S. (1994) 'Giddens, modernity and self-identity: the "hollowing out" of social theory', *Arena Journal*, NS, 2: 45–76.

Hay, J.R. (1975) *The Origins of the Liberal Reforms, 1906–1914*, Macmillan.

Health Education Authority (HEA) (1992) *Tomorrow's Young Adults*, HEA.

Health Education Authority (HEA) (1993a) *Multidisciplinary Team Workshop Programme*, HEA.

Health Education Authority (HEA) (1993b) *The Smoking Epidemic – A Prescription For Change*, HEA.

Health Education Authority (HEA) (1994) *The MESMAC Guide*, HEA.

Health Education Authority (HEA) (1995a) *Health and Lifestyles in the UK*, HEA.

Health Education Authority (HEA) (1995b) *Tomorrow's Young Adults. 9–15 year olds look at alcohol, exercise, drugs and smoking*, HEA.

Health Education Authority (HEA) (1995c) *Awareness of Men's Cancers,* unpublished report.

Health Education Authority (HEA) (1996a) *Health in England 1995*, HEA.

Health Education Authority (HEA) (1996b) *Monitoring Survey*, HEA.

Healthy Sheffield 2000 (1991) *Our City, Our Health*, Sheffield City Council.

Healthy Sheffield 2000 (1993) *Community Development and Health: The Way Forward in Sheffield*, Sheffield City Council.

Hearn, J. and Morgan, D. (1990) *Men, Masculinities and Social Theory*, Unwin-Hyman.

Heginbotham, C. (1996) 'Return to community: the ethics of inclusion and exclusion' in Parker, M. (ed.) *Ethics and Community*, University of Central Lancashire.

Heritage, Z. (1994) (ed.) *Community Participation in Primary Care*, Occasional Paper 64, Royal College of General Practitioners.

HMSO (1991) *O.P.C.S. General Household Survey*, HMSO.

Holroyd, G. (1991) 'Promoting mental health by facilitating participation in planning – the Salford experience', *Roots and Branches*, Papers from the OU/HEA Winter School on Community Development and Health, The Open University.

Holroyd, G. and Lucy, L. (1990) 'A tentative look at men's health', *Men Too*, Autumn.

Hookham, J. (1995) 'Air quality, the commercial vehicle and company car fleets', *Greenhouse*, Issue 5, October, Institute of Earth Sciences, Oxford.

Hornby, S. (1993) *Collaborative Care: Interprofessional, Interagency, and Interpersonal*, Blackwell Scientific Publications.

Hudson, B. (1987) 'Collaboration in social welfare: a framework for analysis', *Policy and Politics*, Vol. 15, No. 3: 175–82.

Hudson, B. (1994) 'Break in the chain', *Health Service Journal*, 104 (5399): 24–26.

Hughes, J. and Gordon, P. (1992) *An Optimal Balance? Primary Health Care and Hospital Services in London*, King's Fund.

Hunt, S. (1990) 'Emotional distress and bad housing', *Health and Hygiene*, 11: 72–9.

Hunt, S. (1993) 'The public health effects of private cars', Beattie, A. *et al.*, (eds) *Health and Wellbeing: A Reader*, Macmillan.

Hunter, D. and O'Toole, S. (1995) 'Rosy outlook', *Health Service Journal* 11 May: 20–21.

Huntington, J. and Killoran, A. (1991) 'Winning at the primaries', *Health Service Journal*, 21 November: 24–25.

Hutton, W. (1995) *The State We're In*, Jonathan Cape.

Independent (1994) 'Gaining benefits of a new system', *Independent* 15 September.

Ineichen, B. (1993) *Homes and Health: How Housing and Health Interact*, E. & F.N. Spon.

Irwin, I. (1996) *Citizen Science*, Routledge.

Jackson, C. (1991) 'Men's health: opening the floodgates', *Health Visitor*. 64 (8): 265–6.

Jackson, C. (1993) 'Pitching the message at men', *Health Visitor* 66 (9): 327–8.

Jacobs, M. (1991) *The Green Economy*, Pluto Press.

Jacobson, B. (1988) *Beating the Ladykillers. Women and Smoking*, Gollancz.

Jacobson, B., Smith, A. and Whitehead, M. (1991) *The Nation's Health*, Kings Fund Publishing.

Johnson, P. and Webb, S. (1993) 'Explaining the growth in UK income inequality 1979–88', *Economic Journal Conference Papers*, 103 (417): 429–35.

Jones, G. (1985) *Social Hygiene in the Twentieth Century*, Sage.

Jones, J. (1991) 'Community development and health education: concepts and philosophy' in *Roots and Branches*, Papers from the OU/HEA Winter School on Community Development and Health, The Open University.

Jones, L.J. (1994) *The Social Context of Health and Health Work*, Macmillan.

Jones, L.J. (1995a) 'Business interests and public policy making' in Jones, H. and Lansley, J. (eds) *Social Policy and the City*, Avebury.

Jones, L.J. (1995b) *Transport and Health: The Next Move*, A report for the Association of Public Health, APL.

Jones, M. (1996) 'Healthy settings, healthy scepticism (a personal view)' in *UK Health For All Network News*, Winter1995/Spring 1996: 11.

Katz, J. and Peberdy, A. (1997) *Promoting Health: Knowledge and Practice*, Macmillan.

Kelly, J.M. (1980) in Miles, A. (1991) *Women, Health and Medicine*, The Open University Press.

Kelly, M. and Charlton, B. (1992) 'Health promotion: time for a new philosophy?', *British Journal of General Practice*, June: 223–4.

Kenny, S. (1994) *Developing Communities for the Future*, Thomas Nelson.

Kickbusch, I. (1984) 'Health promotion – a typology', in WHO Regional Office for Europe *Health Promotion: Concepts and Principles*. A selection of papers presented at the working group on concepts and principles, Copenhagen, 1984.

Kickbusch, I. (1989a) 'Healthy Cities: a working project and a growing movement', *Health Promotion* 4, 2: 77–82.

Kickbusch, I. (1989b) cited in Kaplun, A. and Wenzel, E. (eds) (1989) *Health Promotion in the Working World*, Springer Verlag.

Kimmel, M.S. and Messner, M. (eds) (1993) *Men's Lives*, Macmillan.

Kinman, B.F. and Vinten, G. (1996) 'The role of UK tobacco advertising: no effect on the nation's health?' in *Journal of the Royal Society of Health*, Vol. 116 (1) February.

Klein, R. (1983) *The Politics of the National Health Service*, Longman.

Klein, R. (1995) *The New Politics of the NHS*, 3rd edition, Longman.

Kruger, A. (1994) 'The mid-life transition – crisis or chimera?' *Psychological Reports*, No. 75.

La Berge, A.F. (1992) *Mission and Method: The Early French Public Health Movement*, Cambridge University Press.

Labonte, R. (1991) 'Econology: integrating health and sustainable development. Part two: guiding principles', *Health Promotion International*, 6: 147–56.

Labonte, R. (1993) 'Community development and partnerships', *Canadian Journal of Public Health*, Vol. 84, No. 4: 237–40.

Lalonde, M. (1974) *A New Perspective on the Health of Canadians*, Ottawa, Ministry of Supply and Services.

Lamond, B., cited in Pownall, M. (1985) 'Action men', *Nursing Times*, 4 December.

Lancet, The (1993) 'Rise and fall of diseases' (editorial), The Lancet, 341: 151.

Lancet, The (1994) Population health looking upstream (editorial), The Lancet, 343: 429.

Le Touze, S. (1996) 'Health promotion in general practice – the views of staff' Nursing Times, Vol. 92, No. 1, 3 January: 32–33.

Leathard, A. (1994) 'Interprofessional developments in Britain', and 'Conclusion and future agendas' in Leathard, A. (ed.) Going Inter-Professional: Working Together for Health and Welfare, Routledge.

Lee, P. and Raban, C. (1983) 'Welfare and ideology' in Loney, M., Boswell, D. and Clarke, J. (eds) Social Policy and Social Welfare, Open University Press.

Lewis, J. (1980) The Politics of Motherhood, Croom Helm.

Lewis, J. (1993) 'Community care: policy imperatives, joint planning and enabling authorities', Journal of Interprofessional Care, Vol. 7, No. 1: 7–14.

Lewis, P. et al. (1986) 'Reducing the risks of coronary heart disease in individuals and in the population', The Lancet, 26 April: 956–9.

Lindblom, C.E. (1975) 'Still muddling, not yet through', Public Administration Review, Vol. 39, 6: 517–26.

Linney, J. (1993) 'Gain without pain', Health Service Journal, No.103 (5349): 29–30.

Lipsey, D. (1995) 'Equal measures', Search, Issue 22, Spring.

Lloyd, B. and Duvean, G. (1992) Gender Identities and Education: The Impact of Starting School, Harvester Wheatsheaf.

Local Government Management Board (LGMB) (1995) Indicators for Local Agenda 21, LGMB.

Loney, M. (1983) Community Against Government: The British Community Development Projects 1968-78, Heinemann.

Loney, M. (1986) The Politics of Greed, Pluto Press.

Lorber J. and Farrell, S.A. (1991) The Social Construction of Gender, Sage.

Lovins, A. (1977) Soft Energy Paths: Towards a Durable Peace, Penguin.

Lowry, R. (1994) 'The drive to be greener', Greenhouse, Issue 1, September, Institute of Health Sciences, Oxford.

Lukes, S. (1974) Power: A Radical View, Macmillan.

Lupton, D. (1995) The Imperative of Health: Public Health and the Regulated Body, Sage.

Lupton, D. and Chapman, S. (1995) 'A healthy lifestyle might be the death of you: discourses on diet, cholesterol control and heart disease in the press and among the lay public', Sociology of Health and Illness, 17; 4: 477–94.

Macdonald, G. and Bunton, R. (1993) 'Health promotion, disciplines or discipline?' in Bunton R. and Macdonald G. (eds) Health Promotion: Disciplines and Diversity, Routledge.

Mack, J. and Lansley, S. (1991) Poor Britain, Harper Collins.

MacLennan, W.J. (1986) 'Subnutrition in the elderly', British Medical Journal, 293: 1189–90.

Malpass, P. (1985) Housing Policy in Britain, Macmillan

Marmot, M. (1986) 'Epidemiology and the art of the soluble', Lancet, 19 April: 897–900.

Marmot, M., Shipley, M. and Rose, G. (1984) 'Inequalities in death – specific explanation of a general pattern?', The Lancet, May 5: 1003–6.

Marsh, G.N. and Chew, C. (1984) 'Well Man Clinics in General Practice', *British Medical Journal* 288: 6412.

Marshall, M., Preston, M., Scott, E. and Wincott, P. (eds) (1979) *Teamwork For and Against: An Appraisal of Multidisciplinary Practice*, British Association of Social Workers.

Marshall, T.H. (1965) *Social Policy*, Hutchinson.

Martin, J. and White, A. (1988) *The Financial Circumstances of Disabled Adults Living in Private Households*, HMSO.

Mawhinney, B. (1993) Speech to the Association for Public Health Annual Conference, Chester, APH.

McGrath, M. (1991) *Multidisciplinary Teamwork: Community Mental Handicap Teams*, Avebury.

McKeown, T. (1976) *The Modern Rise of Population*, Edward Arnold.

McKie, L. (1994) *Risky Behaviours and Healthy Lifestyles,* Quay Publishing.

McKie, L. (1995) 'The art of surveillance or reasonable prevention: the case for cervical screening', *Sociology of Health and Illness*, Vol. 17, 4: 441–57.

McKinlay, J. (1993) 'The promotion of health through planned socio-political change: challenges for research and policy', *Social Science and Medicine*, 36: 109–12.

Meadows, D. *et al.* (1993), *The Limits to Growth*, Pan Books.

Meth, R.L. and Pasick, R.S. (1990) *Men in Therapy: The Challenge to Change*, The Guildford Press.

Miles, A. (1991) *Women, Health and Medicine,* The Open University Press.

Milio, N. (1987) *Promoting Health Through Public Policy*, Canadian Public Health Association, Ottawa.

Millar, B. (1995) 'Could do better', *Health Service Journal,* 3 August: 14.

Millett, K. (1969) *Sexual Politics*, Virago.

Mischel, W. (1968) *Personality and Assessment*, Wiley.

Moffat, J. (1980) 'A Well Man clinic – thought for the future', *Health Visitor:* 53: 433–4.

Moon, G. and Gillespie, R. (1995) *Society and Health: An Introduction to Social Science for Health Care Professionals*, Routledge.

Moore, J. (1989) 'The end of the line for poverty', speech delivered by the Secretary of State for Social Security, 11 May, DHSS.

Moore, J.H. (1989) *But What About Men?*, Ashgrove Press.

Moore, W. (1994/1995) 'Making it up as they go along', *Health Matters* Issue 20, Winter: 6–7.

Munn, R.E. (1992) 'Towards sustainable development', *Atmospheric Environment*, 26a(15): 2725–31.

Murray, C. (1994) *Underclass: the Crisis Deepens*, Institute of Economic Affairs.

Nathanson, C.A. (1977) 'Sex roles as variables in preventative health behaviour', *Journal of Community Health.* Vol. 3, No. 1: 142–5.

National Audit Office (1996) *Review of the Implementation of Health Promotion Policies*, HMSO.

National Heart Forum (1995) *Preventing Coronary Heart Disease in Primary Care: The Way Forward*, HMSO.

NCH (National Children's Home) (1991) *Poverty and Nutrition Survey*, National Children's Home.

Nelkin, D. and Tancredi, L. (1989) *Dangerous Diagnostics: The Social Power of Biological Information*, Basic Books, New York.

Nettleton, S. and Bunton, R. (1995) 'Sociological critiques of health promotion', in Bunton, R., Nettleton S. and Burrows, R. (eds) *The Sociology of Health Promotion and the New Public Health*, Routledge.

Neve, H. (1996) 'Community assessment in general practice', in Burton, P. and Harrison, L. (eds) *Identifying Local Health Needs: Community Approaches in Theory and Practice*, The Policy Press.

NHSE (National Health Service Executive) (1994) *Healthy Hospitals Initiative*, NHSE.

Nicholson, J. (1993) *Men and Women. How Different Are They?*, Oxford University Press.

Noakes, J. (1993) 'Health promotion within primary care', *Primary Care Management*, 3, 10: 10–11.

Northern General Hospital NHS Trust (undated) Report of the Board.

Nutbeam, D. (1986) Health Promotion Glossary, *Health Promotion*, 1, pp. 113–27.

O'Brien, M. (1994) 'The managed heart revisited: health and social control', *The Sociological Review*, 43; 2: 393–413.

O'Brien, M. (1995) 'Health and lifestyle: a critical mess? Notes on the dedifferentiation of health', in Bunton, R., Nettleton S. and Burrows, R. (eds) *The Sociology of Health Promotion and the New Public Health*, Routledge.

O'Donnell, O. and Propper, C. (1991) 'Equity and the distribution of UK National Health Service Resources', *Journal of Health Economics*, 10: 1–19.

O'Neil, J. (1981) 'Male sex role conflicts, sexism and masculinity: psychological implications for men, women and the counselling psychologist', *Journal of Counselling Psychology*, Vol. 9, No. 1: 61–80.

Oakley, A. (1994) 'Who cares for health? Social relations, gender and the public health', *Journal of Epidemiology and Public Health* (48).

Office for National Statistics, HEA (1996) *Health in England 1995*, HMSO.

Office of Health Economics (1994) *Health Information and the Consumer*, OHE briefing No. 30. Office of Health Economics.

Ong, B.N. and Humphris, G. (1994) 'Prioritising needs with communities: rapid appraisal methodologies in health', in Popay, J. and Williams, G. (eds) *Researching the People's Health*, Routledge.

Open University, The (1992), *K258 Health and Wellbeing*, The Open University.

OPM (Office for Public Management) (1993) *Healthy Alliances*, Report to the Second Healthgain standing Conference, East Anglia, 1992, OPM.

Orme, J. and Wright, C. (1996) 'Health promotion in primary health care', Scriven, A. and Orme, J. (eds) *Health Promotion: Professional Perspectives*, Macmillan, pp. 54–65.

Ovretveit, J. (1990) *Co-operation in Primary Health Care*, Brunel Institute of Organisation and Social Studies.

OXCHECK Study Group (1995) 'The effectiveness of health checks conducted by nurses in primary care: final results from the OXCHECK study', *British Medical Journal* 310: 1099–104.

Paris, J. and Player, D. (1993) 'Citizens' advice in general practice', *British Medical Journal* 306, 6891: 1518–20.

Parish, R. (1995) 'Health promotion: rhetoric and reality' in Bunton, R., Nettleton, S. and Burrows, R. (eds) *The Sociology of Health Promotion*, Routledge, pp.13–23.

Paton, C. (1995a) 'Present dangers and future threats: some perverse incentives in the NHS reforms', *British Medical Journal*, 310, 13 May: 1245–8.

Paton, C. (1995b) 'Contriving competition', *Health Service Journal*, 30 March: 30–31.

Pearse, L.H. and Crocker, T.H. (1943) *The Peckham Experiment: A Study in the Living Structure of Society*, George Allen & Unwin.

Pederson, D. *et al.* (1988) 'Health Policy in The Netherlands', *Health Promotion International*, Vol. 3.

Percy-Smith, J. and Sanderson, I. (1992) *Understanding Local Needs*, Policy Studies Institute.

Perelberg, J.R. and Miller, C.A. (1990) *Gender and Power in Families*, Routledge.

Phillimore, P. and Beattie, A. (1994) 'Widening inequality of health in Northern England, 1981–91' in *British Medical Journal*, Vol. 308: 1125–8.

Piachaud, D. (1981) 'Peter Townsend and the Holy Grail', *New Society*, 57: 419-21.

Pietroni, P. (1992) 'Towards reflective practice in the language of health and social care', *Journal of Interprofessional Care*, 6(1) Spring: 7–16.

Pietroni, P. (1994) 'Inter-professional teamwork', in Leathard, A. (ed.) *Going Inter-Professional: Working Together for Health and Welfare*, Routledge.

Pintus, S. (1996) personal communication.

Platt, M. (1984) 'Recent research on the impact of unemployment on psychological wellbeing and parasuicide', Berryman, J.C. (ed.) *The Psychological Effects of Unemployment*, Leicester University Press.

Platt, M. *et al.* (1989) 'Damp housing, mould growth and symptomatic health state', *British Medical Journal*, 298: 305–12.

Popay, J. and Williams, G. (1996) 'Public health research and lay knowledge,' *Social Science and Medicine*, 42: 759–68.

Popay, J. and Williams, G. (eds) (1994) *Researching the People's Health*, Routledge.

Popay, J. *et al.* (1993) 'The impact of industrialization on world health', in Beattie, A. *et al.* (eds) *Health and Wellbeing: A Reader*, Macmillan, pp. 272-80.

Powell, M. (1993) *Healthy Alliances: Report to the 2nd Health Gain Standing Committee, East Anglia 1992*, Office for Public Management.

Pownall, M. (1985) 'Action Men', *Nursing Times*, 4 December 1985.

Pratten, B. and Choudhury, S. (1995) 'Listen so that people will talk', *Health Matters* Issue 23, Autumn: 8.

Pritchard, P. and Pritchard, P. (1992) *Developing Teamwork in Primary Health Care: A Practical Workbook*, Oxford University Press.

Public Health Alliance (PHA) (1984) Charter, PHA.

Public Health Alliance (PHA) (1991) *The Health of the Nation Consultation Paper: an evaluation*, PHA.

Public Health Alliance (PHA) (1994) *Poverty and Health*, Birmingham, PHA.

Ranade, W. (1994) *A Future for the National Health Service*, Longman.

Raw, M. (1990) *Cleaning the Air*, British Medical Association.

Rawson, D. (1992) 'The growth of health promotion theory and its rational reconstruction', in Bunton, R. and MacDonald, G. (eds) *Health Promotion: Disciplines and Diversity*, Routledge.

Rawson, D. (1994) 'Models of inter-professional work: Likely theories and possibilities', in Leathard, A. (ed.) *Going Inter-Professional: Working Together for Health and Welfare*, Routledge.

RCP (Royal College of Physicians) (1983) *Health or Smoking: A Follow-Up Report*, Pitman Medical.

RCP (Royal College of Physicians) (1992) *Smoking and the Young*, RCP.

Rehman, H. and Walker, E. (1995) 'Researching black and minority ethnic groups', *Health Education Journal*, Vol. 54, No. 4: 489–500.

Renzetti, C.M. and Curran, D.J. (1995) *Women, Men and Society* (3rd edn), Allyn and Bacon.

Richardson, J. (1987) *Well Woman Centres: A Survey,* Report published by GMB.

Riley, J.C. (1987) *The Eighteenth Century Campaign to Avoid Disease*, Croom Helm.

Rissel, C. (1994) 'Empowerment: the holy grail of health promotion?' *Health Promotion International,* Vol. 9, No. 1: 39–47.

Roberts, H. (1992) *Women's Health Matters*, Routledge.

Root, A. (1995) 'Oxford blues' *Health Service Journal*, 19 January: 32–33.

Rorty, R. (1980) *Philosophy and the Mirror of Nature*, Blackwell.

Rose, G. (1981) 'Strategy of prevention: lessons from cardiovascular disease' in *British Medical Journal*, Vol. 6: 1847.

Rose, G. (1985) 'Sick individuals and sick populations' in *International Journal of Epidemiology*, Vol. 14: 32–38.

Rose, G. (1992) *The Strategy of Preventive Medicine*, Oxford Medical Publications.

Rose, G. (1993) 'Preventive strategy and general practice', *British Journal of General Practice* April: 138–9.

Rosenthal, H. (1983) 'Neighbourhood health projects: some new approaches to health and community work in parts of the United Kingdom', *Community Development Journal*, Vol. 18, No. 2: 120–31.

Rowntree Foundation (1995) *Rowntree Report on Income and Wealth*, Joseph Rowntree Foundation.

Rowntree, B.S. (1901) *Poverty: A Study of Town Life*, Heinemann.

Royal College of Nursing (1994) *Public Health Nursing*, RCN, London.

Royal College of Nursing (1995) *Men's Health: A Survey of District Directors of Public Health*, MORI.

Rudat, K. (1994) *Black and Ethnic Minority Groups in England: Health And Lifestyles*, Health Education Authority.

Russell, J. (1995) *Health Promotion and Primary Health Care*, Greater London Association of Community Health Councils (GLACHC).

Rutten, A. (1995) 'The implementation of health promotion: a new structural perspective', *Soc. Sci. Med.*, Vol. 4, No. 12: 1627–37.

Saan, M. (1986) 'Health promotion and health education: living with a dominant concept', *Health Promotion*, 1, 3: 3–16.

Sabo, D. and Gordon, D.F. (eds) (1995) *Men's Health and Illness: Gender Power and the Body,* Sage.

Sadler, C. (1992) 'Men's hidden illness', *Nursing Times:* 88 (46): 18–19.

Sarafino, E.P. (1990) *Health Psychology,* Wiley.

Savigar, S. and Buxton, V. (1993) 'Public health nursing in grasping the nettle', *Primary Health Care* 3, 5: 6–7.

SCCD (1992) *A Working Statement on Community Development,* The SCCD Charter.

Schrek, R. *et al.* (1950) 'Tobacco smoking as an etiological factor in disease' in *Cancer Research,* No. 10: 49–58.

Schumaker, E.F. (1974) *Small is Beautiful,* Abacus.

Scott-Samuel, A. (1992) 'Still got a long way to go; an international perspective', *The Health of the Nation: are we on target?* Public Health Alliance, pp. 7–18.

Scottish Office (1992) *Scotland's Health: A Challenge to Us All,* HMSO.

Scriven, A. and Orme, J. (eds) (1996) *Health Promotion: Professional Perspectives,* Macmillan.

Secretary of State for Health (1993) *Working Together for Better Health,* DoH.

Shakespeare, H., Tucker, M. and Northover, J. (1989) *Report of a National Survey on Inter-Professional Education in Primary Health Care,* Institute of Community Studies.

Shaw, I. (1994) *Evaluating Interprofessional Training,* Avebury.

Sheldon, J.H. (1948) *The Social Medicine of Old Age. Report of an Inquiry in Wolverhampton,* Nuffield Foundation/Oxford University Press.

Shilling, C. (1993) *The Body and Social Theory,* Sage.

Shipley, P. (1993) *An Evaluation of the Camden Occupational Health Project,* Report for the King's Fund Centre. Department of Occupational Psychology, Birkbeck College and Occupational Health Unit, Royal Free Hospital, London.

Shurtleff, D. (1974) 'Some characteristics related to the incidence of cardiovascular disease and death', *Framingham Study,* Section 30, US Government Printing Office.

Singer, L. (1993) *Erotic Welfare: Theory and Politics in the Age of Epidemic,* Routledge, New York.

Smaje, C. (1995) *Health, Race and Ethnicity – Making Sense of the Evidence,* King's Fund Institute/ SHARE.

Smith, A. and Jacobson, B. (1988) *The Nation's Health,* Kings Fund.

Smith, R. (1994) 'Room at the top', *Health Service Journal,* 24 November: 28–29.

Smith, R., Gaster, L., Harrison, L., Martin, L., Means, R. and Thistlewaite, P. (1993) *Working Together for Better Community Care,* School for Advanced Urban Studies, Bristol.

Smithies, J. (1995) *Moving On: A Report of the National Community Health Conference, Bradford 1995,* Labyrinth Training and Consultancy.

Smithies, J. and Adams, L. (1993) 'Walking the tightrope: issues in evaluation and community participation for Health for All', in Davies, J.K. and Kelly, M.P. (eds) *Healthy Cities: Research and Practice,* Routledge: 55–71.

Social Trends (1994) Central Statistical Office.

Solancke, A. (1996) 'Focus on black women's health', *Health Line,* February: 5.

Soloman, K. (1981) 'The masculine gender role and its implications for the life of older men', *Journal of American Geriatrics Society,* Vol. 29. No. 3: 297–301.

Somerville, G. (1984) *Community Development in Health: Addressing the Confusions,* London Community Health Resource.

Sommers, S. (1993) *World Smoking and Health*, World Council for Tobacco Research.

Sone, K. (1993) 'Assessments and unmet need still causing confusion'. *Community Care*, 1 April: 17.

South East Institute of Public Health (1996) Summary table of health and environment targets, reproduced in FoE press release, FoE, July 8.

Southwark Council (1995) *Benefits Advice Service*, unpublished material from Southwark Consumer Money and Advice Centre.

Stacey, M. (1988) *The Sociology of Health and Healing*, Unwin Hyman.

Standing Nursing and Midwifery Advisory Committee (SNMAC) (1995) *Making it Happen*, DoH.

Stansfield, S.A., Gallacher, J.E.J., Sharp, D.S. and Yarnell, J.W.G. (1991) 'Social factors and minor psychiatric disorder in middle aged men', *Psychological Medicine,* No. 21.

Stewart-Brown, S.L. and Prothero, D.L. (1988) 'Evaluation in community development', *Health Education Journal*, Vol. 47, No. 4: 156–61.

Stott, N. (1994) 'Screening for cardiovascular risk in general practice', *British Medical Journal,* 308: 285–6.

Stott, N. and Pill, R. (1990) 'Advise yes, dictate no: patients' views on health promotion in the consultation', *Family Practice*, 7, 2: 125–31.

Strachan, D. (1989) 'Damp housing and childhood asthma: validation of reporting of symptoms' *British Medical Journal*, 297: 1223–26.

Strassburg, M. (1984) 'The global eradication of smallpox', Black, N. *et al.,* (eds) *Health and Disease: A Reader*, Open University Press.

Styles, B. (1994) 'Viol Bodies', *Health Service Journal*, 3 February: 30–32.

Swift, C. and Levin, G. (1987) 'Empowerment: an emerging mental health technology', *Journal of Primary Prevention,* 8: 71–94.

TAC (Tobacco Advisory Council) (1992) *Facts About Tobacco*, TAC.

Tannahill, A. (1985) 'What is Health Promotion?', *Health Education Journal*, 44: 167–8.

Tannahill, A. (1990) 'Health education and health promotion: planning for the 1990s', *Health Education Journal* 49: 194–8

Tannahill, A. (1994) 'Health education and health promotion: from priorities to programmes', *Health Promotion Country Series* No. 1, Health Education Board for Scotland/WHO.

Taylor, D. and Bloor, K. (1994) *Health Care, Health Promotion and the Future General Practice*, The Nuffield Provincial Hospitals Trust, Royal Society of Medicine Press, London.

Taylor, P. (1984) *The Smoke Ring*, Sphere Books.

Thomas, C. (1993) 'Public health strategies – a comparison of the conceptual foundations of the Sheffield and British Government approaches' in *Health Promotion International*, Vol 8, No. 4: 299–308.

Thompson, E.H. and Pleck, J.H. (1988) 'The structure of male role norms' in Kimmel, M.S. (ed.) *Changing Men. New Directions in Research on Men and Masculinity*, Sage.

Thornley, P. (1987) in Orr, J., *Women's Health in the Community*, Wiley.

Timmins, N. (1990) 'Fixing the poverty line', *Search*, 6, Joseph Rowntree Foundation, pp. 14–16.

Titmuss, R. (1968) *Commitment to Welfare*, George Allen and Unwin.

Tolley, K. (1994) *Health promotion: How to Manage Cost-effectiveness*, HEA.

Tomlinson, D. (1996) 'The dangers of community', in Parker, M., *Ethics and Community*, University of Central Lancashire, pp. 242–6.

Tones, B.K. (1990) *The Power to Choose: Health Education and the New Public Health*, Health Education Unit, Leeds Metropoliton University.

Tones, B.K. and Tilford, S. (1994) *Health Education: Effectiveness, Efficiency and Equity* (2nd edn), Chapman and Hall.

Townsend, P. (1979) *Poverty in the UK*, Penguin.

Townsend, P. (1995) 'Poverty, labour markets and Eastern Europe', in Rodgers, G. and van de Hoeven, R. *The Poverty Agenda: Trends and Policy Options*, IILS, Geneva.

Townsend, P., Davidson, N. and Whitehead, M. (1988) *Inequalities in Health: The Black Report and The Health Divide*, Penguin.

Trade Union Congress (1994) *Better Safety Standards at Work*, TUC.

Transport and Health Study Group (1991) *Health on the Move*, Public Health Alliance.

Tregoran Hospital (1996), interviews with hospital staff, unpublished.

Trevelyan, J. (1985) 'Well Men', *Nursing Times,* 85 (12): 46.

Trichopoulos, D. (1996) 'The future of epidemiology', *British Medical Journal*, 313: 436–7.

Tsouros, A. (1990) *World Health Organization Healthy Cities Project: A Project Becomes a Movement*, SOGESS

Tsouros, A. and Draper, P. (1993) 'The healthy city project: new developments and research needs', Davies, J.K. and Kelly, M. (1993) *Healthy Cities, Research and Practice*, Routledge.

Tudor Hart, J. (1993) 'Health promotion in general practice: well man clinics won't reduce morbidity', letter, *British Medical Journal* 307, 7 August: 379–80.

Turner, B. (1992) *Regulating Bodies: Essays in Medical Sociology*, Routledge.

Twelvetrees, A. (1992) *Community Work*, Macmillan.

UNCED (United Nations Conference on Environment and Development) (1993) (Earth Summit, Rio de Janiero, Brazil) *Agenda 21*, UNO.

United Nations World Commission on Environment and Development (1987) *Our Common Future* (The Brundtland Report), Oxford University Press.

Vanclay, L. (ed.) (1995) 'Research and evaluation issues in interprofessional education', *CAIPE Bulletin*, No. 10, Winter.

Verhagen, K. (1989) 'Evaluation in partnerships: attractive utopias or deceptive illusions', unpublished paper.

Virchow, R. (1848) *Die Mediszinische Reform, Eine Wochenschrift*, Berlin, Duck und Verlag von. G. Reimer.

Wald, N.J. *et al.*, (1991) *Passive Smoking: a Health Hazard*, Imperial Cancer Research Fund/ Cancer Research Campaign.

Walker, A. (1984) *Social Planning, A Strategy for Socialist Welfare*, Blackwell.

Walt, G. (1995) *Health Policy*, Sage.

Walters, S. (1994) 'What are the respiratory effects of vehicle pollution?', Reid, C. (ed.) *How Vehicle Pollution Affects Our Health*, Ashden Trust.

Watt, A. and Rodmell, S. (1988) 'Community involvement in health promotion: progress or panacea?', *Health Promotion* ,Vol. 2, No. 4, Oxford University Press, pp. 359–67.

Watt, G.C.M. (1996) 'All together now: why social deprivation matters to everyone', *British Medical Journal*, 312: 1026–9.

Weale, A. (1988) *Cost and Choice in Health Care: The Ethical Dimension*, Kings Fund.

Webb, A. (1991) 'Co-ordination: a problem in public sector management', *Policy and Politics*, 19: 229–41.

Weinstein, J. (1994) *Sewing the Seams for a Seamless Service. A Review of Developments in Interprofessional Education and Training*, CCETSW.

Wellings, K. (1993) *Sexual Behaviour in Britain*, Penguin.

Wellness Forum (undated) *Press Briefing, Working For Health Awards*, Wellness Forum.

Welsh Office (1989) *Strategic Direction and Intent for the NHS in Wales*, HMSO.

Welsh Office (1994) *Caring for the Future*, HMSO.

West, M. and Anderson, N. (1994) 'Measures of invention', *Health Service Journal*: 28.

White, M. (1996) 'Who's who in public health?', *Healthlines*, May: 14–16.

Whitehead, M. (1987) *The Health Divide*, HEC.

Whitehead, M. (1995) 'Tackling inequalities: a review of policy initiatives', Benzeval, M., Judge, K. and Whitehead, M. (1995) *Tackling Inequalities in Health: An agenda for Action*, Kings Fund, pp. 22–52.

Whitehead, M. and Dahlgren, G. (1991) 'What can be done about inequalities in health? , *The Lancet*, Vol. 338: 1959–63.

Whitehead, M. and Kleinman, M. (1992) *A Review of Housing Needs Assessment*, Housing Corporation.

Wilkinson, R. (1996) *Unhealthy Societies: The Afflictions of Inequality*, Routledge.

Wilkinson, R.G. (1989) 'Class mortality differentials, income distribution and trends in poverty 1921–81', *Journal of Social Policy*, 18 (3): 307–35.

Wilkinson, R.G. (1993) 'The impact of income inequality on life expectancy', in Platt, S. *et al.* (eds) *Locating Health: Sociological and Historical Explorations*, Avebury.

Wilkinson, R.G. (1994) *Unfair Shares*, Barnardos.

Williams, G. (1989) 'Hope for the humblest? The role of self-help in chronic illness: the case of ankylosing spondylitis', *Sociology of Health and Illness*, Vol. 11, No. 2: 135–59.

Williams, G. and Popay, J. (1996) 'Social science and public health: issues of method, knowledge and power', *Critical Public Health* 7,1.

Williams, S. and Calnan, M. (1996) 'The "limits" of medicalization? Modern medicine and the lay populace in "late" modernity', *Social Science and Medicine*, 42: 1609–20.

Williams, S. J. and Calnan, M. (1994) 'Perspectives on prevention: the views of General Practitioners', *Sociology of Health and Illness* 16, 3: 372–93.

Wilson, G. and Dockrell, J. (1995) 'Elderly care', in Owens, P., Carrier, J., Horder, J. (eds) *Interprofessional Issues in Community and Primary Health Care*, Macmillan.

Woodhouse, D. and Pengelly, P. (1991) *Anxiety and the Dynamics of Collaboration*, Aberdeen University Press and Tavistock Institute of Marital Studies.

World Health Organisation (WHO) (1946) *World Health Organisation Constitution: Basic Documents*, WHO.

World Health Organisation (WHO) (1977) *Health For All by the Year 2000*, WHO.

World Health Organisation (WHO) (1978) *Alma Ata Declaration*, WHO.

World Health Organisation (WHO) (1983) *New Approaches to Health Education in Primary Health Care*, Report of a WHO Expert Committee, Technical Report Services 690, WHO.

World Health Organisation (WHO) (1984) *Report of the Working Group on Concepts and Principles of Health Promotion*, WHO.

World Health Organisation (WHO) (1985) *Health For All in Europe by the Year 2000, Regional Targets*, Copenhagen, WHO.

World Health Organisation (WHO) (1986) *Ottawa Charter for Health Promotion*, WHO.

World Health Organisation (WHO) (1988) *Adelaide Recommendations on Healthy Public Policy*, Adelaide, WHO.

World Health Organisation (WHO) (1989) *Charter on Environment and Health*, WHO.

World Health Organisation (WHO) (1990) *Investment 'in Health*, Brochure prepared for International Conference on Health Promotion, 17–19 December, WHO.

World Health Organisation (WHO) (1991) *Revised Targets for Health For All in Europe*, Copenhagen, WHO.

World Health Organisation (WHO) (1992) *'We Can Do It', Sundsvall Handbook* from the 3rd International conference on Health promotion, Sundsvall, Sweden June 9–15, 1991, Stockholm, Karolinska Institute/WHO.

Wyman, L. (1994) 'Training the trainer: module for change', *Primary Health Care* Vol. 4, No. 3, March: 19–20.

Yen, L. (1995) 'From Alma Ata to Asda and beyond: The transition in health promotion services in primary care from commodity to control' in Bunton, R., Nettleton, S. and Burrows, R. (eds) *The Sociology of Health Promotion: Critical Analyses of Consumption, Lifestyle and Risk*, Routledge.

Zola, I.K. (1972) 'Medicine as an institution of social control', *Sociological Review*, 20: 487–504.

Zola, I.K. (1973) 'Pathways to the doctor', *Social Science and Medicine*, No. 7.

Index